Human Computer Interaction Research in Web Design and Evaluation

Panayiotis Zaphiris, Centre for HCI Design, City University, UK

Sri Kurniawan, School of Informatics, The University of Manchester, UK

IDEA GROUP PUBLISHING

Hershey • London • Melbourne • Singapore

Acquisitions Editor:	Michelle Potter
Development Editor:	Kristin Roth
Senior Managing Editor:	Jennifer Neidig
Managing Editor:	Sara Reed
Copy Editor:	Holly Powell
Typesetter:	Sharon Berger
Cover Design:	Lisa Tosheff
Printed at:	Yurchak Printing Inc.

Published in the United States of America by
    Idea Group Publishing (an imprint of Idea Group Inc.)
    701 E. Chocolate Avenue
    Hershey PA 17033
    Tel: 717-533-8845
    Fax: 717-533-8661
    E-mail: cust@idea-group.com
    Web site: http://www.idea-group.com

and in the United Kingdom by
    Idea Group Publishing (an imprint of Idea Group Inc.)
    3 Henrietta Street
    Covent Garden
    London WC2E 8LU
    Tel: 44 20 7240 0856
    Fax: 44 20 7379 3313
    Web site: http://www.eurospan.co.uk

Library of Congress Cataloging-in-Publication Data

Human computer interaction research in Web design and evaluation / Panayiotis Zaphiris and Sri Kurniawan, editors.
    p. cm.
  Summary: "This is a comprehensive book on Human Computer Interaction and Web design focusing on various areas of research including theories, analysis, design and evaluation. It is not a book on web programming; it provides methods derived from research to help develop more user-friendly websites. It highlights the social and cultural issues in web design for a wider audience"--Provided by publisher.
  ISBN 1-59904-246-0 (hardcover) -- ISBN 1-59904-247-9 (softcover) -- ISBN 1-59904-248-7 (ebook)
  1. Web sites--Design. 2. Human-computer interaction. I. Zaphiris, Panayiotis. II. Kurniawan, Sri, 1970-
  TK5105.888.H85 2006
  004'.019--dc22
                    2006019158

British Cataloguing in Publication Data
A Cataloguing in Publication record for this book is available from the British Library.

Human Computer Interaction Research in Web Design and Evaluation

Table of Contents

Section IV: Evaluation

Preface

OVERVIEW AND MOTIVATION

The Web is becoming a medium through which more and more people search for information, communicate with others, and have fun. The complexity of this collection of information has attracted the interest of the human-computer interaction (HCI) research community. Researchers have focused their attention in developing new models and methodologies for describing user behavior on the Web, analyze their needs and expectations, and thus successfully design user-friendly Web sites.

Usability evaluation for the Web presents an additional interesting complexity. Due to the variety in design of Web sites and the variety of user goals while browsing the Web, the task of choosing and properly using the appropriate evaluation method becomes a challenge. New approaches and methodologies for Web evaluation have been developed — this book presents some of those.

This book also points out that beyond the technical aspects of Web design we need to systematically take into account human interaction and activity and the completely renewed social and cultural environments that Web environments and interfaces are calling for and that technologies are now capable of delivering.

The book's objective is to serve university educators and educators in general; university administrators; researchers; lecturers of HCI and user-centered design (UCD); Web system managers; instructional designers; and the general audience with an interest in HCI and Web design. This book is structured in such a way so that it can act as a core textbook in HCI and Web development courses.

DESCRIPTION OF CHAPTERS

Interaction design should always follow a UCD approach that focuses the design activity on the user. This user-centered approach is further broken down into three key activities: analysis, design, and evaluation. Our book is structured into four broad sections. Section I provides an introduction into HCI in Web design and evaluation and provides the theoretical foundations for it. Section II takes those theoretical foundations further by focusing on task analysis. The focus of Section III is on the design stage of UCD. Finally, in Section IV we include chapters that describe evaluation methodologies for the Web.

The book includes 14 chapters from prominent international authors.

The following section presents an overview of each chapter.

Section I: Introduction and Theoretical Foundations

Chapter I, *The Usability Engineering Behind User-Centered Processes for Web Site Development Lifecycles*, is written by Theresa O'Connell and Elizabeth D. Murphy and discusses usability engineering and the processes that it encompasses, such as requirements definition, UCD, and evaluation. The authors define the usability engineer's (UE) role throughout a user-centered, Web site development lifecycle and stress that this lifecycle integrates compatible usability engineering processes into software engineering processes, drawing examples from research and experience in developing for accessibility.

Chapter II, *How Users View Web Pages: An Exploration of Cognitive and Perceptual Mechanisms*, is written by Rebecca A. Grier, Philip Kortum, and James T. Miller. Their chapter presents the basic cognitive and perceptual attentional mechanisms that affect how users view Web pages and the methods used to measure this attention. The primary goal of the chapter is to help the reader gain an understanding of what visual elements on a Web page draw a user's attention, how that knowledge can be collected, and how it can be applied to the design of useful and usable Web sites.

Chapter III, *A Qualitative Study in User's Information-Seeking Behaviors on Web Sites: A User-Centered Approach to Web Site Development*, is written by Napawan Sawasdichai. This chapter introduces a qualitative study of user's information-seeking tasks on Web-based media, by investigating user's cognitive behaviors when they are searching for particular information on various kinds of Web sites.

Section II: Analysis

Chapter IV, *Understanding the Nature of Task Analysis in Web Design*, is written by Rod Farmer and Paul Gruba. This chapter presents an overview of task analysis frameworks in HCI, which are capable of eliciting, describing, and evaluating human factor requirements in Web design. Moreover, the chapter describes existing and emerging paradigms in task analysis, including several prominent methodologies. The chapter concludes with the description of a task analysis framework suited to both the cognitive and sociocultural demands of Web design.

Section III: Design

Chapter V, *From Behavior to Design: Answering the Question of Who and What to Build Human-Centered Products and Information Systems*, is written by Catherine Forsman. In this chapter UCD concepts are explored through case studies illustrating tools and techniques in the Internet industry for the practice of UCD. It argues that by combining techniques from participatory design, persona research, and market research, complex quantitative and qualitative evidence is produced and offers a potentially more substantive approach to understanding the nature of designing interfaces for the Internet in a variety of contexts.

Chapter VI, *Design Methods for Experience Design*, is written by Marie Jefsioutine and John Knight. The chapter describes an approach to Web design and evaluation where the user experience is central. It outlines the historical context in which experience design has evolved and describes the experience design framework (EDF). This is based on the principles of UCD and draws on a variety of research methods and tools to facilitate the design, development, and evaluation of user experiences.

Chapter VII, *Innovations in Collaborative Web Design: Methods to Facilitate Team Learning During Design*, is written by Madelon Evers. In this chapter the link between multi-disciplinary design and team learning, which the authors argue needs to be supported in equal measure during Web design projects, is explored. The chapter introduces a new approach to collaborative Web design, called the design and learning methodology, as a way to support these two processes. The approach involves many stakeholders, including future Web site users, in design decision making. It structures stakeholder participation through multi-disciplinary design teams (MDTs). It uses professional facilitators to guide design and learning processes.

Chapter VIII, *Information Architecture and Navigation Design for Web Sites*, is written by David Benyon. In this chapter the author explores two key issues of Web site design; information architecture and the design of navigation support. In order to do this he draws upon theories of information spaces and theories of navigation in urban spaces. From these theories a number of practical features of Web sites are described.

Chapter IX, *A Methodology for Web Accessibility Development and Maintenance*, is written by Julio Abascal, Myriam Arrue, and Markel Vigo. This chapter introduces the basic concepts related to Web accessibility and proposes a method for including accessibility in standard Web engineering methodologies. The key phases, accessibility, evaluation, and maintenance are described in detail. Finally, a model is proposed for implementing accessibility policy in organizations.

Section IV: Evaluation

Chapter X, *Usability Evaluation*, is written by Zhijun Zhang. This chapter introduces the different ways of conducting usability evaluation, which is categorized under four methods: model- or metrics-based, inquiry, inspection, and testing. Under each method, a list of techniques is described, focusing on when and how each technique should be applied. The chapter also summarizes various studies that compared the effectiveness of different usability evaluation techniques.

Chapter XI, *Walkthroughs in Web Usability: Cognitive, Activity, and Heuristic Walkthrough*, is written by Hokyoung Ryu. Three usability inspection methods — heuristic walk-through (HW), cognitive walk-through (CW), and activity walk-through (AW) — are reviewed in this chapter. This chapter then discusses the relative advantages and weaknesses of all of the techniques, and suggestions for Web evaluation are offered, with a short Web site example. Based on these analyses, the authors suggest some changes to Web site evaluation to improve accuracy and reliability of the current walk-through methods.

Chapter XII, *User-Centered Evaluation of Personalized Web Sites: What's Unique?*, is written by Sherman Alpert and John Vergo. In this paper, based on our experience in usability studies of a personalized e-commerce site, the authors present some of the additional questions and issues that must be addressed for user-centered evaluations of personalized Web sites.

Chapter XIII, *Remote Usability Evaluation of Web Interfaces*, is written by Naouel Moha, Ashraf Gaffar, and Gabriel Michel. While it is prohibitively expensive to conduct usability testing on a global range of users, it is technically possible and is more feasible to remotely collect the necessary information about usability problems and to analyze them the same way we do local tests. In this chapter, the authors present systematic methods and tools to support remote usability testing and evaluation of Web interfaces.

Chapter XIV, *Modeling Interactive Behavior with a Rational Cognitive Architecture*, is written by David Peebles and Anna L. Cox. In this chapter the authors discuss a number of recent studies that demonstrate the use of rational analysis and cognitive modeling methods to understand complex interactive behavior involved in three tasks: icon search, graph reading, and information retrieval on the World Wide Web.

Acknowledgments

Many thanks go to the publishing team and especially Kristin Roth, Idea Group Inc. Development Editor, for all the support and encouragement in this process. Special thanks go to Chee Siang Ang, Andrew Laghos, and Areej Al-Wabil from City University London for their help. Finally, we would like to warmly thank all the authors for making this book possible through their very interesting contributions.

Panayiotis Zaphiris, zaphiri@soi.city.ac.uk

Sri Kurniawan, s.kurniawan@manchester.ac.uk

Section I:

Introduction and
Theoretical Foundations

Chapter I

The Usability Engineering Behind User-Centered Processes for Web Site Development Lifecycles

Theresa A. O'Connell, Humans & Computers, Inc., USA

Elizabeth D. Murphy, U.S. Census Bureau, USA[1]

ABSTRACT

Usability is integral to software quality. Software developers increasingly acknowledge the importance of user-centered, Web site development. The value of usability engineering and the role of the usability engineer (UE) are less understood. A common assumption is that the UE's role is only to be a user advocate. To this role, we add the responsibility of addressing concerns of other stakeholders in Web site design and development. We discuss usability engineering and the processes that it encompasses, such as project planning, requirements definition, user-centered design (UCD) and evaluation/testing within the context of traditional software engineering lifecycles. We define the UE's role throughout a user-centered, Web site development lifecycle. This lifecycle integrates compatible usability engineering processes into software engineering processes, drawing examples from research and experience.

INTRODUCTION

People use the Web in a variety of ways. Their interaction with the Web can be self-motivated or externally motivated; their proficiency novice or expert; their needs and expectations simple or complex. To engineer a successful and satisfactory user experience with a Web site, we need to understand issues such as why people go to a Web site; what they expect and intend to accomplish at the site; and everything impacting on their experience.

A Web site is the result of a set of processes, usually iterative, beginning with conceptualization, planning and requirements definition, then going on to design, version production, and testing/evaluation, before culminating in the site launch. For usability engineering to be fully integrated into Web site development, its practices must be fully integrated into software development lifecycles (Addelston & O'Connell, 2004, 2005). Lifecycles are structured frameworks for software development activities. For example, Figure 1 incorporates elements that iterative lifecycles typically include. In practice, the sequence and frequency of activities can vary. Research and experience show that including usability in software engineering lifecycles is critical (Mayhew, 1992).

Developing a Web site is a team effort. Each team member has roles and responsibilities. The roles of the usability engineer (UE) are integral to these processes and to the team implementing them, primarily because the UE promotes a user-centered perspective. Software engineering of a Web site addresses a variety of purposes: building a new site; upgrading, refurbishing, maintaining or introducing new information or functionality to an existing site; and replacing a legacy site. These purposes track to the goals of the Web site providers. Software engineering is not inherently user centered. It becomes user centered by incorporating usability engineering. User-centered processes for Web site development are compatible and simultaneous with software engineering lifecycle processes.

Building usability into a Web site requires user-centered processes. Such processes require defined roles and activities, which, in turn, depend on common definitions of con-

Figure 1. A generic, variable sequence, iterative Web site development lifecycle illustrates points where usability engineering is most beneficial

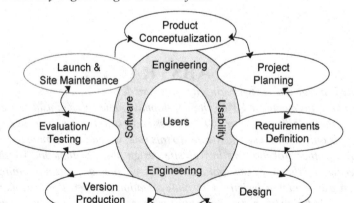

Note: With the exception of version production, each of the activities in the outer ovals includes both usability engineering and software engineering processes. In practice, the sequence and frequency of activities can vary.

cepts, inputs, outputs, and tools. From the start, team members must share an understanding of users' attributes and needs. This understanding underpins the collaboration necessary to incorporate user-centered processes into Web site development.

Guided by Figure 1, this chapter addresses the following topics:

- Usability
- Users
- User interface
- Usability engineering
- Software engineering
- Integrating usability engineering into software engineering lifecycles
- Lifecycle activities

The chapter ends with a summary and references.

USABILITY

People outside the field of usability engineering sometimes consider usability to be obvious, but vague and unstructured — something common sense can recognize and accomplish. Sometimes they are surprised to learn that the field has its own definitions and established processes. Although those people are happy to define usability as "I know it when I see it," for UEs, a strict definition underlies our focus on users' needs and our goal of meeting those needs through usability engineering processes. This chapter discusses users' needs in the context of human-computer interaction (HCI), specifically as users interact with Web sites.

The International Organization for Standardization (ISO) defines usability through the attributes of users' interactions with software products in specific contexts of use: efficiency, effectiveness, and user satisfaction. We "boil these attributes down" to two outcomes: (1) user success and (2) user satisfaction (1998). The ISO definition implies that usable software must be accessible.

Throughout this chapter, we draw illustrations from our work in a specialized branch of usability called accessibility. Accessibility enables people with disabilities to experience success and satisfaction with software to a degree comparable to that enjoyed by people without disabilities. Although some authors treat accessibility as distinct from usability, we consider it to be a subdomain of usability in which the users are people with physical and/or cognitive disabilities (Hix & O'Connell, 2005).

USERS

In the context of this chapter, users are people who interact with Web sites. In the sense in which we use the term, users are also known as *end users*, the people who visit Web sites and interact with their contents. The term *user* excludes people employed in a Web site project, for example, the UEs. It excludes the site's providers and others who have any stake in the Web site. People close to the project can be too technical or too expert in a domain to represent a user who does not have the same training, goals or background. Those close to the project run a high risk of unintentionally clouding their view of users' needs with their own commitment to achieving the project's goals.

Many variables are inherent to users (Bias & Karat, 2005). Some are intrinsic, for example, age; gender; experience with technology; intellectual or aesthetic preferences; interaction styles; and the presence or absence of physical or cognitive disabilities. Other variables, such as employer goals and working environment are extrinsic, but affect the user experience. Many user attributes can decline with age, for example, memory and perception of color contrast (O'Connell, in press).

Each user brings a cluster of capabilities and limitations to any interaction with a Web site. These are the well-documented human capabilities and limitations in perception, manual dexterity, memory, problem solving, and decision making (e.g., Baddeley, 1990; Brown & Deffenbacher, 1979; Mayer, 1992). For example, the limitations of working memory are well known: seven plus or minus two "chunks" (sets of items), with the size of a chunk varying depending on the user's experience (Miller, 1956). Research has found that working memory can be futher limited by environmental characteristics, for example, noise, fatigue, perceived time pressure, and other sources of stress (Bradley, 1990). Correctly applying such research findings to Web site design is the UE's responsibility.

Some user attributes are physical. The term *user* includes people with disabilities as well as people without disabilities. Users with physical disabilities require a Web site that accommodates those disabilities. For example, a user with low manual dexterity may be a skilled problem solver, but have difficulty clicking on small screen elements with a mouse. As content density increases on Web pages, the need for small controls rises. Consider a page with a long list of expandable or contractible menu options. By offering the expanded state as the default, the site accommodates users with low manual dexterity, relieving them of the need to click on the tiny controls. Tradeoffs are inevitable. The user who cannot expand or contract the list must contend with content density. Accommodating users' capabilities and limitations is rarely simple. Sometimes we must accommodate several factors at once. The user with the manual dexterity disability may also have a visual disability brought about by age.

The World Wide Web Consortium (W3C) considers the needs of users with a wide variety of disabilities, the W3C gives guidelines and success criteria for assessing accessibility (W3C, 2004). For users with special needs, an accessible Web site provides perceivable content; operable content components; understandable content and controls; and content compatibility with other technologies (Caldwell, Chisholm, Slatin, & Vanderheiden, 2005).

Publishing a Web site makes it available to the world, but it is not possible to design for the world. Certainly, there are generic commonalities across Web sites. Any Web site can have hyperlinks, controls, and information architecture. But, any Web site will also have unique features to meet the needs of its targeted audience. Designers need to know the characteristics of the site's targeted audience to promote their success and satisfaction at the site. They must also project future user characteristics. For example, the intended audience needs to include users with disabilities, even if none of the current users has a disability. Today's able user may have a disability tomorrow. Age brings disabilities (O'Connell, in press). New employees may have disabilities.

A Web site goal is to enable its users to experience success and satisfaction by accom-modating each user attribute of the set of targeted users as well as the unique constellation of attributes defining each individual user. However, the "average" user is a myth. Designers need to understand the range of each attribute within a group of users and to recognize that users will fall at all points along the range (e.g., low to high spatial ability).

To help us accommodate these ranges while still focusing on targeted users, we group users into classes, rather than design for them as individuals. We define user classes by people's participation in a set of user attributes. For example, for a theater-ticket vending site, the senior citizen user class will include the attributes, aged 65 or over and partial memory loss. The first attribute qualifies these users for a discount; the second tells UEs that the interface needs to remind users of the time of the show. Other user classes for this site would include adults, children, and members of theater clubs, each class having its own attributes.

User Participation in Web Site Design

It is essential to include users in the process of Web site design because users will do what they will, not necessarily what the designers or developers want or expect them to do. User behavior can be anticipated up to a point, but not predicted in exact detail. Not being intimately familiar with the design of a site, users will try to do what seems logical to them, even though their logic may conflict with the designer's or developer's logic. According to Shneiderman (1998), users do not make errors of intention because they are doing what seems logical to them in the context of the task they are trying to complete. Users do not try to get lost, but they do get lost.

User involvement in design extends our understanding of human behavior within the context of the site and its stakeholders' goals. In some projects, users participate in focus groups and interviews or respond to surveys. They join in conceptualization and design discussions. Observing users interact with a Web site provides the most valuable new insight, taking UEs to a level of understanding not otherwise possible. These observations are combined and analyzed to develop profiles of the range of expected interactions. Observing users interacting with the site identifies unanticipated needs and behaviors. Analyzing observational data produces requirements exceeding what programming logic, technical expertise, and the best of intentions can identify.

Some software engineering processes eliminate user participation but purport to accommodate a user orientation. These include assigning a user surrogate and processing user information channeled through a nonuser, such as the user's manager. In contrast, usability engineering relies on close interaction with real users at the strategic points where their input is most crucial. It documents input from the users who actually participated in lifecycle activities.

Knowledge gained from usability engineering cannot be gained by other means. This is not to say that users drive design. Users are not designers. It is a key role of the UE to translate the understanding of users and their needs into design recommendations. It is a key role of designers and developers to incorporate usability recommendations into interactive interfaces that promote users' success and satisfaction.

Users' Mental Models

Along with their capabilities and limitations, users bring with them their previous experience of computers and Web sites. We assume they have built mental models, that is, psychological representations of the ways in which computers and Web sites work (Carroll, 1990; Johnson-Laird, 1983; Van Der Veer & Del Carmen Puerta Melguizo, 2003).

Highly experienced users can have mental models of different categories of Web sites, for example, sites for entertainment, information gathering, and e-commerce. According to the user's mental model, an entertainment site should use bright colors and animation, whereas an information site should use subdued colors and minimal animation, for example, only to demonstrate an integral concept. Abstracting and representing users' mental models is another job for the UE. Tools for doing this include cognitive task analysis (e.g., Crandall, Kline, & Hoffman, 2006).

User expectations for Web sites are based on their experience with the Internet. They have expectations for the behavior of controls, for example, the back and forward button, Tab key, and Enter key. They have expectations for hyperlinks, for example, a link once activated will change its color. Some expect to be told whether clicking on a link will take them outside the site. Sometimes, users worry about whether they will be able to get back to where they are if they click on a link because they have been unable to form a definite mental model for link behavior. This uncertainty can arise when they have experienced links behaving inconsistently across sites.

USER INTERFACE

In one sense, a user interface (UI) is software that people use to interact with technology. For UEs it is a matter of layers. Above the underlying technology is the important look-and-feel layer (Garrett, 2002). Feel refers to more than the point and click paradigm; it also refers to what users hear, for example, a sound associated with an alarm. The UI includes both the user's actual and expected mode of interaction with a Web site, for example, keyboard, mouse, or speech. Whether the designers intend it or not, because of mental models the UI includes implied functionality based on similarities to familiar software. In the broadest sense, the UI is the virtual place where the user's mental model, meets the designers' system model (Bolt, 1984). Aligning these models is a goal of usability engineering (Norman & Draper, 1986).

USABILITY ENGINEERING

Usability engineering is a set of defined, user-centered processes, grounded in research and experience-based principles. The purpose of usability engineering in Web development is to raise the potential for users' success and satisfaction and, thereby, to support Web site providers' goals. The UE must understand the complex set of variables residing in any user group and apply this understanding to promote users' success and satisfaction. This understanding is what makes usability engineering critical to achieving Web site usability. Because people's styles of interacting with technology change as technology progresses, usability engineering is a continually evolving field informed by applied research in human interaction with technology.

The UE applies expertise not usually found in other software development team members to make an essential contribution to the quality of a Web site. As noted by Bias and Karat, "good usability is not standard for most Web sites…" (2005, p. 2). When usability engineering is not part of Web site development, the team faces a high risk that, at the least, the site will not promote users' success and satisfaction; at worst, it will inhibit users' success and satisfaction and thereby prevent achievement of the site providers' goals. This outcome would be a disservice to the providers and other stakeholders.

Usability engineering is practiced by UEs who typically have training and experience in a variety of disciplines. In the case of Web work, relevant experience is in fields such as psychology, HCI, testing protocols, and design. The UEs' work is distinguished by its orientation toward the user, but usability engineering is more than user advocacy. For example, in addition to understanding users' mental models and expectations, the UE must also be well versed in technology, standards, and laws. To create feasible design approaches, the UE must understand organizational and project goals. To integrate usability into the lifecycle, the UE must be able to communicate with users, stakeholders, and other members of the Web site development team.

A Web site has several objectives. While delivering information and functionality, it also bears the responsibilities of putting the site providers' best foot forward and achieving their business goals. A Web site's usability influences users' impressions of the site providers' integrity and trustworthiness. UEs are qualified to coordinate the factors necessary to meet the needs of both users and site providers. As we show later, the means to this end is to incorporate usability throughout a software development lifecycle.

Usability Engineering Principles

Usability engineering is a multi-disciplinary field. With roots in human factors, it also draws on disciplines such as software engineering, linguistics, biology, cognitive psychology, technology, and graphic design. These fields' diverse contributions are documented in usability principles, a set of research and experience-based, widely accepted guidelines for achieving usability (e.g., Koyani et al., 2003; Mayhew, 1992; Shneiderman & Plaisant, 2004). UEs continually update usability principles in response to new research and technologies. Usability principles empower design strategies to meet users' needs and expectations, while avoiding unnecessary, inappropriate features that burden schedules and budgets.

Most usability principles trace to human capabilities and limitations. A user with color deficiencies can detect changes in brightness or shape but cannot distinguish between certain colors. Therefore one usability principle tells us never to rely on color to convey meaning. An important usability principle requires taking steps to assure users always feel in control. Progress bars and hourglasses give users a sense of where they are in a process, contributing to their sense of control. Another principle obliges UEs to direct users through design, for example, leading them through a Web-based form, by following their expectations, for example, whether the family name should precede or follow the last name.

Stakeholders

Everyone who has any interest in a Web site is a stakeholder, whether they are company officers, the marketing team, or the system administrators in charge of maintaining the site. Site providers are the stakeholders who finance the Web site and set the business goals. They stipulate the purpose of the site from the business point of view. They allocate resources and set policy.

Although some consider UEs to be principally user advocates, UEs have another equally important job. That is to address the concerns of stakeholders during software development. It is the UE's responsibility to make sure that the design, while promoting users' success and satisfaction, also promotes the aims of the Web site's stakeholders.

Sometimes stakeholders have misconceptions about the worth of usability engineering or how it integrates with software engineering. Recognizing and addressing this fact is an essential task for UEs; they must remedy these misconceptions or expect little chance of successfully integrating usability engineering in a Web development project (Hix & O'Connell, 2005). For example, it is not uncommon for stakeholders to mistakenly consider usability engineering an expensive add-on that puts users' needs above all others. To counter this misconception, the UE will give examples of usability as a cost-effective and cost-justifiable, integral contributor to achieving the site providers' goals while instilling usability (e.g., Mayhew & Tremaine, 2005; Web Accessibility Initiative, n.d.). Another means to overcoming stakeholder misconceptions is to bring them in to watch early usability evaluation sessions where they see users encountering usability problems. When they return for later sessions after changes have been made to the UI, stakeholders observe users experiencing the benefits of designing for usability.

SOFTWARE ENGINEERING

Software engineering is the "application of a systematic, disciplined, quantifiable approach to the development, operation, and maintenance of software" (IEEE, 1990, p. 70). A software engineer plays two roles, computer scientist and project manager. On a large Web project, software engineers typically oversee both the technical and management aspects of development. They accomplish this by following lifecycles that stipulate, for example, a project's phases, methods, activities, inputs, outputs, milestones, documentation, and risk mitigation strategies.

The software engineering view of usability has not always coincided with the UE's definition or outlook. Historically, software engineering's attention to usability was largely confined to summative testing activities (Hix & Hartson, 1993), validation at project's end that people can use a Web site. Now, software engineers more often consider usability a valuable part of Web site development lifecycles.

INTEGRATING USABILITY ENGINEERING INTO SOFTWARE ENGINEERING LIFECYCLES

Software engineering lifecycles are hospitable to usability engineering. Commonalities between software engineering and usability engineering facilitate this compatibility. The two professions share tools such as use cases, although they sometimes employ them differently. They have the common goal of delivering quality Web sites, on time and on budget, to satisfied users, customers, and other stakeholders. They share terminology, but sometimes with different meanings or connotations. For example, in software engineering, the word *interface* primarily means a connection between two components of a software system, whereas, to a UE, *interface* first and foremost denotes the human-computer interface.

Software engineering and usability engineering processes can occur in parallel because their activities and outputs are compatible. Sometimes these processes are rigid, but the constraints of developing Web sites in real time against tight schedules and tighter budgets drive a trend toward adaptability. This trend emphasizes the need for a UE. In this fast-paced environment, users on the development team can be few and their involvement infrequent. In such a case, a UE draws on knowledge of the field, for example, usability principles and knowledge of users, to aid in the development of usable Web sites.

LIFECYCLE ACTIVITIES

Usability engineering has corresponding activities for most software engineering activities. Not all lifecycles incorporate the same activities. Activity sequence and frequency can vary. Some activities can be simultaneous. Each activity has goals, inputs, processes, and products.

In Figure 1, we present a high-level view of a user-centered software engineering lifecycle. We use a generic lifecycle where all activities are connected to each other, feeding output into subsequent activities. The sequence of activities is adaptable. Within each activity, usability engineering and software engineering processes occur simultaneously.

Table 1 sets out some activities and processes of software development lifecycles. In addition to usability in general, the goal or objective of these activities and processes is to provide accessibility for people with disabilities. This table is not comprehensive, but it demonstrates how some usability engineering processes can be integrated into a software development lifecycle.

Although we maintain the importance of usability engineering throughout Web site development (e.g., Murphy, Marquis, Nichols, Kennedy, & Mingay, 2001), our discussion zooms in on the most critical iterative process areas. These core activities are project planning, requirements definition, design, and evaluation/testing. Although these are a subset of all possible software engineering activities, we designate these activities as core because they represent the "make it or break it" points in a typical software engineering lifecycle where usability engineering must be addressed. However, none of these activities stands alone. So, we place them within the context of other typical iterative lifecycle activities such as product conceptualization and version production.

Project Planning

A Web site project starts as an idea. This can be a new idea encapsulating the site providers' vision. More often, at the end of a lifecycle, a team returns to product conceptualization when they evaluate an existing site and begin to plan future versions. In either case, the team needs a blueprint for the steps between the original concept and the insertion of the final product into the workplace. This blueprint is called the project plan.

Formal software engineering lifecycles start with project planning. Successful project planning depends on a clear understanding by all team members of the site providers' vision as well as an appreciation of the concerns of other stakeholders. Usability engineering and user involvement must be addressed from the start in the plan's schedule and budget. If not, they are excluded early, with little chance of later inclusion. This is true whether development focuses on a new site or an existing site.

Project planning aims to ensure on-time, on-budget delivery of a Web site that meets its providers' organizational goals and fulfills requirements. Usability engineering adds the goals of users' success and satisfaction. Another primary goal is to gain site provider and team acceptance of usability engineering (Hix & O'Connell, 2005). Input to project plan-

Table 1. Usability engineering activities and processes during a software development lifecycle (Partially based on Addelston & O'Connell, 2005; Mayhew, 1992)

Software & Usability Engineering Lifecycle Activities	Examples of Usability Engineering Processes
Product Conceptualization	Literature review, for example, to check latest research results
	Expert review of competition or legacy Web site
	Brainstorming
	Collection and analysis of users' feedback on legacy Web site
Project Planning	Overview planning, for example, project summary with requirements
	Project organization planning, for example, identifying and assigning resources, roles, and responsibilities
	Usability risk management planning
	Technical process planning, for example, accessibility processes, equipment, and tools
	Test planning
	Incorporating UE responsibilities into plan
Requirements Definition	Interviews
	Focus groups
	User profiling
	User class definition
	Translating users' needs into requirements
	Behavioral and cognitive task analysis
	Persona development
	Setting usability goals for evaluation/testing
	Post-release user surveys
	Analyzing usage statistics
	Contextual user observations
Design	User-centered design
	Interaction design (e.g., use cases)
	Participatory design
	Style guide writing
	Story boarding
	Card sorting
Version Production	Instantiating design in Web-authoring tools
Evaluation/Testing (Across versions)	User interface evaluation with user participation (measurement of users' success and satisfaction)
	Expert review
	Automated testing with accessibility tools
Launch & Site Maintenance	No usability engineering processes

ning includes output from product conceptualization such as market analyses and everything learned while maintaining a legacy site.

Typical processes involved in project planning are setting schedules; identifying and allocating resources; and stipulating activities, inputs, outputs, and milestones. Usually, planning is the responsibility of software engineers and managers. However, the UE contributes to planning by identifying the points where usability engineering is necessary and identifying the inputs and outputs needed to proceed from one step to the next. For example, the UE will point out the need to design and produce an accessible version with alt tags (alternative text). An alt tag is HTML code associating words with Web site graphics to describe their content. Alt tags must be present before evaluation with a screen reader, an assistive device that reads aloud the contents of Web pages, including alt tags. Screen reader users include people with little or no eyesight. Assistive hardware, such as a screen magnifier, or software devices, such as screen readers, help people with visual disabilities interact with technology. The UE also alerts the team to the need to schedule users with visual disabilities to participate as evaluators.

The product of these processes is a project plan that integrates usability engineering activities with other scheduled project activities and defines all players' roles, responsibilities, milestones, inputs, and outputs. The unique goals of usability engineering during planning are that the Web site's design will consider the user and be hospitable to user-centered processes, and that the project will fund, schedule, and provide usability engineering. If these goals are to be achieved, the plan must require usability engineering.

Requirements Definition

From the software engineering perspective, requirements definition is a set of processes that identify and document a Web site's goals in terms of how the site will fulfill its providers' vision by delivering information and/or functionality. It focuses on user needs assessment. Usability engineering also looks at the site from the users' perspectives as well to verify that the users' needs and expectations are being met. It addresses user requirements.

Web sites have functional, system performance, and usability requirements. Functional requirements define what a Web site is supposed to do. For example, a functional requirement for an e-commerce site that sells printers stipulates that the site must display photos of the printers. System performance is a measure of how well the Web site does what it is supposed to do. In our example, a system performance requirement stipulates that the site will deliver a specified photo over a 56K modem in less than two seconds. Usability requirements are sometimes called *non-functional* requirements. This term is misleading, however, because it diminishes the importance of usability.

Usability is a measure of users' success and satisfaction with their experience at the site. But usability must also address the goals of the site's providers. For example, the providers of an e-commerce site benefit from having customers revisit their site frequently. To achieve this goal, usability requirements stipulate that a user be able to purchase a product, making no more than one error, and give a satisfaction rating of seven on a scale where nine is the maximum positive rating. Users' success and satisfaction benefit both the users and the site's providers.

Some interface requirements are yes/no, for example, the Web site will provide anchor links on every page at its top two levels. Others are quantified, for example, users will be able to navigate, with only one click, from a product description page to a page where they can order the product.

Some requirements are standards-driven. Standards can be defined by the site provider, for example, an in-house standard for displaying the company logo. Standards can come from groups such as the ISO, which, for example, gives standards for representing names of languages in its ISO 639 (ISO, 2002).

Sometimes requirements are legally mandated. Take the case of "special needs", a term that refers to the needs of users with disabilities. The UI of a U.S. federal government site must comply with Section 508 of the Rehabilitation Act of 1973 as amended in 1998. These requirements aim to provide users who have special needs a quality of information accessibility comparable to that of users without disabilities.

The primary goal of requirements definition for the UE is setting usability requirements, the Web site's obligations to address users' needs. In usability engineering, users' needs and Web site requirements are often the same thing.

Ideally, filling requirements will meet users' needs. However, a Web site can fulfill all functional and system performance requirements, yet still not be usable. In the end, it is the users' experiences of a Web site that determine whether the site has achieved the site providers' vision. So, usability engineering promotes a perspective that incorporates the product concept, but expands it with an understanding of targeted users and their needs. Usability engineering brings an understanding of factors that may otherwise not come into the mix, for example, users' mental models in the context of their capabilities and limitations.

Usability engineering processes during requirements definition start by considering users and their needs within the context of the Web site's intended purposes. Inputs to this process are the providers' goals for the site as well as existing information about targeted users and their needs. As other team members set performance and system function requirements, UEs learn whether proposed content will meet not only providers' goals, but also users' needs. If the provider's goal is to inform users about weather conditions, are users people who need to know only tomorrow's temperature and precipitation forecast, or do they include fishermen interested in tides as well? If the project involves an existing site, UEs address what worked and what did not work for its current users. This understanding empowers UEs to leverage the fact that each user's experience of the site is a reflection of that user's needs and expectations.

Requirements definition brings the UE face-to-face with targeted users during interviews, focus groups, and observations in their workplaces, that is, any place where people interact with the Web. The UE develops surveys and studies existing documentation such as usage statistics for a legacy site. However, existing documentation often omits the users' real-world practices. Therefore, close interaction with users is key. However, the Web introduces the requirement of designing for a wider range of users than a project can usually involve. This factor dictates that the UE rely also on usability principles and knowledge of human capabilities and limitations within the context of Web use. The UE consults resources, such as Web sites on Web usage statistics, to keep abreast of changing interaction behaviors (e.g., Internet World Stats Market Research, 2005; Refsnes Data, 2005). Such resources inform production conceptualization as well as requirements definition.

The UE aims for user-informed requirements, but not necessarily user-driven requirements. Although users' input is integral and respected, the UE must also draw on knowledge of usability engineering to inform recommendations for requirements. For example, when information must be stressed, users may have a preference for many colors and other emphasis techniques on the same display. The UE knows that a user-driven requirement for large blocks of text in upper case, presented in a large variety of strongly contrasting colors will result in adverse effects on user performance (e.g., Koyani et al., 2003). The usability-engineered requirement will specify what portion of the text to emphasize and how to emphasize it in a way that promotes users' success. For example, the requirement will stipulate initial capitals and no more than three or four compatible colors that can be distinguished by most users with visual color deficiencies.

Once the UE has collected data on users, data analysis occurs. The first step is to define user profiles, descriptions of the Web site's target population. User profiles record user attributes such as computer literacy; experience in the subject matter and functionality of the site; physical and cognitive capabilities and limitations; special needs; education; mental models; interaction styles; goals at the site; and tasks — all important factors that impact on user interaction with the site. In another process, user class analysis (also called user group analysis), the UE allocates user profiles into groups according to shared attributes, thereby defining user types, such as patients or policy holders.

In behavioral and cognitive task analysis (also called process analysis), the UE develops descriptions of users' goals and the tasks they perform to accomplish those goals. These definitions are developed within the context of the site providers' intended purposes for the site. During this key requirements definition activity, the UE studies existing documents and observes users to learn the steps and sequences that they take to accomplish goals. Behavioral analysis documents observable tasks such as receiving information and inputting to the computer. Cognitive task analysis documents users' mental transformations and decisions. Doing mental arithmetic is an example of a mental transformation. Do users have to keep a running total in mind of their bill on an e-commerce site or does the Web site do it for them? When comparing products as the basis for decision making, is the product information displayed in a way that facilitates comparison, or does the user have to navigate between pages to find comparative data?

Task analyses include steps and work flows. They describe the users' experience from beginning to end. For example, when users must fill out a form on a secure Web site, the UE documents the experience by identifying the initial steps users need to go through, such as receiving an information package in the mail, locating the URL for the site, locating the user's unique identifying number for login, all long before the user navigates to the form (Gordon & Gill, 1997; Hackos & Redish, 1998; Kirwan & Ainsworth, 1992; Redish & Wixon, 2003; Schraagen, Chipman, & Shalin, 2000; Vicente, 1999).

During requirements analyses, the UE can develop personas, imaginary representatives of highly specified classes of users (e.g., Head, 2003; Pruitt & Grudin, 2003). Personas reflect what has been learned about users during requirements analysis. They are detailed descriptions of typical users, often given names and illustrated with commercial photographs. Personas become almost real to the team, serving as reminders of typical users' needs.

The UE tracks the findings of these processes to the site's intended content to assure that it is presented in a manner that empowers users to achieve their goals at the site. For example, during user class definition, the UE specifies groups of people with disabilities, associating needed assistive devices with the user group. The UE introduces requirements for the site to present content in a way that makes it accessible via these devices.

In translating user needs into requirements, the UE draws on a variety of sources. The site's goals are viewed through the lens of users' needs. For example, consider a case where one of the site's goals is to enhance the organization's image by showing its chief technology officer talking about a new technical approach. Considering users with hearing impairments and users with low bandwidths that rule out multimedia, the UE introduces two usability requirements: (1) captions and (2) a text version of the presentation. Meeting these requirements benefits the organization by spreading the message to some who would not otherwise be able to receive it. Thus, the UE addresses the needs of both the users and the organization that provides the Web site.

Usability requirements become goals for later usability evaluation. Setting specific, measurable usability goals with the client provides a quantitative basis for assessing the design against users' needs (Whiteside, Bennett, & Holtzblatt, 1990).

Although requirements definition produces helpful artifacts such as user profiles, user classes, user task descriptions, and personas, the most important products of requirements definition are the usability requirements that specify the site's look and feel. Usability requirements become a checklist for everything that must be accomplished to promote successful and satisfactory users' experiences at the site.

A project benefits from understanding users, the motives behind their actions, and the rationales behind their opinions about the site. When no requirements reflect users and their needs, a project is at high risk of developing an inappropriate site — a site that does not meet its intended users' needs and expectations. It risks wasting time and resources meeting inappropriate goals. It risks negative impacts on schedule and budget because of the need to retrofit, that is, redesign and recode the UI to correct usability problems.

Although requirements are established at the beginning of a project, they are iteratively reviewed and updated as more is learned about users and the ways that the Web site's look, feel, functioning, and performance impact users' success and satisfaction.

Design

Incorporating users' input from requirements definition, the UE participates in developing the site's information architecture. Information architecture is like a road map; it sets out the paths that users follow to their destinations on a Web site. It is at the heart of design. Impacting more than site navigation, the information architecture impacts a page's content and layout. The UE's role is to assure that the information architecture facilitates navigation and makes finding information natural for users.

Important UCD processes, collectively called interaction design, consider the ways that real users attempt to accomplish goals at a Web site. UEs base interaction design on all that they have learned about the users, for example, their age-based capabilities, mental models, and expectations within the context of the goals of the site's providers. Usability principles provide UEs with rules of thumb that inform UCD decisions. Consider a site intended for senior citizens who expect a prominent link to articles about leisure activities for seniors. The UE considers usability principles on legibility for older users with decreased visual acuity. These principles recommend a large font and a strong contrast between the font and background colors (e.g., Czaja & Lee, 2003).

User-Centered Design

Best practices in usability engineering include UCD, a set of usability engineering processes that focus on understanding users, their goals, their strengths and limitations, their work processes — all user attributes that impact how users will interact with a Web site.

The goal of UCD is to achieve users' success and satisfaction by incorporating the users' perspective into design.

The UE's multi-disciplinary background adds value to interface design. For example, understanding technology is a prerequisite for designing an accessible Web site. Publishing a Web site is simple nowadays. Adding unneeded features is tempting, just because it is so easy to do. The UE knows how to manage the impact of features, such as animations, on users with disabilities. It is a simple matter to give an information site a bright red background with flashing blue bold titles. The UE understands the biological impacts of such an approach, the potential for the eye to become fatigued because it is unable to focus (Travis, 1991). The UE also knows that animations increase download time and, that therefore, on an informational site, animations can reduce users' satisfaction.

The UE brings to UCD an understanding of disciplines such as psychology and semiotics, the science of signs and symbols. When incorporating icons into a UI design, for example, it is important to use standard icons to mean what they usually mean and to test any new designs for user comprehension. If a standard icon is used to mean something different from what the users expect, it is likely to cause confusion. Many users will have no idea how to interpret an ambiguous icon in the context of their tasks. With effort, users can learn arbitrary meanings for icons, but they easily forget arbitrary meanings. Icons need text labels to clearly indicate the actions that will occur when they are activated (Horton, 1994).

The UE applies usability principles to participatory design, a UCD process in which users comment on design concepts and perhaps generate their own sketches. Users offer opinions on mock-ups or prototypes. A prototype Web site is like a preview of coming attractions at the cinema. It includes a sampling, but not all of the features and functions of the planned site. Sometimes it is an experiment to investigate UI concepts.

A typical participatory design process is card sorting, where users sort terms that are going to be used in the Web site into groups which they name. The UE combines results from all participants through a statistical technique. Applying usability principles, the UE then derives a meaningful organization of topics for the Web site to inform the information architecture.

We distinguish between *user-centered* design and inappropriate *user-driven* design where users' input translates directly into design directives. Although user-driven design has the admirable quality of being user-focused, it excludes the input of a UE. In turning users' requests into design decisions without looking at them in light of usability principles, practitioners of user-driven design run a high risk of producing Web sites that, in the end, do not meet users' needs. Another pitfall of user-driven design is requirements creep that extends schedules and strains budgets as users add inappropriate features and functions that, at worse, will have a negative impact on their experience at the site (Andre & Wickens, 1995).

Ideally, a team of designers, developers, and UEs document UCD decisions in a style guide to promote consistent design. For example, a style guide specifies conventions for screen layout; size, spacing, and location rules for screen elements; and fonts, icons, and color palettes. The style guide evolves, continually updated to record new design decisions.

Design is rarely a one-time effort. Design versions are iteratively evaluated and revised throughout the lifecycle. In many lifecycles, design and version production are interspersed or even simultaneous. In these situations, the UE performs design consultations and evaluates iterative products, informing design decisions with knowledge of users and usability principles. UCD results in a plan for the ways that users will interact with the Web site.

The principal product of design is not necessarily a ready-to-publish Web site. It can be a prototype.

Traditionally, during design, the UE has been a user advocate who consults on decisions involving the UI. In this fast-paced age, UEs are more and more involved in design creation and version production, using Web site creation tools.

Although design iterations occur throughout the lifecycle, once part of the site is implemented, programmers are naturally reluctant to make changes. Engineering usability up front reduces the need to request changes after programming. This is why UEs and programmers need to work closely together during UC design.

The principal benefit of having a UE in the loop is that design is more likely to speak to users' needs. Results include increased productivity, shorter learning times, longer and repeated visits, increased profits, and decreased costs (e.g., Bias & Mayhew, 2005; Kalin, 1999; Mayhew 1999).

Use Cases

A use case is a formal description of ways a product can be used. It consists of a statement of goals with a description of the users and the processes the designers expect them to perform to achieve those goals. Sometimes, a use case is expressed in a sketch. Use cases first come into play in task analysis activities during requirements definition. They are referred to during design.

Use cases provide an example of how a UE can prevent a well-intentioned practice from misrepresenting users. Use cases are the product of a process analysis technique to develop a simple, high-level statement of users' goals and processes. Use cases are common to the tool kits of both software engineers and usability engineers.

Basing Web design on use cases has strengths and weaknesses. For each module of a system, common processes are written up with the prerequisites for each process, the steps to take for the users and the system, and the changes that will be true after the process is completed. Use cases help to ensure that frequent processes are supported by the system, that they are relatively straightforward, and that the system architecture reflects the process structure.

Use cases, however, do not account for all possible user interactions at the Web site. Use cases tend to stress behavioral tasks, but do not capture cognitive tasks. Use cases do not leave room for users' unexpected actions at the Web site. Users will naturally do what seems apparent to them, based on the cues given by the UI. A use case does not necessarily represent a natural action for users in the context of the moment. Use cases can put users in the position of having to provide unexpected input to the computer — input that the computer needs but that users do not necessarily know they are supposed to provide.

Use cases make assumptions about the users, for example, that they understand the internal logic of the system the way developers do. Consider novice users who try to use the back button only to discover it does not work because a second browser instance has launched unannounced and without taking focus. The use case depicts users navigating between browser instances, but does not accommodate their expectation to use the back button or the fact that they do not know about the second browser.

The limitations of use cases demonstrate the need for usability engineering. If design relies on use cases but omits a use case for a certain goal/process set, the site will lack important functionality or information. Conversely, use cases not derived from understanding users can result in unnecessary features or information. The UE adds value to use cases by making user-centered recommendations that would not be in the picture otherwise. The UE adds the human dimension to an otherwise limited view of the user as the provider of input to the computer and the recipient of output from the computer. The UE knows that factors such as the user's thoguht processes and physical abilities are key to system success.

As with any other tool, use cases must evolve as a project progresses. During updates, the UE introduces the user perspective, incorporating what has been learned since the last iteration about how users will interact with the site. Without a UE, the project risks misapplying use cases. For example, avoiding a one-to-one relationship between use case and screen, the UE assures that screens accommodate users' decision-making strategies and work flows, not someone else's model of discrete interactions.

Evaluation/Testing

Verification and validation (V&V) are software engineering terms for testing. Verification is iterative testing against requirements. Validation is the final testing against requirements at the end of the lifecycle. Usability evaluation is a set of V&V processes that occurs in conjunction with other V&V activities and is an integral component of an overall V&V approach. In addition to checking for conformance to usability requirements, usability evaluation has the added goal of assessing a wide range of users' experiences at the site. The UE keeps the door open for new requirements based on the way real users interact with the site. New requirements become input to the next cycle. At project's end, they become input for new product conceptualization.

Key user-centered, usability evaluation processes entail observing users interacting with a Web site. Activities for formal user observation include writing a test plan; identifying participant users; working with site providers to set usability goals for each user group and task; defining tasks; writing statements of goals that never tell users how to achieve those goals; preparing a user satisfaction survey; preparing ancillary materials such as consent forms; carrying out the observations; analyzing data, and writing a report (Lazar, Murphy, & O'Connell, 2004). These formal processes entail structuring evaluation activities to reflect the tasks identified during requirements definition.

Evaluation draws on the products of all earlier activities. For example, usability goals are based on input from task analysis (Whiteside et al., 1990). Designers also identify features or functions about which they have usability concerns. The UE makes sure that these concerns are addressed in the scenarios to generate information needed to inform UCD decisions.

During a usability evaluation session, users work with scenarios, sometimes behind one-way glass. On the other side of the glass, UEs often employ click-capture software; record numbers and types of user errors; document latency periods when users pause for a significant period of time trying to figure out what to do next; and record critical incidents where users must stop work because of difficulties with the Web site. Ideally, the providers, developers, and stakeholders observe users as they try to accomplish tasks at the site. Observing users interacting with the site can show them the need for changes. Nothing speaks louder about the quality of a Web site than the experiences of its users.

Using a method called *think aloud*, the UE encourages users to talk about their expectations and reactions while they work with the Web site. The output is metric data on users' success accompanied by anecdotal data, the users' own comments on what they were doing and why and what they think of the site. UEs are specially trained to put users at ease during observations and to facilitate the users' evaluation experience, without telling users how to accomplish their tasks.

After usability observations, users often complete satisfaction surveys on their experience with the Web site. In an effort to foster reliability, the UE only collects and processes feedback on those elements of the site that the user has experienced. These surveys typically collect ratings on a numerical scale to produce metric data. They also offer opportunities for users to elaborate on their experiences.

The UE never relies solely on satisfaction data, but uses it to inform analysis of performance data collected during user interactions with the Web site. Users often report higher levels of satisfaction than would be expected from their observed performance. This is one reason why UEs interview users about their experience at the end of the session. Another reason is to give users opportunities to bring up points that no one else has anticipated. It is common for developers and other stakeholders to talk with users at this point, too.

Formal usability observations can take place wherever users interact with the Web site. With increasing personal computer sales and the proliferation of mobile devices, people are viewing the same sites from different locations: a conventional office, a crowded cyber café, or a subway train. Each location impacts the user experience differently. A conventional office can have lights that glare on the screen, ringing phones, and frequent interruptions from colleagues. The cyber café can have background noise and poor lighting. The subway can cause breaks in connectivity and the need to view only small chunks of information on a small mobile phone screen. Because of this, when possible, UEs try to hold observations in environments where the site will be used. Otherwise, when possible, they simulate the work environment within the evaluation environment to produce more valid findings.

It is unusual to hold formal usability observations at every development iteration. Indeed, some projects find even one or two rounds of user observations to be cost prohibitive. However, other simple, less expensive processes incorporate users' perspectives. In an expert review, one or more UEs independently assess an interface against their understanding of users; usability principles; and applicable laws and standards. If more than one UE has performed the expert review, the UEs then meet to discuss and prioritize their findings before discussing them with the rest of the team. Another kind of expert review employs automated accessibility tools, for example, InSight/InFocus (SSB Technologies, 2004). Such tools inspect the Web site code for the UI for conformance with accessibility regulations. They identify violations and recommend remedies.

A lifecycle typically includes several V&V iterations. The product of usability evaluation is a set of recommendations to improve the potential for users' success and satisfaction with the UI. The principal benefit is an understanding of how users interact with the site (Dumas & Redish, 1999). A unique benefit of usability engineering is the coordination of these recommendations with other stakeholder, organizational, and project goals.

Without a UE, the team risks relying on processes that appear to be usability evaluation, but actually fall short of delivering user-centered products. Examples of pseudo-usability engineering include having stakeholders other than real users provide feedback on interacting with the Web site. Another example is simply asking users to say what they like and dislike. The Web is rife with misinformation about usability engineering. Someone other than a UE trying to engineer usability based on such misinformation can arrive at invalid recommendations that fail to improve the user experience and, at worst, can degrade it. Nothing takes the place of actual success and satisfaction data collected from representative users and interpreted by trained usability engineers.

SUMMARY

We maintain that usability engineering is rigorous, process-based, and addresses needs of stakeholders, such as site providers, as well as users. We have set out a typical software engineering process and discussed key usability engineering contributions. We have demonstrated simultaneous, complementary activities whose products benefit later activities without adversely affecting schedules. We have shown what would be lacking without usability engineering and how the potential of users' success and satisfaction increases with usability engineering. We stress that usability engineering is the means to providing successful and satisfactory experiences for Web site users while fulfilling the goals of the site's providers. The UE's contribution is integral to Web site development.

REFERENCES

Addelston, J. D., & O'Connell, T. A. (2004). Usability and the agile project management process framework. *Cutter Consortium Agile Project Management Executive Report, 5*(10).

Addelston, J. D., & O'Connell, T. A. (2005). Integrating accessibility into the spiral model of the software development lifecycle. In *Proceedings of the 11th International Conference on Human-Computer Interaction* (Volume 8 — Universal Access in HCI: Exploring New Dimensions of Diversity). Las Vegas, NV: Mira Digital Publishers. CD-ROM.

Andre, A. D., & Wickens, C. D. (1995). When users want what's NOT best for them. *Ergonomics in Design, 4,* 10-14.

Baddeley, A. (1990). *Human memory.* Boston: Allyn & Bacon.

Bias, R. G., & Karat, C. M. (2005). Justifying cost-justifying usability. In R. G. Bias & D. J. Mayhew (Eds.), *Cost justifying usability: An update for the Internet age* (2nd ed., pp. 2-16). San Francisco: Elsevier.

Bolt, R. A. (1984). *The human interface: Where people and computers meet.* Toronto, Canada: Wadsworth.

Brown, E. L., & Deffenbacher, K. (1979). *Perception and the senses.* New York: Oxford University Press.

Caldwell, B., Chisholm, W., Slatin, J., & Vanderheiden, G. (Eds.). (2005, June 30). *Web content accessibility guidelines 2.0 (WCAG 2.0).* Working draft. Retrieved July 13, 2005, from http://www.w3.org/TR/WCAG20/#robust

Carroll, J. M. (1990). Mental models in human-computer interaction. In M. Helander (Ed.), *Handbook of human-computer interaction* (pp. 45-65). New York: Elsevier B.V.

Crandall, B., Kline, G., & Hoffman, R. R. (2006). *Working minds: A practitioner's guide to cognitive task analysis.* Cambridge, MA: MIT Press.

Czaja, S. J., & Lee, C. C. (2003). Designing computer systems for older adults. In J. A. Jacko & A. Sears (Eds.), *The human-computer interaction handbook: Fundamentals, evolving technologies, and emerging applications* (pp. 413-427). Mahwah, NJ: Erlbaum.

Dumas, J. S., & Redish, J. C. (1999). *A practical guide to usability testing* (Rev. ed.). Portland, OR: intellect.

Garrett, J. J. (2002). *The elements of user experience: User-centered design for the Web.* Thousand Oaks, CA: New Riders.

Gordon, S. E., & Gill, R. T. (1997). Cognitive task analysis. In C. Zsambok & G. Klein (Eds.), *Naturalistic decision making* (pp. 131-140). Hillsdale, NJ: Erlbaum.

Hackos, J., & Redish, J. (1998). *User and task analysis for interface design*. New York: Wiley.

Head, A. J. (2003). Personas: Setting the stage for building usable information sites. Retrieved July 16, 2005, from http://www.infotoday.com/online/jul03/head.shtml

Hix, D., & Hartson, H. R. (1993). *Developing user interfaces: Ensuring usability through product & process*. New York: Wiley.

Hix, D., & O'Connell, T. A. (2005). Usability engineering as a critical process in designing for accessibility. In *Proceedings of the 11th International Conference on Human-Computer Interaction* (Volume 8 — Universal Access in HCI: Exploring New Dimensions of Diversity). Las Vegas, NV: Mira Digital Publishers. CD-ROM.

Horton, W. (1994). *The icon book*. New York: Wiley.

Institute of Electrical and Electronics Engineers (IEEE). (1990). *IEEE standard glossary of software engineering terminology* (IEEE Standard 610.12-1990). New York: IEEE.

International Organization for Standardization (ISO). (1998). *Guidance on usability*. (ISO 9241-11). Geneva, Switzerland: ISO.

International Organization for Standardization (ISO). (2002). *Codes for the representation of names of languages*. (ISO 639). Retrieved July 20, 2005, from http://www.ics.uci.edu/pub/ief/http/related/iso639.txt

Internet World Stats Market Research. (2005). *Internet User Statistics and Population Stats for 51 Countries and Regions — North America, Central America, South America and the Caribbean*. Retrieved July 11, 2005, from http://www.internetworldstats.com/stats2.htm#north

Johnson-Laird, P. N. (1983). *Mental models*. Cambridge, UK: Cambridge University Press.

Kalin, S. (1999, April 1). Usability mazed and confused. *CIO Web Business Magazine*. Retrieved July 16, 2005, from http://www.cio.com/archive/webbusiness/040199_use.html#price

Kirwan, B., & Ainsworth, L. K. (Eds.). (1992). *A guide to task analysis*. Philadelphia: Taylor & Francis.

Koyani, S., Bailey, R. W., Nall, J. R., Allison, S., Mulligan, C., Bailey, K., et al. (2003). *Research-based Web design & usability guidelines* (NIH Publication No. 03-5424). Washington, DC: U.S. Department of Health and Human Services

Lazar, J., Murphy, E. D., & O'Connell, T. A. (2004). Building university-government collaborations: A model for students to experience usability issues in the federal workplace. *Journal of Informatics Education Research, 6*(3), 57-78.

Mayer, R. E. (1992). *Thinking, problem solving, cognition* (2nd ed.). New York: W. H. Freeman.

Mayhew, D. J. (1992). *Principles and guidelines in software user interface design*. Englewood Cliffs, NJ: Prentice Hall.

Mayhew, D. J. (1999). *The usability engineering lifecycle: A practitioner's handbook for user interface design*. San Francisco: Morgan Kaufmann.

Mayhew, D. J., & Tremaine, M. M. (2005). A basic framework. In R. G. Bias, & D. J. Mayhew (Eds.), *Cost-justifying usability: An update for the internet age* (pp. 41-101). San Francisco: Elsevier.

Miller, G. A. (1956). The magical number seven plus or minus two: Some limits on our capacity for processing information. *Psychological Review, 63,* 81-97.

Murphy, E., Marquis, K., Nichols, E., Kennedy, K., & Mingay, D. (2001). Refining electronic data-collection instruments and data-collection tools through usability testing.
Research in Official Statistics, 4(2), 23-33.

Norman, D. A., & Draper, S. W. (Eds.). (1986). *User centered system design.* Hillsdale,
NJ: Erlbaum.

O'Connell, T. A. (in press). The why and how of senior-focused design: 21st century user
interface design strategies to empower users born in the 20th century. In J. Lazar (Ed.),
Universal usability. West Sussex, UK: Wiley.

Pruitt, J., & Grudin, J. (2003). Personas: Practice and theory. ACM. Retrieved July 20, 2005,
from http://www.aiga.org/resources/content/9/7/8/documents/pruitt.pdf

Redish, J., & Wixon, D. (2003). Task analysis. In J. A. Jacko & A. Sears (Eds.), *The human-
computer interaction handbook: Fundamentals, evolving technologies, and emerg*ing
applications (pp. 922-940). Mahwah, NJ: Erlbaum.

Refsnes Data. (2005). Browser statistics. Retrieved July 11, 2005, from http://www.w3schools.
com/browsers_stats.asp

Rehabilitation Act, 29 U.S.C. §794d (1973). As amended by the Workforce Investment Act,
PL 105-220 (1998).

Schraagen, J. M., Chipman, S. F., & Shalin, V. L. (2000). *Cognitive task analysis.* Mahwah,
NJ: Erlbaum.

Shneiderman, B. (1998). *Designing the user interface: Strategies for effective human-computer interaction* (3rd ed.). Reading, MA: Addison Wesley Longman.

Shneiderman, B., & Plaisant, C. (2004). *Designing the user interface: Strategies for effective
human-computer interaction* (4th ed.). Reading, MA: Pearson Addison Wesley.

SSB Technologies. (2004). InSight (Version 4.0)/InFocus (Version 4.0). [Computer software].
San Francisco: SSB Technologies.

Travis, D. (1991). *Effective color displays: Theory and practice.* New York: Academic
Press.

Van Der Veer, G. C., & Del Carmen Puerta Melguizo, M. (2003). Mental models. In J. A. Jacko
& A. Sears (Eds.), *The human-computer interaction handbook: Fundamentals, evolving
technologies, and emerging applications* (pp. 52-80). Mahwah, NJ: Erlbaum.

Vicente, K. J. (1999). *Cognitive work analysis: Toward safe, productive, and healthy computer-based work.* Mahwah, NJ: Erlbaum.

Web accessibility initiative (WAI). Retrieved July 16, 2005, from http://www.w3.org/
WAI/

Whiteside, J., Bennett, J., & Holtzblatt, K. (1990). Usability engineering: Our experience
and evolution. In M. Helander (Ed.), *Handbook of human-computer interaction* (pp.
791-817). New York: Elsevier B.V.

World Wide Web Consortium (W3C). (2004).

ENDNOTE

[1]   This material is released to inform interested parties of ongoing research and to encourage discussion of work in progress. The views expressed are those of the authors
and not necessarily those of the U.S. Census Bureau.

Chapter II

How Users
View Web Pages:
An Exploration of Cognitive
and Perceptual Mechanisms

Rebecca A. Grier, Aptima, Inc., USA

Philip Kortum, Rice University, USA

James T. Miller, AT&T Labs, USA

ABSTRACT

This chapter presents the basic cognitive and perceptual attentional mechanisms that affect how users view Web pages and the methods used to measure this attention. It describes the groundbreaking work of Faraday (2000), who proposed a visual scanning model of Web pages based on salient visual elements, and summarizes data from eye-tracking techniques that reveal the strengths and weaknesses of the Faraday model. The primary goal of the chapter is to help the reader gain an understanding of what visual elements on a Web page draw a user's attention, how that knowledge can be collected, and how it can be applied to the design of useful and usable Web sites.

DEFINING AN EFFECTIVE WEB PAGE

An effective Web page design meets the goals of both the site owner and the site user. One of the key requirements for ensuring that a user can accomplish the tasks intended by the site owner is an understanding of how users attend to Web pages and designing pages in accordance with this understanding. Designing Web pages that help the user focus on the page elements believed to be critical by the Web site owner is the subject of this chapter. Fundamentally, this process rests on guiding the user's attention to the page elements that are critical for the Web site owner and critical for task completion.

Until Faraday (2000) wrote his theory of how users attend to Web pages, no systematic evaluation of the attentional elements of Web pages had been performed. A greater understanding of these elements might help clarify some of the important underlying principles of Web page design. Faraday's (2000) theory identified a number of salient visual elements (SVEs) that could be found on a Web page and provided a description of how those elements are scanned by a user. In this chapter we discuss Faraday's model and other variables that might have an impact on user's attention. This discussion of Faraday's model is followed by a presentation of the results of a rigorous test of the model (see Grier, 2004 for details) using data from extensive eye-tracking experiments. Findings from these studies have been incorporated into a new theory of the factors that control users' attention on Web pages. Design implications of this theory of attention for the development and evaluation of Web pages are provided. We begin the chapter with a basic discussion of attention and common attention measurement techniques in order to help the reader frame the issues that are relevant to visual attention and Web design.

ATTENTION BASICS

Attention is the result of cognitive processes that guide the user's focus in a controlled fashion. One cognitive model of attention, the spotlight model, uses an analogy of a beam of light to represent attention. The illumination of the center of the beam is strongest and represents the focus of attention. The spotlight (and attention) weakens the farther it is from the center. Once an object has been processed, the attentional spotlight can be shifted from one object to another (Posner, 1978; Styles, 1997). Eye movements can be viewed as an index of attention analogous to the spotlight metaphor and facilitate measuring attentional shifts from one location to another. Attention in the presence of eye movements has been labeled overt attention (Hoffman, 1998; Kramer & McCarley, 2003).

There are also a number of models of attention based on experiments that use stimuli presented at durations too brief for the execution of an eye movement. Experiments of this sort have identified several important results that together are labeled covert attention (Hoffman, 1998; Kramer & McCarley, 2003). Covert attention models describe a number of important phenomena, chief among these being the ability to direct attention to different locations in space in the absence of eye movements (Eriksen & Yeh, 1985; Posner, 1980). This ability would seem to be at odds with the overt attention models that require eye movements in order to focus attention.

The current view, known as the pre-motor theory, reconciles this discrepancy by asserting that both types of attention are controlled by similar mechanisms and that covert attention would normally direct saccadic eye movements to appropriate objects except when task limitations prevent doing so (Palmer, 1999). Support for this view comes from experiments indicating that target detection/discrimination is best when target location coincides with the location of saccades (Hoffman & Subramaniam, 1995; Rorden & Driver, 1999). These and similar results have led Kramer and McCarley (2003) to conclude that covert attention and overt spotlight attention are tightly coupled.

Perceptual Mechanisms

There are a number of physical features in the visual world that draw a user's attention. Faraday (2000) identified six SVEs that draw attention in Web pages. These include motion, size, color, text-style, the presence of images, and the position of components on the Web page. Motion is one of the most frequently discussed of these qualities, because the visual system is so highly sensitive to motion as evidenced by velocity detection thresholds as small as 1 to 2 minutes of arc/sec (Graham, 1965; Hochberg, 1971). Motion has also been shown to attract attention away from other stimuli (Boyce & Pollatsek, 1992; Thomas, 1968), indicating its strength relative to other SVEs.

Like motion, size is also a powerful attractor of attention (Wickens & Hollands, 2000; Wolfe, Stewart, Friedman-Hill, Yu, Shorter, & Cave, 1990). Large images are often fixated before and for longer durations than small ones (Yarbus, 1967). Similarly, when given a choice, participants read large text in advertisements before small text (Rayner, Rotello, Stewart, Keir, & Duffy, 2001).

Images (defined here as nontextual characters such as icons, photographs, and graphics) have also been found to capture attention. In fact, some studies have indicated that they actually help guide a reader's attention in examining newsprint (Garcia, 1993). Other studies have shown that the presence of an image can make a warning stand out from its surrounding text (Bzostek & Wogalter, 1999).

Human factors psychologists have long been aware of are the primacy of color in the design of signs and displays (Wickens & Hollands, 2000). Color "pop-out," where colored objects stand out in an array of nontarget items is a well known phenomenon (Treisman & Gelade, 1980). This phenomenon is used in numerous situations where high attention and detectability are desired, for example, the design of warning labels (Adams & Edworthy, 1995; Laughery, Young, Vaubel, & Brelsford, 1993) and highway signs (Schieber, Larsen, Jurgensen, Werner, & Eich, 2001).

Publishers frequently use text style as a means of capturing attention in printed material by bolding, underlining, or italicizing key words to make them stand out from words in plain text. Similarly, graphic designers know that the saliency of different positions can convey importance (Fleming, 1997). For example, in Western culture the top left corner of a display is typically looked at first and elements within this area are perceived as more important than those in other areas; whereas the top right corner plays a similar role in Eastern culture (Megaw & Richardson, 1979; Wallsten & Barton, 1982).

MEASURES OF ATTENTION

Attention must be measured in order to determine where it is directed. This section describes some of the most common methods used and the relative strengths and weaknesses of each. As with most psychological measures, many researchers utilize a combination of these techniques to best match the task at hand.

Indirect Measures

Indirect measures of visual attention rely on inferences about the impact attention has on the performance of a specific task or on a person's own assessment of what was being attended to at any given moment. These measures, particularly ones based on performance, are often the appropriate measure of attention that a Web designer should use, because these measures have a direct relationship with real-world user behavior.

Performance

Performance is one of the most widely used measures of attention, because the data (1) are usually easy and inexpensive to collect, (2) are not subject to the vagaries of memory or report bias, and (3) have high face validity since there is direct applicability to the successful completion of the task being measured. Performance-based measures simply indicate whether or not a person completed a given task — the inference being that successful task completion required the users' attention. Failure to complete the task suggests that insufficient attention was allocated for successful completion. For example, in Benway and Lane's (1998) studies of banner blindness a participant's click on a link or banner ad was used as the performance measure. Successful users, as indicated by those who quickly clicked on the information, likely paid attention to the banner ad. Conversely, users who were slow to click on the information probably did not direct sufficient attention to the banner ad on the Web page.

While seemingly simple, performance-based measures must be constructed and recorded carefully to insure that the selected performance measure is valid as a measure of attention. For example, if a person was asked to locate a camouflaged hunter in an image, success might not be a good measure of attention. Although the participant may have devoted considerable attentional resources to the task, even in the correct areas of the image, the participant might not have been able to detect the hunter. In this case detectability would have been inappropriately measured, rather than attention.

Self-Report

In self-report, participants tell the experimenter whether or not they attended to a specified target. This reporting does not need to take place in real time, but can happen later. For example, after using a Web site to order pizza, a survey might ask the user if he noticed a coupon for free breadsticks. An affirmative response would imply that the user did attend to the coupon, while a negative response would suggest that he did not. The survey could be administered immediately after the user visited a Web site, or, as is frequently done, administered some time after the task was completed.

Recall is a variation of self-report in which a user is asked to describe one or more Web pages after the pages have been viewed. This method has the advantage of pinpointing items that gained a user's attention and were salient enough for the user to remember when reconstructing the page.

Both self-report and recall measures have the advantage of being relatively easy to collect and inexpensive because a large number of users can be queried without direct contact. Because data collection is done after the completion of a task, the method has the significant advantage of answering posthoc questions about user's behaviors. As easy as these procedures are to use, however, self-report and recall have four significant deficiencies that need to be considered.

First, what participants recall about their attention may not be accurate. In other words, (a) they may not have attended to the target at all but thought they did, (b) they may have simply forgotten that they attended to a specific target, or (c) they may not have attended to the target on the visit to the site in which the experimenter was interested.

Second, they may be primed or prompted by another user of the site, thereby altering the attention process. For example, the participant may not have attended to the target initially, but someone might have mentioned the target to the user. Thus primed, the user is prompted to attend to the target on a subsequent visit.

Third, users may have bias concerning the target and (either intentionally or not) incorrectly report their attention to the target. This bias could be either positive or negative — they report attending to it when they did not or they report not attending to it when they did. For example, customers standing in line at a grocery checkout stand might be asked if they saw the article about the alien spacecraft landing in Nebraska. Even though a customer might have seen and read the article, he/she may have a bias against these kinds of publications (i.e., he/she is embarrassed to acknowledge that they read the article) and report not seeing the story. This bi-directional response bias is important to note because it means that no correction factors can be applied to get more accurate data since neither the size nor the direction of the bias can be easily estimated.

Finally, in the use of recall tasks, users frequently generalize from the entire Web browsing experience; so items attributed to a specific page may have come from other pages in the site or even from other Web sites entirely. In general, self-report and recall measures should be used cautiously and, where practical, should be verified with performance-based sample measurements.

Recognition

Recognition tasks are essentially hybrids of performance and self-report measures. In recognition, a participant is shown a target and asked if that target was seen while the task was being performed. In a variation of this task, the user is shown several targets and then asked which one was seen while performing the task. As with all indirect measures, the inference is made that a correct recognition means that the user attended to the target. This kind of indirect measure has the benefit of being somewhat more robust than self-report measures because "blanks" or trials with no "good" targets can be presented to help minimize and estimate response bias. Further, this type of attentional task can also get to the heart of the degree of attention if multiple targets have high confusability. This is especially valuable in Web sites where navigation elements might be confused with content elements or other similar navigation elements on the page.

Recall and recognition tests are frequently performed together during an evaluation. Bayles and Chaparro (2001) used recall and recognition to determine the ability of animated and unanimated banner ads to attract attention. Participants correctly recalled the animated elements, but only about a third could recognize the banner. These results suggest that attention to the banner ad occurred, but only minimally.

Direct Measures of Attention: Eye Tracking

In all of the indirect methods for measuring attention that were just described, attention is inferred from the data. A more direct measure of visual attention (as supported by the pre-motor theory) can be gained by recording where the eye is looking at any given time. These measures can be taken for short viewing experiences or over the course of time of a complete Web site visit. Eye-tracking equipment is now commercially available with sufficient accuracy for most Web-viewing tasks and the equipment has minimal impact on the user's viewing experience.

Before using eye tracking as a measure of attention it is important to understand a few basics about eye movements. Two eye movements that are of prime importance in eye tracking are saccades and fixations (see Dember & Warm, 1979 for a complete review). Saccadic movements are very rapid and abrupt; their primary purpose is to keep objects of interest on the fovea. These saccades may be small (less than three min of visual angle) or large (20° of visual angle) with a person typically making about three to five saccades per second (Fischer & Weber, 1993; Schiffman, 2000).

Between saccades, the eyes fixate an object of interest for varying periods of time depending on the task at hand. During a saccade, vision is attenuated, a phenomenon known as saccadic suppression. This is important because it means that some items on a Web page may not be fully attended to even though the eye may pass over them during a saccade. Once the eye starts a fixation, the majority of the attentional resources go towards processing the information in the center part of that fixation (the foveal image). However, there is still some processing of the information in the areas surrounding the direct focus of attention as demonstrated by Kortum and Geisler (1996). Visual perception, and thus attention to specific elements on a Web page, happens during each of the fixations that occur as a person uses a Web page (Fischer & Weber, 1993; Palmer, 1999).

Eye Tracking in Web Evaluation

Human factors specialists have used eye tracking to study visual attention in a wide variety of domains including flight control (Fitts, Jones, & Milton, 1950; Harris, Tole, Stephens, & Ephrath, 1982), radiological diagnosis (Kundel & LaFollete, 1972), automobile driving (Recarte & Nunes, 2000), and athletic performance (Abernethy, 1988). With the development of the current generation of robust, affordable eye trackers, eye tracking has become practical for studies of visual user interfaces as well, with Yammoto and Kuto (1992) performing some of the first early experiments in this area.

Yammoto and Kuto's (1992) work focused on determining if a text-based DOS interface could be evaluated for usability by an eye-tracking procedure. They determined that scan paths reflected different levels of usability for different layouts. Similarly, Kotval and Goldberg (1998) found that scan path data were effective in evaluating the usability of a layout in a graphical user interface.

Other studies have provided potentially important insights into elements that affect interface observers' scanning behavior as well. Joseph, Knott, and Grier (2002) demonstrated that text formatting could influence the scan efficiency of readers. The Stanford-Poynter project (Lewenstein, Edwards, Tatar, & Devigal, 2000) evaluated the layout of online news sites and determined that textual material is fixated before images (icons, photographs, graphics, etc.). Clearly, studies such as these indicate that eye-movement tracking can be of significant value to designers in the development of computer interfaces, including Web pages.

A MODEL OF VISUAL ATTENTION
TO WEB PAGES

Faraday (2000) published the first model of visual attention to Web pages. Faraday's model postulated that users scanned Web pages in two stages. In Stage 1, the initial entry point to the Web page is determined by the SVEs of the Web page. Faraday proposed that

Figure 1. Poorly designed Web page

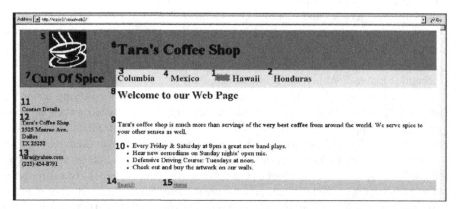

Note: Numbers are the in which order elements will be fixated according to the Faraday (2000) model.

Figure 2. Well-designed Web page

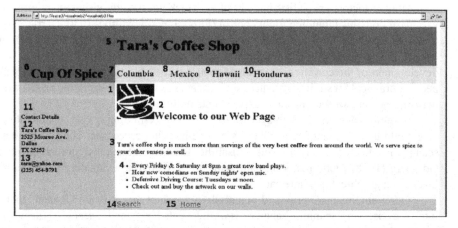

Note: Numbers are the order in which elements will be fixated according to the Faraday (2000) model.

features fell into the following hierarchy: motion, size, image, color, text style (e.g., bold, italics, etc.), and position. That is, if a page element has motion it would be fixated first. If there is no motion on the page, then the largest element on the page will be fixated first, and so forth until the hierarchy is exhausted.

In Stage 2, the area around the entry point is defined and searched. The area around the entry point is defined by Gestalt grouping principles (e.g., background color; see Wertheimer, 1923/1938 for complete review). After it is defined, the area is scanned in normal reading order until all items in the area have been fixated. If the target is not located within the area around the initial entry point, the process iterates. A new fixation point is selected from the hierarchy described in Stage 1. Then the area around this new entry point is defined and scanned. This process repeats until the target is found or the user abandons the search.

To illustrate the model, two versions of a simple e-commerce Web page with predicted scan paths are shown in Figure 1 and Figure 2. These pages are very similar to those used by Faraday (2000) to demonstrate his model. Figure 1 shows a poorly designed page in which the word "new" flashes (has motion) and should serve as the initial entry point in Stage 1. At first, Stage 2 search is limited to the elements sharing the same background color with the initial entry point and proceeds in traditional reading order. Faraday claimed that this was a "poorly designed" page because of the need for recursive eye movements in order to make the transition from "Honduras" to "Columbia," since this movement is counter to traditional Western reading order.

Figure 2 shows a "well-designed" Web page since there are no recursive eye movements within the areas around entry points. Because this page has no motion, the initial entry point is at the "Coffee Cup," the largest component on the page. If the search target is not found within the first entry point, the next entry point would be "Tara's Coffee Shop" since it is the next largest component.

AN EMPIRICAL TEST
OF THE FARADAY MODEL

The Faraday (2000) model provided an initial framework for several empirical studies that were conducted in order to further expand our knowledge regarding how individuals interact with Web pages. The first of these studies (Grier, 2004) used an eye tracker to analyze the scan path of users as they searched one of two Web pages (Figure 1 and Figure 2) for a recent order that they had placed. However, order status information was not available on the site to ensure that an exhaustive search was conducted. Analysis of the scanning sequences was limited to the initial fixation in a given look zone (the page components) and subsequent fixations were not considered. Despite the methodological efforts to force an exhaustive search, not all participants did so.

Grier (2004) analyzed the scan paths by calculating the individual rank order correlations between the predicted and observed fixations for each Web page. A nonsignificant mean rank order correlation for the poorly designed page was found. The rank order correlation for the well-designed page was marginally significant. At best, these findings provide weak support for Faraday's model.

To gain a more complete understanding of the differences between the observed scan paths and the predicted scan paths, Grier (2004) further analyzed specific aspects of the scan paths and fixations. For example, Faraday's (2000) model predicted that "Hawaii" and "Coffee Cup" would be the first look zones to be fixated on for the poorly designed and well-designed Web pages respectively. However, on the poorly designed page, "Welcome" was fixated first significantly more often than chance. On the well-designed page, the "Coffee Cup" was fixated more than any other element (which is in agreement with Faraday's prediction), but this percentage was not significantly greater than chance. Thus, Faraday's model failed to accurately predict the initial fixations.

Another analysis of the scan path components compared the intermediate transitions from one look zone to another. For the poorly designed page, only 4 of the 14 transitions predicted from the Faraday (2000) model significantly exceeded chance. Only 1 of the 14 transitions exceeded chance for the well-designed page. These data suggest that the transition pattern for these participants was far more intricate than that proposed by Faraday. However, the fixation patterns obtained support the notion of areas being searched together (i.e., more within area transitions occurred than between area transitions).

Faraday's (2000) model provided an interesting framework for approaching the problem of visual attention to Web pages. The basic premises of the model seem appropriate given that the SVEs have been found to influence search in other environments such as drawings of natural scenes (Henderson, Weeks, & Hollingworth, 1999) and fractals (Parkhurst, 2002).

These studies suggest that salience may indeed be a key factor in Web search, but that the salience order selected by Faraday (2000) (motion, size, image, color, text-style, and position) may be incorrect. Specifically, Faraday weighted position lowest in the hierarchy but other studies have shown that Web page users examine the center of the page first and more frequently than other areas (Lim & Wogalter, 2000; Schroeder, 1998). Further, the user may have expectations as to where information may be based on experience with the Web in general or that page in particular.

However, it is uncertain how position impacts the viewers scan path. It is possible that some positions are dominant over others as noted previously. It could also be that users' expectation about the specific location of information is based on what is being viewed (Schroeder, 1998). This suggests that the effect of the purely visual elements should be disambiguated from the effects of position and context. In order to more fully examine this hypothesis, four subsequent studies were performed by Grier (2004) to separate the effect of the perceptual features of elements themselves from the position of those elements. Three of these four studies used stimuli that were presented in a simple, context-free display to better understand the impact of position on attention, while the fourth used more natural Web stimuli.

DIAGNOSING THE FAILURE
OF THE FARADAY MODEL

Experiment 1: Perceptual Features and Initial Gaze

The first of these four experiments evaluated the ability of the five SVEs of the Faraday (2000) model — motion, size, image, color and text-style — to attract attention in a visually sparse, context free environment. Position was not included as a factor in this experiment since Faraday considered it to be a default determiner of initial gaze when no other salient visual element is present.

The target page (Figure 3) was not a Web page as before, but rather a display of combinations of the five SVEs (120 in all). An instance of each type of SVE cited by Faraday (2000) was randomly selected and presented on each target array. On each trial, participants were instructed to look at a fixation target presented in the center of the screen. The target screen was presented immediately after the termination of the fixation screen and participants were instructed to look at the items of the screen in any order they wished.

Results indicated that the mean percentage of fixations on the motion SVE was significantly greater than for the other SVEs, which did not differ from each other. Faraday's

Figure 3. Example of the target stimulus in experiment 1

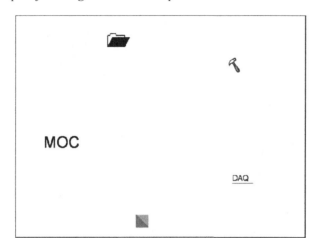

Note: Folder opened and closed.

(2000) assertion that motion is the dominant SVE was substantiated within the relatively austere visual environment of this experiment. Even so, support for the priority of motion was not strong, since the mean first fixation to the motion SVE was only 34.1%. No support at all was obtained for prioritizing the other SVE elements within the SVE hierarchy proposed by Faraday.

Experiment 2: The Effect of Position on Initial Gaze

The second experiment was performed to determine the effects of position on initial gaze to a screen (This experiment was not reported in Grier, 2004). It has been previously shown that first fixation is typically near the center of a monitor screen (Lim & Wolgalter, 2000; Schroeder, 1998). However, the center of the screen was not clearly defined in the previous research and there were no controls for eye position prior to the presentation of the target screen. Although Faraday (2000) did predict that the center of the screen would dominate initial fixation if the screen was mostly images, he also stated that the upper left corner would dominate if the screen was mostly filled with text.

In this experiment, one of four fixation screens (Figure 4) was presented for 1 second prior to the presentation of the stimulus screen. The 20 experimental screens (e.g., Figure 5) displayed five instances of the same SVE, one in each of the four corners and one in the center of the screen. The study used the four corners of the video display terminal (VDT), because of research (e.g., Lim & Wogalter, 2000) demonstrating that these positions are looked at by Web users once the dominant position of the center is removed.

Participants' initial fixations were overwhelmingly to the center of the screen (90.13%) regardless of the initial fixation point or target screen SVEs. These findings strongly support the powerful effect of position in controlling initial gaze within an austere environment.

Figure 4. The four fixation screens used in experiments 2 and 3

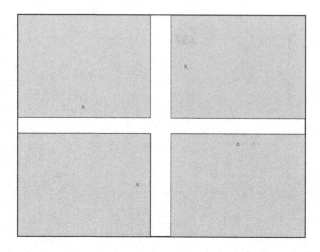

Figure 5. Example of a target page used in experiment 2

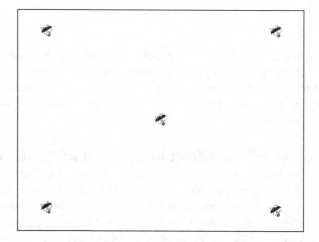

However, they do not address the interaction among position and the SVEs proposed by Faraday (2000).

Experiment 3: Interaction Between SVE Salience and Location

It seems clear that position may play a far more important role in determining first fixations on a Web page than Faraday (2000) supposed. Henderson et al. (1999) and Parkhurst (2002) have suggested that position may be a moderator variable for salience, such that the effectiveness of different salience dimensions may depend upon their spatial location. Experiment 3 tested that possibility with regard to the SVEs described by Faraday.

Results from the experiment showed that there was a statistically significant main effect for SVE and a significant main effect for position with no interaction between these two factors. Motion was fixated first significantly more often than any other SVE; the other SVEs did not differ significantly from each other. The center position was viewed first significantly more often than each of the other positions and the top left position captured first fixations significantly more often than the three other positions. There were no significant differences among the remaining positions.

This experiment replicated the findings of the first experiment in this series, demonstrating again that motion attracted a greater percentage of initial fixations than each of the other SVEs. As in the second experiment, the center was fixated first. However, unlike the previous finding, a clear position hierarchy in determining first fixations was observed. As suggested by Schroeder (1998) and Lim and Wogalter (2000), the center position was looked at first more often that any of the other positions. Additionally, the first-fixation rate of top left position exceeded that of the remaining positions. Moreover, while position did not modify the differences among the SVEs, it did exert a more powerful influence on first fixation than did other SVEs. However, contrary to the suggestion by Henderson et al. (1999) and Parkhurst (2002) the effects associated with the SVE dimension were independent of spatial position. This study clearly demonstrated that position, in particular the center of the screen, has a far more critical impact on initial fixations than described in Faraday's model.

Experiment 4: Validation Using Real Web Pages

There are two possible reasons why these three experiments failed to fully support Faraday's (2000) model. First, the stimuli used have little in common with the complex Web pages typically found on the Internet. Second, participants were asked to freely view these displays, but a vast majority of Internet users are usually searching for particular items of information (U.S. Department of Commerce, 2002) when they use the Web. Accordingly, the final experiment in this investigation featured a realistic Web page in which observers had the opportunity to actually locate the information for which they searched.

Sixteen high-fidelity examples of an e-commerce Web page were created (e.g., Figure 6). Each example was presented as if in Internet Explorer 6.0 and typified a portal style Web page with a navigation bar. The content on each page was the same, but content organization was different (see Grier, 2004 for details). On each page the participant was required to search for a single designated target — one of the page links or components. The target was presented equally often at the four corners or the center of the screen. All possible combinations of position of target and position of motion were tested. Both indirect measures (accuracy and speed) and direct measures (eye tracking) of attention were recorded. The overall mean accuracy of finding the designated target was 94.5%. Because of this high accuracy rate, search time was used as the principal performance measure in this study.

Contrary to predictions, significant main effects were found for target position and motion position with a significant interaction between these factors. Based on the previous experiments in the series, Grier (2004) had hypothesized that performance would be best when targets appeared in the center of the screen. Conversely, Faraday's (2000) model would lead one to believe that the congruence of motion and target position would lead to the fastest detection times regardless of position of target. Neither of these predictions held

Figure 6. Example of a target stimulus screen in experiment 4

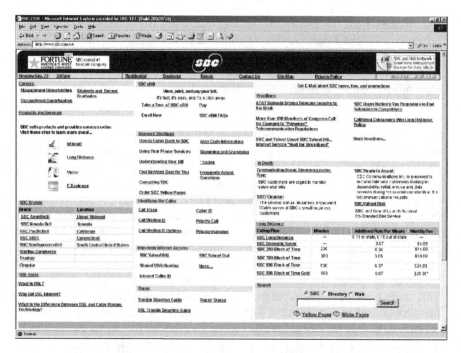

Note: Frequently asked questions flashed.

true. Indeed, the overall fastest detection times were for targets in the top left and bottom left positions. However, the advantages of these positions depended upon the concurrent motion position. The nature of this interaction was very complex, supporting the theory that something other than perceptual features is driving users' scan paths.

In order to better understand this complex interaction, the eye-tracking data were analyzed. The first analysis determined if participants gazed at the animation on each stimulus screen as would be predicted by Faraday's (2000) model. The overall frequency of fixations on motion was 52.53%, which is significantly less than the 100% asserted by the Faraday model. Analysis indicated that the frequency of motion fixations seemed to depend on the position of the motion SVE. When motion was in the bottom right it was fixated on significantly less often than when motion was in the top left, bottom left, or center of the screen. Motion in the center of the screen was fixated significantly more often than when motion was in the top right corner of the screen. This finding is counter to that which was observed in Experiment 3, which suggests that the context of Web pages does indeed influence visual attention.

While position served as a moderator variable for motion, it too did not fare well as a dominant determinant of participants' attention. For each participant, the area in which the first fixation occurred on any given presentation was identified. Although first fixations for the center screen position occurred significantly more often than chance, first fixations found here were much less frequent than found in Experiments 2 and 3. Moreover, the top left corner position did as well as or slightly better than the center position in attracting first fixations, a result not seen with the simpler content-free displays employed in Experiments 2 and 3. The center right, bottom left, bottom center, and bottom right were all fixated on first significantly less than chance.

Summary of the Experiments

The final experiment in this investigation utilized realistic Web pages to evaluate Faraday's (2000) model of users' scan paths in light of the earlier findings that position was the dominant initial fixation area. However, a complex pattern that is not readily explainable simply on the basis of target/motion or target/position congruencies was found. In addition, the eye-tracking data also provided little support that scan paths are determined on the basis of SVEs alone.

One of the critical differences between the two studies using Web pages and the three studies using the austere visual environments is the task assigned to the user. In the two studies that failed to support the Faraday (2000) model, the users' task was to search the Web page for specific information. Support for the Faraday model was, at best, weak in these two studies. In the other three studies with the austere visual environment, the user was asked to freely view the "page." In those studies, slightly better support for the Faraday model was obtained. These findings suggest that Faraday's model may be accurate when users are viewing Web pages with no particular goal in mind.

EHS THEORY

As noted earlier, Web pages are not usually randomly viewed, but rather are primarily used to search for specific information (U.S. Department of Commerce, 2002). Therefore, an understanding of how users view Web pages when casually browsing the Internet is not sufficient. One must also appreciate how users attend to Web pages with an explicit goal in mind. It is possible that when users search Web pages their scan paths are idiosyncratic as has been observed when users free-view line drawings (Noton & Stark, 1971), or in search tasks in other environments (Chun & Wolfe, 1991).

Although inexperienced users may engage in random scanning of a Web site, the participants in these studies were highly experienced Web users. Consequently, it is possible that their past experience with Web pages may have led them to develop expectations that played crucial roles in determining where they looked for information. As Wickens and Hollands (2000) have pointed out, cognitive factors related to expectancies of where useful information might be located in the visual field have been found to control target search in a variety of activities such as scanning of X-rays for tumors (Kundel & LaFollete, 1972), automobile driving (Mourant & Rockwell, 1972), athletic endeavors (Walker & Fisk, 1995), chess playing (Matthews, Davies, Westerman, & Stammers, 2000), and photographs and drawings (Yarbus, 1967). Further analysis of data from the initial test of Faraday's (2000) model and Experiment 4 show that search patterns by expert users are consistent with our proposed theory of visual search, which we call EHS theory. According to EHS theory (represented in Figure 7), individuals search an e-commerce or portal Web page in three stages: (1) expected location, (2) heuristic search, and (3) systematic search.

The location of the first fixation on a newly opened Web page is based upon user experience. That is, the user will first look for the item in an "expected" location. If the user is familiar with the site, then the first gaze will be where information has been previously found. If the user is unfamiliar with the site, the first gaze will be to locations where information of that type was found on other Web pages (see Markhum & Hall, 2003 and Bernard, 2001 for a more detailed discussion). Finally, if the user does not have an expected location, then the first stage is skipped and the user starts with the heuristic search.

The first action within the heuristic search is to determine which section of the page contains the main content. The user then searches this area in a pattern that appears arbitrary, but is not, since heuristic rules are being applied. The first heuristic is "the top left corner is dominant." As such, the top left corner of the main content area is the starting point. The next heuristic used by the individual is that "low level information has a low visual salience, but advertisements have a high visual salience." Because of this rule, those elements that stand out as being too different in visual saliency from the surrounding information will be ignored. Likewise, information that blends in too much with other content will be overlooked. These two heuristics mean that the user's attention will be drawn to the items that have a mid-level of salience. The final heuristic is that "information of similar type will be grouped together," suggesting that there is a cognitive salience factor that manifests in the heuristic search as well.

When the user has viewed all items that fall into the mid-range of cognitive-visual salience in the main content area, the third stage, systematic search, begins. In this stage, the user chooses a pattern and conducts a serial search of the main content area. This pattern varies across individuals, but all items in the main content area are viewed. If, after completing a systematic search of the main content area, the user still has not found the object, then the user will search the other areas of the page. Another area will be chosen and a heuristic

Figure 7. The EHS theory

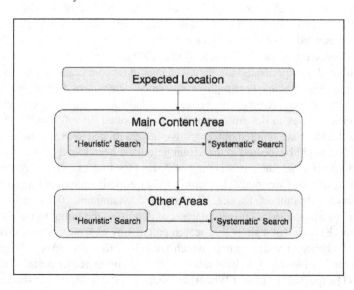

search of that area will be performed as described previously. If the object is still not found, a systematic search of that area will be conducted. This process will be repeated until the user finds the information, gives up, or views every item on the page.

As noted, evidence in favor of the EHS theory can be found in Experiment 4 and Grier's (2004) initial test of the Faraday (2000) model. Several results from both studies support the idea that users have expectations when searching Web pages. For example, in the initial experiment, despite methodological efforts to promote an exhaustive search, users failed to look at each item on the page. The percentage of participants that failed to look at each look zone was computed for each of the pages used in the initial test of the Faraday model (Grier, 2004). The findings indicate that seven look zones on the poorly designed page and six on the well-designed page were not viewed significantly more often than would be expected if the participants were performing an exhaustive search. Moreover, the pattern of omitted zones was similar, suggesting that users expected that the task relevant information would not be found in these locations.

More specific evidence in support of user expectations can be found in the fourth experiment reported previously, primarily from the task of searching for the current date on the page. In this experiment, the date was in the expected location (i.e., in the navigation bar on the right) and was found quickly. Considering the banner blindness phenomena (Benway & Lane, 1998), the date should have been among the most difficult to find. In fact, the two targets that took the longest time for users to find were in the navigation bar. As such, it seems clear that when users were looking for the date, they knew to look in the navigation bar.

The fact that users spent less than 3% of their time searching the navigation bar, which took up approximately 11% of the page, suggests that this area was deemed less likely to contain the required information in most instances (Grier, 2004). This result not only supports the claim that expectations guide search, it also corroborates the notion that users divide the page into areas and weight these areas as to likelihood of finding information. Further evidence for the independence of areas is found in Grier's initial test of the Faraday (2000) model. Specifically, more fixation sequences were observed between items within an area than between items across areas.

The first heuristic of the EHS theory is that the top left corner of the main content area is the dominant position after the expected location. This has been observed in previous research (e.g., Schroeder, 1998) as well as in Grier's (2004) studies. Specifically, in Experiment 4, more first fixations were in the top left corner than any other area. In the test of the Faraday (2000) model, on both pages the items that were fixated first most often were in the top left of the main content area.

Experiment 4 also supports the second heuristic of the EHS theory, that "overly salient items do not contain information." The target that took the third longest to find was in a block of color with animated text. With these visual characteristics the visual salience should have been significantly greater than the rest of the page. In observing the participants' eye movements it was clear that they tended to skip over this item, fixating all items around it, until the heuristic search terminated. Even when the participants' eye movements indicated a switch from heuristic to systematic search, the users would skip this item in some cases, and fixate on items immediately above and below it.

IMPLICATIONS FOR THE DESIGN OF WEB PAGES

These experiments have provided us with additional knowledge about how participants attend to Web pages and provide us with some simple concepts that should be followed in the design of Web pages. First, location on a Web page of certain global elements (e.g., shopping cart, home link, etc) should be established in a consistent location. Where available, these should follow what Nielsen (1999) has termed the "de facto standards of the web" since users have come to expect items to be in certain positions (see Bernard, 2001; Markhum & Hall, 2003) because of their experiences with other Web pages.

Second, the designer should determine the goals of the users who will visit the site. In some cases, there will be no particular goal. Rather, the users will most likely just casually view the site. In this case, the business goals of the site should be used to determine the design of items on a page. Those items that are of most importance should be animated and in the center or top left corner of the page. Those items of less importance should be more subtlety designed and placed on the periphery and bottom of the page.

However, if it is known that users have a purpose for visiting the page (e.g., to make a purchase, to learn how to use an item they have purchased, etc.), these goals should be considered first in the creation of the Web page. The border areas should be reserved for global or navigational elements of the site. The information that is searched for most often should be placed in the top left corner of the main content area. The remainder of the information should be grouped in accordance with how users group the information. Finally, the design of the information within the main content area should be consistent. If something is more or less salient, it will likely be skipped as noted.

Using the user's goals as the primary design criteria does not mean that business goals should be ignored. Rather, the design should aid the user in accomplishing his goal quickly and easily. Once his goal has been accomplished, the user will be more likely to explore the site. This is what Spool and Schroeder (1998) call the Seducible Moment. If users cannot find the information that they are seeking, they will abandon the site and not return. With this in mind, designing a site to help the user meet his/her goals quickly and easily will help both the business and the customer reach their goals.

CONCLUSION

This chapter has described the ways in which users look at Web pages and the methods used to collect attentional data. A number of recommendations for designing pages are provided based on the results of extensive experimentation. Using these data-driven recommendations, Web designers can now more accurately understand and predict how users will look at their Web pages. This knowledge will help Web page designers construct pages that meet the goals of both the site owner and the site user.

REFERENCES

Abernethy, B. (1988). The effects of age and expertise upon perceptual skill development in a racquet sport. *Research Quarterly for Exercise and Sport, 59*(3), 210-221.

Adams, A. S., & Edworthy, J. (1995). Quantifying and predicting the effects of basic text display variables on the perceived urgency of warning labels: Tradeoffs involving font size, border weight, and colour. *Ergonomics, 38*(11), 2221-2237.

Bayles, M. E., & Chaparro, B. (2001). Recall and recognition of static vs. animated banner advertisements. In *Proceedings of the Human Factors and Ergonomics Society 45th Annual Meeting* (pp. 1201-1204). Santa Monica, CA: Human Factors and Ergonomics Society.

Benway, J. P., & Lane, D. M. (1998). Banner blindness: Web searchers often miss "obvious" links. *Internetworking, 1.3.* Retrieved January 28, 2002, from http://www.internettg.org/newsletter/dec98/banner_blindness.html

Bernard, M. L. (2001). Developing schemas for the location of common Web objects. In *Proceedings of the Human Factors and Ergonmics Society 45th Annual Meeting* (pp. 1161-1165). Santa Monica, CA: Human Factors and Ergonomics Society.

Boyce, S. J., & Pollatsek, A. (1992). Identification of objects in scenes. The role of the scene background in object naming. *Journal of Experimental Psychology: Learning, Memory, & Cognition, 18,* 531-543.

Bzostek, J. A., & Wogalter, M. S. (1999). Measuring visual search time for a product warning label as a function of icon, color, column and vertical placement. In *Proceedings of the Human Factors and Ergonomics Society 43rd Annual Meeting* (pp. 888-892). Santa Monica, CA: Human Factors and Ergonomics Society.

Chun, M. M., & Wolfe, J. M. (1991). Visual attention. In E. B. Goldstein (Ed.), *Blackwell handbook of perception* (pp. 272-311). Oxford, UK: Blackwell.

Dember, W. N., & Warm, J. S. (1979). *Psychology of perception* (2nd ed.). New York: Holt, Rinehart, & Winston.

Eriksen, C. W., & Yeh, Y. Y. (1985). Allocation of attention in the visual field. *Journal of Experimental Psychology: Human Perception and Performance, 11,* 583-597.

Faraday, P. (2000, June 19). Visually critiquing Web pages. *Proceedings of the 6th Conference on Human Factors and the Web*, Austin, Texas.

Fischer, B., & Weber, H. (1993). Express saccades and visual attention. *Behavioral and Brain Sciences, 16*(3), 553-610.

Fitts, P. M., Jones, R. E., & Milton, J. L. (1950). Eye movements of aircraft pilots during instrument-landing approaches. *Aeronautical Engineering Review, 9*(2), 24-29.

Fleming, J. (1997, July 25). In defense of Web graphics. *Webreview.* Retrieved August 24, 2001, from http://www.webreview.com/1997/07_25/index.shtml

Garcia, M. (1993). *Contemporary newspaper design: A structural approach* (3rd ed.). Englewood Cliffs, NJ: Prentice Hall.

Graham, C. H. (1965). *Vision and visual perception.* New York: Wiley.

Grier, R. A. (2004). *Visual attention and Web design.* Retrieved January 24, 2005, from http://www.ohiolink.edu/etd/view.cgi?ucin1092767744

Harris R. L., Tole, J. R., Stephens, A. T., & Ephrath, A. R. (1982). Visual scanning behavior and pilot workload. *Aviation — Space and Environment Medicine, 53*(11), 1067-1072.

Henderson, J. A., Weeks, P. A., Jr., & Hollingworth, A. (1999). The effects of semantic consistency on eye movements during complex scene viewing. *Journal of Experimental Psychology, 25,* 210-228.

Hochberg, J. (1971). Perception: Space and movement. In J. W. Kling & L. A. Riggs (Eds.), *Experimental Psychology* (pp. 475-550). New York: Holt, Rinehart, & Winston.

Hoffman, J. E. (1998). Visual attention and eye movements. In H. Pashler (Ed.), *Attention* (pp. 119-154). University College London Press.

Hoffman, J. E., & Subramaniam, B. (1995). The role of visual attention in saccadic eye movements. *Vision Research, 57*(6), 787-795.

Joseph, K. M., Knott, B. A., & Grier, R. A. (2002). The effects of bold text on visual search of form fields. *Proceedings of the 46th Human Factors and Ergonomics Society Meeting* (pp. 583-587). *Santa Monica, CA: Human Factors and Ergonomics Society.*

Kortum, P. T., & Geisler, W. S. (1996). Search performance in natural scenes: The role of peripheral vision. *Investigative Ophthalmology & Visual Science Supplement*, 37/3, S297.

Kotval, X. P., & Goldberg, J. H. (1998). Eye movements and interface component grouping: An evaluation method. *Proceedings of the Human Factors and Ergonomics Society 42nd Annual Meeting* (486-490).

Kramer, A. F., & McCarley, J. S. (2003). Oculomotor behavior as a reflection of attention and memory processes: Neural mechanisms and applications to human factors. *Theoretical Issues in Ergonomics Science, 4*, 21-55.

Kundel, H. L., & LaFollete, P. S. (1972). Visual search patterns and experience with radiological images. *Radiology, 103*(3), 523-528.

Laughery, K. R., Young, S. L., Vaubel, K. P., & Brelsford, J. W., Jr. (1993). The noticeability of warnings on alcoholic beverage containers. *Journal of Public Policy and Marketing, 12*, 38-56.

Lewenstein, M., Edwards, G., Tatar, D., & Devigal, A. (2000). Front page entry points (Initial analysis). Retrieved June 12, 2006, from http://www.poynterextra.org/et/i.htm

Lim, R. W., & Wogalter, M. S. (2000). The position of static on-off banners in WWW displays on subsequent recognition. In *Proceedings of the XIVth Triennial Congress of the International Ergonomics Association and 44th Annual Meeting of the Human Factors and Ergonomics Society* (pp. 420-424). Santa Monica, CA: Human Factors and Ergonomics Society.

Markum, J., & Hall, R. H. (2003). *E-Commerce Web objects: Importance and expected placements.* Laboratory for Information Technology Evaluation Technical Report. Retrieved July 19, 2005, from http://campus.umr.edu/lite/tech_reports/LITE-2003-02.pdf

Matthews, G., Davies, D. R., Westerman, S. J., & Stammers, R. B. (2000). *Human performance: Cognition, stress, and individual differences.* Hove, East Sussex, UK: Psychology Press.

Megaw, E. D., & Richardson, J. (1979). Target uncertainty & visual scanning strategies. *Human Factors, 21*(3), 303-316.

Mourant, R. R., & Rockwell, T. H. (1972). Strategies of visual search by novice and experienced drivers. *Human Factors, 14*, 325-335.

Nielsen, J. (1999, November 14). When bad designs become the standard. *Alertbox.* Retrieved June 25, 2005, from http://www.useit.com/alertbox/991114.html

Noton, D., & Stark, L. (1971). Scanpaths in eye movements during pattern perception. *Science, 171*(3968), 308-311.

Palmer, S. E. (1999). *Vision science: Photons to phenomenology.* Cambridge, MA: MIT Press.

Parkhurst, D. J. (2002, September). Selective attention in natural vision: Using computational models to quantify stimulus driven attentional allocation. *Dissertation Abstracts International: Section B, The Sciences and Engineering, 63*(3-B), 1593.

Posner, M. I. (1978). *Chromametric explorations of mind.* Hillsdale, NJ: Erlbaum.

Posner, M. I. (1980). Orienting of attention. *Quarterly Journal of Experimental Psychology, 32,* 3-25.

Rayner, K., Rotello, C. M., Stewart, A. J., Keir, J., & Duffy, S. A. (2001). Integrating text and pictorial information: Eye movements when looking at print advertisements. *Journal of Experimental Psychology: Applied, 7,* 219-226.

Recarte, M. A., & Nunes, L. M. (2000). Effects of verbal and spatial-imagery tasks on eye fixations while driving. *Journal of Experimental Psychology: Applied, 6*(1), 31-43.

Rorden, C., & Driver, J. (1999). Does auditory attention shift in the direction of an upcoming saccade? *Neuropsychologia, 37,* 357-377.

Schieber, F., Larsen, J., Jurgensen, J., Werner, K., & Eich, G. (2001). Fluorescent colored highway signs don't 'grab' attention; They 'guide' it. In *Proceedings of the Human Factors and Ergonomics Society 45th Annual Meeting* (pp. 1622-1626). Santa Monica, CA: Human Factors and Ergonomics Society.

Schiffman, H. R. (2000). *Sensation and perception: An integrated approach.* New York: John Wiley & Sons.

Schroeder, W. (1998). Testing Web sites with eye tracking. *Eye for Design, 5.* Retrieved August 2, 2001, from http://www.uie.com/eyetrack1.htm

Spool, J., & Schroeder, W. (1998). Seductive design for Web sites. *Eye for Design, 5.* Retrieved November 27, 2001, from http://www.uie.com/articles/seductive_design/

Styles, E. A. (1997). *The psychology of attention.* Cast, Sussex, UK: Psychology Press.

Thomas, E. L. (1968). Movements of the eye. *Scientific American, 219,* 88-95.

Treisman, A., & Gelade, G. (1980). A feature-integration theory of attention. *Cognitive Psychology, 12,* 97-136.

U.S. Department of Commerce. (2002). *A nation online: How Americans are expanding their use of the Internet.* Retrieved March 15, 2002, from http://www.ntia.doc.gov/ntiahome/dn/nationonline_020502.htm

Walker, N., & Fisk, A. (1995, July). Human factors goes to the gridiron. *Ergonomics in Design,* 8-13.

Wallsten, T. S., & Barton, C. (1982). Processing probabilistic multidimensional information for decisions. *Journal of Experimental Psychology: Learning, Memory, & Cognition, 8,* 361-384.

Wertheimer, M. (1938). Untersuchungen zur Lehre von der Gestalt II [Laws of Organization in Perceptual Forms]. In W. Ellis (Ed.), *A source book of Gestalt psychology* (pp. 71-88). London: Routledge & Kegan Paul. (Original work published 1923)

Wickens, C. D., & Hollands, J. (2000). *Engineering psychology and human performance* (3rd ed.). Upper Saddle River, NJ: Prentice Hall.

Wolfe, J. M., Stewart, M. I., Friedman-Hill, S. R., Yu, K. P., Shorter, A. D., & Cave, K. R. (1990). Limitations on the parallel guidance of visual search: Color x color and orientation x orientation conjunctions. *Journal of Experimental Psychology: Human Perception and Performance, 16,* 879-892.

Yammoto, S. & Kuto, Y. (1992). A method of evaluating VDT screen layout by eye movement analysis. *Ergonomics, 35,* 591-606.

Yarbus, A. L. (1967). *Eye movements and vision.* New York: Plenum Press.

Chapter III

A Qualitative Study in User's Information-Seeking Behaviors on Web Sites:
A User-Centered Approach to Web Site Development

Napawan Sawasdichai,
King Mongkut's Institute of Technology, Ladkrabang, Thailand

ABSTRACT

This chapter introduces a qualitative study of user's information-seeking tasks on Web-based media, by investigating user's cognitive behaviors when they are searching for particular information on various kinds of Web sites. The experiment, which is a major part of the recently completed doctoral research at the Institute of Design-IIT, particularly studies cognitive factors including user goals and modes of searching in order to investigate if these factors significantly affect users' information-seeking behaviors. The main objective is to identify the corresponding impact of these factors on their needs and behaviors in relation to Web site design. By taking a user-based qualitative approach, the author hopes that this study will open the door to a careful consideration of actual user needs and behaviors in relation to information-seeking tasks on Web-based media. The results may compliment the uses of existing quantitative studies by supplying a deeper user understanding and a new qualitative approach to analyze and improve the design of information on Web sites.

INTRODUCTION

When visiting a Web site, each user has a specific goal that relates to a pattern of needs, expectations, and search behaviors. They also approach with different modes of searching based on varied knowledge, experience, and search sophistication. This leads to differences in information-seeking strategies and searching behaviors. Since information on Web sites is traditionally structured and presented based on Web sites' goals and contents, it may or may not match with user goals or search behaviors.

Because of these problems, information structuring is the essence of Web design since these problems cannot be solved by the development of technically sophisticated systems alone. User search behaviors need to be studied and deeply understood in order to design systems that allow them to perform their information-seeking tasks easily, without struggle and frustration. The contents need to be authored, organized, structured, and presented to fit their needs, expectations, and search behaviors, while being able to carry out the goal of the Web site simultaneously. Both the provider and user must benefit at the same time to ensure the Web site success. As a result, user-centered design process is important in Web development to help people succeed within an information context that seeks to achieve business goals (Brinck, Gergle, & Wood, 2002).

In attempts to move toward user-centered design, many studies have been developed to establish design principles that better serve Web-based media. Among these attempts, Web usability, grounded in human-computer interaction (HCI), has currently assumed a significant role underpinning the design of many Web sites in order to maximize efficient use. Web usability studies and practices are primarily concerned with people performing a task accurately, completely, and easily. These may involve making information accessible, retrievable, legible, and readable, ensuring that all Web pages are reachable and practically navigated, or dealing with technical aspects of media interface and Web system by ensuring that all system functionality can be operated correctly and easily.

User Research in Web Development

User research in relation to Web site development is mostly conducted by using quantitative methods or automated programs, such as data mining and Logs File Analysis (analyze usage data), GOMS analysis (predict execution and learning time), and Information Scent modeling (mimic Web site navigation) serve different purposes. These automated methods are particularly essential to usability testing (evaluation), especially in cases where numerous users are involved since they can reveal a substantial amount of information with regard to usage patterns by representing the actual usage characteristics. Some also provide in-depth statistical analysis of usage. For example, *logs file analysis* can show overall hits, conversion rates, entrance pages, search terms, peak times, demographics, and system down-time (see Figure 1 and 2). These develop an understanding of how the Web site is being used by the actual users, which helps identify potential problems of the Web site, and may assist in suggesting a change or directing the future design (Brinck et al., 2002).

However, the limitations of these automated methods are that they cannot be employed without an existing Web site; the Web site needs to be prototyped or implemented at some level before these methods can be applied since they are intended as an analytical means rather than a generative one. More importantly, these automated methods cannot capture important qualitative and subjective information such as user preferences and misconceptions (Ivory & Hearst, 2001). They tend to yield a higher

Figure 1. An example page from logs file analysis: Visits

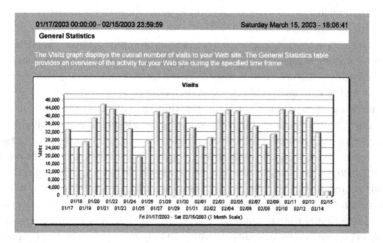

Figure 2. An example page from logs file analysis example: Top entry pages

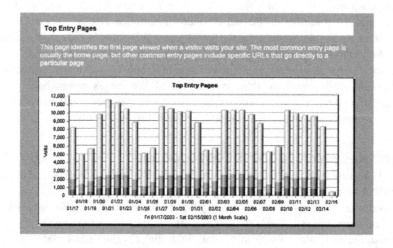

level of user data — what they do or what they do not do — but they usually fail to capture and analyze user cognitive behaviors such as their satisfaction, decision-making pattern, or reasons that underpin their needs and behaviors.

Therefore, qualitative study using nonautomated methods such as user observation, focus groups, user interviews and surveys still play an important role in Web development. These nonautomated methods can be used in the design process to capture, analyze, and conceptualize Web structure before usability evaluation takes place. They can be employed in the evaluation process as complements to the automated methods as well, in order to help capture and analyze qualitative and subjective user information that is missing from the automated methods alone. Applying both quantitative and qualitative studies can significantly improve the quality and quantity of user input and feedback that may help suggest a change or direction that better supports user satisfaction. As a result, this study investigates a relatively new area of user research in Web-based media, offering a user-centered perspective with consideration of user goals, user modes of searching and their search behaviors by taking a user-based qualitative approach. The study expects to expand understanding within the area of user studies, and accordingly investigates how these user cognitive factors contribute to differences in user information needs and their information-seeking behaviors on Web-based media, particularly in view of user search strategies and user search methods. Understanding within this area will contribute to the further development of information architecture and interface design.

SCOPE OF THE RESEARCH

The practices of Web site development are fundamentally concerned with two equally important and interrelated parts: (1) Web functionality and (2) Web information. In the user-centered perspective, usability, accessibility, sustainability, suitability, credibility, and usefulness of both Web functionality and Web information for its intended users are important for the Web to succeed. In most current practices, the user-centered approach is usually taken into design consideration in a general sense; for example, by conducting user studies to establish who are the intended users of the Web site (user profiles), and what do they want to achieve (user goals)? Others may perform user testing with regard to usability evaluation in terms of what is working, and what is not (usability of Web functionality). These current user-centered approaches are concerned with Web functionality rather than Web information. Furthermore, they pay considerably more attention to usability aspects while the Web information content receives less attention. Therefore, this research primarily focuses on the design of Web information, particularly in view of the importance, suitability, and usefulness of information design provided on Web sites (see Figure 3).

The study is particularly concerned with user information needs and user information-seeking behaviors; it also investigates whether the design of information provided on the Web site supports these needs and behaviors. Secondly, the research is also concerned with the suitability and usefulness of Web functionality necessary for users to gain access to the information they need. The research also looks into different types of search methods or search tools provided on Web sites to investigate whether these search methods or tools are useful and suitable to user search strategies.

When searching, each user has a different search plan: For instance, they lightly explore or seriously search and they select search methods and tools in order to easily achieve their goal. This search plan is primarily based on their search strategy, which is the scheme that generally distinguishes user search patterns. Besides search strategies, each user may use a particular search method, which is the procedure for how they actually perform their search. User search method is based on the types of search tools they choose for their search, which may include menu bar, table of contents, index, or search engine. User search strategies can range from general or less-focused search to more specific or purposeful search. Furthermore, it may change from time to time based on the current context or situation that unfolds while they are searching as well as the search results that they find or retrieve. Based on user search strategies and its results, user search methods are

Figure 3. Primary focuses of the research: The design of Web information-based on user-centered approach, particularly with regard to usefulness and suitability

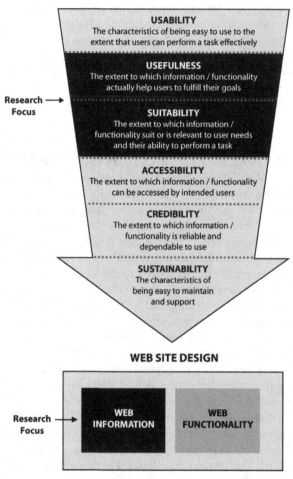

changed accordingly. As a result, this research is aimed to uncover the primary factors governing or influencing these user search strategies and methods.

More importantly, in order to understand and eventually determine what types, characteristics, formats, and presentation methods for information is suitable and useful for users, the research needs to investigate the relatively new areas of user-centered approaches to Web site design: user goals and user modes of searching (see Figure 4).

Information scientists have studied user modes of searching for decades, and these ideas are well categorized by Rosenfeld and Morville (1998) in their book *Information Ar-*

Figure 4. Primary focus of the research: User goals and user modes of searching

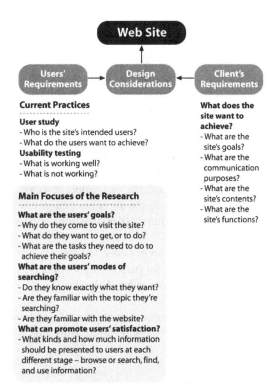

chitecture for the World Wide Web. However, since the notion of user modes of searching has never been elaborated in terms of what to expect from their differences, it needs further investigation — this becomes the primary focus of this research to uncover its substantial impact on user needs, expectations, search strategies, or information-seeking behaviors in this medium. In addition, typical user profiles are also categorized in order to determine whether these profiles exert any substantial impact on user needs, expectations, or search patterns. These profiles particularly focus on user demographic and technographic data, including prior knowledge in the content they are searching, prior experience in the particular or similar Web site interface, and sophistication in general Internet use.

RESEARCH ANALYTIC FRAME

The research begins with defining and categorizing the important elements or factors of the study, including user goals, user modes of searching, as well as Web site goals and contents. Accordingly, the research analytic frame is established to help identify potential cases for the study. User goals and modes of searching were investigated within the context of specific Web site goals to reveal common user search patterns, search strategies, and search methods associated with each case and to identify the primary problems that occur in each pattern.

User Goals

Each user has a specific goal when visiting a Web site. Different goals suggest different kinds of needs, expectations, and search behaviors, which are factors in Web usage and success. Further, users may access the same Web site with different goals at different times; moreover, they often link several goals and explore them sequentially. User goals may be categorized as follows:

- **To seek specific information:** In this category, users may engage a Web site to search for specific information that helps them to stay updated, make decisions, fulfill a specific inquiry, perform tasks, learn, or conduct research.
- **To fulfill personal interests:** Some users may engage a Web site as a resource for pleasure to fulfill a personal interest (e.g., watching a video clip or listening to music on an entertainment Web site).
- **To communicate and/or perform tasks:** Others may use Web sites as a channel for communicating or as a means for performing tasks (e.g., connecting to a community Web site or paying bills on a company Web site).

Among these three categories of user goals, the information-seeking goal is prevalent and poses the greatest problem for users. Consequently this is the primary investigative focus in this research.

User Modes of Searching

Besides user goals, users also approach a Web site with varied levels of specification of their needs and different levels of search specification and determination, this leads to differences in information-seeking behaviors including search strategies, search methods, and selection of search tools. Some users may know exactly what they are looking for and where to find it, while others are without a clue. Since these search behaviors and user expectations vary widely, it is important to recognize and distinguish among them noting their differences.

A current study (Rosenfeld & Morville, 1998) has delineated users' different modes of searching as known-item searching, existence searching, exploratory searching, and comprehensive searching (research). Based on Rosenfeld and Morville's model, user modes of searching are modified and extended in this research to include topical searching which falls between existence and known-item searching. User modes of searching may be categorized as follows:

- **Exploratory searching (browsing):** Users have a vague idea of their information needs. They do not know exactly what they are hoping to find, but some may know how to phrase their question. They want to explore and learn more.
- **Existence searching:** Users have an abstract idea or concept of what they are hoping to find, but do not know how to describe it clearly or whether the answer exists at all. They want to search for what matches their idea or mental image.

- **Topical searching:** Users know what they want in general. Some may want to search for an answer to their specific question. They know what they are hoping to find, but do not know where/which categories they should look for.
- **Known-item searching:** Users know exactly what they want, and usually know where/which categories they should look for. Users' information needs are clearly defined and have a single, correct answer.
- **Comprehensive searching (research):** Users want to search for specific information, and they want everything available regarding this information. Users' information needs are clearly defined, but might have various or many answers.

Users Search Behaviors

When users are searching for information and trying to accomplish their goals, they move between two cognitive states (thoughts/decisions — with regard to their goal and interest) and physical states (interactions — concern with functions, navigation, and computer performance) with regard to information provided on each Web page.

For instance, some users may want to keep searching because they need detailed information, while others may be satisfied with only a short descriptive text presented on the first page. Some may prefer textual information, but others may feel more satisfied with visual information. These search behaviors may be identified as shown in Table 1. These cognitive and physical behaviors with regard to user search, previously observed from initial user observation, will be further used to establish a coding scheme used in an analytical process of the research.

Web Site Goals and Contents

While this research focuses on the relatively new areas of user studies: user goals and user modes of searching, other factors such as site contents, site goals, and site functions nevertheless play a significant role in determining the design of a Web site. Each Web site contains unique contents and goals depending on the nature of the company, institution, or individual that owns that Web site. Based on the book *Web Navigation: Designing the User Experience* (Fleming, 1998), these Web sites can be distinguished and generalized by the similarities of their goals and contents into six categories: (1) commercial Web site, (2) identity Web site (Web site for company or institution), (3) information Web site, (4) education Web site, (5) entertainment Web site, and (6) community Web site. However, only the first four categories, in which the problems of information-seeking tasks are primarily found, will be investigated in this study. Moreover, entertainment and community Web sites are quite different from other Web sites because of their unique goals, contents, and functions.

By simultaneously considering the three important factors of information design on Web sites: (1) Web site goals and contents, (2) user goals, and (3) user modes of searching, an analytic frame is constructed. Different aspects of each factor are systematically combined with one another to establish prominent cases or scenarios for the study; each of which presents a unique combination of the three factors: (1) Web site goals and contents, (2) user goals, and (3) user modes of searching.

Nevertheless, these cases are not mutually exclusive; they might overlap or combine since one Web site may consist of two or more combinations (see Figure 5). As shown in Figure 6, case 1 represents the scenario in which users with exploratory searching

Table 1. Users' cognitive and physical search behaviors

Users' Cognitive Behaviors (thoughts/decisions)	Users' Physical Behaviors (interactions)
— Some information is found, and they want to learn more, or want to know the details of the retrieval documents. — The intended information is found. Users' primary information needs are fulfilled, but users are interested in finding other relevant or related information. — The intended information is found. Users' primary information needs are fulfilled. Users are ready to use information they found to take further action(s). — The intended information is not found, or not enough to take further action(s). Users' primary needs are not fulfilled. Users need to keep searching. — Users make a positive decision (decide to proceed) about something according to information they found. — Users make a negative decision (decide not to proceed) about something according to information they found. — Users are satisfied. All users' needs are fulfilled. Users are able to accomplish their goals based on the information they found. — Users are not satisfied. Users' needs are not fulfilled. Users are unable to accomplish their goal(s).	— Users keep searching in the current retrieval results. — Users keep searching by changing search strategy. — Users record the information they found. — Users go back to the selected (bookmarked) page or results. — Users give up.

mode visit a commercial Web site in order to find information to make a decision. Case 2 represents a similar scenario to case 1; however, users in case 2 arrive with an existence mode of searching. Cases 3, 4, and 5 represent similar scenarios in which users visit identity (company) Web sites to find information to fulfill a specific inquiry.

However, each case has a distinctive search mode. Users in case 3 approach with an existence mode; case 4 with a topical mode; while case 5 approaches with a known-item mode. Cases 6, 7, 8, and 9 represent the scenarios in which users visit information Web sites to find information to stay updated. Though, they are assigned different modes of searching, which include exploratory, existence, topical, and known-item modes respectively. Case 10 represents a scenario in which users with a comprehensive mode of searching approach an educational Web site to find information for learning or researching a specific content. Each of these 10 cases will be investigated and analyzed to uncover similarities and differences in patterns of user information-seeking behaviors, as well as to identify user information needs, user search strategies, and user search methods associated with different user goals, modes of searching, and Web site characteristics.

RESEARCH QUESTIONS

The study is specifically conducted within these selected 10 cases generated from the research analytic frame shown in Figure 5 in order to find the answers to these research questions:

- What are the common patterns of user information-seeking behavior presented in each study case?
- What are the user search strategies, search methods, or selected search tools commonly found or employed in each study case?
- What kinds of information do users need in each study case in terms of the types, characteristics, formats, presentation methods, quantity and quality of information?
- What are the key factors in each study case that help or obstruct users to accomplish the information-seeking task?

The research findings that answer these questions will be analyzed to identify the relationships existing among user goals and user modes of searching with their information needs, search strategies, and search methods. These results will help establish the classification of cognitive factors, as well as provide an analysis framework for information design on Web sites.

RESEARCH METHODOLOGY

Research Methods

A qualitative research method is used in this study to explore the similarities and differences of user search patterns. Users' information-seeking behaviors are observed through controlled observation, through video observation combined with protocol analysis. User profiles are also collected through a series of questionnaires. Ten scenarios are designed to create the 10 study cases originating from the research analytic frame to help the participants enter the situation and the tasks they needed to accomplish. Each scenario is embedded with a particular mode of searching, and a different search goal resulting in the performance of a task, ranging from open-ended to very specific purpose and search.

- *Scenario 1* **explores a commercial Web site:** Expedia.com. User goal is to make a decision; user search mode is exploratory searching.
- *Scenario 2* **explores a commercial Web site:** Toyrus.com. User goal is to make a decision; user search mode is existence searching.

Figure 5. The research analytic frame: Generating 10 different study cases for the research

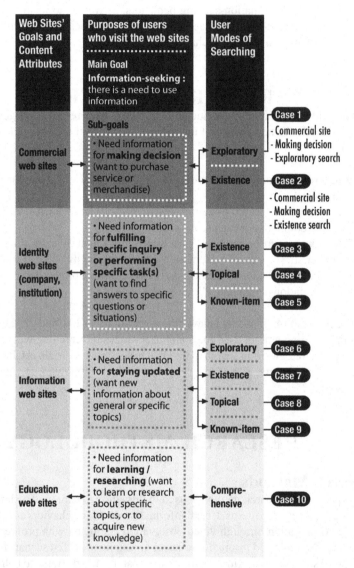

- *Scenario 3* **explores an identity Web site:** Paris-ile-de-France.com. User goal is to fulfill a specific inquiry; user search mode is existence searching.
- *Scenario 4* **explores an identity Web site:** Apple.com. User goal is to fulfill a specific inquiry; user search mode is topical searching.
- *Scenario 5* **explores an identity Web site:** FoodTV.com. User goal is to fulfill a specific inquiry; user mode is known-item searching.

Figure 6. An example scenario

<table>
<tr><td>

Scenario 1

User goal : Information-seeking to make a decision
User mode of searching : Exploratory searching
Web site characteristic : Commercial website

You have been working very hard this year. Your boss surprised you with a $5,000 bonus and a 2-week vacation. You're thinking about taking a trip, but don't know what kind of trip, or where to go because you just went to your favorite place last month. You want to go somewhere that you've never been to before. So you visit the website "Expedia.com" to see if there is anything interesting. You want to explore more before you decide what you should do.

What would you do on your vacation ?

</td></tr>
</table>

- *Scenario 6* **explores an information Web site:** TVGuide.com. User goal is to stay updated on some interesting topics; user search mode is exploratory searching.
- *Scenario 7* **explores an information Web site:** ABCNews.com. User goal is to stay updated on a specific topic; user search mode is existence searching.
- *Scenario 8* **explores an information Web site:** DiscoveryHealth.com. User goal is to stay updated on a specific topic; user search mode is topical searching.
- *Scenario 9* **explores an information Web site:** CNN.com. User goal is to stay updated on a specific topic; user mode is known-item searching.
- *Scenario 10* **explores an information/education Web site:** WebMD.com. User goal is to research and learn about a specific topic; user search mode is comprehensive searching.

Fifty participants from different cultures, all of whom were literate in English, are observed regarding how they search for information and try to accomplish the tasks defined by the scenario they received. The participants approached the selected Web site with unspecified and various modes of searching and searched for information with goals appropriate to the selected scenario. Ten participants are randomly selected to participate in each scenario, with each participant doing two cases or two different scenarios.

As a result, the research collects in total 100 observation cases, which consist of 10 cases for each of 10 scenarios. The participants' interactions (physical behaviors) on Web sites are simply captured through a video recorder. Furthermore, by using protocol analysis, the participants express verbally what they think while performing tasks in order to reveal their thoughts (cognitive behaviors) and comments, which are extremely important for the analytical process.

Analysis Methods

Since the research data collected from participants is qualitative in nature, several methods of qualitative analysis are used in this research to carefully analyze various aspects of the data, in order to obtain integrated research findings that answer the related but different research questions on which this research focuses. Each analysis method used in the study delivers distinctive analytical results answering a specific research question. The analytical results obtained from these different analysis methods are also cross-examined in order to accumulate further findings. This collective analysis process helps to uncover the pattern

Table 2. The coding scheme used in thematic analysis

Thematic Analysis: Coding Scheme	
User's Search Behaviors: **Cognitive Behaviors (Thoughts, Decisions)**	**Physical Behaviors (Interactions)**
(SR) Some information is found and they want to learn more, or want to know about the details of the retrieval documents.	(SR) Users keep searching in the current retrieval results.
[C] The intended information is found. Users' primary information needs are fulfilled, but users are interested in finding other relevant or related information.	[C] Users record the information they found.
[C] The intended information is found. Users' primary information needs are fulfilled. Users are ready to use information they found to take further action(s).	▲? Users keep searching by changing search strategy or search methods.
/?\ The intended information is not found, or not enough to take further action(s). Users' primary needs are not fulfilled. Users need to keep searching.	◆ Users go back to the selected (bookmarked) page or result.
◇D Users make a positive decision (to proceed) about something according to information they found.	
◇D Users make a negative decision (not to proceed) about something according to information they found.	**Integrated Behaviors** Initial searching (SR) (SR)
☆S Users are satisfied. All users' needs are fulfilled. Users are able to accomplish their goals based on the information they found.	Information-collecting [C] [C] [C]
★S Users are somewhat satisfied, but not completely satisfied. Users' primary needs are fulfilled, and users are able to accomplish their goals based on the information they found. However, users still need more information to fulfill all their needs completely.	Struggling /?\ ▲? Decision-making ◇D ◇D ◆D
✳U Users are not satisfied. Users' needs are not fulfilled. Users are unable to accomplish their goal(s).	Satisfactory / Unsatisfactory ☆S ★S ✳U

of relationship that exists among various user cognitive factors, as well as to identify their substantial impact on user search behaviors and information needs.

Thematic analysis (Boyatzis, 1998), the process used for encoding qualitative information, is performed in this study to analyze the overall user search behaviors including user task list and process. In order to uncover the differences and similarities in user search behaviors, a thematic analysis framework with a coding scheme is designed based on an initial observation on user search behaviors. Participants' search behaviors are captured through video and sound recording, then analyzed and encoded by using the coding scheme (see Table 2).

User search behaviors are analyzed at each Web page the user visited as cognitive behaviors (thoughts/decisions) and physical behaviors (interactions). Each behavior is encoded using the preset coding scheme. The result is the sequence of user tasks performed by each user when searching for specific information on the particular Web site as described in the scenario they received (see Table 3).

The results, displayed as the encoded information of user search behaviors, are then further analyzed and generalized to determine the common patterns of information-seeking tasks that are associated with each study case (scenario) by using a *time-ordered matrix* (Robson, 1993). The time-ordered matrix is used to systematically display the encoded information of user search behaviors in *time-ordered sequences* by presenting various types of user search behaviors, both physical and cognitive behaviors, observed in each Web page from the start to completion of the task (see Figure 7).

Color coding is also added to help identify and group the same or similar tasks together. This enables one to see the overall task list and its sequence visually and practically in order to compare the differences and similarities that occur within and across different scenarios.

In addition, the results gained from thematic analysis are eventually summarized as *procedural analysis*, which presents the common process or pattern of user search behaviors in each study case (scenario) including search methods and task descriptions (see Figure 8).

The encoded information of user search behaviors is also further transformed into Chernoff Faces (Chernoff, 1973; Wainer & Thissen, 1981) in order to further identify and compare the common patterns of search behaviors that are associated with each user goal and mode of searching. Chernoff Faces are another coding scheme that is, in this case, used to help identify user's search behaviors holistically with regard to how frequent each behavior occurs, or which behavior occurs more often than the others.

Chernoff Faces also help visualize the frequency of tasks performed within and across different scenarios. For example, in this coding scheme, the face is used to represent the user's information-collecting state. The bigger the face, the more information has been collected by the user. The eyes represent how much the user searches, while the eyebrows represent a struggling state (see Tables 4.1, 4.2, and Figure 9).

As shown in Figure 9, Chernoff Face Analysis reveals the patterns of user's prominent tasks performed in each different scenario. For example, users in scenario 2, as shown in the top row, need to perform an extensive decision-making task indicated by the gray and black hair they are all wearing; in contrast to users in scenarios 4 and 9 who all appear with no hair signifying that they do not perform any decision-making task at all. The analysis also visually addresses user search struggle or satisfaction clearly. As seen clearly in Figure 9, all users in scenario 9 appear with complete satisfaction while most users in scenario 4 are unsatisfied with their search.

Table 3. An example analysis of thematic analysis by using the pre-designed coding scheme

Information display on Web page	User's key actions	User's key speech/thoughts	User's cognitive and physical behaviors
page 1 **Homepage** • Menu bar • Table of contents • Search field • Recommend features	scrolling up-down select table of content	• "Well ... I want to look around first." • "There're lots of categories to choose from here, but I think I should start searching by 'Ages.'"	(SR) Some information is found, and they want to learn more, or want to know about the details of the retrieval documents. (SR) Users keep searching in the current retrieval results.
page 2 **Result Page** • Table of contents • Recommend products (small image + short description)	scrolling up-down read table of content look at image select table of content	• "Let's see if anything interesting is here." • "Visual stimulation ... um ... it sounds interesting." • "Well ... let's see what's in it."	(SR) Some information is found, and they want to learn more, or want to know about the details of the retrieval documents. (SR) Users keep searching in the current retrieval results.
page 3 **Result Page** • Small images + short descriptions	scrolling up-down look at image read short text select related categories	• "Well ... nothing interesting here." • "Maybe I should try another category to see if it has more interesting items."	(?) The intended information is not found, or not enough to take further action(s). Users' primary needs are not fulfilled. Users need to keep searching. (?) Users keep searching by changing search strategy.

In order to identify the patterns of user search strategies and methods commonly used in each scenario, a checklist with a sequence record (Robson, 1993) is designed to record participants' frequency and sequence of use of various search tools available on each Web site. The recorded data is then further analyzed to identify the common patterns of user search strategies and search methods primarily used in each scenario, as well as to compare the differences and similarities of user search patterns within and across different scenarios (see Table 5).

Figure 7. An example use of time-ordered matrix used for further analyzing and generalizing the encoded information gained from the earlier thematic analysis by presenting user search behaviors in the time-ordered sequences

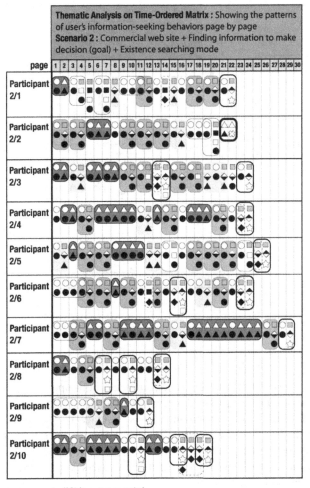

Participant N/n means scenario 'N' / participant 'n'.

Similarly, in order to identify the patterns of user information needs commonly found in each study case, another Checklist Record (Robson, 1993) is designed to record the frequency of use of different kinds of information available on each Web site. Different types, characteristics, formats, and presentation methods of information display that are viewed by users while performing information-seeking tasks are captured by using the Checklist Record. This process is used to analyze and identify the main types, characteristics, formats, and presentation methods of information needed by users to accomplish the given task within and across different scenarios (see Table 6).

Figure 8. An example of procedural analysis used for presenting the process of user search patterns

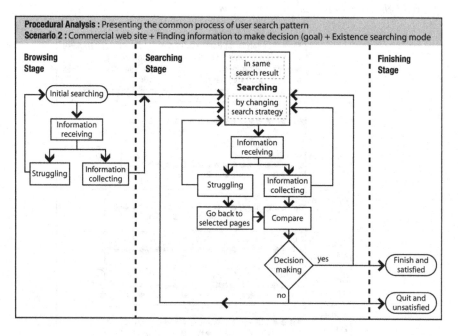

The analysis of user profiles is collected and built upon user data acquired through a series of questionnaires provided to the research participants when the observation took place (see Figure 10). The questionnaire was designed to acquire user demographic and techno-graphic data focusing on different aspects of user experience, including users' prior knowledge and experience in the specific content they are searching, users' prior experience in the particular or similar Web site interface, and users' general experience in Internet use for information-seeking purposes.

Furthermore, qualitative comparison is conducted by constructing truth tables (Ragin, 1987, 1994) to help further identify additional insights and various factors that may reveal additional information about user search struggle or success, and help confirm the results from other analytical methods (see Table 7). This particular analysis is important for the research since it looks across all 100 cases simultaneously, in contrast to other analyses that examine 10 observation cases of each scenario collectively.

Validation of Coding System

Reliability and validity of coding schemes specifically designed to use for analysis in this research is fundamentally important and needs to be examined before the study proceeds further. In qualitative research, the observer's consistency and bias in interpreting user behaviors and using coding schemes to code events are a primary concern. As a result, to

Table 4.1. The coding scheme used in Chernoff Face Analysis

Chernoff Faces Analysis: Coding Scheme	
Users' cognitive states and physical states	**Chernoff Faces coding system**
Initial searching states (SR) Some information is found, and they want to learn more, or want to know about the details of the retrieval documents. (SR) Users keep searching in the current retrieval results.	**EYES** less often ● ● 5 ⊙ ⊙ 10 ⊙⊙ 15 more often ⊙⊙ 20
Information-collecting states [C] The intended information is found. Users' primary information needs are fulfill, but users are interested in finding other relevant or related information. [C] The intended information is found. Users' primary information needs are fulfill. Users are ready use information they found to take further action(s). [C] Users record the information they found.	**HEAD** ◯ 5 less often ◯ 10 more often ◯ 15 ◯ 20
Struggling states /?\ The intended information is found. Users' primary information needs are fulfill. Users are ready use information they found to take further action(s). ▲? Users keep searching by changing search strategy.	**EYEBROWS** less often ⌒⌒ 0 − − 5 ⌣ 10 \/ 15 more often \/\/ 20

Table 4.2. The coding scheme used in Chernoff Face Analysis

Chernoff Faces Analysis: Coding Scheme	
Users' cognitive states and physical states	**Chernoff Faces coding system**
Decision-making states Users make a **positive** decision (to proceed) about something according to information they found.	**CHEEK** less often ↕ more often 1 More than 1
Users go back to the previously selected or recorded (bookmarked) pages or results, and/ or compare the selected pages or results side by side in case there are more than one page or result selected.	**NOSE** less often ↕ more often 1 More than 1
Users make a **negative** decision (not to proceed) about something according to information they found.	**HAIR** less often ↕ more often 5 10 15
Satisfactory states Users are satisfied. All users' needs are fulfilled. Users are able to accomplish their goals based on the information they found.	**MOUTH** ‿
Users are somewhat satisfied, but not completely satisfied. Users' primary needs are fulfilled, and users are able to accomplish their goals based on the information they found. However, users still need more information to fulfill all their needs completely.	**MOUTH** ⊢⊣
Users are not satisfied. Users' needs are not fulfilled. Users are unable to accomplish their goal(s).	**MOUTH** ⌢

Figure 9. Examples of Chernoff Face Analysis used to visually identify various types of user search behaviors regarding the frequency of each behavior

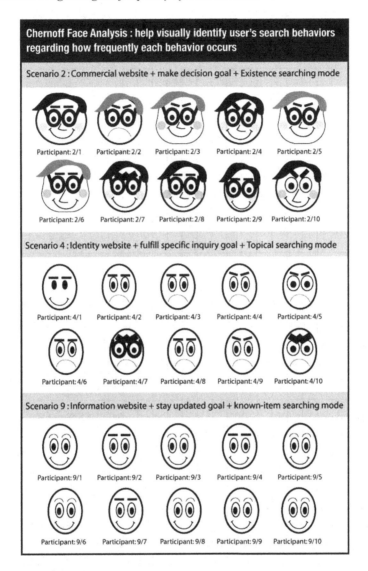

Table 5. An example analysis of user search strategies and user search methods by using the Checklist and Sequence Record

Checklist and Sequence Record: Showing the frequency and sequence of use of different search tools — **Scenario 2: commercial** Web site + **making decision** goal + **existence searching** mode

	Exploring/Browsing							Purposeful searching						Auxiliary			Sequence
	Menus	Table of content	Feature items/topics	list of items/topics	Advertising	Related items/topics	Table or diagram w/ link text	Search field	Simple search function	Advanced search function	Index	Shortcut	Site map	"Back" button	"Next" button	"See more" button	
Participant 2/1*	2**	5						1						7		7	browsing categories → browsing results ↔ purposeful searching
Participant 2/2		2						6						6		9	purposeful searching → retrieval results ↔ exploring, browsing
Participant 2/3		3	2			4		2						5		7	browsing categories → browsing results ↔ purposeful searching → retrieval results
Participant 2/4		4				2		1	1					4	6	5	browsing categories → browsing results ↔ purposeful searching → retrieval results
Participant 2/5						2		2	3					8		10	purposeful searching → retrieval results ↔ exploring, browsing
Participant 2/6		6												14		11	browsing categories → browsing results
Participant 2/7		13						1						15	1	7	browsing categories → browsing results ↔ purposeful searching
Participant 2/8		3						1						6		7	browsing categories → browsing results ↔ purposeful searching
Participant 2/9		4												5		6	browsing categories → browsing results
Participant 2/10		8						1						10	2	7	browsing categories → browsing results ↔ purposeful searching
Central tendency: mean	0.2	4.8	0.2	0	0	0.8	0	1.4	0	0.4	0	0	0	8	0.9	7.6	browsing categories → browsing results ↔ purposeful searching; purposeful searching → retrieval results ↔ exploring, browsing; browsing categories → browsing results ↔ purposeful searching → retrieval results
	6.0							**1.8**						**16.5**			

Table 6. An example analysis of user information needs by using the Checklist Record

Scenario 2
Commercial Web site, making decision goal, existence searching mode

	Characteristics of Information								Formats of Information display					Presentation Methods of Information display				Types of Information			Remarks: Users thoughts, comments on their information needs
	Quick references, Bullet points	FAQs, questions and answers	Step-by-step instructions	Comparison information	Recommendations, feature articles	Glossary explanations	Stories, sequence information	Complete descriptions	Topics, keywords, headlines	Abstracts, summaries	Short or brief text/information	Full or long text/information	Biography references	Textual descriptions	Diagrams, maps	Matrix, tables	Images, icons, illustrations	Opinions, reviews recommendations	News, reports	Facts, scientific information	
Participant 2/1	8				2			7	15	9	23	7		24			21	YES		YES	Many users would like to see more and bigger pictures, or some interactive displays showing the usage of product.
Participant 2/2	25				2			3	14	8	22	3		22			23	YES		YES	
Participant 2/3	22				4			7	11	11	22	7		22			24	YES	YES	YES	
Participant 2/4	22				4			3	15	7	23	3		23			24	YES		YES	
Participant 2/5	24				1			4	11	15	26	4		26			27	YES		YES	
Participant 2/6	25				6			2	19	11	30	2		30			30	YES	YES	YES	Some users expect to see the same or similar information to what they would see on the package of the product when they buy in a store.
Participant 2/7	29				10				30	6	36			35			36	YES		YES	
Participant 2/8	36				4			2	9	7	16	2		16			18	YES	YES	YES	
Participant 2/9	16				4				8	4	12			12			15			YES	
Participant 2/10	27				8				21	6	27			26			30	YES		YES	
Central tendency (mean)	23.8				4.5			2.8	15.4	8.4	23.7	2.8		23.6			24.8				Most users want to see comparison information or want a comparison tool.

measure reliability and validity of the coding scheme and analysis methods, a second observer is invited to independently interpret and code the same video data. The scripts encoded by both observers are then compared to identify the degree to which both observers agree in their interpretation and coding. This validation process is called *double coding,* which is perhaps the most used technique to attain sufficient reliability to proceed with analysis and interpretation (Boyatzis, 1998; Miles & Huberman, 1984).

After the double coding process is completed, the *confusion matrix* is constructed to show where the two observers are different in their judgment when coding the events. Agreement takes place when both observers use the same code for the same event. On the contrary, disagreement occurs when observers use different codes to code the same event. To read the confusion matrix, the scores on the diagonal from top left to bottom right indicate agreement between the two observers, while the scores off this diagonal indicate their disagreement (Robson, 1993) (see Figure 11).

Figure 10. An example of analysis of user profiles

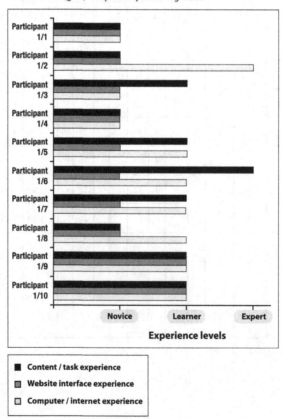

User Profile Analysis
Scenario 1 : Commercial web site + Finding information to make decision (goal) + Exploratory searching mode

Table 7. The construction of truth table 1

Causal conditions				Total instances among 100 cases	Output code: presence/absence of instance (P)	Output code: achieving goal–search success (S)
A	**B**	**C**	**D**			
Have prior knowledge and/or experience in content?	Have visited the Web site before (return user)?	Utilize different kinds of search tools?	Read text or detailed information thoroughly?			Achieve original goal–search success?
1*	1	1	1	3	1*	1*
1	1	1	0	3	1	1
1	1	0	1	6	1	1
1	0	1	1	8	1	1
0	1	1	1	0	0	n/a**
1	1	0	0	9	1	0
1	0	0	1	12	1	1
0	0	1	1	3	1	1
1	0	1	0	15	1	1
0	1	0	1	3	1	1
0	1	1	0	0	0	n/a**
1	0	0	0	22	1	1
0	0	0	1	6	1	1
0	1	0	0	0	0	n/a**
0	0	1	0	3	1	1
0	0	0	0	7	1	0
				= 100 cases		

*Number '1' indicates the presence of a causal condition or an output, and '0' indicates its absence. **Code 'n/a' indicates that the output code for the particular row is not applicable or it cannot be identified because the instance of the causal combination on that row is absent.*

As shown in Figure 11, the scores on the diagonal from top left to bottom right appearing in coding 'A', 'B', 'C', 'D', and 'L' indicate agreement between the two observers. However, for the coding 'E', there is also a score appearing off this diagonal which indicates an event of their disagreement. Note that in this particular case, both observers do not assign coding 'F', 'G', 'H', 'I', 'J', 'K', and 'M' to any events. Therefore, there is no score for unused coding in the matrix; this will be different from one case to another.

Then, based on the scores on the confusion matrix, the proportion of agreement, the proportion expected by chance, and the Cohen's Kappa are respectively calculated to measure inter-observer agreement (see Figure 12). "The inter-observer agreement is the extent to which two or more observers obtain the same results when measuring the same behaviors (e.g. when independently coding the same tape)." (Robson, 1993, p. 221).

In order to assess the significance of Kappa scores, Fliess (1981) has suggested the following rules of thumb: the Kappa scores of 0.40 to 0.60 is considered "fair"; the Kappa scores of 0.60 to 0.75 is considered "good"; and the Kappa scores above 0.75 is considered

Figure 11. An example construction of the confusion matrix showing the scores of agreement and disagreement between two observers in their judgment when coding the events

C o n f u s i o n   M a t r i x

Observer 1	Observer 2 A ○	B ●	C △	D ▲	E □	F ▣	G ■	H ◇	I ◇	J ◆	K ☆	L ⊗	M X	Total
A ○	6				1									7
B ●		8												8
C △			4											4
D ▲				4										4
E □					2									2
F ▣														
G ■														
H ◇														
I ◇														
J ◆														
K ☆														
L ⊗												1		1
M X														
Total	6	8	4	4	3							1		26

"excellent." The results obtained from this validation process show that validity of the coding schemes used in this study, in the view of inter-observer agreement, is positively strong. The Kappa scores of seven observation cases acquire "excellent" points (0.75-0.95), and the other three cases also show "good" scores (0.64-0.71).

However, the extent of agreement between two observers who use the coding scheme to code the same events independently is also affected by some other factors. One primary factor may be the observer's learning curve with regard to the coding scheme; one observer is more familiar with the coding scheme while the other observer is new and still learning to use the codes and/or interpret the events. Another important factor may be the observer's lack of experience or direct contact with the actual participants in the prior observation when the events were recorded. This occurs when one observer attended the observation in person when the events were recorded while the other observer was absent. The observer who had experience or direct contact with the actual participants when the events were recorded will be able to capture the participants' emotions or thoughts that are hard to detect through watching video data alone. As a result, the two observers may interpret the same user behavior differently since the first observer also makes judgments based on experi-

Figure 12. An example calculation of the proportion of agreement, the proportion expected by chance, and the Cohen's Kappa Score to measure the extent of inter-observer agreement

Proportion of Agreement

$$Po = \frac{(\text{number of agreements})}{(\text{number of agreements}) + (\text{number of disagreements})}$$

$$Po = \frac{6+8+4+4+2+1}{26} = \frac{25}{26} = 0.96$$

Proportion of Expected by Chance

$$Pc = (P1A \times P2A) + (P1B \times P2B) + (P1C \times P2C) + (P1D \times P2D) + (........)$$

P1A = the probability the **first** observer using code '**A**'
P2A = the probability the **second** observer using code '**A**'
P1B = the probability the **first** observer using code '**B**'
P2B = the probability the **second** observer using code '**B**'

$$Pc = (0.26 \times 0.23) + (0.30 \times 0.30) + (0.15 \times 0.15) + (0.15 \times 0.15) + (0.11 \times 0.07) + (0.03 \times 0.03) = 0.1969$$

Cohen's Kappa

$$K = \frac{Po - Pc}{1 - Pc}$$

$$K = \frac{0.96 - 0.1969}{1 - 0.1969} = \frac{0.7631}{0.8031} = 0.95$$

ence with the actual participant. These are factors that may play an important role in the inter-observer agreement.

ANALYSIS OF RESEARCH DATA

Patterns of User Search Behaviors

The research provides a new perspective on design considerations for a Web site by incorporating requirements from both Web site (client) intentions and user goals.

The results from this study in which user goals and their modes of searching were investigated simultaneously with Web site goals to reveal common search patterns associated with each case and significantly show that the patterns of user search behaviors are uniquely different depending on their goals and current modes of searching. Even though each user performed his/her task in isolation and in his/her own way, similar search patterns appeared based on a shared goal and/or the same mode of searching. Different search patterns were associated with different user goals and modes of searching, as well as Web site intentions.

In this research, user search behaviors are primarily analyzed by using the thematic analysis (Boyatzis, 1998) with time-ordered matrix (Robson, 1993) (see Table 3 and Figure 7), along with procedural analysis (see Figure 8), and Chernoff Faces (Chernoff, 1973, Wainer and Thissen, 1981) (see Figure 9), to uncover the patterns of user tasks in each scenario, while Checklist and Sequence Record (Robson, 1993) (see Table 5) is used to identify the types of user search strategies and methods. The analyses (see an example in Figure 7) show that users who begin with the same goal will perform their search similarly in terms of what tasks are necessary to reach the goal. However, if they use different modes of searching, which depend mainly on how precisely they know what they want, they will have different search strategies and consequently choose different kinds of search methods even though they begin their search with the same goal. Therefore, based on these research findings, user goals and modes of searching are the main mechanisms that play an important role in determining user behaviors and the resulting search patterns.

While user goal is the main factor regulating their task description, user mode of searching provides the major impact on search strategies and search methods. User goals determine the different tasks they need to perform to achieve their goal. Simultaneously, user

Figure 13. User goals and user modes of searching, the main factors regulating user search behaviors and the resulting search patterns

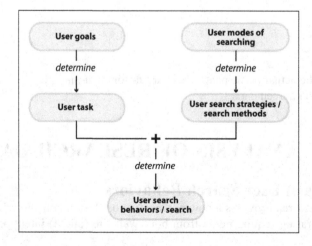

modes of searching influence their search strategies, or the plans of their search, determining how hard or easy the search can be and how much time is spent on their search, which accordingly results in selecting different search methods based on their search strategies (see Figure 13).

The analyses are collectively done on 10 observation cases of each of 10 scenarios which are systematically fabricated according to the research analytic frame previously demonstrated, in order to uncover the patterns of similarities or differences of user search behaviors. Based on research findings, the participants in scenarios 1 and 2 share the same search goal. As a result, even though they have different modes of searching and perform their tasks on different Web sites, the patterns of their task descriptions are very alike. Likewise the participants in scenarios 3, 4, and 5, or the participants in scenarios 6, 7, 8, and 9 have different modes of searching on different Web sites but have very similar tasks. Each group of these participants who share the same search goal, perform their tasks similarly although they do not share the same search modes and they visit different Web sites.

Patterns of User Search Strategies and Methods

When performing their search, individuals need a search plan — how to perform their search and which kinds of search tools to use in order to easily achieve their original goal. This plan is different from person-to-person based on user search strategy. However as stated earlier, one's search strategy is influenced by one's mode of searching (see Figure 13).

As a result, when visiting a Web site, individuals who arrive with different modes of searching will form different intentions as well as plan different search strategies, and accordingly perform their search in different ways to reach the same goal. Search strategies range from a general or less objective search (browse) to a more specific or purposeful search. These are directly proportional to user modes of searching which range from open-ended to specific search. They may also plan a fast or slow search based on time available and the urgency of their need. Users who plan a slow search usually want to record their search results by using the bookmark function or simply print out the results of retrieval pages for later use. Search strategy may change from time to time in accordance with modes of searching, which are based on the current context or situation that unfolds while they are searching as well as in response to the search results they find or retrieve.

While search strategy is the scheme that generally characterizes user search patterns, search method is the procedure for how they actually perform their search. This concerns the types of search tools chosen for use in their search. These search tools may include a menu bar, table of contents, index, site map, shortcut, search engine, and so forth. Users select from a combination of these search tools to perform their search based on their strategy. For example, users who are in the mode of exploratory searching (open-ended search), will likely plan a slow and general search (search strategy) and explore by browsing the menu bar and table of contents (search method). On the other hand, users who are in the mode of known-item searching (specific search), will usually plan a fast and purposeful search (search strategy) and comfortably use the index or shortcut (search method) to pursue their search.

The analyses (see an example in Table 5) show that users who begin with the same mode of searching have similar search strategies and choose similar methods. Based on research findings, the participants in scenarios 1 and 6 begin their search with the same mode of searching. As a result, even though they have different search goals and perform their tasks on different Web sites, they choose similar search strategies and methods. Each group of participants who share the same mode of searching chooses similar search strategies and methods although they do not share the same search goals and they visit different Web sites. However, note that even though the participants in scenarios 2, 3, and 7 have different modes of searching from the participants in scenarios 4 and 8, they also share similar search strategies and methods.

Patterns of User Information Needs

In this research, user information needs are primarily analyzed by using the Checklist and Sequence Record (Robson, 1993) (see Table 6) to identify the types, characteristics, formats, as well as quality and quantity of information preferred or needed by users to fulfill their original goals. Besides having different search strategies and methods, users also have different needs for information that can fulfill their goals. The findings demonstrate that user goals, modes of searching, and prior knowledge and experience in the contents they search are collectively the main mechanisms that play an important role in determining their information needs. Consequently, each user who comes to visit a Web site with a different goal, mode of searching, and prior knowledge and experience will need different kinds of information in order to fulfill his/her goal. Information provided on a Web site may be categorized based on various aspects of information including the characteristics of the information; formats and presentation methods of information display; types of information; as well as quality and quantity of given information.

Information characteristics differ widely including quick reference information such as short or brief information organized and presented using bullet points; frequently asked

Table 8. Boolean minimization process applied to the primitive expressions from truth table 1

Minimization : Step 1	Minimization : Step 2
ABCD *combines with* ABCd *to produce* ABC	ABC *combines with* AbC *to produce* AC
ABCD *combines with* ABcD *to produce* ABD	ACD *combines with* ACd *to produce* AC
ABCD *combines with* AbCD *to produce* ACD	ACD *combines with* AcD *to produce* AD
ABCd *combines with* AbCd *to produce* ACd	AbC *combines with* Abc *to produce* Ab
ABcD *combines with* aBcD *to produce* BcD	AbC *combines with* abC *to produce* bC
ABcD *combines with* AbcD *to produce* AcD	AcD *combines with* acD *to produce* cD
AbCD *combines with* AbCd *to produce* AbC	BcD *combines with* bcD *to produce* cD
AbCD *combines with* abCD *to produce* bCD	bCD *combines with* bcD *to produce* bD
AbcD *combines with* abcD *to produce* bcD	bCD *combines with* bCd *to produce* bC
AbcD *combines with* Abcd *to produce* Abc	
abCD *combines with* abCd *to produce* abC	
AbCd *combines with* Abcd *to produce* Abd	
AbCd *combines with* abCd *to produce* bCd	
aBcD *combines with* abcD *to produce* acD	

question (FAQ); glossary or explanation; procedural guideline or step-by-step instruction; comparison information; recommendation; sequential story or report; and complete description. Based on the research findings, user need for different characteristics of information is influenced by their different goals.

Types of information can be categorized into three different groups. The first group includes information that comes from personal or expert opinion, critique, review, or recommendation such as an editor's choice or customer's review. The second group may include the information that is collected from news or reports such as today's news or weekly reports, and the last group includes the information that presents the facts or scientific information for any given topic or item. Similar to user need for different information characteristics, the research findings demonstrate that user information needs for different types of information are influenced by different user goals.

Formats of information display range from an abstract level, including keyword; topic or headline; abstract; summary, to the detailed level including brief/short text or information, full/long text or information, reference, and bibliography. Based on the research findings, user needs for different formats of information display are influenced by different modes of searching. Presentation methods for information display range from textual to visual presentation, including textual or descriptive information (text), diagram, matrix, table, icon, image, illustration, or combinations of these methods. The research findings show that information needs for different presentation methods of information display are influenced by the type and character of the site contents.

Quality and quantity of information range from shallow information, which is usually not enough to help individuals to take further actions, to a variety of deep and detailed information. Based on the research findings, user information needs for different levels of quality and quantity of given information are influenced by various factors related to both the user and the Web site simultaneously. These factors include user goal; modes of searching; prior knowledge and experience in the contents they search; as well as the characteristics of Web contents — simple, everyday topics, or complicated, hard topics.

Discussion on Relevant Factors for User Search Success

Even though the accuracy of a search engine is one of the most recognized factors determining user search success or failure, qualitative comparison conducted by constructing truth tables and applying *Boolean algebra method* (Ragin, 1987, 1994) demonstrates that there are other relevant factors that play an important role to influence user search success or struggle. These influencing factors derive from both user profiles and behaviors as well as Web site attributes.

The qualitative comparison method is used in this study to examine among cases the combinations of causal conditions that help produce the positive outcome (users achieve the goal). These causal conditions include user prior experience in the content and Web site interface, their behaviors while searching, and several Web site attributes. Two truth tables (truth table 1 [see Table 7], and truth table 2 [see Table 10]) are constructed from observation data, which is recorded into nominal-scale and represented in binary form, to display different combinations of values on the conditions and outputs.

A presence-absence dichotomy is used in the tables to specify what outcomes and causal conditions are either present or absent in each observation case. Code number 1 indicates

Table 9. Prime implicant chart showing coverage of original terms by prime implicants

Primitive Expressions

	ABCD	ABCd	ABcD	AbCD	AbcD	abCD	AbCd	aBcD	Abcd	abcD	abCd
AC	X	X		X			X				
AD	X		X	X	X						
Ab				X	X		X		X		
bC				X		X	X				X
bD				X	X	X				X	
cD			X		X			X		X	
ABD	X		X								
Abd							X		X		
Acd		X					X				

Prime Implicants

the presence of a condition or an output; code number 0 indicates the absence (see Tables 7 and 10). Truth table 1, as demonstrated in Table 7, is constructed to examine the causal conditions of user prior experience and search behavior and identify the combinations that significantly contribute to user search success.

With uppercase letters indicating presence and lowercase letters indicating absence of a particular causal condition shown in the combination, the data on user search success (S) from truth table 1 can be represented in the Boolean equation as follows:

$$S = ABCD + ABCd + ABcD + AbCD + AbcD + abCD + \\ AbCd + aBcD + Abcd + abcD + abCd$$

This equation for S (search success) shows 11 primitive combinations of causal conditions that help users to achieve their goal. In order to simplify these primitive expressions, the concept of Boolean minimization is used. The most fundamental of Boolean minimization rules is (Ragin, 1987):

If two Boolean expressions differ in only one causal condition yet produce the same outcome, then the causal condition that distinguishes the two expressions can be considered irrelevant and can be removed to create a simpler, combined expression (p. 93).

The *Boolean minimization process* is conducted in a bottom-up fashion until no further stepwise reduction of Boolean expression is possible. This process is applied to the primitive expressions derived from truth table 1 as demonstrated in Table 8. With the Boolean minimization process applied, the reduced expressions (prime implicants) on user search success (S) from truth table 1 can be represented in the simpler equation as follows:

$$S = AC + AD + Ab + bC + bD + cD + ABD + Abd + Acd$$

Then, the final step of Boolean minimization is conducted by using the prime implicant chart (see Table 9) to map the links between nine prime implicants (see the second equation previously shown) and 11 primitive expressions (see the first equation). This process helps to eliminate redundant prime implicants in order to produce a logically minimal number of prime implicants which cover as many of the primitive Boolean expressions as possible.

Eventually, with the final process of Boolean minimization applied, the final equation (S) from truth table 1 demonstrates six combinations of causal conditions that produce the positive outcome (user search success) as follows:

$$S = AC + AD + Ab + bC + bD + cD$$

This final equation significantly demonstrates the result showing that causal condition 'A' (users have prior knowledge and/or experience in the content), condition 'C' (users utilize different kinds of search tools), and condition 'D' (users read text or detailed information thoroughly) are the important variables that help users to achieve their goals.

Contrary to the traditional view on user experience with Web site interface (first-time versus return users), the result shows that causal condition 'B' (users have visited the Web site before) is not the primary factor contributing to users' accomplishment in their search.

In addition, the second truth table (truth table 2) is constructed to examine the impact of various causal conditions including user prior knowledge in the contents they search (condition 'A') and prior experience in Web interface (condition 'B'), combined with different causal conditions from various Web site attributes (see Table 10). These variables include condition 'E' (Web site provides different approaches to content classification), condition 'F' (Web site has well-organized search retrieval results), and condition 'G' (Web site provides search tips or examples).

With all processes of Boolean minimization applied, the final Boolean equation (S) from truth table 2 demonstrates six combinations of causal conditions that produce the positive outcome (user search success) as follows:

$$S = AeF + AEFg + AEfG + BeFg + bEFg + Abefg$$

Significantly, this final equation derived from truth table 2 also confirms that causal condition 'A' (users have prior knowledge and/or experience in the content) is the important variable that helps users to achieve their goals. Besides the condition 'A,' the Web site variables that have significant impact on user search success include condition 'E' (Web sites that provide different approaches to content classification) and condition 'F' (Web sites that have well-organized search retrieval results). The result also shows that condition 'B' (users have visited the Web site before), and 'G' (Web sites provide search tips or examples) have

Table 10. The construction of truth table 2

Causal conditions					Total instances among 100 cases	Output code: presence/ absence of instance (P)	Output code: achieving goal– search success (S)
A	**B**	**E**	**F**	**G**			
Have prior knowledge and/or experience in content?	Have visited the Web site before (return user)?	Provide different approaches to content classifi-cation?	Have well organized search (retrieval) results?	Provide search tips or examples?			Achieve original goal– search success?
1*	1	1	1	1	0	0	n/a**
1	1	1	1	0	5	1*	1*
1	1	1	0	1	1	1	1
1	1	0	1	1	1	1	1
1	0	1	1	1	0	0	n/a
0	1	1	1	1	0	0	n/a
1	1	1	0	0	0	0	n/a
1	1	0	0	1	0	0	n/a
1	0	0	1	1	9	1	1
0	0	1	1	1	0	0	n/a
0	1	1	1	0	0	0	n/a
1	1	0	1	0	7	1	1
1	0	1	0	1	9	1	1
0	1	0	1	1	0	0	n/a
1	0	1	1	0	9	1	1
0	1	1	0	1	0	0	n/a
1	1	0	0	0	7	1	0
1	0	0	0	1	0	0	n/a
0	0	0	1	1	0	0	n/a
1	0	0	1	0	5	1	1
0	0	1	0	1	0	0	n/a
0	1	0	0	1	0	0	n/a
1	0	1	0	0	0	0	n/a
0	0	1	1	0	6	1	1
0	1	1	0	0	0	0	n/a
0	1	0	1	0	3	1	1
1	0	0	0	0	25	1	1
0	1	0	0	0	0	0	n/a
0	0	1	0	0	0	0	n/a
0	0	0	1	0	5	1	0
0	0	0	0	1	0	0	n/a
0	0	0	0	0	8	1	0
					= 100 cases		

*Number '1' indicates the presence of a causal condition or an output, and '0' indicates its absence. **Code 'n/a' indicates that the output code for the particular row is not applicable or it cannot be identified because the instance of the causal combination on that row is absent.*

less impact on user search success compared with other variables. These analytical results as well as others are further summarized and synthesized, in order to develop explanatory frameworks of user search behaviors and needs, as well as to establish classifications of substantial user factors and analytical frameworks to evaluate information design on Web sites.

CONCLUSION

This investigation demonstrates that a user-centered approach can improve information design on Web-based media through study of various factors, especially user cognitive factors including user goals and modes of searching, to identify the corresponding impact of these factors on information and functional needs in terms of user behaviors. As an attempt to solve the problems of information-seeking tasks in Web-based media, the research is successful in providing a new perspective on Web site design considerations by strongly taking a user-centered approach to incorporate a careful consideration of actual user needs and behaviors together with requirements from a Web site.

By conducting extensive qualitative research on user study in relation to search needs and behaviors on Web sites as well as employing various analytical methods to uncover different aspects of the research data, the study answers the research questions. The common patterns of user information-seeking behavior, user search strategies and methods, as well as user information needs presented in different cases are revealed. These valuable findings will be further synthesized to develop frameworks and classifications.

Deeper understanding of these various factors, especially user cognitive factors, may complement the use of existing analytical or design methods such as task analysis and scenario-based design, by helping Web developers to recognize the important factors that may be subtle or previously unidentified yet substantially affect user task performances. By recognizing these elements, Web developers can identify the useful and appropriate functions and/or information to include in each particular case, in order to support user needs and task performances and eventually promote their satisfaction.

REFERENCES

Boyatzis, R. E. (1998). *Transforming qualitative information: Thematic analysis and code development*. Thousand Oaks, CA: Sage.

Brinck, T., Gergle, D., & Wood, S. D. (2002). *Usability for the Web: Designing Web sites that work*. San Francisco: Morgan Kaufmann.

Chernoff, H. (1973). The use of faces to represent points in k-dimensional space graphically. *Journal of the American Statistical Association, 68,* 361-368.

Fleming, J. (1998). *Web navigation: Designing the user experience*. Sebastopol, CA: O'Reilly & Associates.

Fliess, J. L. (1981). Statistical methods for rates and proportions. New York: Wiley.

Ivory, M. Y., & Hearst, M. A. (2001). The state of the art in automating usability evaluation of user interface. *ACM Computing Surveys, 33*(4), 470-516.

Miles, M. B., & Huberman, A. M. (1984). *Qualitative data analysis: A soursebook of new methods*. Newbury Park, CA: Sage.

Ragin, C. C. (1987). *The comparative method: Moving beyond qualitative and quantitative strategies*. Berkeley; Los Angeles: University of California Press.

Ragin, C. C. (1994). *Constructing social research: The unity and diversity of method*. Thousand Oaks, CA: Pine Forge Press.

Robson, C. (1993). *Real world research: A resource for social scientists and practitioner-researchers*. Malden, MA: Blackwell.

Rosenfeld, L., & Morville, P. (1998). *Information architecture for the World Wide Web*. Sebastopol, CA: O'Reilly & Associates.

Wainer, H., & Thissen, D. (1981). Graphical data analysis. *Annual Review of Psychology, 32*, 191-241.

Section II:

Analysis

Chapter IV

Understanding the Nature of Task Analysis in Web Design

Rod Farmer, The University of Melbourne, Australia

Paul Gruba, The University of Melbourne, Australia

ABSTRACT

Designing usable Web-based interfaces challenges practitioners to carefully consider end-user behaviour and requirements. Unfortunately, in meeting this challenge, human-computer interaction (HCI), task analysis is often poorly understood and applied during Web design activities. Rather than purely evaluating usability against prescriptive guidelines, we argue that designing for Web-based interaction requires a more holistic and descriptive approach. This chapter provides an overview of cognitive and postcognitive HCI task analysis frameworks, and their respective abilities to capture a systemic view of stakeholder requirements. As such, this chapter provides a valuable resource for researchers and practitioners alike.

INTRODUCTION

Although improved system design results when researchers and developers understand how users use technology (Raeithel & Velichkovsky, 1996), understanding individual user traits, such as motivation and other contextual factors that guide user participation during computer-mediated activities can be deceptively complex. Simply asking users what they want and how they use a system is further complicated by the fact that users are often incapable of vividly and objectively describing their experiences with the system (Sommerville, 2004). Expertise, sociocultural, and organisational policy factors may impact perception of purpose, meaning, and context, and hence influence the quality of user feedback (Gasson, 1999). Therefore, determining whether a system is *fit-for-purpose* for a particular end-user population can be extremely challenging.

As developing fit-for-purpose systems is a principal concern of human-computer interaction (HCI), the system design process must ensure that end-user requirements are validated against those who have a vested interest in its use (stakeholders). Therefore, choosing the right HCI framework for eliciting, analysing, and modelling stakeholder requirements is critical for ensuring overall system quality (Farmer, Gruba, & Hughes, 2004). The process of seeking to understand the human nature of these requirements is referred to in HCI as *task analysis*. There is a wealth of frameworks, models, methodologies, and tools that can be applied to assist in this process. However, choosing the "most appropriate" approach is dependent upon several factors, including: the domain, context of use, and available resources.

Task analysis is arguably the most important aspect of HCI as it provides the analyst, researcher, or developer with insights into the nature of human behaviour. A major benefit of conducting task analysis throughout the software development life cycle (SDLC) is its communicative power and ability to elicit and elucidate requirements throughout each phase of development via a set of formalised attributes and notations. Unfortunately, comparing and choosing the right task analysis approach during system design is frequently hampered by the lack of universal notations and user attributes that can be applied across frameworks (Balbo, Ozkan, & Paris, 2004).

The aim of this chapter is to provide a critical overview of task analysis in HCI and its application to Web design. Specifically, the chapter will discuss the cognitivist origins of task analysis, and the recent shift towards more ecologically valid approaches. We discuss several leading approaches within each paradigm and describe their general applicability to Web design. We conclude with an integrative approach to task analysis that attempts to bridge the divide between cognitive and postcognitivist perspectives.

TASK ANALYSIS IN HCI

The term *task analysis* is commonly used to denote a wide range of activities and processes that attempt to either describe, equate, or predict human performance during task-based interaction (Diaper, 2004). A direct corollary of early cognitive psychological research concerning cognition and procedural knowledge (Kirwan & Ainsworth, 1992; Miller, 1953, 1962), task analysis has been applied successfully to numerous fields of research, including:

- Interactive system design (Newman & Lamming, 1998)
- Safety critical systems design and evaluation (Paternò & Santoro, 2002)
- Cognitive engineering (Rasmussen, Pejtersen, & Goodstein, 1994; Vicente, 1999)
- Computer-assisted language learning (Corbel, Gruba, & Enright, 2002; Farmer & Hughes, 2005a, 2005c)
- Multi-modal interaction (Farmer, 2005)
- Intelligent learning object classification (Farmer & Hughes, 2005b)

Table 1. Types of task analysis (MITRE, 2003)

Types of Task Analysis	
Cognitive task analysis	System evaluation methods
Knowledge elicitation	Descriptive analysis
Computational cognitive modelling	Human reliability analysis
Task analysis	Cognitive-oriented methods
Computational task simulation	System-oriented methods

- Social intimacy (Vetere et al., 2005)
- Web design (Dix, 2005)

It is therefore not surprising to see an increasingly divergent array of theoretical perspectives emerging on the nature of human-machine interaction. Observing that methodologies in HCI have already reached a sufficient level of sophistication and application, Whittaker, Terveen, and Nardi (2000) have argued that it is time to address existing problems, rather than develop additional idiosyncratic models and notations. Indeed, renewed focus has recently been applied to the problem of integrating and grouping task analysis theories and techniques, which at first glance may appear fundamentally incommensurate (Farmer, 2006; Wild, Johnson, & Johnson, 2003).

The primary aim of task analysis is to produce a reliable procedural description of human praxis. However, unlike mere procedural functions, tasks incorporate the notion of *purpose* (Preece, Rogers, Sharp, Benyon, Holland, & Carry, 1994, p. 411), hence goals and planning. Many task analysis techniques are built on the belief that systems are reducible to their constituent parts, promoting a systematic, linear decomposition of human praxis (Watts & Monk, 1998). However, systems can never be logically decomposed into subsystems without losing some implicit value, whether operational (knowledge) or functional (capability) (Latour, 1987). This said, linear reductionist descriptions of work may be appropriate for developing highly constrained, well-defined environments, such as interactive voice response (IVR) systems that typically restrict users to inhabiting a single state. Such cognitive environments therefore promote a strong adherence to a narrow view of user behaviour (Robinson, 1993). Table 1 shows a variety of task analysis approaches typically employed within HCI.

Disregarding the actual methods applied within these frameworks, we can further collapse these approaches onto two conceptual axes: *descriptive/analytical* and *cognitive/system*. The descriptive/analytical axis reflects whether the purpose of the analytical framework is to describe or to empirically analyse interaction behaviour. The cognitive/system axis reflects whether the framework is cognitively oriented, concerned with modelling mental processes during work activity, or system oriented, concerned with modelling how individuals relate cognitively to their social, organisational, and environmental work contexts. As these axes represent continuums, more fine-grained categories of task analysis now emerge.

Low-level a*nalytic/cognitive* approaches such as *goals, operators, methods and selection rules* (GOMS) and *hierarchical task analysis* (HTA) tend to treat task interaction as a series of linearly sequenced actions from which we can derive the sense of the activity, and thus effective system design. Higher-level *system/descriptive* approaches, such as soft systems methodology (Checkland, 1999), tend to take a more holistic perspective, focusing on situated activity rather than actions. The growing importance of modelling situation awareness during HCI is representative of a paradigmatic shift away from individual, information processing accounts of interaction, towards more socially relevant, tool-mediated representations of activity.

Gathering Requirements via Task Analysis

Requirements engineering (elicitation, analysis, and specification) is essential to developing quality Web-based systems as it (1) helps to elicit possible user groups and their level of involvement; (2) provides insight into user and system requirements; and (3) places the development effort within a contextual environment (Balbo et al., 2004; Farmer et al., 2004). Schach (1999) provides a case-based analysis of software development projects, highlighting that the origin of 80% of all software defects can be traced back to earlier requirements engineering and design phases. In addition, the cost of fixing a defect during the maintenance phase, as opposed to these earlier phases, is an order of magnitude. As both requirements engineering and task analysis serve to determine which features of a system will render it fit-for-purpose, it is necessary to ensure they are conducted appropriately throughout the SLDC (see Table 2).

According to Mager (1991), there are four distinct fields of work analysis: (1) *performance*, (2) *critical incident*, (3) *task*, and (4) *goal analysis*. Performance analysis attempts to describe aspects of human activity that are directly related to understanding and improving human performance. Traditionally, this area of research has focused on two aspects of work:

Table 2. Purpose of task analysis various stages of the SDLC

Phase	Purpose
Discovery and definition	To elicit, analyse, and specify functional and nonfunctional stakeholder requirements within the context of use and the existing limitations and constraints upon the activity. To generate high-level, coarse-grained descriptions of the main tasks and objectives that are relevant to the user(s)
Design	Traditionally, the role of this phase has been to develop the user-interface design, however it should also include high-level, system architecture specification, documentation and additional resource design. These activities should all occur concurrently. To define and model the generic functionalities of the system, especially consistency and learnability (affordance, usability) when the system is to be deployed across several platforms
Development and Deployment	To analyse the implemented functionality of the system in terms of efficiency. To automatically generate parts of the architecture and subsystem components related to the functional stakeholder requirements
Evaluation and prediction	Through the use of specific task modelling notations, to produce a series of design tests which evaluate user performance and ensure that the final product is fit-for-purpose

operator awareness and capability modelling; and human-system simulation environments. Operator modelling is for the most part a behavioural activity, using techniques such as time analysis and operator function models (Kirwan & Ainsworth, 1992). Human-system simulation environments, on the other hand, require sophisticated, computational-task simulation tools and theories to evaluate human decision making, including recognition-primed decisions and naturalistic decision making (Zsambok & Klein, 1997).

Critical incident analysis focuses on developing causal models of relationships within complex systems to prevent accidents or error states in safety-critical environments (Shrayne, Westerman, Crawshaw, Hockey, & Sauer, 1998). As such, this work requires a higher-degree of probabilistic modelling and stochastic analysis than the other fields. More than any other work analysis related field, critical incident analysis attempts to reduce complex activities to discrete, measurable events.

Perhaps the most difficult category to define, however, is task analysis. Researchers and practitioners have failed to agree upon a universal definition of "task," including an appropriate unit of analysis (Carroll, 2002). As a result, the term *task analysis* has been used to describe all four categories of work analysis, especially goal analysis. Accordingly, contention has arisen concerning the structure of tasks, and their relationship to goals and planning (Nardi, 1996; Suchman, 1987).

What is a Task?

Figure 1 depicts a traditional structural view of *task* in HCI where it is seen as a conscious act (Kirwan & Ainsworth, 1992; Watts & Monk, 1998). Task-as-activity is comprised of some goal that must be achieved through mediated interaction via agents and artefacts of the environment (Flor & Hutchins, 1991; Hutchins, 1995). Planning is implied as goals reflect the system state to be achieved through effecting some combination of actions (events). Unfortunately, here we run into trouble. Preece et al. (1994) conceive activities as devoid of control structures and not requiring thought. While this may be true of some activities where procedural knowledge has reached a certain level of automaticity through habituation, it cannot be true of all interactive systems, such as Web environments.

Goals require constant monitoring and evaluation (Suchman, 1987), which implies conscious decision making. Indeed, it is more logical to assume that tasks are constructed and maintained within a frame of reference that includes planning (Filkes, 1982). Planning requires knowledge of when and how to initiate tasks. We therefore question the correctness of this traditional view of *Task*, and propose Figure 2 as an alternative. Here the term *task*

Figure 1. Traditional structural view of task

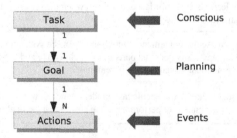

Figure 2. Activity-oriented structural view of task

is substituted for *activity*. As activities are motivated social constructs (Leont'ev, 1978), it is appropriate that they appear superordinate to goals, individual goals being a subset of collective goals. As activities exist at the social level, they are less temporal than subjective individual acts. Planning is therefore rooted firmly within specific communities of practice, and less open to change and violent fluctuations in behaviour. Given their degree of permanence, we classify conscious decision making conducted at this level, *meta-planning*. Furthermore, Suchman (1987) argues that individuals plan reflexively rather than deliberatively, responding to immediate changes in environmental conditions. As such, planning at the goal level is likely to be affected by micro changes during an activity. We classify this within-activity planning, *micro-planning*. Figure 2 suggests that tasks are subordinate to goals, thus inverting the traditional view. Moreover, Figure 2 distinguishes between two types of task: conscious and unconscious.

The mediating variable in task classification is habituation. The more one practices an event, the fewer attentional (cognitive) resources need to be assigned to performing that task. Conversely, when an error or breakdown in information flow occurs, these tasks are raised into consciousness and associated with an existing or newly formed goal (Engeström, 1987). Raising unconscious actions into conscious goal-oriented behaviour has been shown to significantly impact task performance (Farmer, 2005).

Divisions within HCI on Task Analysis

The notion of Task has historically been dependent upon the predominant theoretical models of the time. According to Goguen (1996), there are today two dominant theoretical perspectives within HCI: the cognitive (cognitive science and experimental psychology) and the postcognitive (sociology and anthropology). These perspectives exist along a continuum polarised by the split between the natural and social sciences (Raeithel & Velichkovsky, 1996). Selecting between cognitive and ecological theories of human praxis can have considerable impact upon system development. For instance, the view that participation within an activity is not isolated, yet inexorably bound to external relationships and sociocultural conditions poses serious questions for how we model both functional and nonfunctional requirements during online system design.

Cognitive approaches to task analysis primarily focus on aspects of user performance (Diaper, 2004), often neglecting sociocultural phenomenon essential to meaningful interaction. Postcognitivist, or ecological, approaches underscore the importance of context in evaluating human praxis. Postcognitive approaches hold that meaningful interaction can only be derived from careful consideration of the environmental, sociocultural, and historical contexts in which an activity occurs. Moreover, activity itself is distributed among various cognitive systems within the environment, and not just at the user interface, as interaction requires the accessing of information and/or anticipation of events that may be beyond the user's experience. Hence, measuring the meaningfulness of interaction is not merely an empirical measure of performance (human or technological), rather an evaluation of the appropriateness of an activity in relation to a set of established goals. Furthermore, meaning during online activity is negotiated through the user interface, and not at the user interface.

Contrary to the more behaviouristic views of cognitivist approaches, postcognitive perspectives are driven primarily by sociological considerations, including how work is shared, organised, and completed within communities of practice (Wegner, 2003). This shift is also indicative of increased research into how we can better capture the context of interaction; develop greater understanding of user behaviour — in situ — ; and how tool mediation impacts knowledge acquisition and management (Kaptelinin, 1996b).

The cognitivist dialogue maintains an assumption that derived task models can be universally applied across different user groups, implying a greater degree of similarity between individuals than should otherwise be accorded (Preece et al., 1994). Carroll (1997) suggests that designing systems upon the notion of universally applicable task models implies certain cognitive equivalences between humans and computers, yet maintains that artefacts lack self-awareness, and should never be thought to possess knowledge of their behaviour. Although some may suggest that artefacts possess certain cognitive affordances, this is often a misinterpretation of the impact of social process, such as cultural conventions, on object use (Norman, 1999).

APPROACHES TO TASK ANALYSIS IN HCI

As previously highlighted, the two primary task analysis movements within the field of HCI are cognitive (behaviourist) and postcognitive (sociocultural). Methods employed within the cognitivist paradigm promote action-oriented analyses of interaction (Kaptelinin, Nardi, & Macaulay, 1999). Postcognitive frameworks represent not so much an opposing view, but rather an argument for greater emphasis on modelling human activity as it occurs *in situ*. Postcognitivist methodologies favour goal-oriented or object-oriented analyses. To better understand how these paradigms differ from one another, we now consider related methodologies.

Behavioural Task Analysis

Behavioural, or cognitive task analysis frameworks focus primarily on how human behaviour is determined by the user's internalisation and transformation of input, and how this information results in output as action. Cognitive approaches to HCI mostly focus on the user-computer interface, as it forms the critical point of coherence between two discrete

Table 3. Common objectives of task models (Bomsdorf & Szwillus, 1998)

Objective	Purpose
To inform	To inform users and designers about potential problems. Common themes involve needs analysis, usability, and affordance.
Evaluation of human performance	To establish the impact of new or existing tools upon task performance in some work practice
System design support	To provide a detailed and structured conceptual model of the task, including behavioural (time, errors, feedback, etc.) and structural modelling (functionality, visibility, etc.)
System generation	To help develop prototypes, user interfaces, and elements of the system architecture

models of processing — that of the human and the computer. While this is true of most underlying cognitive task models, differing purposes of use have resulted in considerable variation between approaches.

Cognitive Task Models

There are various levels of behavioural task analysis approaches within HCI. These include low-level cognitive methodologies, such as HTA (Annett, 2004; Annett & Duncan, 1967; Shepherd, 2001), and higher-level, meta-cognitive frameworks, such as *scenario-based design* (Carroll, 1996, 1997, 2000, 2002; Rosson & Carroll, 2002).

Behavioural frameworks are structured upon specific task models, structured descriptions of the interactive task to be performed by the user(s). It encompasses the notion of task and as such represents the specific set of actions that the user may undertake in a goal-directed activity. Task models may also include a task hierarchy, indicating task sequencing and any additional constraints upon usage (Limbourg & Vanderdonckt, 2004). Although most vary substantially in their depth of analysis, degree of formalism, and purpose, all task models comprise a set of common objectives (Table 3).

According to Table 3, these common objectives imply that task models can be used for a variety of purposes, from requirements engineering through to system evaluation, representing varying levels of abstraction and serving different purposes within the SDLC (Balbo et al., 2004).

The underlying theme within behaviourist frameworks is that users have an overarching system goal they wish to achieve, which through intentionality is transformed into action. Decision making occurs through comparison of intention and perceived system behaviour (feedback) (Norman, 1999). As such, interaction is modelled as a closed information-processing loop — input, transformation, and output. These types of analysis are effective for modelling and evaluating the primitive tasks that determine user behaviour in well-structured activities. Here, we briefly describe a set of highly influential, cognitive task analysis frameworks. With the possible exception of *cognitive work analysis* (CWA), we argue that these approaches fail to sufficiently support decision making and problem solving in unstructured and dynamic environments.

Goals, Operators, Methods and Selection Rules

GOMS-based approaches have received considerable attention in the HCI literature (John & Kieras, 1996a, 1996b), as it can be used quantitatively to predict efficient user interaction with a system design (task performance), and qualitatively as a means of modelling low-level tasks (Kieras, 2004). GOMS-based approaches are also effective at predicting future task performance. However, models of interaction derived from a GOMS analysis tend to be abstract, rather than specific. Moreover, GOMS — as initially conceived — does not account for motivational factors involved in computer-mediated activities, nor is it well suited for modelling social and collaborative work practices.

The unit of analysis in GOMS is the task. Like HTA, GOMS describes task-based interaction as a hierarchically ordered sequence of actions, aligned with specific goals (and subgoals) (Card, Moran, & Newell, 1983). Briefly, GOMS views tasks as comprising:

1. **Goals:** Desired outcomes within some computer-mediated activity;
2. **Operators:** Actions that must be executed in order to achieve some goal;
3. **Methods:** The set of operators that are required to achieve some larger (system) goal; and
4. **Selection rules:** Logic rules used to choose between competing methods given some system feedback.

Within GOMS, input is received from the system, which is processed and associated with internalised representations of the system (mental models). This internal system information is aligned with immediate and overarching goals, and subsequently associated with competing possible actions. Selection rules serve as transformation functions, helping to determine which actions possess the greatest utility, and thus provide the most effective means of interaction. Output is the corollary of some cognitive utility evaluation, representing the most effective path to achieving the desired goal.

For GOMS, generating meaning from interaction occurs at the man-machine interface and is highly determined by subjective internal representations of the activity. Unfortunately, GOMS is highly prescriptive and fails to consider distributed models of interaction, which consider environmental artefacts, organisational behaviour, and social conventions that reflect historical decision-making processes and cultural conventions (Hutchins, 1995).

Hierarchical Task Analysis

HTA is an action-oriented, decompositional framework primarily concerned with the training of people in system design and use. Initially developed for analysing nonrepetitive operator tasks (Annett, 2004; Annett & Duncan, 1967), HTA grew out of the need for a more expressive model for describing mental processes during man-machine interaction. HTA's theoretical foundations lie in system theory and information processing, seeing task performance "as the interaction between human and machine, the latter becoming increasingly complex as computers and automation develop[ed]" (Annett, 2004, p. 68). With relation to task performance, the term *analysis* in HTA refers to the process of problem identification and structuring. HTA is an effective process for proposing empirical solutions to existing specified problems (Annett, 2004).

In HTA, *goal* refers to an expected outcome, or system state. Goals and subgoals, may be active or latent, arising when the need presents itself to achieve some expected outcome.

HTA frequently models this goal-oriented behaviour as tree structures, such as decision trees. Goals are established and acquired through an information processing cycle similar to that in our discussion of GOMS (Annett & Duncan, 1967; Kieras, 2004). As with goals, *actions* in HTA may also be decomposed into nested actions, each maintaining their direct relationship to an established system state. Being nested, actions are available at both the current node of activity, and at their super node (parent task). Therefore, according to HTA, user behaviour can be reduced to a cycle of monitoring for new input, deciding upon available alternatives and controlling subsequent behaviour.

Although an attractive framework, there are a number of problems HTA practitioners typically encounter. Firstly, when a parent goal becomes active, all subgoals (and their related actions) become active as well. However, it is seldom the case that a user is simultaneously aware of current and future goals. Rather, user behaviour is typically more anticipatory and reflexive (Endsley, 2000; Suchman, 1987). According to HTA, subgoals and their actions are maintained as conscious constructs available to the user. Again, this is unlikely to be the case, as many procedural actions essential for effective task completion are habituated or unconscious even when the associated goal is being actioned (Whittaker et al., 2000).

GroupWare Task Analysis

Developed by van der Veer, Lenting, and Bergevoet (1996), *GroupWare task analysis* (GTA) attempts to incorporate cooperative strategies within cognitive task models. Within GTA, complex tasks are decomposed into low-level unit tasks (Limbourg & Vanderdonckt, 2004). However, by assigning roles to both tasks and agents in the environment, GTA differs from HTA in its ability to model aspects of collaboration and cooperation. As roles change within the organization and across activities, traits that link specific tasks to activity structure, agents, and artefacts can be identified. This process contributes a social dimension to task performance analysis. Unfortunately, GTA currently lacks sufficient formalism, and therefore expressive power, to handle complex environments. Additionally, GTA is presently only effective when evaluating existing systems. It is therefore not appropriate for exploratory modelling activities.

Cognitive Task Analysis

Cognitive task analysis (CTA) refers to a host of techniques that can be applied to investigating expert system usage (Gordon & Gill, 1997). Examples include *naturalistic decision making, recognition-primed decisions*, and *schema theory* (Zsambok & Klein, 1997). CTA techniques address many of the weakness inherent to HTA and GOMS by explicitly modelling procedural knowledge and complex information-processing structures (Hollnagel, 2003). Decision ladders capture the central characteristic of information processing, yet incorporate short circuits, or experience-based patterns of action that permit experienced individuals to move between goal structures in response to changing action and planning resources. CTA is therefore highly suited to modelling expert behaviour. However, analysing sociocultural features of an activity is not sufficiently developed or formalised in CTA. Although HTA and GOMS may be cast as derivatives of the CTA approach, CTA is inherently more adaptable, as seen through (1) its advocacy of methodological plurality; (2) promotion of task heterarchies over hierarchies; and (3) its consideration of both cognitive and environmental artefacts within an activity. As CTA models activities in terms of cognitive architectures, it is less applicable to investigating exploratory, descriptive, and ill-structured social activities.

Cognitive Work Analysis

CWA is a work-centred framework that represents a major advancement upon traditional CTA approaches. It is designed specifically for analysing work environments that require significant human behavioural adaptation to new and existing tasks (Rasmussen et al., 1994; Vicente, 1999; 2004). It is built upon a meta-cognitive task model that integrates both cognitive and ecological practices within a holistic framework for work practice analysis.

CWA differs from other cognitive approaches in that it does not merely focus on *normative modelling* (how HCI should proceed); *descriptive modelling* (how HCI currently occurs); or *formative modelling* (how specific actions are sequenced during an activity). Rather, the aim of CWA is three fold:

1   Identify the properties of the work environment
2.   Define likely work boundaries
3.   Evaluate boundary effects on HCI

In CWA, actor-system interaction is always situated within some activity; hence, it considers not just the tasks actors perform, but also the situation in which they are undertaken. In conducting a work analysis, activity is broken down into five levels of analysis: (1) *work domain analysis*; (2) *control task analysis*; (3) *strategies analysis;* (4) *social-organisational analysis;* and (5) *work competencies analysis*. In practice, these five levels are used to constrain possible human-computer design considerations. Although prescriptive methods are formalised and integrated within CWA, the framework itself advocates a plurality of analysis techniques, so long as they fulfil a practical purpose. As conceptual levels are interdependent (soft boundaries), analysis progresses from one layer to another in an iterative fashion — all layers activated to some lesser or greater extent at any point in time. Moreover, in applying CWA, there is no explicit ordering of analysis activities (Vicente, 1999). This renders the approach extremely flexible and reduces the learning curve required to apply its principles in practice.

Work domain analysis seeks to establish the structural limitations of the work domain. This stage identifies the type of users expected to participate in the activity, the activity problem, and additional logical and physical constraints upon the system. Control task analysis represents the set of abstract tasks that control the general flow of information within an activity. Strategies analysis investigates how individuals or groups overcome a problem when presented with a set of alternatives. This decision-making process is similar to that of selection rules in GOMS. However, unlike GOMS, this process considers prior experiences, spatio-temporal constraints upon operation, motivation, aptitude, and other similar criteria. Social-organisational analysis seeks to establish how tasks are shared between actors and artefacts in a cooperative and collaborative manner. Finally, work competencies analysis examines the degree of training and experience actors bare upon some activity.

Table 4. Overview of cognitive task models

Criteria	Approaches				
	GOMS	HTA	GTA	CTA	CWA
Expressive power	LOW	LOW	MEDIUM	HIGH	HIGH
Complexity	LOW	LOW	MEDIUM	HIGH	HIGH
Collaboration	NO	NO	YES	NO	YES
Timing	YES	YES	NO	NO	NO
Roles and responsibilities	NO	NO	YES	NO	YES
Evaluation	YES	YES	YES	YES	YES
Requires Training	LOW	LOW-MED	MED-HIGH	HIGH	HIGH
Scalable	NO	NO	NO	YES	YES
Social Orientation	NO	NO	NO	NO	YES

Summary of Approaches

To determine which approach may best be used within a particular Web design project, Table 4 provides a brief overview of the cognitive approaches previously mentioned and demonstrates their shared and unique attributes.

Ecological Task Analysis

Until recently, task analysis in HCI has focused almost exclusively upon deriving reductionist cognitive representations of individual tasks (Hollan, Hutchins, & Kirsch, 2001). Although HCI is currently moving towards more ecologically valid models of human praxis, postcognitivist theorists have yet to agree upon the most promising alternatives (Kaptelinin, 1996a). Resolving this issue depends on two factors:

1. Establishing a common unit of analysis
2. Constructing integrative frameworks that model both cognitive and social phenomena

The need for integrative frameworks is especially relevant to Web designers who must not only support existing social practices through a novel medium, but also the cognitive demands imposed by semiotic constraints when delivering information via the Web (Smart, Rice, & Wood, 2000). Table 5 outlines the required properties of an integrative framework.

At the heart of the postcognitive movement lies the notion of *situation awareness.* Situated awareness represents an understanding of social norms and rules, or a state of knowledge about the context, situation, and environment in which an activity takes place (Erickson & Kellogg, 2001). Situation awareness does not describe, per se, the process of acquiring knowledge, but rather is the end result of invoking any number of cognitive and meta-cognitive processes during active participation in a practice (Endsley, 2000). Furthermore, situation awareness is distributed among individuals, and hence, actionable and relevant only within specific communities of practice (Gasson, 1999). Situation awareness

Table 5. Postcognitive task analysis criteria

Property	Description
Formalised notation system	Common, accessible notation that facilitates conceptual modelling and communication of knowledge between interested parties (Balbo et al., 2004; Erickson & Kellogg, 2001)
Methodological flexibility	The ability to adopt existing methodologies rather than constantly reinvent the wheel (Whittaker et al., 2000)
Cost-effective practices	Cost-effective practices that encourage the use task analysis during system design, thus increasing return-on-investment (Stanton, 2004)
Expressive power	Practical methodologies with sufficient expressive power to support novice and expert usage (Balbo et al., 2004)
Integration within formal software engineering frameworks	An ability to be applied across the SDLC, including integrative mechanisms that facilitate software engineering practices (Farmer, 2006; Farmer et al., 2004; Flor & Hutchins, 1991; Kazman, Abowd, Bass, & Clements; 1996; Rosson & Carroll, 2002)
Reuse	The ability to support that HCI claims reuse (Carroll, 1996; Sutcliffe, 2000)
Ecological validity	Research findings and technology must support existing social processes and cultural practices (Nardi, 1996)

requires individuals to maintain an awareness of the continuously unfolding characteristics of an activity. Summarising Endsley (2000), situation awareness entails:

1. Perceiving relevant contextual information
2. Understanding how the roles and relationships between actors impacts information presentation and communication
3. An ability to use social cues to assist in planning for future events

Albers (1998) states that the quality of an individual's situation awareness is governed by their ability to comprehend, integrate, and reconstruct new information. This three-step process involves extracting the relevant basic information from the task/activity, integrating the information into the individual's conceptual understanding of the problem, subsequently generating new rules and beliefs so as to extrapolate the information into future problem-solving situations. As situations change and new information is presented, so must the individual's awareness of emerging conditions that are likely to impact upon their effective participation in an activity. The problem of situation awareness is highly relevant to developers of Enterprise Content Management systems where the most critical factor impacting successful deployment and integration is user adoption. Postcognitive task analysis frameworks that maintain the centrality of situation awareness are more likely to succeed at meeting this challenge.

Goals, experiences, expectations, and motivations are interdependent constructs that produce localised expectations about situated action, and as such influence situation awareness (Endsley, 2000). Goals help to orientate an individual across a series of tasks, including error recovery. For example, when a user encounters an error during interaction with a Web-based form, a breakdown in planning occurs. In assessing available feedback, the user must evaluate available actions against their goals and state of knowledge about the activity. In overcoming the breakdown or conflict, emergent behaviour may not only result in a reprioritisation of individual goals, but may also lead to new interaction strategies.

Expectations are influential in the division of attention during HCI, acting as a selection mechanism, reducing demand on cognitive resources to efficiently respond to new information. Experience is also influential in the development of automaticity. For instance, expert system users are expected to demonstrate better skills compared to novices, as they are likely to have developed more efficient strategies and greater responsiveness to overcoming breakdowns. The difficulties novices face may be a result of their lack of habituated actions during HCI, rendering the task more cognitively demanding. Situation awareness among novice users typically increases through gradual exposure to, and experience with, the system. However, increased situation awareness does not imply good task performance. It is a probabilistic construct, making good performance more likely, yet not assured.

The notion of situation awareness is found within several postcognitive HCI frameworks. Here, we present a broad comparison of a few notable frameworks. We examine how each of the competing frameworks conceives of an appropriate *unit of analysis*, and how this unit of analysis impacts each framework.

Situated Action Models

The *situated action* view of HCI treats knowledge as a subjective construct. Knowledge is inexorably linked to interpersonal communication and contextual activity. Knowledge is not only subjective, but specifically relevant to a particular situation in which some work practice occurs (Gasson, 1999). Nardi (1996) notes that situated action perspectives are more focused on context-sensitive practices than on the cognitive properties of the artefacts with which individuals interact.

The unit of analysis in situated action is the motivated activity within a relevant community of practice (Lave, 1988), supplanting the largely cognitivist unit of analysis, task. Within each of the ecological perspectives treated in this chapter, the notion of task is redefined or appropriated to mean action. Subjugating the importance of task to activity promotes the influence of actor roles, relationships, and sociocultural cues within a particular setting.

One of the key characteristics of the situated action model is its adherence to reflexivity in system design. Experience, cultural and historic beliefs and anticipatory planning on behalf of the individual are therefore de-emphasised within this perspective. Rather, situated action focuses on the immediacy of interaction, the fluctuating conditions of the situation, and the learning opportunities provided by an individual's creative response(s) to alternative paths through the activity (Lave, 1988; Nardi, 1996; Suchman, 1987). An activity's structure is not something that precedes interaction but emerges directly out of the immediacy of the situation. Planning and goals are produced in the course of action, and thus are work products, rather than characteristics that orient the activity (Bardram, 1998). This view implies that people are basically opportunistic. Planning and goals either emerge concurrently out of participation in the activity itself, or by conscious reflection upon previous interaction.

As situated action subscribes to the view that analysts should only be concerned with recording observable behaviour (Endsley, 2000), we believe that it is not appropriate for analysing exploratory domains, where it is crucial to first identify the contextual problem under investigation and subsequently determine the expected outcomes of the activity. Similarly, we feel that the approach is not sufficiently descriptive to examine large collaborative work activities where knowledge and planning are often spread across actors. In large organisations, activity is seldom seen as a knee-jerk reaction to current events.

Distributed Cognition

Distributed cognition is concerned with how knowledge is propagated and transformed by agents within activity. An agent is any cognitive artefact of the system, be it human, machine, or other work product. The unit of analysis is the cognitive system. Distributed cognition relaxes the assumption that the individual is the best or only useful unit of analysis and thus extends the reach of what is considered cognitive to both systems that are smaller and larger than the individual (Hollan et al., 2001; Hutchins, 1995). The cognitive system in distributed cognition is thus more akin to the term *complex cognitive system*.

Goals, according to distributed cognition, are not merely maintained within the mind of the subject (individual or group), but rather embedded within the cognitive system. Distributed cognition posits that artefacts may themselves possess goals. The cognitive system can only be understood when we know the contributions of individual agents, their shared contributions and collaboration strategies, and the nature agent behaviour in the environment. In contrast to situated action, distributed cognition incorporates culture, context and history, but from within an embedded perspective (Hollan et al., 2001).

There are striking similarities between the distributed cognition and activity theory (Nardi, 1996). Both are activity-centric: they recognise activity as a hierarchical, goal-oriented structure; align physical, verbal, and nonverbal actions with specific goals; and they distinguish between conscious and unconscious actions. Additionally, neither framework prescribes a particular set of methodological practices. Nevertheless, there are two notable differences between the approaches:

- Activity theory is essentially human-centric, individuals motivating activity.
- In activity theory, artefacts are not seen as goal-oriented, cogent entities.

In contrast to activity theory, distributed cognition holds that in cooperative environments, individuals maintain only partial models of the problem. Hence, for distributed cognition, complex systems rather than individuals are the appropriate unit of analysis.

Latour (1987) provides theoretical support for this last argument, stating that part of what is technological is social, and what is social is technological. As relationships in actor-networks constitute human-human and human-artefact interaction, a change in content structure, user interface, pedagogy, or number of participants in an activity has the potential to change the nature of an activity. While not implying that an artefact is cogent, actor-network theory suggests how a work product may impact social and cognitive processes (Tatnall, 2002).

Activity Theory

Activity theory is a descriptive conceptual framework that has emerged primarily from contributions by Vygotsky (1986), Leont'ev (1978), and Engeström (1987). Activity theory serves to describe the different forms of human praxis and developmental processes involved in HCI. Activity theory represents a truly ecological approach to task analysis, providing a broad theoretical framework for examining collaborative activities (Stanton, 2004). As the name suggests, the unit of analysis in activity theory is the activity itself. Individual and social processes are interwoven in the generation of contextualised meaning. Similar to distributed cognition, individual knowledge and meaning cannot be separated from the context of an activity.

Activity theory (depicted in Figure 3) is an object-oriented, task analysis framework. The importance of goals is present, however they are subordinate to motivated outcomes, or objective purpose (object) (Whittaker et al., 2000). Unlike situated action, interaction is not opportunistic, but purposeful. Purpose is context specific as activities define context, and context defines an activity. Therefore, the act of doing in one context cannot be considered congruous with the act of doing in another (Lave & Wegner, 1991). This is in direct contrast to cognitive task models such as GOMS.

One of the principal tenets of activity theory is *tool mediation*. Activities are mediated by individuals carrying out their tasks through the use of available artefacts in the environment. When an artefact is used to mediate interaction, it is said to become a tool. A tool can be any material or mental process used to transform or convey information (Kaptelinin, 1996b). As tools exist only through purposeful activity, they contain cultural and historical residue. They are therefore capable of imparting external sociocultural beliefs and historic conventions upon an activity.

Activity theory posits a hierarchical structure of activity, consisting of three primary elements: activity, object-oriented actions, and operations (Leont'ev, 1978). As shown in Figure 3, activity is motivated by the subject (individual or group). An activity is comprised of mediated, object-oriented actions. Each action is associated with one or more parent and subgoals. This implies that actions are polymotivated; each action (task) may be applied to accomplish several goals. This is important as it provides a way of supporting alternative paths or strategies within an activity for obtaining the purposeful outcome. Accordingly, we cannot focus purely on the action itself, as its purpose or role is ambiguous. Lastly, *operations* are habitual behaviours or unconscious actions.

According to activity theory, there is constant interaction between these three elements of human praxis. This dynamicism is critical to our understanding of human behaviour in interactive environments. However, despite the advantages of applying an activity theoretic

Figure 3. Activity theory framework

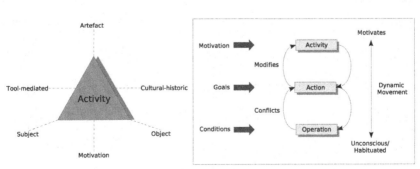

approach to interactive system design, there is as yet no systematic way of interfacing the approach with rigorous software engineering methodologies (Turner, Turner, & Horton, 1999).

Scenario-Based Design

Scenario-based design (SBD) promotes the use of scenarios (or structured narratives) in HCI as a way of understanding human activity and creating computer systems (Carroll, 2000). Today, they are widely used across disciplines. In an attempt to render software development more social, Carroll (1996, 1997) argues that activity theory can be applied effectively to SBD. While Carroll does not describe how this can be accomplished, suggestions are found elsewhere (Carroll, 2000; Go & Carroll, 2004; Kazman et al., 1996; Rosson & Carroll, 2002). Admittedly, natural language narratives are not the most scientific notation used within HCI or software engineering; however, it is often by these means that technical information is conveyed throughout the development effort (Carroll, 1996). Moreover, scenarios provide a flexible mechanism for integrating "real life" accounts of activity with the more empirically discrete views employed within software engineering.

During discovery and definition (see Table 1), scenarios can be used speculatively at the start of the SDLC to document expected user behaviour or to describe hypothetical activities. In the absence of an existing system, this process improves ecological validity during requirements engineering (Stanton, 2004). To assist with requirements engineering, Kaptelinin et al. (1999) suggest that Activity Checklists can assist practitioners to focus on salient aspects of an activity, thereby constraining the process of requirements engineering during SBD.

Scenarios represent purposeful interaction within a system, and are inherently goal-oriented. Scenarios are always particular to a specific situation, and thus situated within a particular frame of research. Because scenarios are actor-driven, describing interaction from the perspective of at least one individual, they can be effectively integrated with an activity

Table 6. Overview of postcognitive task models

Criteria	Approaches			
	Situated Action	Distributed Cognition	Activity Theory	Scenario-Based Design
Expressive power	LOW	LOW	MEDIUM	HIGH
Complexity	LOW	LOW	MEDIUM	HIGH
Collaboration	NO	NO	YES	NO
Timing	YES	YES	NO	NO
Roles and responsibilities	NO	NO	YES	NO
Evaluation	YES	YES	YES	YES
Requires training	LOW	LOW-MED	MED-HIGH	HIGH
Scalable	NO	NO	NO	YES
Social orientation	NO	NO	NO	NO

theory framework. Finally, as scenarios use a common notation, natural language, all stake-holders in the development process can easily communicate requirements, experiences, and other opinions/beliefs without requiring extensive training. Consequently, scenarios serve as an excellent lingua franca for communication between all project stakeholders; a primary goal of any good task analysis framework (Balbo et al., 2004).

Summary of Approaches

Table 6 provides a brief overview of the postcognitive approaches described previously and demonstrates their shared and unique attributes.

TOWARDS SITUATED TASK ANALYSIS IN WEB DESIGN

In this chapter we have outlined the limitations associated with both cognitive and postcognitive approaches to task analysis. Cognitive approaches suffer from their inability to model dynamic social processes; to consider aspects of interaction which are not reducible to discrete cognitive events; and to elicit and describe user goals and their limited extensibility and transferability to new domains. Postcognitive approaches on the other hand suffer from a lack of tools and techniques that bridge theoretical frameworks and practical design and evaluation methods. Although promoting increased reuse of HCI knowledge, postcognitive frameworks are less computationally powered, thus possessing a significant barrier to their integration into standard Web design practices as described in Vora (1998). The challenge therefore is to promote integrative, task analysis frameworks that support both cognitive and ecological perspectives (Czerwinski & Larson, 2002). This new breed of task analysis frameworks is referred to as situated task analysis (Farmer & Hughes, 2005b).

Situated task analysis incorporates the view that in natural settings, problems are fre-quently ill defined, requiring communication, collaboration, negotiation, and prioritisation. This broadens the field of regard from the individual to include organisational and social contexts. This situated view can be seen as an example of macrocognitive architecture, de-

Figure 4. Concept/goal generation during requirements engineering

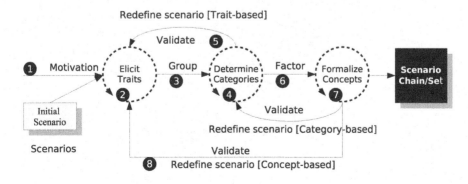

scribing cognitive functions as they are performed in natural settings (Klein, Ross, Moon, Klein, Hoffman, & Hollnagel, 2003). This is in opposition to the traditional microcognitive view of task analysis that focuses on the building blocks of cognition. A detailed account of a situated task analysis framework: cognition, activity, social organisation, environment (CASE) is provided in Farmer (2006).

A Simple Approach to Situated Task Analysis in Web Design

A major obstacle in developing Web sites that are both usable and fit-for-purpose is capturing stakeholder requirements and communicating them to other project team members, especially designers. User requirements are often qualitatively produced, resulting in rich descriptions of functional and operational requirements. While this assists with understanding the nature of activity, it does not always suit developers who are required to describe the system in terms of discrete, verifiable behaviour. In the following, we describe an iterative five-step process that facilitates communication and integration of both static and dynamic views within the requirements engineering and design phases of Web site development.

Step One: Requirements Engineering and Goal Generation

The first step in our process is requirements engineering. Scenarios are ideal in this situation as they are written in natural language and are therefore highly accessible and require little practitioner training (Go & Carroll, 2004).

Figure 4 describes the iterative process of eliciting user requirements using activity checklists (Kaptelinin et al., 1999) and scenarios. Scenario descriptions are iteratively refined until they are stable, the outcome being a set of scenarios reflecting multiple viewpoints of interaction. Using an initial Activity Checklist, containing likely questions and statements related to the purpose of the activity, and a minimal-use scenario, we initiate the requirements elicitation process. As shown in Figure 4, our first aim is to elicit initial traits or themes that emerge out of the user's perception of the activity. Users may be additionally asked to develop

Figure 5. Iterative goal-driven scenario development

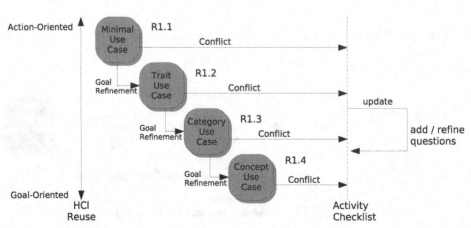

their own use scenario to increase participation and contextuality during the development process. This process continues, redefining the scenarios and checklists, until we are able to group these traits into sets of themes or categories. At each stage, the new scenarios are validated against the users themselves in order to maintain internal consistency.

In a similar manner, once no further traits emerge from our analysis, we proceed by reducing these initial categories to a core set of salient concepts. These concepts can be considered high-level objectives within the activity or goals. These concept-goals can be considered fairly stable and transferable between users, as they will have been derived from multiple perspectives. Finally, we arrive at a set of scenarios that represent the key concept-goals of our activity. These scenarios can be linked together to provide a chain or hierarchical view of the scenarios relative to a particular requirement. The corollary of this process becomes increasingly important as we move towards the initial design phase.

In Figure 5 we see more clearly this process of scenario refinement and linkage. Our initial minimal use scenario (R1.1) is iteratively refined to reveal particular traits of the activity (R1.2). As this ultimately is an exploratory process, each stage can be seen as a form of goal refinement. We notice in Figure 5 that within this process of refinement, conflicts between scenario views (i.e., between users or between users and developers) result in an update of the Activity Checklist. In this way, we are able to capture the context of use and apply this knowledge to subsequent elicitation cycles. As we move towards concept-based scenarios in our analysis, we move away from action-oriented perspectives towards more holistic, goal-oriented views of activity.

Step Two: Determine Salient Features of Interaction

Having constructed a core set of requirements containing both low and high-level views of interaction, the next step is to determine which concepts are most critical to the success of the Web application. Although we already possess relatively stable concept-goals with which to initiate our design process, some concepts may be more salient than others. Techniques for determining salient cognitive and social features during interaction are described in Farmer (2006).

Step Three: From Scenarios to UML Use Cases

Upon establishing the most salient concept-goals with the system, the next step is to transform these rich textual descriptions into static, structural views, amenable to inclusion in the design process. This can be achieved using unified modeling language (UML), use case diagram notation (Rumbaugh, Jacobson, & Booch, 1999). We start by modelling the high-level use cases. These typically correspond to the concept-goal scenarios previously elicited, and hence provide a goal-oriented system view. Subsequently, we drill down into each of these use cases, decomposing them into their subsystems and determining their structural constraints.

Use case decomposition, as shown in Figure 6, is the process of iteratively decomposing an activity into its constituent parts. This process has already been achieved via the bottom-up process of concept-goal generation. Therefore, use case decomposition may easily be achieved by associating each concept-goal with its related categories and traits. This information is present within the previously constructed scenario chains. Designers are therefore able to isolate requirements at particular levels of granularity as well as investigate

Figure 6. Example of use case decomposition

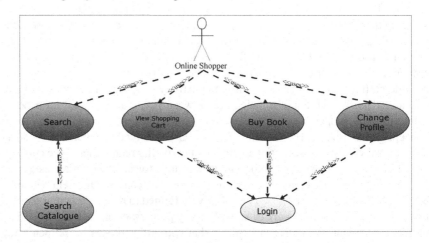

the structural relationships between use cases (implements, depends, generalises) via the rich descriptions provided in the scenarios.

Figure 6 provides an example of a use case decomposition for an online shopping activity. In this instance, the user has only four concept-goals. These are search catalogue, view shopping cart, buy book, and change profile. Common concepts that are shared among requirements, such as login, can be modelled via a dependency relationship. Modelling the relationship between a concept and a category (see Figure 4) can be achieved through inheritance, or implementation. In addition to modelling relationships, designers may choose to isolate particular concept areas, such as social organisation, to further narrow the design perspective.

Step Four: From Use Cases to Design

After constructing the UML use cases at various levels of granularity (from goals to actions), the next step involves transforming these formal decompositions into design elements. One way to manage this complex process is to establish distinct viewpoints, modelling the system from various perspectives (Rumbaugh et al., 1999). Here, we only consider the structural and behavioural system views. The major distinction between these views is that the former emphasises object-oriented interaction, whereas the latter describes event-driven interaction.

The structural view provides a physical description of how the Web site will be made up of various components, including relationships between those components. This is primarily achieved using UML class diagrams that provide an object-oriented view of the system. While primarily promoting a static view of the system, object methods and attributes can also be shown. Using the use cases generated previously from the concept scenarios, it is possible to rapidly construct a high-level representation of the site structure, objects acting as placeholders for each concept goals.

Figure 7. UML Class diagram representation of concepts

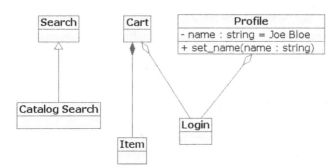

Having modelled at a conceptual level the key user requirements as UML classes or objects, we use the link structure provided during the initial requirements engineering phase to determine additional objects, methods, and attributes of the system. For instance, we can model category-based scenarios in UML class notation via aggregate relations ("is-part-of") to our concept-based objects (Figure 7). Additional techniques, such as noun extraction (noun=object, verb=method, adjective/adverb=attribute), may be used to extract structural information from the scenarios themselves (Schach, 1999).

Figure 7 provides a simple demonstration of this process. In this instance, the class objects *Login* and *Search* represent complex objects associated with login management and searching a Web site. We note these relationships could have been modelled alternatively as methods (login and search are verbs) within other classes, or as interfaces that could be implemented by other objects, as shown in Figure 6.

This process can be extended to the trait-based scenarios to establish additional object attributes. This process has several benefits: it provides a rapid means of determining initial site structure within a goal-oriented framework; it permits designers to link design decisions back to initial requirements, as well as examining requirements from various stakeholder points of view and at various levels of granularity; and designers may link additional design-centric scenarios to each requirement, providing details such as event sequencing and information flow, therefore improving traceability between the SDLC phases.

In examining methods and attributes more closely using our scenarios, we are likely to become more focused on event-driven behaviour. In developing a behavioural system view, we are interested in modelling the flow of system information through event or function-driven interaction. We typically see functional flows (Appendix A) and sequence diagrams used at this point in the initial design phase. These techniques constrain interaction to a finite-state representation, limiting users to predetermined paths through the system. Where multiple paths may initially exist, functional flow analysis and task models may be used to determine optimal paths through the system in order to reduce variability and improve site effectiveness and efficiency. At this point, our design analysis has moved away from modelling goals to modelling actions and evaluating task performance.

Finally, these event-driven views may be abstracted to form UML dialog models or activity diagrams, providing a means of aggregating task models or flow analyses. These dialog models may then be linked into our initial scenario/requirements chain to provide additional system information. This process ensures a multi-view representation of requirements that are linked forwards and backwards to design. Moreover, it ensures that both goal-oriented and action-oriented perspectives of interaction are conveyed during development.

Step Five: Start Over

We recall that task analysis is not a once-off process (Balbo et al., 2004). This is especially true of interactive systems and environments, such as the Web. It is important to note that most people actually learn by doing (Lave & Wegner, 1991). Rather than thinking of a site's design as merely being usable, we should consider how the site or application, as a tool, facilitates participation in an activity.

Developing effective Web sites requires consideration of both novice and expert users. Most users, however, do not arrive at a site as experts. They reason, use past experiences, and explore through interaction. Their ability to gain expertise in these virtual environments is partially governed by how well the design supports and extends the user's current capabilities. This can only be achieved when there is sufficient coherence between the context of use and the virtual environment's design. Taking a user-centred approach to Web design, including an appropriate task analysis framework and set of methodological practices, ensures that developers will never be too far away from their users. Ultimately, it is they who will judge the relative merits of your site/application.

CONCLUSION

Web design is a complex activity at the best of times. Not only do designers frequently encounter technological limitations imposed by a novel communication medium, but also they are highly isolated from their users. Moreover, arguably more than with any other technological medium, the Web application target audience is extremely heterogeneous. Therefore, the ambiguous and diverse nature of Web application use imposes critical limitations on Web design practices. Shadowed by the importance of developing quality, fit-for-purpose systems, this chapter has highlighted the considerable benefits to be gained by incorporating task analysis in Web design. Specifically, this chapter has described how task analysis is not a single process that can be applied indiscriminately of context and use. It is a highly stylised and domain-dependent activity that occasionally suffers from conflicting theoretical and methodological approaches.

We have argued that task analysis is not a silver bullet, rather a means of "getting to know" your users and communicating this information through product development and evaluation. Rather than describing a core set of prescriptive guidelines for conducting task analysis in Web design, this chapter has set out to inform the reader via a critical examination and principled discussion of various approaches to task analysis. Consequently, our hope is that the reader as practitioner will be both more aware and appreciative of the role task analysis can and should play in Web design.

ACKNOWLEDGMENTS

We would like to thank Baden Hughes and Sandrine Balbo for their collaboration and comments on related work. Special thanks go to Sandrine Balbo for her presentation on task models in HCI, which spawned an insightful and lively afternoon of discussions that stimulated aspects of our discussion here.

REFERENCES

Albers, M. J. (1998). Goal-driven task analysis: Improving situation awareness for complex problem solving. In *Proceedings of the 16ᵗʰ Annual International Conference on Computer Documentation* (pp. 234-242). Quebec, Canada: ACM Publishing.

Annett, J. (2004). Hierarchical task analysis. In D. Diaper & N. Stanton (Eds.), *The handbook of task analysis for human-computer interaction* (pp. 67-82). Mahwah, NJ: Lawrence Erlbaum Associates.

Annett, J., & Duncan, K. (1967). Task analysis and training design. *Occupational Psychology, 41*, 211-227.

Balbo, S., Ozkan, N., & Paris, C. (2004). Choosing the right task-modelling notation: A taxonomy. In D. Diaper & N. Stanton (Eds.), *The handbook of task analysis for human-computer interaction* (pp. 435-465). Mahwah, NJ: Lawrence Erlbaum Associates.

Bardram, J. E. (1998). Plans as situated action: An activity theory approach to workflow systems. In J. A. Hughes, W. Prinz, T. Rodden, & K. I. Schmidt (Eds.), *Proceedings of the 5ᵗʰ European Conference on Computer Supported Cooperative Work* (pp. 17-32). Dordrecht, The Netherlands: Kluwer Academic Publishers.

Bomsdorf, B., & Szwillus, G. (1998). From task to dialogue: Task-based user interface design. *SIGCHI Bulletin, 30*(4), 40-42.

Bonaceto, C., & Burns, K. (2003). Mapping the mountains: A survey of cognitive engineering methods and uses. In R. Hoffman (Ed.), *Expertise out of context: Proceedings of the 6th Conference on Naturalistic Decision Making*. Hillsdale, NJ: Lawrence Erlbaum Associates.

Card, S. K., Moran, T. P., & Newell, A. L. (1983). *The psychology of human computer interaction*. Hillsdale, NJ: Erlbaum.

Carroll, J. M. (1996). Becoming social: Expanding scenario-based approaches in HCI. *Behaviour & Information Technology, 15*(4), 266-275.

Carroll, J. M. (1997). Human-computer interaction: Psychology as a science of design. *International Journal of Human-Computer Studies, 46*, 501-522.

Carroll, J. M. (2000). Five reasons for scenario-based design. *Interacting with Computers, 13*, 43-60.

Carroll, J. M. (2002). Making use is more than a matter of task analysis. *Interacting with Computers, 14*, 619-627.

Checkland, P. (1999). *Soft systems methodology in action*. New York: John Wiley & Sons Ltd.

Corbel, C., Gruba, P., & Enright, H. (2002). *Taking the Web to task*. Sydney, Australia: National Centre for English Language Teaching and Research, Macquarie University.

Czerwinski, M. P., & Larson, K. (2002). Cognition and the Web: Moving from theory to Web design. In J. Ratner (Ed.), *Human factors and Web development* (pp. 147-165). Mahwah, NJ: Erlbaum.

Diaper, D. (2004). Understanding task analysis for human-computer interaction. In D. Diaper & N. Stanton (Eds.), *The handbook of task analysis for human-computer interaction* (pp. 5-49). Mahwah, NJ: Lawrence Erlbaum Associates.

Dix, A. (2005). Human-computer interaction and Web design. In R.W. Proctor & K.-P. L. Vu (Eds.), *Handbook of human factors in Web design* (pp. 28-47). Mahwah, NJ: Lawrence Erlbaum Associates.

Endsley, M. R. (2000). Theoretical underpinnings of situation awareness: A critical review. In M. R. Endsley & D. J. Garland (Eds.), *Situation awareness analysis and measurement* (pp. 3-33). Mahwah, NJ: Lawrence Erlbaum Associates.

Engeström, Y. (1987). *Learning by expanding.* Helsinki, The Netherlands: Orienta-Konsultit.

Erickson, T., & Kellogg, W. A. (2001). Social translucence: Designing systems that support social processes. In J. M. Carroll (Ed.), *Human-computer interaction in the new millennium* (pp. 324-336). London: Addison-Wesley.

Farmer, R. A. (2005). Multimodal speech recognition errors and second language acquisition: An activity theoretic account. In *Proceedings of the 6th Conference on Using Technology in Foreign Language Teaching.* Compiegne, France: Université de Technologie Compiègne.

Farmer, R. A. (2006). Situated task analysis in learner-centered CALL. In P. Zaphiris & G. Zacharia (Eds.), *User-centered computer-assisted language learning* (pp. 43-73). Hershey, PA: Idea Group Publishing.

Farmer, R. A., Gruba, P., & Hughes, B. (2004). Towards principles for CALL software quality improvement. In J. Colpaert, W. Decoo, M. Simons, & S. Van Beuren (Eds.), *CALL and Research Methodologies: Proceedings of the 11th International Conference on CALL* (pp. 103-113). Belgium: Universiteit Antwerpen.

Farmer, R. A., & Hughes, B. (2005a). A situated learning perspective on learning object design. In P. Goodyear, D. G. Sampson, D. Yang, Kinshuk, T. Okamoto, R. Hartley, et al. (Eds.), *Proceedings of the 5th International Conference on Advanced Learning Technologies,* Kaohsiung, Taiwan (pp. 72-74). CA: IEEE Computer Society Press.

Farmer, R. A., & Hughes, B. (2005b). A classification-based framework for learning object assembly. In P. Goodyear, D. G. Sampson, D. Yang, Kinshuk, T. Okamoto, R. Hartley et al. (Eds.), *Proceedings of the 5th International Conference on Advanced Learning Technologies* (pp. 4-6). Kaohsiung, Taiwan. CA: IEEE Computer Society Press.

Farmer, R. A., & Hughes, B. (2005c). CASE: A framework for evaluating learner-computer interaction in Computer-Assisted Language Learning. In B. Plimmer & R. Amor (Eds.), *Proceedings of CHINZ 2005 — Making CHI Natural,* Auckland, New Zealand (pp. 67-74). New York: ACM Press.

Filkes, R. E. (1982). A commitment-based framework for describing cooperative work. *Cognitive Science, 6,* 331-347.

Flor, N., & Hutchins, E. (1991). Analysing distributed cognition in software teams: A case study of team programming during perfective software maintenance. In J. Koenemann-Belliveau, T. Moher, & S. Roberson (Eds.), *Proceedings of the 4th Annual Workshop on Empirical Studies of Programmers* (pp. 36-59). Norwood, NJ: Ablex Publishing.

Gasson, S. (1999). A social action model of situated information systems design. *The DATA BASE for Advanced in Information Systems, 30*(2), 82-97.

Go, K., & Carroll, J. M. (2004). Scenario-based task analysis. In D. Diaper & N. Stanton (Eds.), *The handbook of task analysis for human-computer interaction* (pp. 117-134). Mahwah, NJ: Lawrence Erlbaum Associates.

Goguen, J. A. (1996). Formality and informality in requirements engineering. In *Proceedings of the 2nd International Conference on Requirements Engineering (ICRE'96)* (pp. 102-109). Silver Spring, MD: IEEE Computer Society Press.

Gordon, S. E., & Gill, R. T. (1997). Cognitive task analysis. In C. E. Zsambok & G. Klein (Eds.), *Naturalistic decision making* (pp. 130-140). Mahwah, NJ: Lawrence Erlbaum Associates.

Hollan, J., Hutchins, E., & Kirsch, D. (2001). Distributed cognition: Toward a new foundation for human-computer interaction research. In J. M. Carroll (Ed.), *Human-computer interaction in the new millennium* (pp. 77-94). London: Addison-Wesley.

Hollnagel, E. (Ed.). (2003). *Handbook of cognitive task design*. Mahwah, NJ: Lawrence Erlbaum Associates.

Hutchins, E. (1995). *Cognition in the wild*. Cambridge, MA: MIT Press.

John, B. E., & Kieras, D. E. (1996a). Using GOMS for user interface design and evaluation: Which technique? *ACM Transactions on Computer-Human Interaction, 3,* 287-319.

John, B. E., & Kieras, D. E. (1996b). The GOMS family of user interface analysis techniques: Comparison and contrast. *ACM Transactions on Computer-Human Interaction, 3,* 320-351.

Kaptelinin, V. (1996a). Activity theory: Implications for human-computer interaction. In B. A. Nardi (Ed.), *Context and consciousness: Activity theory and human-computer interaction* (pp. 103-116). Cambridge, MA: MIT Press.

Kaptelinin, V. (1996b). Computer-mediated activity: Functional organs in social and developmental contexts. In B. A. Nardi (Ed.), *Context and consciousness: Activity theory and human-computer interaction* (pp. 45-69). Cambridge, MA: MIT Press.

Kaptelinin, V., Nardi, B., & Macaulay, C. (1999, July/August). The activity checklist: A tool for representing the "space" of context. *Interactions,* 27-39.

Kazman, R., Abowd, G., Bass, L., & Clements, P. (1996, November). Scenario-based analysis of software architecture. *IEEE Software,* 47-53.

Kieras, D. (2004). GOMS models for task analysis. In D. Diaper & N. Stanton (Eds.), *The handbook of task analysis for human-computer interaction* (pp. 83-116). Mahwah, NJ: Lawrence Erlbaum Associates.

Kirwan, B., & Ainsworth, L. K. (1992). *A guide to task analysis*. London: Taylor & Francis.

Klein, G., Ross, K. G., Moon, B. M., Klein, D. E., Hoffman, R. R., Hollnagel, E. (2003, May/June). Macrocognition. *IEEE Intelligent Systems, 18*(3)81-84.

Latour, B. (1987). *Science in action: How to follow engineers and scientists through society*. Milton Keynes, UK: Open University Press.

Lave, J. (1988). *Cognition in practice: Mind, mathematics and culture in everyday life*. Cambridge, UK: Cambridge University Press.

Lave, J., & Wegner, I. (1991). *Situated learning: Legitimate peripheral participation*. Cambridge, UK: Cambridge University Press.

Leont'ev, A. N. (1978). *Activity, consciousness, and personality*. Englewood Cliffs, NJ: Prentice Hall.

Limbourg, Q., & Vanderdonckt, J. (2004). Comparing task models for user interface design. In D. Diaper & N. Stanton (Eds.), *The handbook of task analysis for human-computer interaction* (pp. 135-154). Mahwah, NJ: Lawrence Erlbaum Associates.

Mager, R. F. (1991). *Goal analysis.* London: Kogan Page.

Miller, R. B. (1953). *A method for man-machine task analysis* (TR 53-137). Wright Patterson Air force Base, OH: Wright Air Development Center.

Miller, R. B. (1962). Task description and analysis. In R. M. Gagne (Ed.), *Psychological principles in system development* (pp. 187-228). New York: Hold, Rinehart, & Winston.

MITRE. (2003). *Mental models for naturalistic decision making.* Centre for Air Force Command and Control. Retrieved October 12, 2005, from http://mentalmodels.mitre.org/

Nardi, B. A. (1996). Studying context: A comparison of activity theory, situated action models, and distributed cognition. In B. A. Nardi (Ed.), *Context and consciousness: activity theory and human-computer interaction* (pp. 69-102). Cambridge, MA: MIT Press.

Newman, W. M., & Lamming, M. G. (1998). *Interactive system design.* Essex, UK: Addison-Wesley.

Norman, D. A. (1999, May/June). Affordance, conventions and design. *Interactions, 6*(3), 38-43.

Paternò, F., & Santoro, C. (2002). Integrated support based on task models for the design, evaluation, and documentation of interactive safety-critical systems: A case study in the air traffic control domain. *International Journal of Systems Science, 33*(6), 513-527.

Preece, J., Rogers, Y., Sharp, H., Benyon, D., Holland, S., & Carey, T. (Eds.). (1994). *Human-computer interaction.* London: Addison-Wesley.

Raeithel, A., & Velichkovsky, B. M. (1996). Joint attention and co-construction of tasks: New ways to foster user-designer collaboration. In B. A. Nardi (Ed.), *Context and consciousness: Activity theory and human-computer interaction* (pp. 199-234). Cambridge, MA: MIT Press.

Rasmussen, J., Pejtersen, A. M., & Goodstein, L. P. (1994). *Cognitive systems engineering.* New York: John Wiley & Sons.

Robinson, M. (1993). Design for unanticipated use. In G. D. Michelis, C. Simone, & K. Schmidt (Eds.), *Third European Conference on Computer Supported Cooperative Work* (187-202). Dordrecht, The Netherlands: Kluwer.

Rosson, M. B., & Carroll, J. M. (2002). *Usability engineering: Scenario-based development of human-computer interaction.* San Diego, CA: Academic Press.

Rumbaugh, J., Jacobson, I., & Booch, G. (1999). *The unified modelling language: User guide.* Upper Saddle River, NJ: Addison-Wesley.

Schach, S. R. (1999). *Classical and object-oriented software engineering* (4th ed.). Singapore: McGraw-Hill International.

Shepherd, A. (2001). *Hierarchical task analysis.* London: Taylor & Francis.

Shrayne, N. M., Westerman, S. J., Crawshaw, C., Hockey, G. R. J., & Sauer, J. (1998). Task analysis for the investigation of human error in safety-critical software design: A convergent methods approach. *Ergonomics, 41*(11), 1719-1736.

Smart, K. L., Rice, J. C., & Wood, L. E. (2000). Meeting the needs of users: Toward a semiotics of the web. In *Proceedings of the 18th Annual ACM International Conference* on Computer Documentation: Technology & Teamwork (pp. 593-605). Piscataway, NJ: IEEE Educational Activities Department.

Sommerville, I. (2004). Software engineering (7th ed.). New York: Addison-Wesley.

Stanton, N. (2004). The psychology of task analysis today. In D. Diaper & N. Stanton (Eds.), The handbook of task analysis for human-computer interaction (pp. 569-584). Mahwah, NJ: Lawrence Erlbaum Associates.

Suchman, L. A. (1987). Plans and situated actions: The problem of human-computer communication. New York: Cambridge University Press.

Sutcliffe, A. (2000). On the effective use and reuse of HCI knowledge. ACM Transactions on Computer-Human Interaction, 7(2), 197-221.

Tatnall, A. (2002). Actor-network theory as a socio-technical approach to information systems research. In S. Clarke, E. Coakes, M. G. Hunter, & A. Wenn (Eds.), Socio-technical and human cognition elements of information systems (pp. 266-283). Hershey, PA: Idea Group.

Turner, P., Turner, S., & Horton, J. (1999). From description to requirements: An activity theoretic perspective. In Proceedings of the International ACM SIGGROUP Conference on Supporting Group Work (pp. 286-295). Phoenix, AZ: ACM.

Van Der Veer, G. C., Lenting, B. F., & Bergevoet, B. A. J. (1996). Groupware task analysis: Modelling complexity. Acta Psychological, 91, 297-322.

Vetere, F., Gibbs, M. Kjeldskov, J., Howard, S., Mueller, F., Pedell, S., et al. (2005). Mediating intimacy: Designing technologies to support strong-tie relationships. In Proceedings of CHI 2005 (pp. 471-490). Portland, OR: ACM Press.

Vicente, K. J. (1999). Cognitive work analysis: Toward safe, productive, and healthy computer-based work. Mahwah, NJ: Lawrence Erlbaum Associates.

Vicente, K. J. (2004). The human factor revolutionizing the way people live with technology. New York: Routledge

Vora, P. R. (1998). Designing for the Web: A survey. Interactions, 5(3), 13-30.

Vygotsky, L. S. (1978). Mind and society. Cambridge, MA: Harvard University Press.

Vygotsky, L. S. (1986). Though and language. Cambridge, MA: Harvard University Press.

Watts, L. A., & Monk, A. F. (1998). Reasoning about tasks, activities and technology to support collaboration. Ergonomics, 4(11), 1583-1606.

Wegner, E. (2003). Communities of practice: Learning, meaning and identity. Cambridge, UK: Cambridge University Press.

Whittaker, S., Terveen, L., & Nardi, B. A. (2000). Let's stop pushing the envelope and start addressing it: A reference task agenda for HCI. Human-Computer Interaction, 15, 75-106.

Wild, P. J., Johnson, H., & Johnson, P. (2003). Understanding task grouping strategies. In S. McDonald, Y. Waern, & G. Cockton (Eds.), People and computers XIV (pp. 3-21). Bath University, UK: Springer-Verlag.

Zsambok, C., & Klein, G. (Eds.). (1997). Naturalistic decision making. Mahwah, NJ: Lawrence Erlbaum Associates.

APPENDIX

Task analysis matrix adapted from a survey conducted by Bonaceto and Burns (2003).

Key (applicability): ■ High ▧ Medium ☐ Low

Category	Method	Concept Definition	Requirements Analysis	Task Design	Interface Development	Workload Estimation	Training Development	Problem Investigation
Cognitive and Cognitive-Oriented task Analysis	Cognitive Task Analysis							
	Task-Knowledge Structures (TKS)							
	HTA							
	GOMS							
	Cognitive Work Analysis (CWA)							
	Applied Cognitive Work Analysis							
Knowledge Elicitation and Structuring	Interviews							
	Think-Aloud Protocols							
	Mock-ups, Prototypes, Storyboards							
	Wizard of Oz Technique							
	Cluster Analysis/Repertory Grids							
	Cognitive Ladders							
	Cognitive walk-throughs							
	Functional Flow Analysis							
Performance Analysis	Timeline Analysis							
	Operator Function Model (OFM)							
	Perceptual Control Theory (PCT) Approach							
Descriptive, Goal-Oriented Analysis	Activity Theory							
	Situated Action							
	Distributed Cognition							
	Scenario-Based Design							
Human Reliability and Critical Incident Analysis Category	Failure Modes and Effects Analysis							
	Work Safety Analysis							
	Generic Error Modelling Systems							

Section III:

Design

Chapter V

From Behavior to Design:
Answering the Questions of *Who* and *What* to Build Human-Centered Products and Information Systems

Catherine Forsman, USA

ABSTRACT

This chapter illustrates and discusses the historical context of human computer interaction (HCI) concepts such as ethnography, personas, scenarios and task analysis. It also offers a case study of the HCI process for creating products and information systems requirements for a variety of environments and people. Within the case study some of the questions that are focused on are: (1) How do we know who our users are? (2) How are demographic / psychographic identifications different than personas? and (3) How do we get to the "what" or prototype of a product or interface from the research findings. Understanding what these HCI concepts are, their history and how they are used illustrates how the HCI professional can envision, prototype, and create a clear understanding of the environment that a person uses a future product in and types of people who use that product. Additionally, this process and HCI concepts are illustrated in hopes of stimulating further thinking and processes within the HCI field.

INTRODUCTION

Today we are connected to rich information sources at a technical level. To tap into these sources, humans need an interface that is easily accessible and secure for what we are trying to accomplish. In the technology world the nexus of the human need for appropriate information and how to retrieve that information is fashioned by HCI professionals. They create the interface or product that helps humans tap into the rich information sources. Yet, there are questions in the HCI field of how best to do this. What has emerged is a mixture of anthropology techniques (ethnography), design techniques (visual design), information architecture techniques (library science), human factors techniques (usability studies), and HCI techniques (participatory design). In other words, a multi-disciplinary field forming and emerging in order to clearly meet the end goal of usable information systems, interfaces and products for human beings. This type of emerging and changing is witnessed in the posting of jobs in the field ranging from Interaction Designers to Information Architects to Human Factors Specialists to Designers. Many times, the resulting job descriptions will be similar with slightly different focuses, but with the same end goal: create an interface to an information structure or develop interfaces for an existing product that is usable.

One area that is of particular interest to business and HCI professionals is the phase before a team and management creates an interface or product. The question is: What should be built? This chapter illustrates how a HCI professional identifies and understands what is needed before an interface or product is envisioned.

This is the phase where the following questions are asked and answered: "Who and what are we building this for and why?" From this starting point, HCI professionals create the framework for what meets human and business needs for a particular population.

It is one of the more challenging and debatable areas of HCI, but also one of the more exciting opportunities for both businesses and practitioners because identifying the landscape of human need and context means human need is understood first and technology enables and supports those needs. This influences innovation as a process, user adoption, and usage when the resulting interface or product is built. This human-centered approach to technology has its roots in practices started years before this publication, and that, until the 1990s, were disparate fields of study. Out of necessity and common sense, the HCI community has merged different tools and techniques through the years to create a multi-disciplinary approach to answer fundamental questions such as "who and what." "Who" being the understanding of people that will eventually use the technology and the "What" being how to solve and innovate to create the appropriate thing that will meet their needs.

This history is a necessary starting point because it informs where we are today and offers a core understanding of how HCI professionals may go forward to craft their own methodologies to further the practice. Not all the questions and answers have been asked in how to best assess what is appropriate to build to meet human needs. In fact, we may only be at the beginning of understanding this process and in the next decades to come HCI processes may formalize further and more investigation and case studies can inform the field as to what works best.

SOME HISTORY

Businesses from Microsoft to St. Jude's Medical embrace the idea that understanding the human requirements of any technological innovation, or the "what" and "who" for that technology needs to be understood before the "how" of building that technology is answered. To answer the first questions, more essential questions must be asked by HCI professionals that address the idea of who we are building the product for. In order to answer the question of "who" we must ask ourselves what the best ways are to discover this. How companies and UCD professionals go about answering these central questions varies given the direction of management within the organization and the tools that are used.

A set of tools can be deployed that help both management and HCI professionals answer and resolve these questions into blueprints that make sense to engineers, managers, and users. Finding the right tools for the questions and the answers for each situation means understanding where we are now and some of the historical background. By understanding how we got to today, our choices become more solid and beneficial to the challenges that we face developing usable interfaces and products.

Before the 1990s, specialists were trained in such things as ergonomics and task analysis. Understanding these two aspects of machine operation in a nondistributed environment qualified many professionals to understand how a machine operated when someone used it, and whether or not the user could easily operate the machine and interfaces. Most of the studies and work were done after the technology or machine was built. Social movements, such as participatory design (meaning, users participate in the design of the machine and interface) in Scandinavia, took on the challenge of social dynamics in organizations because they saw a direct link between the sociological/anthropological organizational structure and environment and the group of workers who used machines that would be most needed and operated successfully or unsuccessfully within the work environment. Without involving the workers using the machines in the requirements analysis, most early Scandinavian HCI practitioners believed workers within organizations could suffer needless injury, task failure, and fatigue. These early practitioners — although performing their studies in nondistributed environments — realized that the sociological/anthropological underpinnings and creation of machines in specific environments could not be separated from studying how well someone completed a task on a well-designed interface or machine.

In the 1990s, Jonathan Grudin argued that HCI had passed through a number of stages in its development and was, at that time, moving into a fourth stage, which he characterized as "a dialogue with the user" (Grudin, 1990, p. 262). From that point onward, user experience has encompassed the study of how people perform tasks and engage in activities in their environment before a technology is built. Findings are then modeled on these behaviors and translated into knowledge that is disseminated both in political dialogues and practical blueprints.

Seminal works worth further examination are: Lucy Suchman's *Plans and Situated Action*, published in 1987. Her interest in moving HCI practices into the realm of social research rather than end-user testing still resonates today. Bonnie Nardi writes about the value of researching communities to understand requirements. Karen Holtzblatt and Hugh Beyer in their book titled, *Contextual Design: Defining Customer-Centered Systems*, (1998) lay out the fundamental need and use of ethnographic research to both generate questions and produce answers for systems built in context of the user's world. Paul Dourish writes eloquently about the philosophical underpinning and paradoxes of "context" in his book, *Where the Action Is: The Foundations of Embodied Interaction*. These references all deal with the incorporation of anthropology, psychology, and social techniques as they are incorporated into the HCI practice.

While the books mentioned are helpful for understanding the larger issues of context and collaboration, another type of study that influences the current set of tools available comes from Scandinavian efforts in participatory design. Scandinavian and North American professionals undertook efforts to marry collaborative practices to product development. HCI professionals and designers worked closely with intended users of the resultant product during the product design phases, using such methods as card sorting and paper prototyping to create wire frames and blueprints for systems. Many tools resulting from these efforts play a large role today in so far as each user experience team usually gets user input on wire frames before they go into development. However, some aspects of the Scandinavian movement have been lost, such as the full emersion into the culture of the "worker," including eating lunch with factory workers, playing football with workers, and forming relationships with management over an extended period of time. These issues, including long-term commitment to a community of users, attention to the sociopolitical, and "quality of life," marked much of the early work, including values, fears, and aspirations (Grudin & Pruitt, 2002).

Personas were first mentioned in Cooper's (1999) book, *The Inmates are Running the Asylum*. He presents the idea of a persona, or a fictitious character made from parts of subjects from a test group of people. He does not propose the way to accomplish making a persona, but introduces the importance of the concept. His concept is widely influential because it aids HCI teams in envisioning the "who," or the user as a character, with distinct goals and intentions in context of their environment. Before the adoption of personas as a viable means to represent users in context with goals, motivations, and scenarios of action, understanding groups of Internet users was untenable. This problem made it impractical for companies to consolidate a clear understanding of the user because there were so many users from different demograpics and no simple. Determining the user was a difficult and prohibitively expensive endeavor, usually involving market research, where statistics showed the usage of the Web site or online product, but did not inform companies of the goals, motivations, actions, and environments of the users that are most valuable in the innovation of new interactions and products. Persona development adds another piece to the puzzle in the advancement of HCI in today's networked environment.

Today, with the Internet, we live in a massively-distributed computing situation. In order to meet the needs of understanding the user, in various contexts, and with specific identifiable segments, the question really is, "How does a user-experience professional understand and represent users and get to know a segment of people well enough to understand what they do and how they do it in order to make the appropriate interfaces and software that meet their needs?" A concept that brings historical threads together and aids in representing an accurate idea of a user is personas. This chapter proposes that personas can be used to identify the "who" for product design and participatory design can be used to specifically identify the interaction within that product.

This is not an exhaustive list of resources, but it does exhibit the flourishing richness of resources used to create and question the tools and techniques that work best for any organization or individual searching to craft a HCI methodology in this manner. The thread of thought and practice that runs through all of these resources is the idea that HCI professionals focus closely on the context in which people live and work in order to fully understand the requirements for building a highly desirable and usable product. The UCD professional is no longer simply an engineer who tests the end result of an engineering-dominated product cycle, but the first member of the team to address the concerns of what a product can be and what social constructs and environments impact the needs of users.

Additionally, HCI designers are not constrained by a nondistributed environment where interfaces are built upon systems that are for one organization. They essentially became members of teams interested in HCI in the context of users' needs and environment in a massively distributed network.

THE WHO AND WHAT

"Who are you and how did you get in here?" "I'm a locksmith. And, I'm a locksmith."
~ Leslie Nielsen (1926), as Lieutenant Frank Drebin, *Police Squad.*

Given previous research in the area of HCI, history teaches us that asking "Who are we building this for?" is a top priority for the project team because all requirements and visions of the product or information system stem form this knowledge. But, in today's environment, answering this question is not simple. Before the 1990s, many software products had a more readily definable user population because software was built for a defined group within an organization. Today, organizations creating software that is commercial and widely distributed may have an indefinable amount of users ranging from a few thousand to millions comprised of various demographics, speaking different languages, with various cultural orientations. The question of "who" becomes highly complex. The problem is compounded when the HCI team begins the process of setting up a schedule that meets the financial needs of the project. Who do they interview and perform ethnographic research and participatory design with and how long will it take to find these representative users?

As mentioned in the Introduction, Cooper (1999) introduced the practice of persona development as a viable tool for understanding users that is manageable both in time and effort. Much iteration has been made on the initial ideas Cooper introduced. Any organization deploying personas will have varying ways of accomplishing the task because there is no de facto way to create a persona in the industry. However, the importance of personas cannot be underestimated in their ability to represent a user group in a comprehensible form to both management and technology teams.

In order to explain the power of personas, a case study is illustrated in this chapter highlighting the following areas in persona development:

- Many sources of both quantitative and qualitative information are needed to identify users and generate accurate personas
- Ethnographic research plays a vital role in the development of personas
- Scenario development is dependent upon persona development
- Task analysis can be combined with scenarios for an accurate visualization of what a character does and what context they exist in
- Participatory design can be informed by personas and the research used to develop the personas

Who Are You?

When identifying "who," a company may want to understand it is important to stress that both online and off-line behavior is important to the research. This means that, not only to observe as a classifying feature of who they are will the persona research team need to understand people who use the product online (identified through online usage logs), but they will also need to study people that meet the segment definition but may not yet use the product. This is important because research results should show a task or flow of processes that are both online and off-line, but represent the experience a person goes through in the entire experience in order to stimulate new ideas and create better products that solve usage problems.

For this case study, the experience is "shopping." Within the experience of shopping many people go through phases where they use the Internet for research but also use word-of-mouth recommendations and repeat certain behaviors many times at varying intensities. Understanding how these behaviors work together in a whole process, when and where, will ultimately lead to more robust findings that help organizations build to the need of users.

Pinpointing who should be studied in their environment is where most teams begin. Although strict market research, such as online survey results, does not aid in understanding people's tasks and goals in their environment, various forms of this data do aid in identifying who to study. A research methodology can include both a psychographic segmentation analysis, which identifies segments of users through the use of intercept Web surveys, as well as a field ethnographic study, which evaluates the goals and motivations of shoppers on and off-line. The psychographic survey helps identify what type of person should be studied in an environment whereas the ethnograpy survey shows what a person does. The ethnographic study includes visiting people in their homes, conducting one-on-one interviews, collecting artifacts, analyzing behavior, and developing personas along with scenarios. From identifying "who and what", a personal can be created. The overall process, or experience, the persona travels through can be illustrated visually by something in this chapter called an "experience diagram." They are designed and created from patterns evidenced in the ethnographic research by clustering individual behaviors based upon factors determined important to the overall research agenda. The diagrams help form personas, scenarios, and requirements. These diagrams also help in visualizing and exploring the basic interactions of the persona in the world.

The reason it is important to identify who will be studied in any persona study is that studying the correct users affects the accuracy of the persona. Personas are characters created from observing the daily activities of a selected group of people. They embody a grouping of real people's characteristics into one character that anyone within an organization can readily comprehend. What extends the persona into time and space from simply a character representation is the creation of scenarios. A scenario tells the story of how the persona operates in a specific situation. Yet, scenarios formed without personas based in ethnographic research are simply best guesses at what a user might do. Given this, accurately selecting people to study in the real world relates directly to the accuracy of personas. Ultimately, identifying the "who" to study creates better opportunities for accurate scenarios leading to a fuller requirements set and ideas for innovations that involve interactions in a place (e.g., signs posted in specific areas, cell phone interfaces, tone and style of communication, kiosks). Everything revolves around the "who" at the beginning of the user-centered research cycle.

To begin the search for "who", intercept surveys can be launched, then review Web logs and customer demographics launch surveys with specific demographic questions, then a guide a team in statistical representations of segments (based on demographics) and psychographics (based on behavioral questions). These segments can then be used for recruiting four to six participants to visit during field research. An example of a real-world research project is as follows:

Example of Survey Timeframe
- The total time frame for survey and analysis is three months.
- The online intercept survey is launched on Brand A, B, C, D, and E on Web sites in the U.S. and Canada for 1 month.
- The psychographic survey constitutes 6,192 responses with minimum sample sizes of 250 respondents per brand.
- Surveys and demographic data are analyzed for cultural, demographic differences and similarities, and representative size.
- Meanwhile, the team goes through market analysis on demographics and segments performed over the last year.
- All data is gathered together and analyzed for representative segments and the make-up of those segments.

The following is a representative set of segments developed from both psychographic analyses and demographic data. Psychographic analysis means here, that key psychological questions were asked of identified segments in order to determine their orientation to shopping, status, acquisition, and behaviors towards money:

1. Get Me from Point A to Point B
2. It Keeps Working on a Budget
3. Work Hard, Play Hard
4. Soccer Moms
5. Make it Fun
6. Status Conscious

This type of survey identifies demographics and some psychological information, but the goals people have and the actions taken for a specific task are missing. For example, little is known about what specifically Status Conscious people do or why they do those things. Without information about actions in context, it is very difficult for a UCD process to ensue. These findings inform a team about user population and identify who should be recruited for a team with whom to visit and perform ethnographic research.

Recruiting Participants

The question of who is to be studied is coupled with the understanding of what questions are to be answered. This is the phase where initial strategic questions often need to be analyzed and discussed with management and among the HCL team. What questions were missed in the initial business strategy sessions? Can these questions be answered during ethnographic research sessions? What questions need to be asked to get at what a person does and where they do it in regards to the overall project goal? In other words, now that the "who" is initially identified, what is it that needs to be known in order to inform the final design of the product? Once the user research team answers these strategic questions, the following actions can be taken.

1.   The team creates a screener with questions with a format for recording timestamps from videotape and quotations
2.   The team will begin contacting recruiting firms that will aid in recruiting participants in the given demographic

For example, the questions and the recruiting efforts will be dictated by the information found in the previous question and answer phase where strategic questions were brainstormed. The team should know such things as what they are curious to find a hypothesis, representative groups of people by location, gender, marital status, number of children, household income, age, and brand they prefer. Resulting decisions around these characteristics help to fashion questions to be studied within the field research and identify where the team goes to complete their study.

Ethnographic Research

Ethnographic research, or the act of going into the "field" and studying people has been used in software development to capture user requirements (Blomquist & Arvola, 2002) for the last 10 years. By observing behavior and people in context, rich amounts of information are uncovered about decision making; behaviors; analysis of conversations and environmental impact; and examination of artifacts, as well as an overall idea of what people do, when they do it, and why (Beyer & Holtzblatt, 1998).

Example of Ethnographic Timeframe

•   Research conducted over one month
•   Thirty-six people interviewed with six participants per segment
•   Two cities chosen based upon statistical analysis from survey demographic information
•   1.5 to 3 hour observations
•   Participants asked to collect "artifacts" prior to the team arriving

Conversational Journey Guide: Developing a Set of Questions

To ensure consistency and to set expectations, developing a conversation guide to serve as a loose outline of questions for the team to ask in the field is recommended. The goal in deploying a semi-structured interview format is that it allows the researchers to experience each interaction as a dynamic conversational journey, yet more structured in order to consistently collect information across a range of participants. Once all information is collected, it will be analyzed to discover patterns.

Some of the topics covered in the conversational guide include:

•   **Participant background:** day-in-the-life walk-through, family, interests, life stage, and Internet usage
•   **Psychographic questions:** role of product in one's life, relationship to product, and psychological orientation toward areas such as life, product, family, and status

- **Online information process:** trigger for purchases, research behaviors, tasks performed, information needs, online and off-line sources, people consulted, and information sharing
- **Context:** self-description of contexts throughout a day, such as what is done in certain places
- **Hopes, dreams, fears:** dreams for self, family, friends; dream interaction with product, preparation and coping strategies for certain events pertaining to product

In the Field

Entering people's homes or workplaces is a vital component of the team's research process. Videotaping is used to record one-on-one conversations and note taking to record observations of people that illustrate their day-to-day activities. Additionally, collecting artifacts (online printouts, any tools or notes the participants deems as extremely important) from participants help to identify their needs and how they use information. Talking with the participant before the visit will ensure that they collect objects of importance. Discussing each artifact will help determine importance, priority, and why they believe the artifact helps them in their process.

While the ideal team for this type of work consists of a moderator, videographer, and note taker, executive-level members should be encouraged to accompany the team. Many times asking the managerial team to dress down in jeans and t-shirts and instructing them how to work with the team or asking them to take notes during the visit will help bridge the gap between the immediate impact of research on product development and user acceptance. Additionally, including management in the process ensures that the power and impact of this type of research can be socialized within the organization. They inevitably will be able to give reports on the progress and discuss with others within the organization how the research may impact more than their area of product development.

As a team continues fieldwork, field notes are written and the videotape is annotated. This information will later comprise the backbone of the persona character. Though there are varying approaches to taking field notes, the goal of ethnographic research is best illustrated in Emerson, Fretz, and Shaw's (1995, pp. 64-65) *Writing Ethnographic Fieldnotes*. Their strategy is as follows:

The ethnographer's central purpose is to describe a social world and its people. But often beginning researchers produce field notes lacking sufficient and lively detail. Through inadvertent summarizing and evaluative wording, a fieldworker fails to adequately describe what she observed and experienced. The following strategies enable a writer to coherently depict an observed moment through vivid details: these strategies are description, presentation of dialogue, and characterization.

While ethnographic field note taking can be rigorous, additional aspects of ethnographic work can pose problems for persona development. They include:

1. The notes are "just descriptive." It is equivalent to instructing the researcher to describe those and only those aspects of the setting that can be used to demonstrate its self-ordering properties, and to organize the description such that it emphasizes

those properties. It does, therefore, specify not only how to look but also what to find (Cooper, 1999).

2. People rarely recount life in a linear fashion. Characters, events, interruptions, and ad hoc moments are part of living, and decision-making.

3. As Suchman (1993) has described, the role of *The Coordinator* takes place when making sense of people's descriptions or actions. This means that other details outside of classified categories will be observed and that difficulties in categorizing those events will follow. Yet, these categories retain meaning and have implications in the way information is classified regarding actions, people, and environments.

There is no "pure" ethnomethodology to follow when observing people in the field.

The alternative is to combine in some form with messy, contestable, provisional, iterative scenes in which formation and deployment of concepts struggle to carve workable entities and relations out of the seamless flow, and to cope with its simplifications, indexicabilities, inconstancies, and a priori theorizing; all for the prize of having something to say across a wide range of sociological concerns. (Shapiro, 1994, p. 419)

Faced with this problem, field notes became the backbone of accurate qualitative research results; much like data is for segmentation analysis. Yet, each user research team needs to deploy rigorous methods in order to "categorize, index, understand" what was observed. The more rigorous the field notes, the more specific the final persona will be. The more accurate the final persona the more likely user acceptance and user requirements accurately influence for the final product.

Example of Field Note Information
- A report on the day in the life of a participant. This describes what the person does during with the day starting with something akin to, "I get up at 8:30 am," and so forth
- Relationships in the person's life and how they exchange information
- Perception of self in the world and to product (e.g., says everything, says nothing)
- Memories
- Dream aspirations and real scenarios
- Attitudes about technology, level of technology experience, and expertise
- How they research, look for information, who looks with them, how they share

Beginning Analysis and Writing Profiles

After finishing research in the field, the team can use the field notes and artifacts to generate user profiles that include references to artifacts, quotes, photos, and an overall narrative. The purpose of these profiles is to help solidify details and to support recall for the team during data analysis and persona development (Tahir, 1997).

After the analysis of field notes, commonly raised questions among team members have to do with the meaning of a certain artifact, a story (conversational analysis), or the importance a reported interaction may have. These questions should be encouraged and

Figure 1. An example of profile notes

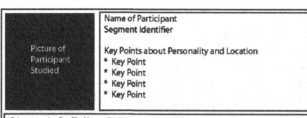

| Name of Participant |
| Segment Identifier |
| |
| Key Points about Personality and Location |
| * Key Point |
| * Key Point |
| * Key Point |
| * Key Point |

Ethnographic Profile Notes Area

Jenny wakes up at 6:30 am every day and begins her motherly duties for the household which include preparing breakfast for her children and waking them for school. She has a son, Jeremy, who is 6 months old, and a daughter, Alea, who is 5 years old. By 10 am Jenny is in her home office beginning her work day. <u>Jenny has found a way to adapt to remote colloboration software out of neccesity because she is usually spend 1/4 of her work year working on location.</u> She uses computer video cameras, conference software, mind mapper brainstorming software and many other types of software she cannot remember the name of. She finds it particularly difficult to stay connected to her colleagues in a meaningful way if all of her communication is remote. She believes she misses out on a lot of office "chit chat" that is vital to some of her decision-making. She says, "I think I have lost a lot <u>of the type of "touch"</u> people have who are relating directly with coworkers, but I find I cannot do my job and take of my family at the same time if I were to go to the office every day. I wish there was a better way to do this, but I have not found anything yet that will allow me to accomplish my work as quickly as a face-to-face meeting."

Jenny has worked for Corporation X for six months at the Troy location. When she talks about how she shops for important items for her family she talks about researching items on the internet. "Some times, if it is something I know someone in my family is interested in I'll ask them to send me website links over e-mail. Most of the time they stand behind me while I am surfing. Then I print out the <u>specifications and the price and start an excel spreadsheet on it."</u> <u>She hands the excell spreadsheet printout to a researcher and continues highlighting for us</u> what she finds important information on the websites about the products she is researching. "Given that I am a mom, worker, etc.... I always find myself juggling researching my family's big purchase decisions during the day."

<continue notes>

Side annotations:

Notice that she uses remote collaboration software but mentions she does most of her "meaningful" negotiations face-to-face.

Rates high (9 or 10) for touch category.

Notice how she organizes information and how that may inform an interaction or information architecture schema in the prototype.

---

team members should compare their observations with others in order to mitigate bias in the observations. At this point, the team is focused on telling a story, but the story may have varying angles. Also, during this phase allowances need to be made to not know the order of events; yet focus on the core pattern of how people explained the core behavior and their interaction with the important aspects identified before the research was conducted. These processes of analysis leave teams open to discoveries of the core behaviors that emerge organically and "clump" together.

By thinking about how the patterns relate to a current design situation, the research can gain analytic leverage on socially-oriented design problems. Patterns of cooperative interaction can be basically thought of as ways of highlighting regularities in the organization of work, activity, and interaction among persons taking part with, through and around artifacts. (Martin & Sommervile, 2004, pp. 66).

As the team reviews the profiles, important data are uncovered which lead to key insights. Information that appeared important in the field may simply not pertain to questions

Figure 2. Participant's environment

relevant to the product or development of personas. Subsequent phases determine what data pertains to persona development.

Along with profiles, taking many ethnographic photographs, or distilling photographs from videotape of key observations will help tell the participants' story in visual terms. Mixing photographs with written profiles adds to the understanding and recall of field research. For example, from the photograph in Figure 2, one can immediately see the environment this participant finds herself in while trying to meet with coworkers. This photograph also shows how her laptop is her office and her relationship to others is done through artifacts she carries with her on her laptop. And, although these observations may seem obvious at the time of recording information, they become less and less trivial as finer details and patterns emerge while researching many different participants in the field. Documenting everything well and thoroughly will ultimately be invaluable in the analysis phase because much is forgotten after interviewing an individual.

Further Analysis

Identifying important factors that identify a person's process and needs for a specific product means that the team must become clear about the hypothesis they believe form the personas. For example, a team may now begin asking, "Does a person's attitude towards this product affect their research behavior?" "Has the Internet affected how this person approaches this process?" "Do they need more information or less information?" "How do they approach that information?" "What do they do before they begin this process and who are they asking to help or coordinate this for them?" "What types of information do they need and how do they get this information?"

Taking these questions into account, the team must then determine what factors of data will give them the information they need. For example, some key factors that might play into answering these questions are:

- Age
- Gender
- Life stage

- Approach to information and the Internet
- Sharing of information or dependence upon others
- Marriage
- Previous experience going through this purchase/research process
- Research style
- Level of information required
- High tech/high touch
- Places people visit and what information they bring with them

Because people have different responses (e.g., level of information needed) mapping those individual responses can aid in identifying what personas exist among all researched participants. For example, mapping each person's responses for the level of information needed to accomplish the goal to a semantic differential, where one attribute is diametrically opposed to another helps a team begin to identify which people group together and for what reasons. In this way, clusters of similar traits form and personas form from this. For example, *fear factor* measures the level of fearful (lowest =1) to how fearless (highest=5) the subjects approach toward gathering information was based on their statements. This could be matrixes with age, marital status, previous experiences, and whether they purchased or not. The important point to notice here is that personas are not created from grouping participants from the same segment together, but from grouping participants based upon their behavior and approach to performing activities.

What results from this analysis is a set of diagrams. These diagrams help determine what primary influencing factors may be in a person's approach to dealerships gathering information, how they do this, and what leads them to accomplish their goal. Many variables can be tested from the information gathered in field research and mapped to quantitative scales. What the team begins to yield are distinct groupings of people around a cluster of characteristics. When these characteristics emerge, the factor can be explored and can potentially influence the personas later.

Task Flows

After grouping participant's characteristics and analyzing the clusters, individual task flows for important processes can be created where the sequence of behaviors for each person is mapped.

Often, participants studied in the field share their experience in a nonlinear fashion. The task-flow analysis reconstructs their stories as a sequence of *events and behaviors* leading to a visit and/or a purchase (if that is the chosen goal) (Hackos & Redish, 1998).

Throughout this analysis what becomes important is:

- What steps are taken in the shopping research process? What order did these occur? When did an individual visit a store or place to accomplish what they could not accomplish on the Internet? What research occurred before and after the visit?
- What were people's experiences (e.g., thoughts, emotions, and impressions) as they carried out each action?
- What observations can we make about users' implicit needs and experiences?

Next, analysis can be conducted across task flows, grouping them for their commonalities and differences. Through this comparative analysis, patterns in behaviors emerge that directly influenced the persona's scenario. Grouping similar tasks flows together and comparing to the previous cluster analysis immediately shows similarities in groups. Essentially what these persona groups show is a type of behavior influenced by emotional approaches.

From Analysis to Persona

Personas are defined as a singular human representative for a group of people who share a similarity in needs and behaviors. When pattern searching, numerous "lenses" can be used to explore patterns in activities, attitudes, and behaviors. The key to defining a useful persona is in identifying which parameters serve as the critical building blocks for a specific topical persona (e.g., for a shopping persona).

When looking at the qualitative research, important aspects are determined to be the most relevant parameters:

Store Visit

The purpose of a store Web site is to help drive store visits that ultimately lead to product sales. Because of this, a crucial component of the experience model captures store visits and addresses the following key questions:

- When in the process does a shopper visit the store?
- What is the frequency of store visits?
- What are the reasons for the visits?
- What attitudes and approaches accompany each store visit?

Research

- What types of information is needed prior to visiting a store?
- How much research is done before and between store visits?

Figure 3 shows clusters of people as plotted from information analyzed in the field notes. For example, on a scale of 1 to 5 we can now see the amount of information an individual needs and gets through technology in their shopping process and quickly certain people may buy or not.

Thing to notice:

1. People who are older tend to require much more personal interaction and use less technology in their decision process.
2. A large group of younger (20 to early 30s) people is relatively high tech and this could explain why they need less interaction with sales people when shopping.

Plus, many other observations can be made by understanding what combinations add to each person's placement within Figure 2. The main question the team should be asking themselves at this point is: What is similar and what is different? By answering these questions a fuller understanding of the cluster emerges. Each cluster will eventually inform the character of the persona. Some questions that could additionally be asked of this cluster diagram would be:

Figure 3. An example a diagram used to plot people researched

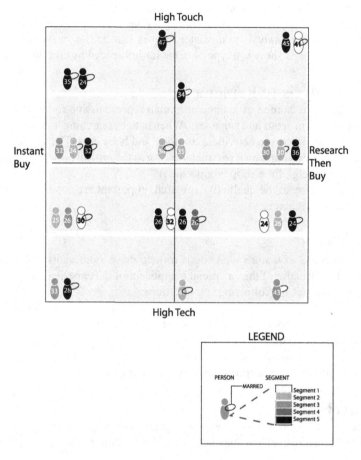

- What type of research and information is needed by different shoppers?
- How are shoppers gathering this information?
- What resources do they specifically use?

General Behavioral/Experience Model

After going through the data analysis exercise, tasks will also aid in helping the team understand what is similar about these clusters. For example, the cluster of very high tech and instant buyers can now be analyzed to see if their experience models tell the team more about why these people are clustered together. Many diagrams with clusters may not pertain, but the work of putting together the data and then analyzing similarities in order to undercover personas is a crucial step in the persona development.

As the team rereads the notes, plotting out an experience model should be based upon what they have learned during the diagramming exercise. For example, now that the team

Figure 4. An example of the core experience model as found by analyzing Participants' notes, profiles, and diagrams

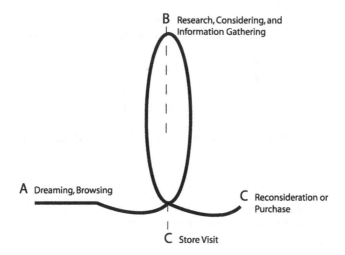

fully understands a group of instant buyers who are high tech, going back over the notes and profiles to understand this process will be crucial. Plotting out this process in a visual format will also help to organize the information.

The components lettered A, B, and C in the General Behavioral/Experience Model (see Figure 4) are:

A.   **Dreaming, browsing (e.g., building a consideration set):** The lead-in to a loop represents shoppers' "dreaming" and "browsing" phase where shoppers develop ideas to explore for large ticket items. Lead-ins to subsequent loops represent further looking around, consideration, and planning.

B.   **Research and information gathering:** The loop represents the online and off-line research a shopper conducts. From the initial lead-in, this research can serve to find out more information on the item of interest, or to begin conducting side-by-side comparisons. Of particular interest is the amount and type of research a shopper conducts before they feel ready to visit a store.

C.   **Store visit:** The close of each loop at the bottom represents a store visit. As the loops closes, shoppers move from research and information gathering to a prepared "moment of contact." Shoppers have multiple reasons to go into a store and may spread these visits out or condense them into fewer visits.

As further analysis is done on the core experience model, it will become obvious what type of experience a certain persona will exhibit. For example, those who were high touch, married, and also high tech, tended to research thoroughly all of their high-priced purchases and then include their spouse in the final decision-making process. The experience model

Figure 5. A experience model for a persona. The goal with the illustration is to build a visual signature, including designers in this visual thinking process.

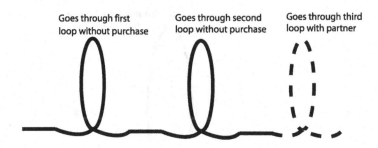

for this persona is created to quickly convey to everyone the "signature" of the personality. An example of how one might do that is in Figure 5.

Once all experience models are created for the identified personas, the final stages of defining the persona can now take place.

Team Notes

Some information from field research is intangible (e.g., cannot be easily translated to concrete findings because transcripts are lengthy or videotape needs to be edited). However, the intangibles gently influence our understanding of the persona and design requirements. Given this, including designers and engineers into the persona process is an important element in transitioning the intangible information to the design team. Including the design team when experience models are created is an optimal time to do this. Including other members of the product development team into the research phase ensures that the knowledge learned during the initial research is brought into the design of the interface at a later time.

Persona Experience Scenarios

Experience models emerge from the research. These are the "signatures" for each of the personas. They illustrate an overall experience informed by a task flow and clustering as seen in Figure 6. Later on, these core models are used in tandem with the personas to create scenarios, suggesting requirements and influencing design decisions. By linking all of these elements together (experience model, cluster analysis, and task flows), personas are ensured to be based upon research and more accurately representative of user needs in any new product development.

Example:

Here are the building block parameters of Store Visit. They are the three key reasons shoppers visit a store.

1.   Browse merchandise
2.   Test, feel, and/or try-on merchandise
3.   Negotiation and purchase

Figure 6. Combining the experience model with a scenario to illustrate requirements

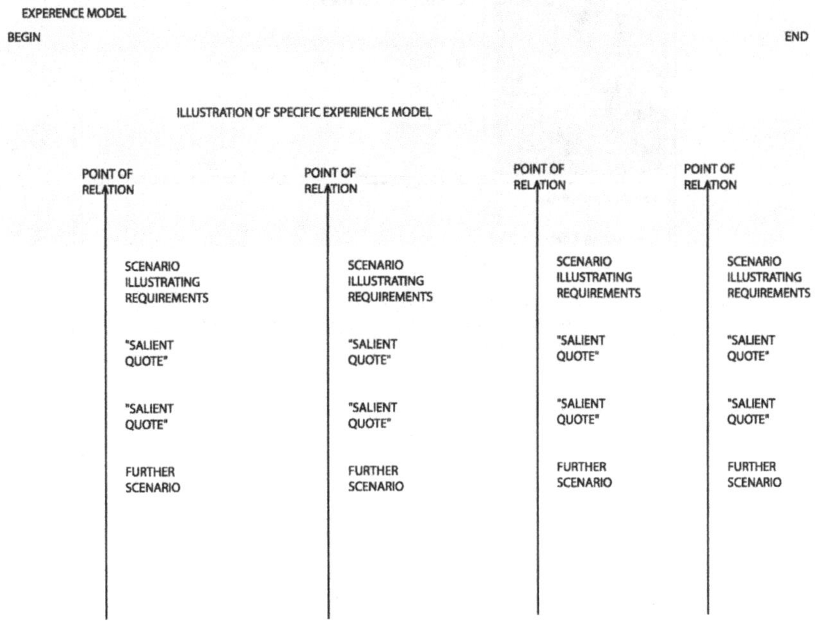

EXPERENCE MODEL
BEGIN   END

ILLUSTRATION OF SPECIFIC EXPERIENCE MODEL

POINT OF RELATION	POINT OF RELATION	POINT OF RELATION	POINT OF RELATION
SCENARIO ILLUSTRATING REQUIREMENTS	SCENARIO ILLUSTRATING REQUIREMENTS	SCENARIO ILLUSTRATING REQUIREMENTS	SCENARIO ILLUSTRATING REQUIREMENTS
"SALIENT QUOTE"	"SALIENT QUOTE"	"SALIENT QUOTE"	"SALIENT QUOTE"
"SALIENT QUOTE"	"SALIENT QUOTE"	"SALIENT QUOTE"	"SALIENT QUOTE"
FURTHER SCENARIO	FURTHER SCENARIO	FURTHER SCENARIO	FURTHER SCENARIO

The key differentiators for these personas can be found in how quickly they visit a store and for what purpose, as well as the amount and type of associated research conducted both online and off-line.

Write the Persona

After all the analysis, task analysis, and fieldwork are complete the persona description can be written as illustrated in template form in Figure 7. Waiting until the last step to write the persona ensures that the character is:

1. Based on field research, and is therefore imbued with a multi-faceted, yet real character;
2. is fully formed in the minds of many of the team members and creates very little confusion; and
3. is a character that is walking through time and completing goals in a specific experience.

Outcome

As mentioned earlier, including executive members of the team in the field research helps the research team as they visit people in their homes. They attend interviews and write notes when needed. After a long day in the field they can meet with the research team to

Figure 7. An example of a persona template

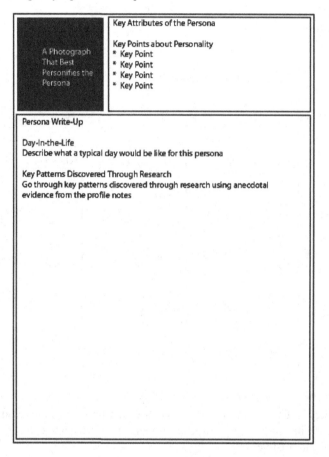

discuss findings and hand over their notes thereby creating both a deeper understanding of this type of research and acting as early advocates to the rest of the company as they return ahead of the team.

The outcome of this is:

- Executives quickly understand the importance of first-hand observation and the enormous value it brings to requirements gathering.
- They are able to advocate the research before the lengthy analysis phase of research. This includes becoming interested in users' lives and concerns, which will ultimately affect the attachment the company will have to the product and the people who use it. It is a humanization of both the user and their needs.
- They socialize the process as a whole and are able to tell anecdotal stories to others within the company. This some times adds to the interest within different departments because the research is no longer seen as simply something done for one product.

Interest grows and many times can be seen as adding benefits to other products and areas within the company.

As word spreads throughout an organization, other employees often ask for updates on the field process as it is interesting and accommodates the human element of product development. These e-mail notes can easily take the form of status reports and interesting narratives of travels or anecdotal records of observances. In this way, a design team can create a grass-roots reporting effort, interesting even to those who are skeptical of the validity of this type of research to their business concerns. People will often forward the initial field-note e-mails to others in the company they believe are interested simply because the information is more compelling and less boring than drier types of research.

When the finalized personas are presented, interested parties attend the meeting including those who initially did not know the research would encompass their concerns due to the socialization of research.

While design research has specific goals and answers it accomplishes by answering the "who" of software development, it is also a human interest story that unfolds, with many requirements that can bridge political barriers within an organization. In two or three projects where persona research was conducted, a full ecosystem of information and technology was uncovered that was otherwise not known to be associated due to political barriers within an organization.

Decisions about design are essentially about organizations and the people who approach these organizations on a one-to-one level either through a technology or not, at some time and in some space. As we move forward as user-experience professionals, the possibility of crafting scenarios around hybrid places is emerging such as the home then the office in one day, or online shopping in an office with saved information for mobile devices. The Internet has offered many possibilities for understanding the core experience a persona is involved in and the information needs they have in order to fulfill that experience, but personas may also answer more complicated questions that earlier research methods could not help us understand.

Personas and experience models are based on observances of real people in the world. There is a "slice of time" in which we observe these people, but there may be even larger slices of time ahead of us. The early Scandinavian design teams understood a larger grouping of time as inherently influencing design decisions. For the early Scandinavian participatory design teams, design was viewed as both a community/social practice and a research process. If longer periods of research times are involved in HCI practices, experience models could be tested against the reality of "experience." What I am proposing is that iterate research for personas may very likely be a method to understand the "what if" scenarios, enhance our understanding of people and places, and help us understand whether an experience truly works the way we envision. To this idea, longer periods of research may answer more questions, tasks analysis could also benefit from a lengthier period of research. Observing the changing and ad hoc process of completing tasks both with technology and outside of what we consider the domain of technology can potentially fit into interesting research that creates a broad and more specific understanding of how people complete goals in different places.

The What

Now that the "who" of the HCI process has been completed, the question is how to translate this information into prototypes that both designers and engineers understand. From each of the personas some of the outcomes that can be expected are a listing of technology priorities, features, and functionality that will meet those priorities. In many cases, features needed by one persona are also needed by another. Finding this overlap in requirements will help design prototypes that satisfy all user groups.

After understanding the requirements needed by each persona low-fidelity prototypes can be made. These prototypes should show both the information needed by each persona and initial ideas of interactions that will take place within each interface. Once the initial low-fidelity prototypes are created, they will need to be brought back into the field to test with persona representatives. This test group of participants should not be the initial segment participants, but people who match the criteria shown in the persona.

From this point forward, traditionally described participatory design and task analysis will help the user-experience professional begin to refine each prototype to a finished product.

CONCLUSION

At the beginning of this chapter a reference was made to Grudin's comment about the third stage of HCI becoming one in which the HCI professional enters into a conversation with the user. The question, hopefully answered in this chapter is, "What can one learn in having a conversation with the user?"

Hopefully, the conversation will become a continuous dialogue. The models, assumptions, activities, and methodologies of HCI work will continue to shift through time in order to more deeply understand how human beings can more easily operate machines. The more distributed computing becomes, the more varied the methods will be to understand the user, the location, and the overall experience of each person through time. The attempt to understand is probably the most important part of this type of work. We attempt to more fully understand who is using a product, where they live, work, and experience portions of the important tasks they need to accomplish each day in order to meet their goals. And, finally, we attempt to fashion usable and desirable requirements for products, communicating those findings to all concerned constituents. More user research models will hopefully develop as we move further and further into how we attempt to understand who uses a product and what it is before building it.

REFERENCES

Beyer, H., & Holtzblatt, K. (1998). *Contextual design: Defining customer-centered systems*. San Francisco: Morgan Kaufmann.

Blomquist, A., & Arvola, M. (2002). Personas in action: Ethnography in an interaction design team. In *Proceedings of NordiCHI*, (pp. 197-200). Chapel Hill, NC: ACM Press.

Cooper, A. (1999). *The inmates are running the asylum: Why high tech products drive us crazy and how to restore the sanity*. Indianapolis, IN: Macmillan Publishing Co.

Dourish, P. (2001). *Where the action is: The foundations of embodied interaction.* Cambridge: MIT Press.

Emerson, R. M., Fretz, R. I., & Shaw, L. (1995). *Writing ethnographic fieldnotes.* University of Chicago Press.

Grudin, J. (1990). *The computer reaches out: The historical continuity of interface.* CHI.

Grudin, J. & Pruitt, J. (2002). Personas, participatory design and product development: An infrastructure for engagement. *Proceedings of the PDC 2002,* (pp. 144-161). Palo Alto, CA: CPSR.

Hackos, J., & Redish, J. (1998). *User and task analysis for interface design.* New York: John Wiley & Sons.

Martin, D., & Sommervile I. (2004), Patterns of cooperative interaction: Linking ethnomethodology and design. *ACM Transaction on Computer-Human Interaction, 2*(1), 59-89.

Nardi, B. A., & O'Day, V. L. (1999). *Information ecologies: Using technology wtih heart.* Cambridge: MIT Press.

Shapiro, D. (1994). The limits of ethnography: Combining social sciences for CSCW. *Proceedings of CSCW* (pp. 417-428).

Suchman, L. (1993). Do categories have politics? The language/action perspective reconsidered. In G. DeMichelis, C. Simone, & K. Schmidt (Eds.), *Proceeding of ESCSCW. The Third European Conference on Computer Supported Cooperative Work* (pp. 1-14). Amsterdam, The Netherlands: Kluwer.

Suchman, L. A. (1987). *Plans and situated actions.* Cambridge: Cambridge University Press.

Tahir, M. F. (1997). Who's on the other side of your software: Creating user profiles through contextual inquiry. In *Proceedings of UPA '97,* Bloomingdale, IL, (pp. 99-112). UPA Press.

Chapter VI

Design Methods for Experience Design

Marie Jefsioutine, University of Central England - Birmingham, UK

John Knight, University of Central England - Birmingham, UK

ABSTRACT

The following chapter describes an approach to Web design and evaluation where the user experience is central. It outlines the historical context in which experience design has evolved and describes the authors' experience design framework (EDF). This is based on the principles of user-centred design (UCD) and draws on a variety of research methods and tools to facilitate the design, development, and evaluation of user experiences. It proposes that to design usable, accessible, engaging, and beneficial Web sites, effort needs to focus on visceral, behavioural, reflective, and social factors, while considering contexts such as the who and why; what and how; when and where; and with what of Web site use. Research methods from a variety of disciplines are used to support exploration, communication, empathy, and speculation. Examples of the application of the EDF, to various stages of the Web design process, are described.

INTRODUCTION

"Although change is afoot, designers (including design engineers) — still worry that corporate bosses and clients see them as merely 'making things pretty.'"
~ Molotch, 2003, p. 28

Producing Web sites is a process that involves a range of skills and disciplines. Design is not an add-on to make the screens look good. Design impacts on what people do, how they do it, and with whom they do it. Products, whether they are Web sites, toasters, or services embody a range of values and our interaction with them is a form of communication. When interacting with a Web site, for example, we may be communicating with other people, real or imagined. As we type with the keyboard, we hear and feel the keys and may vent our frustration through the force of our tapping. While reading the words on a screen we are also taking in all kinds of nonverbal messages from the layout — images, colours, fonts, icons, language, and style of language. Our experience is also affected by our surroundings, our memories of past actions, our current knowledge, and our expectations of the future.

Interaction with a Web site is mediated by a network of people, machines, and systems. The Internet works because of the design of protocols, browsers, laws, technical standards, security mechanisms, machines, communication technologies, and physical infrastructure as much as it does because of the design of the Web pages. Our experience of a Web site is therefore a product of our personal understanding of its context. Givechi and Velázquez (2004) describe the "positive space" of a product, which becomes more significant than the product itself, "the aura of a product, the sum of its physical attributes plus its intangible essence — or the meaning it hosts for each of its users" (p. 43). The meanings we attach to a product change with time, in part due to our changing experiences, the wider socioeconomic and political context of a product, and our changing expectations. To build a successful product, a designer needs to be aware of as many of these factors as possible, and this is why a consideration of the whole user experience is important.

FROM SOFTWARE ENGINEERING TO EXPERIENCE DESIGN

Concepts like "user experience" and "design of experience" are common in the design and business communities now (Fulton-Suri, 2004, p.14), but this has not always been the case, and in some software development circles *designer* still has negative connotations. It is important to recognise the context in which Web design has emerged, to understand why these concerns are so topical.

The development of computer software and interfaces in the 1960s emerged from fields traditionally associated with engineering and science. This era was typified by optimism for technology, and even in the traditional design disciplines there was a movement towards rationalising design methods. Hailed as the "design science decade" (Fuller, 1969, p. 305) the emphasis was on objectivity, rationalism, and technology.

The term *software engineering* can be traced back to an international conference convened by NATO in 1968, to solve the "software crisis" (Campbell-Kelly & Aspray, 1996, p. 200). The crisis emerged from large scale (often military) software projects that encountered problems in management and quality. In response to these failings a number of risk management strategies were advocated including the *waterfall development lifecycle*. Here design and development flowed through a predetermined course of phases. The formalised nature of the process was predicated by each phase having specified inputs and outputs, which could be checked along the way.

A design approach based purely on linear, logical problem solving did not work for the new technologies (e.g., computing, software, and solid state electronics), where problems were nebulous and constantly evolving through technological development and changing requirements. Brooks' (1975) experience on IBM's System/360 project was typical. He describes how software defied traditional logical engineering approaches. Even increasing resources did not improve the success of the approach.

In design disciplines such as product design and architecture, there was a growing realisation that some problems were unsolvable by logical deduction (Cross, 2001). Rittel and Webber (1973), for example, contrasted the "wicked problems" of design with the "tame" ones of science and engineering. In software design attention was turning to human factors. Whereas traditional engineering and industrial design focussed largely on external and measurable ergonomic factors, computer interaction required an understanding of internal, cognitive aspects. In 1969 the *International Journal of Man Machine Studies* was launched and a new field emerged, looking at what is now called human-computer interaction (HCI).

The idea that the computer interface could be modelled on human needs rather than driven by system capabilities led to the development of the graphical user interface (GUI) launched with one of the early commercially available personal computers, the Xerox Star, in 1981. Although the product itself was not successful, the concept of the GUI became almost universally adopted. This interface had been developed using usability engineering methods, including paper prototyping and testing on potential users. The design process was iterative and responsive.

In 1985, Gould and Lewis codified their own approach to software development, identifying the following key principles: early focus on users and tasks; empirical measurement through early and continual user testing; integrated design; and iterative design (Gould 1995; Gould & Lewis, 1985). UCD, as it came to be called, is now embodied in international standards for software development. International Organization for Standarization (ISO, 1999) 13407, for example, describes it as:

> *an approach to interactive system development that focuses specifically on making systems usable. Whatever the design process the allocation of responsibilities and roles adopted, the incorporation of a human-centred approach is characterised by the following:*
>
> a. *the active involvement of users and a clear understanding of user and task requirements;*
> b. *an appropriate allocation of function between users and technology;*
> c. *the iteration of design solutions; and*
> d. *multidisciplinary design.*

Usability became a high profile issue in the 1990's (see Knight & Jefsioutine, 2002) and much of the HCI literature aimed at supporting interaction designers, focused on cognitive and behavioural models of human interaction with attempts to formalise methods (e.g.,

Harrison & Thimbleby, 1990) and generate guidelines about human behaviour, much like the rational approaches to design.

The relationship between humans and computers is not entirely rational or logical however. Reeves and Nass (2002), for example, describe the ways in which people treat computers and software like real people with feelings and personalities. Jordan (2000) argues that usability is no longer sufficient as a design goal. He argues that customers now expect products to be easy to use and claims that "usability has moved from what marketing people call a 'satisfier' to being a 'dissatisfier'" (Jordan, 2000, p. 3). People no longer notice when a product is usable, just when it is difficult to use. Fulton-Suri (2004) points out "established products have become more similar in technology, functionality, price and quality, companies have turned to design to differentiate, their offerings…to create stronger emotional connections with their customers" (p. 13). Lastly, the notion of a problem that can be identified and solved through logical deduction is often at odds with how successful products are developed and adopted by consumers.

The challenge for Web designers is no longer just to produce a functioning and usable product, they must now meet the needs of an increasingly sophisticated and demanding audience and a competitive market place. The EDF was developed by the authors to address these challenges by collating useful methods and approaches to designing products like Web sites and by considering the whole user experience (Jefsioutine & Knight, 2004).

THE EXPERIENCE DESIGN FRAMEWORK

The EDF advocates the principles of UCD already described, and adds another set of considerations: qualities, dimensions of experience, research contexts, and research methods. These are described hereafter.

Qualities

Each product will have its own specific user requirements. The EDF proposes that four fundamental qualities underlie these requirements.

Usable

To go beyond usability does not mean that it is no longer necessary. The benefits of usability are well documented (e.g., Bevan, 2000). Usability is defined as "the extent to which a product can be used by specified users to achieve specified goals with effectiveness, efficiency and satisfaction in a specified context of use" (ISO, 1998) and "the capability of the software product to be understood, learned, used and attractive to the user, when used under specified conditions" (ISO, 2000). Indeed, in long-term use of a product, there is evidence that usability becomes more important than style in predicting users' satisfaction (Maguire, 2004). Usability cannot be ignored as a design goal.

Accessible

The Web relies on a level of standardisation such that pages can be accessed by anyone, on whatever browser or device they use, be it a PC, Mac, or mobile phone. As the Web has grown, so have the standards and so have the number of inaccessible Web sites. Despite the publication of guidelines for accessible web design by the World Wide Web Consortium

Figure 1. The experience design framework (Jefsioutine & Knight, 2004)

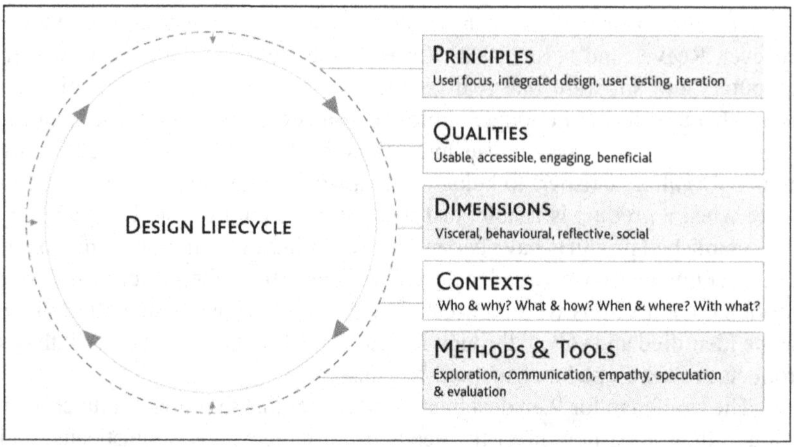

(W3C, 1999), a survey of Web designers found that difficulty interpreting guidelines was a major barrier to implementing them (Knight & Jefsioutine, 2003). Furthermore, the UK's Disability Rights Commission (2004) found that nearly half of the usability and accessibility problems were not violations of any of the WCAG's checkpoints. DiBlas, Paolini, Speroni, and Capodieci (2004) argue that "W3C guidelines are not sufficient to ensure an efficient — even less satisfactory — Web experience" (p. 89). It is important that accessibility is seen as part of the user experience rather than a series of technical checkpoints to cover.

Engaging

Shedroff (2001, p. 4) suggests an experience comprises of "an attraction, an engagement, and a conclusion". What attracts someone to a product could be a need to perform a task, an aesthetic quality, or an affordance. The engagement is then sustained over a period of time, beyond the initial attraction. Csikszentmihalyi (1991) describes the experience of optimal experience and flow: "Concentration is so intense that there is no attention left over to think about anything irrelevant, or to worry about problems. Self-consciousness disappears, and the sense of timing becomes distorted" (p. 71).

Although this level of engagement may not be appropriate for all products, it is useful to consider the properties of an experience that make it engaging. Fiore (2003) suggests that an experience includes a number of dimensions: it is educative and memorable; whole, unique and nonreproducible; historical; meaningful/aesthetic; contextual; physical/sensual/embodied; and situated in time and space. Jones, Valdez, Nowakowski, and Rasmussen (1994) suggest that engaged learning tasks are *challenging, authentic, and multidisciplinary. Such tasks are typically complex and involve sustained amounts of time... and are authentic.* Quinn (1997) suggests that engagement in learning applications comes from two factors — *interactivity and embeddedness,* where the user perceives that they have some control over the system, and it is relevant and meaningful to them.

Beneficial

According to Csikszentmihalyi (1991), an optimal experience is so gratifying that "people are willing to do it for its own sake, with little concern for what they will get out of it" (p. 71). One might assume that what they are getting is some degree of pleasure. Jordan (2000) identifies pleasure as the ultimate quality of the user experience, and DeJean (2002) points out that pleasure is a complex concept. Apparently unpleasant aspects of the user experience, such as difficulty, challenge, and fatigue can all be pleasurable in certain contexts, for example, by generating feelings of achievement or superiority.

Bonapace (2002) adapts Maslow's (1970) hierarchy of human needs to product use qualities. His pyramid begins with safety and well-being, moves up to functionality, and then usability which leads up to an apex of pleasure as the ultimate quality. Dunne (1999) explores the "aesthetics of use" and argues, "The most difficult challenge for designers of electronic objects now lies not in technical and semiotic functionality, where optimal levels of performance are already attainable, but in the realms of metaphysics, poetry and aesthetics, where little research has been carried out" (p. 7).

Liu (2003) describes qualities of "psychosomatic soundness," referring to the extent that a product contributes to the "wholesomeness" or well-being of a person (from "harmful" to "healthful") and the degree to which it is ethical ("bad/wrong" to "good/right") (p. 1296). Knight (2004) too, argues for a reconsideration of the ethics of HCI design. The EDF uses the term *benefit* to include such concepts as ethics, psychosomatic soundness, pleasure, and self-actualisation.

The EDF, therefore, advocates designing for the four fundamental qualities of product use of accessibility, usability, engagability, and benefit. To do this it becomes necessary to widen the focus of research beyond cognitive and behavioural interaction, typical of usability, and HCI studies, to include a multi-dimensional approach to experience.

Dimensions of Experiencing

McDonagh-Philp and Lebbon (2000) suggest that emphasis must change "from *hard* functionality, to *soft* functionality" (p. 38). Rather than focussing on what a product does and how it does it, the focus is on less tangible aspects like emotional associations, familiarity, aesthetics and taste. Fiore's (2003) framework of experience considers physical, emotional, and intellectual aspects. In a similar vein, Norman (2004) describes emotional design in terms of its "visceral, behavioural, and reflective" elements (p. 63). He points out that these three levels of experience are not discrete but interact with each other. Spillers (2004) suggests, for example, that a new icon on a screen could arouse a state of curiosity or annoyance, producing a change in the user's emotional state "which can either propel the user toward a feeling of satisfaction (success) or disappointment (failure)" (p. 2).

Jordan (2000) develops Tiger's (1992) concept of pleasure, and describes four ways in which pleasure can be experienced: "Socio-Pleasure" arises from interaction with others or from a product that represents a social grouping; "Pyscho-Pleasure" comes from the satisfaction felt when a task is successfully completed or from a product that makes a task more pleasurable. "Physio-Pleasure" is derived from the senses; and "Ideo-Pleasure" is derived from entities such as books, art and music or the values that a product embodies (p. 13-14).

The EDF uses Norman's (2004) classification and adds a social dimension. The EDF, therefore, directs attention to the visceral, behavioural, reflective, and social dimensions of experience. Furthermore, it suggests that they be considered in the context of the use qualities. For example, considering *accessibility* in the context of each dimension may generate design goals such as:

- **Accessible/visceral:** legibility and visual clarity, text alternatives to audio content
- **Accessible/reflective:** limiting cognitive overload /clear, simple language use
- **Accessible/behavioural:** keyboard alternatives to using a mouse, shortcuts, voice input
- **Accessible/social:** culturally inclusive, secure, private, moderated

Research Contexts

This section describes a set of key questions that can be asked throughout the design process to develop an understanding of the contexts of product use. The questions are derived from a number of models including Rothstein's (2002) model consisting of the four As of "activity, artefacts, atmosphere and actors" (p. 3), and Ortony, Clore, and Collins (1998) cognitive model comprising "events, agents and objects (p. 63). The EDF advocates four key contexts: (1) who and why (users and stakeholders and their motivations); (2) what and how (content, tasks, task flow, actions, functionality); (3) when and where (situation, frequency, environment); and (4) with what (tools, knowledge, and skills).

Who and Why

In order to be user centred it is necessary to identify who the users and stakeholders are and what motivates them to use a product. It is important to include everyone, however limited their involvement with a product might be. Users of a software system, for example, might include people that buy it, use it at home or at work, communicate through it, people who sell it, or sell on it, administrate it, repair it, install it or support it (e.g., Hackos & Redish, 1998).

When the focus of UCD goes beyond usability, it becomes necessary to collect data that pertain to the qualities and dimensions of the EDF. This might include: demographics (such as age, gender, ethnic origin, and culture); behaviour and skills (such as computer literacy, typing skills, embedded knowledge of a task or system); knowledge and experience (such as novice or domain expert, tacit knowledge); personal characteristics and motivations (such as personality, learning style, attitude, aspirations, values, beliefs, tastes, and preferences); and physical characteristics (such as dexterity, physical abilities, height).

What and How

This refers to the tasks or activities that will be supported, influenced, or affected by the product and how users carry out these tasks. Tasks are typically mapped from a behavioural perspective or cognitive dimension. Liddle (1996) suggests, "The most important component to design properly is... the user's conceptual model. Everything else should be subordinated to making that model clear, obvious, and substantial" (p. 21). The EDF suggests that activities be considered in all dimensions. For example, an airhostess may be performing complex emotional tasks as well as checking in baggage (customer relations, anxiety reduction, risk assessment, etc.) (Hochschild, 1983).

When and Where

The role of context in understanding tasks was emphasised by Suchman's (1987) notion of *situated actions*, that activity is conditional on the situation in which it takes place and is of an improvised rather than planned nature. What people say they are doing or how they do it, is an after-the-event rationalisation. Context should be considered in terms of all of the dimensions. For example, what is the user's current frame of mind? What ideological factors will influence their experience? What aspects of the environment affect their visceral experience — are there loud distracting noises around or reflections on the screen? What emotional state is the user in? What other behaviours are they performing? What is the social context — is the product being used with friends to communicate, to play, to learn, or to work cooperatively?

With What

This refers to objects, artefacts, or tools that are being used or are influencing use (such as software, browsers, input devices, assistive technologies), and to knowledge, expertise, and skills that are used to carry out tasks. Considered in the context of qualities and dimensions, brainstorming, for example, might suggest that a haptic interface or 3D glasses (visceral) may improve engagability when viewing a virtual museum object. Conversely, users' knowledge of existing interface conventions (reflective) may create expectations that reduce the usability of an innovative interface.

Methods and Tools

Reeves and Nass (2002) point out that people are rarely aware of their less rational motivations, so attempts to model what people are thinking or doing by asking them will not necessarily capture the reality of an experience. They advocate the use of methods from the social sciences to establish what people really think. The EDF suggests casting a wide net across many disciplines to find appropriate and useful methods.

Rather than prescribing a process or method, the EDF suggests that a range of tools and techniques can be employed provided they cover four basic purposes — exploration, empathy, communication, and evaluation. Furthermore, by applying these methods to the dimensions, qualities, and research perspectives, a better understanding of the user experience as a whole can be achieved.

Exploration

These methods are about discovery and can be drawn from demography, ethnography, market research, psychology, and HCI. They include surveys, interviews, questionnaires, focus groups, task analysis, field observation, user testing, affinity diagramming, laddering, and experience diaries. A key area of exploration is in understanding users' mental models of a domain. This can be explored by, for example, in depth elicitation techniques and card sorts.

Contextual interviews are conducted during the activity or in the environment in which the product will be used. Users are able to refer to artefacts, such as the documents, memos, and equipment that they normally use in their workflow, and indeed may be encouraged by the researcher to describe what they are doing. One of the most common methods of achieving this is to use the "think aloud protocol" (where users verbalise their actions). This has the advantage that the user is not relying on memory to describe his or her actions, and the researcher is able to note and probe omissions. There are some disadvantages however. The act of conscious reflection may change the way the task is performed and may create excessive cognitive load, or compete for the same cognitive channel as the task.

Both ethnography and ethnomethodology have been applied to eliciting contextual data. Ethnography is the study of a culture achieved by researchers immersing themselves in that culture in order to understand it, while ethnomethodology studies the ways in which participants give order to and make sense of their social worlds (Garfinkel, 1967). The focus of ethnomethodological studies is often at a very detailed level of interaction, including interaction between people and artefacts, technologies, and systems. For this reason it is a useful approach for the study of complex work situations, for example, air traffic or train control systems (Heath & Luff, 2000). The researcher may also use the artefacts produced by organisations, such as manuals and training materials; policies and procedures; and forms and documentation to enrich the detail of the observation. The rationale for applying these approaches to design is that the knowledge acquired will enable designers to work with, rather than against, users' ways of understanding and making sense of the activities in which they are engaged.

Nevertheless, integrating these methodologies within the design process is not without its problems. The skills of trained ethnographers are often underestimated. Done properly, ethnographic methods involve sophisticated and skilful observation and recording techniques. The data may be far more detailed than the designer needs, and in a form that is difficult to interpret. Furthermore it can take many years to do a full ethnographic study, and for most software development projects, this amount of time is unrealistic. A simpler version may include shadowing target users for a short time, noting what they do and use, taking photographs, asking questions, and using techniques to elicit their values or emotional responses (Beyer & Holtzblatt, 1998).

Communicating

Design involves communication with a wide range of people, from users to software engineers. Design teams need to accommodate different viewpoints and share a common language. Curtis (2002) emphasises the importance of actively listening to a client and finding out the story behind a product. Hammer and Reymen (2004) stress the importance of designers expressing their emotional as well as rational reflections on design decisions. Communication methods serve to clarify and share the goals of stakeholders, the exploratory research data, design requirements, and ideas to a multi-disciplinary team who may not have a common vocabulary. It is important to ensure good communication throughout the process to ensure the product itself communicates the design goals effectively. Methods include story telling; user profiles and personas; use cases or task scenarios; scenario-based design; mood boards; written briefs and specifications; storyboarding; and prototypes.

User profiles are generated from demographic data and lifestyle surveys. They can include textual and visual descriptions of key user groups. They are used to think through design solutions and for recruiting users for research. Mood boards are normally collages of photographic information that aim to generate a visual "personality" for the product or service. Mood boards can be created by designers or users or be the result of collaboration between the two. Mood boards are useful because they work at a nonverbal level where people may otherwise have difficulty expressing their wants and needs. Storyboards are time-based often with a narrative aspect. Storyboards can be sketches or low-fidelity screen shots of a user's interaction. Prototypes range from paper sketches to working interactive replicas. Information architecture can be communicated through formalised diagrams and charts or simple tree structures and hierarchies.

Empathy

These methods represent an approach aimed at gaining a deeper understanding and empathy for users. They include focus groups, diaries, workshops, participatory design, and immersion. Diaries can be used to record users' interaction with a product over time while workshops and participatory design involve users in the development team either directly or through a user advocate that champions their perspective. Participant observation, or "eat your own dog food," involves taking part in the activity or culture being observed, where the designer becomes a user. Molotch (2003) describes a method used by Ford designers in which they test products "dressed in what they call a 'third age' suit, with glasses and gloves, to simulate having the body and eyesight of a 70-year old" (p. 49).

Crossley (2004) describes a technique used to help designers develop an awareness of the target audience for male grooming products. It involved:

> rapidly immersing the design team into the lives, hearts and minds of people in a short space of time. The challenge for this project was to get young men inspired to tell us their own stories and express their emotions about a mundane functional activity"... "Character modelling [was used] ... where the team and sometimes the user has a kit with questions, cameras and collages, [that enabled them] to frame and understand the lifestyle of the person they are creating for. (pp. 38-39)

Personas are used to develop a shared vision of end users among development teams. They can be textual, visual, animated, or acted. One of the most important functions of personas is to get teams to think differently about people, as Cooper (1999) notes:

A fully realized, thoroughly defined user persona is a powerful tool. Until the user is precisely defined, the programmer can always imagine that *he* is the user. A completely pronounced user persona is key to the suppression of any tendency for the developer to usurp or distort the user persona's role. Long before a single line of code is written, a well-defined user persona becomes a remarkably effective tool for interaction design. (pp. 128-129)

Role-play is often used to encourage designers to empathise with users. Dramatic techniques can also help teams get into the minds of users and their values. Carmichael, Newell, Morgan, Dickinson, and Mival (2005) describe how the UTOPIA project improved designers' understanding of requirements. Using professional actors the project developed video scenarios of elderly people using technology. This was then shown to design teams to encourage them to design for others rather than themselves.

Speculation

In addition to understanding users' wants and needs, designers also need to speculate about new solutions and future trends. The Sony Walkman, for example, introduced an entirely novel mode of behaviour that no users had asked for. The decision to add text messaging to mobile phones was based on a speculation of how that functionality might be needed and by whom. The success of text messaging, however, was based on its uptake by an entirely different user group with its own needs and method of use. Designers may need to predict how users will adopt and adapt to a new product.

Here the solution is not tied to a particular technology or need but to reconceiving it. Good design requires up-to-date knowledge of what is possible and the ability to see beyond the obvious. There are a number of methods that achieve this. Jones (1990) sees speculation as "divergence, transformation and convergence" (p. 64-68) and suggests methods such as brainstorming (search for alternatives) and synetics (search for alternatives by analogy).

Rosson and Carroll (2002) describe scenario-based design in which scenarios are deployed throughout the design process to speculate the future. Scenarios can be used to challenge existing practices and encourage users and designers to think beyond the confines of the current situation. Dunne (1999) describes the use of scenarios to communicate design ideas and to stimulate thinking beyond the preexistent reality. He suggests that they can "push the viewer towards a more complex, emotional or revolutionary understanding of the problems posed" (p. 75). By testing design ideas rather than prototypes, the user's attention is shifted from the "aesthetics of construction" to the "aesthetics of use" (p. 73).

Speculation and innovation are, in part, about predicting the future, and a number of methods have been developed for this. The UK Cabinet Office published a Futurist's toolkit (UK Cabinet Office, 2001) describing six key methodologies for futures work, including quantitative and qualitative trend analyses, the Delphi survey method, scenario methods, wildcards, and future workshops. Cayol and Bonhoure (2004) describe a methodology which used sociological studies predicting the evolution of French people for the year 2025, to identify and evaluate future product concepts.

De Bono (1995) uses lateral thinking to generate different scenarios and ways of thinking about problems. De Bono's "Six Thinking Hats" (pp. 78-79) is a method for creative thinking but is also useful for developing empathetic intelligence. This method involves six team members role-playing different aspects of the design process. Thus the white hat is neutral and reflects back opinions and ideas, whereas the black hat is judgemental, cautionary and avoids mistakes. Speculative methods are important because design teams need to be able to see beyond user requirements and consider latent needs and potential opportunities.

Evaluation

Evaluation methods include auditing, standards compliance, and user testing. Evaluating may also use similar methods to exploration, with a shift in emphasis from discovery to checking outcomes against intentions. Does the product meet the design goals and/or the user expectations? Evaluation can be formative, conducted during the development of a product, or summative, conducted when a product is complete and is being used. Summative testing of an earlier version or a similar product can be useful to identify design goals, while summative testing of the product at the end of its design lifecycle is usually done for auditing and verification purposes. Feedback at this stage is of little use to the designer, the deadline has passed and the money is spent. Clearly formative testing is most helpful to a designer/developer. Gould and Lewis (1985) stress the importance of empirically testing design iterations throughout the design process. Evaluative tools such as heuristics are often used, although evidence suggests that they are no substitute for testing real users (e.g., Lee, Whalen, McEwen, & Latremouille, 1984). The EDF broadens the test and evaluative criteria from the traditional focus on cognitive and behavioural measures. Bonapace (2002) describes a method aimed at tapping into the four pleasures described by Jordan (2000), called the Sensorial Quality Assessment Method (SEQUAM) applied to the design of physical products in car manufacturing. User testing can combine empirical methods of behavioural observation with techniques such as co-discovery, think aloud and empathic interviewing, to tap into the subjective aspects of experience.

Establishing evaluation criteria at the beginning of a design process helps to focus the evaluation process from the beginning, although it is wise to allow some freedom for the evolution of design goals through iteration and to allow evaluative concerns to emerge (Hall 2005). The EDF can be used to generate evaluative criteria for qualities in each dimension and context of use.

APPLYING THE
EXPERIENCE DESIGN FRAMEWORK

The authors have used the EDF to adapt and focus methods for requirements research, brief development, ideation, and testing and have developed a range of services and training based on it. The EDF has been particularly useful in generating design goals, aiding decision making, and developing user-testing scenarios. Some examples of applications follow.

Visioning Workshops

Visioning workshops usually take place at the beginning of the design process, preferably before the brief is finalised. The workshop is structured around the experience design framework and fulfils a number of functions. Techniques are adapted to improve communication; to build literacy and a common language to describe the medium; and to build an empathic understanding of users and other contexts of use. Individual and group activities are facilitated by a researcher and recorded by a scribe. Activities include the following:

- Participants identify their vision of the project goals and their personal objectives, roles, and stories.
- Participants share their personal preferences and tastes by discussing examples of the product type or medium from visceral, behavioural, reflective, and social perspectives, and in so doing, build up a shared language for product qualities.
- Participants discuss the nature of the design problem from different perspectives and use speculative techniques to generate new ideas.
- Participants identify audience and stakeholders; then develop personas and scenarios based on different contexts of use.
- Participants share desired product qualities, functionality, and content from the perspective of the stakeholders identified.
- Participants identify and prioritise product goals and develop evaluative criteria.

By the end of the workshop, participants have prepared the foundations of a creative brief, have started working together as a team, and have formed a common language and shared understanding of the project goals.

Contextual Interviews

Contextual interviews take place prior to detailed requirements specifications and may follow a visioning workshop. Firstly, stakeholders are identified and a representative sample recruited. The aim is to survey a large sample and to iteratively develop knowledge about the design problem. In this context, as many as 50 users may be involved and the focus is to gain as full a set of requirements as is possible in a short space of time. The interviews are semi-structured over approximately 30 minutes and are conducted within the context of use. Their exact format is dependent on whether the product is a new one or a refinement of an existing one. In the former case, the researcher works with low-fidelity prototypes and in the latter case with the existing product. Activities include the following:

- Stakeholders are asked to provide documents, processes, and artefacts involved in the tasks.
- Interviewees are asked to complete a persona template with details about themselves, their interests, and their lives.
- Interviewees are asked to identify critical tasks, events, and work-arounds with the existing product.
- Interviewees identify relationships with other users/stakeholders in their use of the product, and what other tools or products they use in association with the tasks.
- Interviewees are asked to describe key tasks with the product and/or walk through a task. The interviewer elicits details of any prior knowledge, expertise, or skills being applied to the tasks and probes for emotional responses to aspects of the activity.
- Interviewees are asked to describe how the product fits in with their daily life.

The results of interviews inform the production of anonymous personas and use scenarios, which are used to communicate the requirements to the development team and build their empathy with the users.

Conceptual Design Workshops

Conceptual design workshops involve development teams rethinking the design problem and considering potential solutions. The aim is to generate a number of alternative design concepts. These are then evaluated and then "worked up" for initial user testing or participatory prototyping (see what follows). Workshop members usually include members of the development team plus representatives of key stakeholders. The workshops are structured around the EDF and activities include the following:

- Participants reconceptualise the design problem in terms of the EDF's contexts.
- Participants brainstorm and develop a number of design concepts.
- The concepts are discussed and similar solutions are merged together and evaluated against the EDF's qualities.
- The process is repeated until a number of distinctly different and viable concepts have been generated and can be tested on users.

Participatory Prototyping

Participatory prototyping combines the skills of the development team with user feedback. Prototypes are developed of content structures, interaction flow, and layouts. Initial prototypes are developed and users are asked to critique or adapt the prototype with specific reference to the qualities of the EDF and the dimensions of experience. Designers interpret this feedback and develop further prototypes, with the focus on interaction and structure, and later on look and feel issues. Activities include the following:

- Users are asked to card sort content or to map out their expectations of content domains and structures.
- Users are asked to "walk through" prototypes in order to carry out their key tasks, using the think aloud method.
- Responses to the organisation of the interface and the terminology used are elicited.
- Users perform tasks with the prototype and are asked to speculate on improvements, applications, or additional features.
- Where trade-off or multiple interfaces exists users sort the prototypes on the basis of their preference.

By the end of the process a complete low-fidelity prototype has been developed that has been iterated around the qualities of the EDF.

Audience Reception Workshops

Audience workshops review the final prototype design. Users are recruited to represent the key stakeholder groups. The prototype then undergoes a group critique that tests the solution against the initial requirements and evaluative criteria gathered by the visioning workshop and contextual interviews. As well as ensuring that the prototype is suitable the workshops gauge barriers and opportunities to take up and adoption of a new product or design. In addition, it provides the development team with a rationale and evidence of the suitability of the final design solution. Activities include the following:

- Group walk-throughs of the prototype
- Identification of conflicts and trade-offs
- Comparison of look and feel prototypes
- Quantitative research methods and user attitude measurement

Post Implementation Research

Post implementation research reviews the application after launch. Unlike traditional usability that focuses on requirements and development, this research is necessary to monitor changing user needs throughout the product's lifecycle. A user cohort is recruited and is asked to provide regular feedback based on the EDF. As well as ensuring that maintenance and new features are accepted by users this research is important to identify new products and user needs. Activities include the following:

- User diaries
- Online discussion groups and surveys
- Focus groups and ongoing user testing

CONCLUSIONS AND THE FUTURE OF WEB EXPERIENCES

The EDF was created in response to the needs of clients and has generated research, which has fed back into the design of services. The EDF has been applied to a number of internal and external products and has been refined through practice. The EDF is meant to provoke discussion, raise questions, challenge assumptions, and generate alternatives.

Every design problem is different and so it is necessary to deploy a range of research methods to support the work of the digital media designer. Nevertheless, these methods should be focused around the key issues for UCD, which is to understand users, the tasks they undertake, and the contexts in which they function. They provide a rich understanding of users from which the creative designer can create usable and desirable products. The EDF helps teams focus requirements research and can be used in a workshop environment with a range of stakeholders and users. The EDF can be used as a brainstorming tool that aims to map out the requirement and the process, and possible solutions from the team and stakeholders.

If methods are focused around qualities, dimensions, and contexts of experience, they provide a richer understanding of users from which the designer can create usable and desirable products. The EDF provides a reminder of the complexity of the user experience and can be used throughout the design lifecycle.

REFERENCES

Bevan, N. (2000). *Esprit Project 28015 Trump: Cost benefit analysis*. Retrieved April 26, 2002, from http://www.usability.serco.com/trump/documents/D3.0_Cost%20benefit_v1.1.doc

Beyer, H., & Holtzblatt, K. (1998). Contextual design: Designing customer-centred systems. In S. Card, J. Grudin, M. Linton, J. Nielson, & T. Skelley (series Eds.). *Morgan Kaufmann series in interactive technologies*. San Fransisco: Morgan Kaufmann.

Bonapace, L. (2002). Linking product properties to pleasure: The sensorial quality assessment method — SEQUAM. In W. S. Green & P. W. Jordan (Eds.), *Pleasure with products: Beyond usability* (pp. 187-217). London: Taylor & Francis.

Brooks, F. P. (1975). *The mythical man-month: Essays in software engineering*. London; Reading, MA: Addison-Wesley.

Campbell-Kelly, M., & Aspray, W. (1996). *Computer: A history of the information machine*. New York: Basic Books.

Carmichael, A., Newell, A. F., Morgan, M., Dickinson, A., & Mival, O. (2005, April 5-8). *Using theatre and film to represent user requirements*. Paper presented at Include 2005, Royal College of Art, London. Retrieved from http://www.hhrc.rca.ac.uk/programmes/include/2005/proceedings/pdf/carmichaelalex.pdf

Cayol, A., & Bonhoure, P. (2004). Prospective design oriented towards customer pleasure. In D. McDonagh, P. Hekkert, J. van Erp, & D. Gyi (Eds.), *Design and emotion: The experience of everyday things* (pp. 104-108). London: Taylor & Francis.

Cooper, A. (1999). *The inmates are running the asylum. Why high-tech products drive us crazy and how to restore the sanity*. Indianapolis, IN: SAMS.

Cross, N. (2001). Designerly ways of knowing: Design discipline versus design science. *Design Issues, 17*(3), 49-55.

Crossley, L. (2004). Bridging the emotional gap. In D. McDonagh, P. Hekkert, J. van Erp, & D. Gyi (Eds.), *Design and emotion: The experience of everyday things* (pp. 37-42). London: Taylor & Francis.

Csikszentmihalyi, M. (1991). *Flow: The psychology of optimal experience*. New York: Harper Collins.

Curtis, H. (2002). *MTIV: Process, inspiration and practice for the new media designer*. Indianapolis, IN: New Riders.

De Bono, E. (1995). *Serious creativity. Using the power of lateral thinking to create new ideas*. London: Harper Collins.

DeJean, P. H. (2002). Difficulties and pleasure? In W. S. Green & P. W. Jordan (Eds.), *Pleasure with products: Beyond usability* (pp. 147-150). London: Taylor and Francis.

DiBlas, N., Paolini, P., Speroni, M., & Capodieci, A. (2004). Enhancing accessibility for visually impaired users: The Munch exhibition. In D. Bearman & J. Trant (Eds.), *Museums and the Web 2004: Selected papers* (pp. 89-97). Ontario, Canada: Archives and Museum Informatics.

Dunne, A. (1999). *Hertzian tales: Electronic products, aesthetic experience and critical design*. London: Royal College of Art.

Fiore, S. (2003). *Supporting design for aesthetic experience*. Paper presented at HCI, the Arts and the Humanities, International HCI Workshop, King's Manor, York, UK.

Fuller, B. (1969). *Utopia or oblivion*. New York: Bantam Books.

Fulton-Suri, J. (2004). Design Expression and human experience: Evolving design practice. In D. McDonagh, P. Hekkert, J. van Erp, & J. Gyi (Eds.), *Design and emotion: The experience of everyday things* (pp. 13-17). London: Taylor & Francis.

Garfinkel, H. (1967). *Studies in ethnomethodology*. Englewood Cliffs, NJ: Prentice Hall.

Givechi, R., & Velázquez, V. L. (2004). Positive space. In D. McDonagh, P. Hekkert, J. van Erp, & D. Gyi (Eds.), *Design and emotion: The experience of everyday things* (pp. 43-47). London: Taylor & Francis.

Gould, J. D. (1995). How to design usable systems (Excerpt). In R. M. Baecker, J. Grudin, W. Buxton, & S. Greenberg (Eds.), *Readings in human-computer interaction: Toward the year 2000* (2nd ed., pp. 93-121). Morgan Kaufmann.

Gould, J. D., & Lewis, C. (1985). Designing for usability: Key principles and what designers think. *Communications of the ACM, 28*(3), 300-311.

Hackos, J. T., & Redish, J. C. (1998). *User and task analysis for interface design*. New York: John Wiley & Sons.

Hall, R. (2005). *The value of visual exploration: Understanding cultural activities with young people*. UK: The Public.

Hammer, D. K., & Reymen, I. M. M. J. (2004). The role of emotion in design reflection. In D. McDonagh, P. Hekkert, J. van Erp, & D. Gyi (Eds.), *Design and emotion: The experience of everyday things* (pp. 421-425). London: Taylor & Francis.

Harrison, M., & Thimbleby, H. (1990). *Formal methods in human-computer interaction*. Cambridge, UK: Cambridge University Press.

Heath, C., & Luff, P. (2000). *Technology in action*. Cambridge, UK: Cambridge University Press.

Hochschild, A. R. (1983). *The managed heart: Commercialization of human feeling*. London; Berkeley: University of California Press.

International Organization for Standardization (ISO). (1998). *Ergonomic Requirements for Office Work With Visual Display Terminals (VDTs) — Part 11 Guidance on Usability* (9241-11). Geneva, Switzerland: ISO.

International Organization for Standardization (ISO). (1999). *Human-Centred Design Processes for Interactive Systems* (13407). Geneva, Switzerland: ISO.

International Organization for Standardization (ISO). (2000). *Software Engineering — Product Quality — Part 1: Quality Model* (9126-1). Geneva, Switzerland: ISO.

Jefsioutine, M., & Knight, J. (2004, November 17-21). *Methods for experience design: The experience design framework.* Paper presented at Future Ground, Design Research Society International Conference 2004, Melbourne.

Jones, J. C. (1990). *Design methods* (2nd ed.). London: Design Council, David Fulton Publishing.

Jones, B., Valdez, G., Nowakowski, J., & Rasmussen, C. (1994). *Designing learning and technology for educational reform.* Oak Brook, IL: North Central Regional Educational Laboratory.

Jordan, P. W. (2000). *Designing pleasurable products.* London: Taylor & Francis.

Knight, J. (2004, September). *Design for life: Ethics, empathy and experience.* Paper presented at Design for Life, British HCI Group Conference, Leeds, UK.

Knight, J., & Jefsioutine, M. (2002, September). Relating usability research to design practice. In M. Maguire & K. Adeboye (Eds.), *European Usability Professionals Association Conference Proceedings* (Vol. 3, pp. 2-7). EUPA Conference. London: British Computer Society.

Knight, J., & Jefsioutine, M. (2003, October 14). Attitudes to Web accessibility. *Usability News.* Retrieved October 2003, from http://www.usabilitynews.com/news/article1321.asp.

Lee, E. S., Whalen, T., McEwen, S., & Latremouille, S. (1984). Optimizing the design of menu pages for information retrieval. *Ergonomics, 27,* 1051-1069.

Liddle, D. (1996). Design of the conceptual model; An interview with David Liddle. In T. Winograd (Ed.), *Bringing design to software* (pp. 17-31). New York: Addison-Wesley.

Liu, Y. (2003). The aesthetic and the ethic dimensions of human factors and design. *Ergonomics, 46*(13/14), 1293-1305.

Maguire, M. (2004). Does usability = attractiveness? In D. McDonagh, P. Hekkert, J. van Erp, & D. Gyi (Eds.), *Design and emotion: The experience of everyday things* (pp. 303-307). London: Taylor & Francis.

Maslow, A. (1970). *Motivation and personality* (2nd ed.). New York: Harper & Row.

McDonagh-Philp, D., & Lebbon, C. (2000). The emotional domain in product design. *The Design Journal, 3*(1), 31-43.

Molotch, H. (2003). *Where stuff comes from: How toasters, toilets, cars, computers and many other things come to be as they are.* London; New York: Routledge.

Norman, D. (2004). *Emotional design: Why we love [or hate] everyday things.* New York: Basic Books.

Ortony, A., Clore, G. L., & Collins, A. (1988). *The cognitive structure of emotions.* Cambridge; New York; Melbourne: Cambridge University Press.

Quinn, C. N. (1997). Engaging Learning. *Instructional Technology Forum (ITFORUM@ UGA.CC.UGA.EDU),* Invited Presenter. Retrieved June 19, 2003, from http://itech1.coe.uga.edu/itforum/paper18/paper18.html

Reeves, B., & Nass, C. (2002). *The media equation: How people treat computers, television, and new media like real people and places.* Stanford, CA: Center for the Study of Language and Information Publications.

Rittel, H., & Webber, M. (1973). Dilemmas in a general theory of planning. *Policy Sciences, 4,* 155-169. Amsterdam: Elsevier Scientific Publishing Company Inc., 155-169.

Rosson, M. B., & Carroll, J. M. (2002). *Usability engineering: Scenario-based development of human computer interaction*. San Francisco: Morgan Kaufmann.

Rothstein, P. (2002, September 5-7). a (x 4): Combining ethnography, scenario-building, and design to explore user experience. In D. Durling & J. Shackleton (Eds), *Common Ground Proceedings of the Design Research Society International Conference 2002* (pp. 945-960). Stoke-on-Trent: Staffordshire University Press.

Shedroff, N. (2001) *Experience design 1*. Indianapolis, IN: New Riders.

Spillers, F. (2004). *Emotion as a cognitive artifact and the design implications for products that are perceived as pleasurable*. Paper presented at Design and Emotion 2004, Ankara, Turkey.

Suchman, L. A. (1987). Plans and situated actions: The problem of human machine communication. Cambridge, UK: Cambridge University Press.

Tiger, L. (1992). *The pursuit of pleasure*. Boston: Little, Brown and Company.

UK Cabinet Office. (2001). *A futurist's toolbox: Methodologies in futures work*. United Kingdom: Performance and Innovation Unit, Strategic Futures Team. Retrieved June 12, 2006, from http://www.strategy.gov.uk/downloads/files/toolbox.pdf

UK Disability Rights Commission. (2004). *The Web: Access and inclusion for disabled people*. London: TSO.

World Wide Web Consortium (W3C). (1999). *Web Content Accessibility Guidelines 1.0.* Retrieved August 26, 2004, from http://www.w3.org/TR/WAI-WEBCONTENT/checkpoint-list.html

Chapter VII

Innovations in Collaborative Web Design:
Methods to Facilitate Team Learning During Design

Madelon Evers, Human Shareware, Kapelstraat, The Netherlands

ABSTRACT

In this chapter we analyse the link between multi-disciplinary design and team learning, which, we argue, need to be supported in equal measure during Web design projects. We introduce a new approach to collaborative Web design, called the Design and Learning Methodology, as a way to support these two processes. The approach involves many stakeholders, including future Web site users in design decision making. It structures stakeholder participation through multi-disciplinary design teams (MDTs). It uses professional facilitators to guide design and learning processes. Facilitation tools are drawn from a combination of action learning methods, which help MDTs reflect and act on new knowledge gained from design experiences and human centred design, which is an international protocol for achieving quality in interactive systems design (International Organization for Standardization, 2000). Based on our research, we describe how facilitating the process of learning from design contributes to continuous improvement in collaborative competencies needed for Web design.

INTRODUCTION:
THE NEED FOR A NEW APPROACH TO
COLLABORATIVE WEB DESIGN

One of the main challenges in Web design projects is to "align" technical, human, and business requirements into one central design. To achieve this, theorists and practitioners alike point to a need for a collaborative approach to Web design. The assumption is that by stimulating collaboration between technical and nontechnical disciplines, companies can improve the quality and usability of designs and achieve early acceptance of technology by customers. Companies increasingly set up multi-disciplinary design teams (MDTs), in order to bring a wide range of expertise to bear on Web design problems. MDTs are seen as a logical and efficient way to achieve design success. However, most Web design projects continue to fail, as is well known from years of reports in business and design research literature. Why is this so?

A number of design research studies show that when nontechnical specialists and other stakeholders participate in an MDT, they expect to be allowed to co-determine the design (Bekker & Long, 1998; Valkenburg, 1996). However, when nontechnical people and other stakeholders participate in multi-disciplinary design, decisions tend to not reflect input from these people; instead, they often end up accepting solutions generated by technical decision makers, who tend to veto or ignore the critical advice team members try to give them (Ball & Ormerod, 2000; Buchanan, 1991; Cooper, 1999). Design becomes a process of "contested collaboration" between MDT members (Sonnenwald, 1993), which is difficult to sustain when intensive differences in opinion must be negotiated (Toerpel, 2001).

Other studies indicate that design projects typically do not generate decisions through participation of all MDT members (Ball, Lambell, Reed, & Reid, 2001; Olson et al., 1996; Turner & Cross, 2000). Walz, Elam, and Curtis (1993), Marchman (1998), and Steiner, Gabriele, Swersey, Messler, and Foley (2001) indicate, MDTs do not engage in knowledge sharing as a team. Rather, individuals carve off a small piece of the work and avoid interacting much with other team members. Shared understanding is defined by Flood (1999) as consisting of three types of understanding. These are:

- **Consensus:** in which there is strong agreement between team members and where the agreement sacrifices individual needs and identities for a meta-definition of what is needed
- **Accommodation:** where finding some common ground between people is achieved while preserving some differences in opinion, so that individuals can change the meaning in repeated cycles of negotiation and learning
- **Tolerance:** which means maintaining diverse identities with no necessary overlap, allowing disagreement to exist within a plethora of viewpoints

Eisenberg (1990) suggests that tolerance is probably the most important form of shared understanding for multi-disciplinary work. Tolerance puts less emphasis on achieving complete consensus and more on making connections and facilitating communication among team members. Tolerance for diversity implies that people from different disciplines feel mutual respect for each other and trust in knowledge from other disciplines, even when they do not feel empathy with people representing that knowledge (Hill, Song, Don, & Agogino,

2001; Homan, 2001; Olsen, Cutkosky, Tenenbaum, & Gruber, 1994; Valkenburg, 1998; Walz et al., 1993). Marchman (1998) found that engineering students working in MDTs lack confidence in the value team-based decision making, harbouring serious doubts about the abilities of other MDT members and showing little respect for the knowledge represented by other disciplines assigned to their project. This attitude causes inefficiency as it means that people must first overcome their personal hesitations before being able to collaborate on a design project.

Our research (Evers, 2004) shows that managers consider most design project failures as resulting from a persistent lack of design-related skills in MDTs, including their ability to:

- Define clear objectives for a design project
- Tackle complex problems as a team
- Develop insight into the scope of a project
- Streamline communication between stakeholders
- Manage collaborative decision making
- Share and integrate knowledge productively

Notably, the design-related skills that MDTs tend to lack are not the technical expertise and content-oriented skills that are generally well developed in programmers, interaction designers, Web developers, and other engineering professionals. Rather, these are collective, process-oriented, management, and social skills that develop through interaction in groups and through cumulative design experience on the job, not from theoretical knowledge or technical specialisation. We argue that if a lack of these collective skills is such a significant cause of Web project failure, then a concerted effort to stimulate MDTs to develop these skills *as a team* is critical for project success. The question is, how can we help MDTs improve these skills in practice?

To answer this question, we explore the important link between multi-disciplinary design and team learning processes, which, we argue, need to be supported in equal measure during Web design projects. Using a case study of a failed Web design project, we described how certain approaches to design do not (adequately) support multi-disciplinary team learning within the multi-disciplinary design process, and may actually work *against* the ability of MDTs to collaborate and find appropriate design solutions. The case is based on our professional experiences with an MDT involved in a Web design project that was recently carried out in a large European broadcasting company. After discussing the case, we will go on to propose our new approach to collaborative Web design as a way to alleviate this problem over time.

The Case of a Failed Web Design Project

Context: Cross Media Design
A Web design project is launched by a European broadcasting organisation to develop a new online community resource Web site, as a complimentary medium to support a new television series. The MDT assigned to the design project consists of creative and technical professionals from various disciplines and departments, including a project leader; a team leader who acts as a human resources manager from the new media department; program-

mers; senior editors; interaction designers; a marketing and communications manager; and a television producer responsible for ensuring brand quality on the Web site.

The Design Meetings

Before the first meeting, an agenda is set by the team leader and the project leader to brainstorm about the content and structure of the future system. The project leader is in charge of the kick-off meeting, presenting a consumer and business case for a solution he has in mind, with a complete scenario; statistics for Web site use and television viewer rates; and technical options for Web site design. A deadline is set for Web site launch within 7 months. The site must coincide with the first television broadcast of the new programme.

After the presentation, the programmers and the interaction designer have many questions: Is this really the kind of Web site that the broadcaster wants? What kind of interaction does the public expect? How does the Web site support the television programme? How will the Web site be implemented? Can this project be carried when expenditures are being cut in the new media department? The project leader's first response to these questions is that he does not want to go back into fundamental questions about research and planning; he feels he has done his homework and is presenting the best first step. The television producer and the marketing and communications manager agree with the project leader; they perceive the desire to delve into what they see as organisational and marketing questions as a waste of time. The marketing and communications manager suggests that the "techies" focus on developing a solid interactive solution as quickly as possible, since the television show cannot be delayed by Web site production. The project leader emphasises that there is little time for the MDT to consider too many innovative options. The point is to compliment the existing television show with Web site material and to make sure that a community of fans grows up around the programme.

At the second meeting, the project leader asks for ideas from the technical specialists about how to fill in the solution he presented at the first meeting. Their analysis of design problems for the Web site indicates that the issues are quite complex and not as simple as "complimenting the television show" might suggest. The MDT spends over 3 hours discussing details, with no conclusions drawn at the end of the session, but with much confusion about what needs to be done during production. After the meeting, the team leader, the senior editor, and the interaction designer meet separately to discuss their discontent with the project. They decide to brainstorm to come up with a more creative solution for the Web site. As the interaction designer hears her colleagues' ideas, however, she rapidly dismisses their ideas, stating that they do not offer a realistic technical picture of the navigation involved on the Web site. The team leader argues that the concept is far too complex and he is worried about delaying implementation. The senior editor emphasises that budget cuts in their department are coming up and argues for a simpler design and lower-cost development of the Web site content.

Shift in Design Meeting Dynamics

The design discussion now shifts to how to make the simplest system, in the shortest time, on existing content, at the cheapest price. The interaction designer tends to dominate the discussion, and the meeting ends with the decision to make a downscaled version of the initial plan presented by the project leader in the first meeting. The trio briefly discuss their concept with the project leader, who then writes an adjusted project plan and sends this by e-mail to the rest of the MDT. In the plan, tasks are divided among the different disciplines and departments represented by MDT members, and instructions are given for delivering the elements of the Web site set out in the plan.

There is no follow up meeting to discuss the project plan with all MDT members present. Instead, over the next 6 months, MDT members work in their own departments, with separate priorities and tasks. At most design meetings, the project leader invites mainly the interaction designer, the senior editor, and the television producer, reserving consultation with programmers and other team members for ad hoc feedback on decisions. When other MDT members do attend a design meeting they tend to not contribute, preferring to remain quiet to hear what it is they have to do. When the project leader asks if there are questions during these design meetings, there are hardly any. The project leader reports to his managers that he is satisfied; people seem to be getting on with it now; there is not much contention between the new media and television departments, and subteams are executing tasks relatively within budget. E-mail communication is limited to a checklist of technical deliverables, updated periodically, and discussions within the MDT are limited to separate meetings to discuss specific design deliverables per specialisation.

Dealing with Unexpected Problems

Near the end of the project, however, the project leader discovers that the graphical user interface made by the interaction designer is not compatible with the systems interface developed by the programmers. As a result, the database technology underlying the Web site does not mesh with the navigation set-up designed for the interface. MDT members get into heated discussions about this problem and disagree on how to solve it. The project leader cannot solve the problem either, as he disagrees with both the programmers and the interaction designer on their solutions.

Seeing potential disaster looming for the television broadcast date, the project leader puts more pressure on the MDT members to deliver the final version of the Web site. Deliverables are, however, increasingly delayed. The interface designer refuses to deliver multimedia content as long as it is unclear how the modules will be deployed in the Web site interface. The marketing and communications manager cannot organise communication about the Web site, as it is still unclear how the Web site will work and whether it will be online by the time the television programme airs. After weeks of interpersonal conflict between the new media and television departments, in which the project leader for the Web site project unsuccessfully tries to force a solution, upper management steps in. The decision is made to outsource the project to a third-party, Web development company who guarantees to design and deliver before the television broadcast date. This executive decision gets the Web site work done, but does not make the MDT happy about the project at all.

Rapid Closure of the Project

Rather than dealing with this disappointment, there is no further contact between the members of the television department and the new media department. Communication with the third party company goes entirely through the project leader, the marketing and communications manager, and upper management. After deliverables are completed, there is a rush to implement before the television show airs. The project leader informs management when to expect the Web site launch. Within the television and new media departments, there is no time to do another test to ensure that the Web site really fits with the television show, that it meets user needs, and that it can be updated and maintained by editors across the organisation, in the manner intended. Instead, instructions for testing and editing are e-mailed to those responsible. Due to delays, there is also no time left to introduce the Web site to the public before television broadcasts begin.

After the launch, Web site users appear confused about how to use the content on the site, and visitor statistics for the Web site fall far below the viewer rates achieved for television. It is difficult to force viewers to join the online community, and the new media department, frustrated with the complexity of the technology delivered, increasingly opt not to maintain or update content from the television programme on the Web site. There is no capacity or money left to develop the Web site further after the television programme has aired for a number of months. The team leader of the new media department considers the project failed and refuses to accept costs of the system as part of his annual budget. Television refuses to accept the costs as well because they feel the third party company is responsible for the interaction accompanying their broadcasts. The third party company has, however, delivered according to demands from upper management, and point to a lack of solid briefing from upper management and from the MDT, with which they could meet the broadcaster's needs. Discussions reach an impasse.

Project "Success"

The project leader writes a technical and financial report, indicating that the project was, in fact, successful, since required technical components for his original plan were delivered (almost) on time and within budget. Upper management makes no comment on the project leader's report and the project is considered closed. Within a month after launching the Web site, the MDT is formally disbanded. New projects immediately demand full attention, so there is no time to evaluate what happened and how the project failed. There is also little time for informal evaluation and contact between MDT members, as they are not assigned to the same productions in the next year.

Analysis of the Case

What does this case illustrate about the ability of MDTs to collaborate effectively during Web design? Firstly, the project was characterised by a group dynamic in which certain dominant team members imposed preconceived solutions on others, seeking consensus rather than drawing on input from the whole MDT to discover viable solutions for design problems. Since there was no concerted effort to work in a truly multi-disciplinary manner, specialists did not invest in sharing knowledge and therefore could not solve these problems effectively.

Secondly, ad hoc meetings and the pressure on individual team members led to a lack of openness and questioning of assumptions, as well as an inability to deal with interpersonal conflict. Without a shared understanding, MDT members lost the desire to learn from each other. The downward spiral of miscommunication was exacerbated by top-down decisions made by upper management. This ended up having the opposite effect than was undoubtedly intended. Rather than ensure quality in design and improve the design process, MDT members were divided and left out of the process still more. The project leader lost control of the team, and discontent mounted rapidly as the project progressed.

Thirdly, as the MDT had no clear strategy or design approach for thinking and acting collaboratively on design issues, the design process became a series of reactionary actions from start to end of the project.

This case indicates the importance of being able to learn from one another as a team, during multi-disciplinary design work. Management certainly felt the full impact of the lack of team learning that went on by the time the project failed. However, even after failure, there was no evaluation at management level or within the MDT. No learning came out of the collective experiences with this Web design project, and no structured and serious consideration was given about how to improve design performance in the future. Instead, the project was simply "written off."

The Link Between Project Failure and Lack of Learning in MDTs

Lei (1994) notes that many design projects fail because teams are incapable of faithfully reflecting and integrating multiple types of knowledge and perspectives in their design decisions. Knowledge integration cannot take place without learning (Homan, 2001). Learning involves exploring as many known elements and solutions as possible, integrating these, and then creating something new out of that mix. It requires people to develop the collective skill to leap into a new frame of thinking about something that did not exist before. In teams, people need to draw on both individual and team-based learning, in order to create relevant knowledge.

In individual learning, people focus on in-depth information from their own discipline or specialisation. For example, an interface designer learns more about technical usability testing, to expand their understanding of how graphics and text displays in an interface are used. This information is needed to be able to meet changing needs of customers in relation to Web design. A person's capacity to learn individually and to represent what he/she is learning determines the quality of information available to the whole team about the state of knowledge they have at any point in time. However, individual learning gives only limited insight into the whole, complex process of design. It does not provide complete insight or experience with all facets of design; it simply presents a mosaic of decisions made and does not guarantee shared understanding in the MDT. It is therefore ineffective to rely only on individual learning during collaborative Web design projects. It is equally important to enhance the MDT's capacity to learn as a team. When the MDT tries to understand design problems *as a team*, rather than separating communication processes and remaining within specialised or personal models of knowledge and experience, the team can create a shared memory, or collective mental model, of the whole, complex design process.

A collective mental model emerges from the process of intensive communication and participation in the MDT. It is then constantly modified through ongoing social interaction inside and outside the team (Homan, 2001). According to Van der Veer and Puerta Melguizo (2003), a collective mental model can be made explicit when expressed through some form of representation or language agreed upon beforehand. By making collective mental models explicit, a team shares experiences, memories, and stories and finds out whether they are capable of working, as a team, towards a mutually acceptable solution. However, research by Sole and Edmonson (2002) shows that team learning tends to remain ad hoc and informal in nature, depending on the personal interests of MDT members to look beyond their own individual specialisation, to stimulate knowledge exchange with people in a network. Team learning shaped by individual initiatives brings only an individual understanding of design problems to the MDT. Schwalbe (2000) states that team members need to develop skills in working proactively to share expertise beyond the individual's personal "island of knowledge" and to contribute knowledge to other disciplines and processes in an organisation.

In our design consultancy work, we therefore focus on helping MDTs create and share representations of collective mental models from the very start of their design project. We notice that when sufficient attention was paid to the process of team learning, team members began to learn in a more productive and sustainable manner, over time. We have found that, once a MDT learns to share collective mental models, new team members could draw on the knowledge developed later on in the project or in future design situations. We will now describe the new approach we have developed to facilitate MDTs to achieve collaborative team learning during multi-disciplinary design work.

EXPLORING A NEW DESIGN APPROACH: INTEGRATING HUMAN-CENTRED DESIGN AND ACTION LEARNING METHODS

The approach we introduce in this section moves away from traditional technical engineering methods to embrace a different philosophy of design. Our approach sees design fundamentally as a learning process, in which the key is to manage the creation of relevant and new human knowledge by supporting social interaction and integrated organisational processes. As shown in the aforementioned case study, MDTs depend on effective team learning in order to be able to accommodate divergent or conflicting views in the process of collaborative decision making. Indeed, the quality of a design can be said to depend on the MDT's collective skills in learning as a team to develop mutual trust, maintain productive relationships, and share knowledge effectively throughout a design project, as opposed to only developing specialised skills in the production of technology. We call our approach the Design and Learning Methodology, as modelled in Figure 1.

The approach is based on three main components: (1) human-centred design, (2) action learning, and (3) facilitation. Each component of the model is described hereafter.

Human-Centred Design

Human-centred design is a participatory and holistic design method, described in quality process management norms published by the International Organization for Standardization of Geneva (ISO, 2000). The difference between human-centred design and other design approaches is that it moves the translation of a design solution into functional, technical specifications up to later phases of a project. More time is taken in first phases to consider quality of design as related to human needs, and to ensure that the design process is managed appropriately to address these needs at all times. Other design methodologies tend to rush or skip these considerations, moving rapidly to functional modelling and to building and implementing technology.

In human-centred design, the goal is to produce a set of design solutions that has multiple, rather than singular solutions contained within it. Solutions represent changes in social, organisational, as well as technical systems. Human-centred design focuses on the usability and usefulness of a design, as determined by personal, group, and organisational contexts of use, rather than being determined only by technical considerations. Although usability focuses on how humans understand technology, usefulness counters this by focusing on how technology is suited to support human needs. Human-centred design demands that the balance between usability and usefulness is made at all times. Hence the impact of a human-centred design project is generally more encompassing than traditional technical engineering contexts, in which the emphasis is on usability, not necessarily on usefulness of design.

Limitations of Human-Centred Design

Although human-centred design appears to be well suited to facilitating MDTs to collaborate effectively during Web design, it is important to consider the context in which human-centred design tends to be implemented in organisations. The protocol for human-centred design, as described in the ISO 9000 series (2000) documentation and certification procedure, places enormous demands on the capability and maturity level of organisations. One can question whether MDTs have the competencies required to achieve human-centred design in the first place, that is, from the start of a design project. As established earlier, the absence of these collective skills means that design projects can continue to fail. To help MDTs master the process of human-centred design, we draw on action learning methods and integrate this into our model of the design and learning methodology.

Figure 1. Basic model of the design and learning methodology

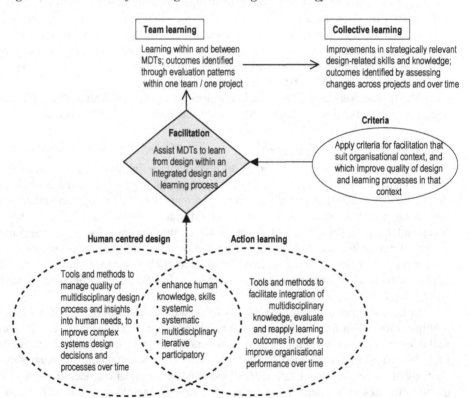

Action Learning

Action learning is a process in which multi-disciplinary teams plan actions, follow up on actions, and evaluate actions in strategically relevant ways (McAdam & Leonard, 1998). Action learning involves small groups of people working as a team, or *set*, to solve real, complex problems in their organisation. At the same time, the set evaluates what they are learning from their problem-solving process, and how their learning can benefit their *set* and the larger organisation or context in which they work. It requires teams to commit to questioning actions and assumptions in a critical manner, and to synthesising questions and answers into a holistic perspective of the whole problem they are dealing with (Garvin, 2000).

As shown in Figure 1, human-centred design and action learning methods have a number of common elements:

- Both methods aim to enhance human knowledge and skills, rather than seeking ways to reduce learning or replace human involvement in organisations through automation.
- Both methods are systemic, aiming for holistic insights into complex design/learning problems.
- Both methods are systematic, structuring design/learning processes in consistent cycles of planning, action and review.
- Both depend on multi-disciplinary teams to represent diverse points of view on a problem.
- Both aim for iteration or multiple adjustments, in plans, actions, and reviews produced during learning/design processes.
- Both processes are participatory, assuming intensive group interaction and communication will take place, rather than allowing passivity in, or exclusion from, team processes to emerge.

Facilitation

Facilitation is modelled in the design and learning methodology as a way in which to guide action learning and human-centred design processes simultaneously. Facilitation is not meant to be dramatic and sudden, but dynamic, flexible, and continuous. Facilitation is essential at the beginning of a collaboration process, when human-centred design and action learning methods may be completely new to an MDT, and the MDT itself is not yet a cohesive group with a shared understanding of the context in which they work. Facilitators must have skills in mentoring or coaching teams, as well as having extensive experience in design. At Human Shareware we identify this combination of skills in our design coaches. According to Zuber-Skerritt (2002), the key role of a facilitator is to ask open-ended questions about what is being done, about how achievements can be improved upon, and about how the team can help each other to change. Facilitation is a key process because, as we found in our research (Evers, 2004), MDTs have difficulty developing collaborative design skills on their own and require support to learn these skills as a team, on the job. Facilitators are responsible for creating and introducing tools for supporting design and learning in one, integrated process. The tools must be learned and applied easily by MDT members, in daily design practice.

Criteria

A facilitator can support both action learning and human-centred design, by helping an MDT to clarify the criteria by which they wish to improve their design process, by which they wish to develop their design skills, or by which they wish to expand their knowledge of the design problems by learning more about them as a team. The facilitator also helps MDTs carry out consistent design reviews, based on clear criteria that are defined before-hand and planned as a part of a process of achievable actions taken in the context of their particular organisation.

IMPLEMENTING THE NEW DESIGN APPROACH IN EUROPEAN ORGANISATIONS

To date, the design and learning methodology has been developed and applied through action research and design consultancy work in a range of European companies, including financial service organisations such as Achmea NV, broadcasting companies such as the British Broadcasting Corporation, Danish Radio and Television, and Dutch broadcasters such as IKON and NCRV, as well as in professional engineering training programmes at institutes such as SAE Technology College, Media Academie Hilversum, and Lusofona University Portugal. In this section, we share results of introducing the design and learning methodology into a range of European companies and then describe three practical tools we developed to facilitate MDTs to engage in action learning and in human-centred design in one, integrated process.

Table 1 is a general summary of results gained from using the design and learning methodology in a range of European companies. Data in Table 1 represent verbatim feedback gained from MDT members and managers who evaluated their own design projects.

Methodology

Now we will now describe three practical facilitation tools selected from a much larger set of methods that we have developed for the Design and Learning Methodology over the past decade.

Tool 1: Co-Creating a "Physical" Design Scenario

One facilitation tool that we find to be extremely useful for guiding MDTs in collab-orative Web design is a modified process of design scenario development. Traditionally, a design scenario is a written document that describes and analyses the aspects of design that need to be taken into account, before functional specification of technology can begin. In our facilitation tool, the design scenario is not developed as a written document, but is co-created through a physical collaboration process that involves the whole MDT in a brainstorm ses-sion that lasts 2 to 3 hours. The aim of the process is to solicit and aggregate a wide variety of viewpoints on human needs and other issues that relate to a Web design problem.

The MDT starts off with a set of physical objects, made up of elements such as string, wooden blocks in different colours or shapes, small toys, and other gadgets, which are laid out on one side of a large, empty table. The facilitator stands to one side to guide the MDT through the process. The MDT is asked by the facilitator to stand (not sit!) around the table

Table 1. Overview of results gained from implementing the design and learning methodology

EVALUATION QUESTION	ORGANISATION: FINANCIAL SERVICES	ORGANISATION: ENGINEERING TRAINING INSTITUTE	ORGANISATION: BROADCASTING
Did facilitation support both design and learning?	Yes	Yes	Yes
What types of design-related skills were developed?	Communication skills	Collaboration skills	Process management skills
Which design and learning activities were facilitated?	Team-based creative work; self-sufficiency; decreasing negative attitudes to learning as a team; making effective presentations; training in action learning methods.	Learn to streamline decision making; structure feedback from stakeholders; learn to apply nontechnical solutions to design problems; training in participatory and human-centred design methodology.	Negotiation processes; ensuring participation of nontechnical specialists; breaking patterns in design work; taking time to determine the design problem more precisely at the start.
What type of team learning was achieved?	Cooperative and transformative—we changed our way of thinking and acting in design projects.	Cooperative, but not much more than that.	Collaborative: we are more aware of the potential of learning across departments and how to bring disciplines together.
What changes did you notice in the organisation after using the approach for 6 months?	More awareness of bureaucracy and island culture that is company culture; more frequent attempts to tackle lack of communication between departments; more bottom-up initiatives and decision making.	Failed to apply approach to whole curriculum within the year—change is too great to achieve quickly; mentoring helped but using design review checklists created too much administration; institute has more insight into why team projects may not succeed.	We now have a new system of mentoring for concept development sessions; we are drawing in more experienced professionals from different departments on each project; we are more aware of how we communicate (productively or not) as a team.
Did the approach make sense in this setting?	Yes, because it fit with "networked knowledge strategy" we are trying to implement; it supported input from wide range of stakeholders; it smoothed interaction between layers of management and professionals in departments; it encouraged pro-active knowledge management.	Yes, however, intensive mentoring is required to help trainees change attitudes; use of tools does not guarantee that an MDT can achieve transformation in 6 months. Yes, the institute is more capable of supporting team learning process related to design, whereas before we only supported and assessed individual learning.	Not always: top-down management decisions prevent MDTs from taking initiatives; more and more aspects of work in the organisation need to be changed to accommodate the approach; different style used by facilitators can create tension between the project leader and the rest of the MDT; more tools are needed.

Table 1.continued

Which criteria were established for facilitation?	Facilitators must use a common list of questions to evaluate process; management condones use of approach beforehand; group decision support systems software should be used to increase input into design discussions by nonmanagers.	Roles and tasks must be described and understood beforehand, including facilitation role; each facilitated session with one MDT must be followed up by a presentation to share knowledge between MDTs; mentoring sessions need to take place at least once a week; use a Web site forum to increase knowledge sharing.	Use face-to-face methods; do not overload MDT with e-mails; increase time frame for facilitation during a project; hold a brainstorm first to establish group feeling before dealing with content of design; develop tools to bridge levels (management/employee).

to work together to create a physical landscape of their design scenario, using the physical objects. MDT members are requested not to focus on writing down what is going on, but to focus on the co-creation process. They are also asked not to propose or comment on solutions in an ad hoc manner. Instead, people take turns picking up and placing objects on the table, at the same time explaining how these represent human needs or other design issues. The other team members then analyse how this design element can be supported and how this impacts future Web site users. The solutions that come out of this discussion are then physically represented on the table as well.

By creating a physical representation of their collective mental model on the table, MDT members practice sharing complex and abstract concepts with each other, by showing each other how to interpret these concepts in a concrete and easy-to-understand manner. At the end of the session, the facilitator asks the MDT to take at least 30 minutes to review what they have created together and to mark each element on the table with a short description written on a yellow Post-It note that is stuck next to the (clusters of) object(s). Then the facilitator takes a digital photograph of the whole design scenario, as laid out on the table, so that the MDT can use it as a reference to negotiate and clarify what is useful and usable in their Web design in future design meetings.

Tool 2: Implement a Plan, Do, Check, Act Cycle in Each Design Meeting

The Plan, Do, Check, Act (PDCA) cycle is a well-known quality process management tool that was originally developed by Shewhart (1980). It involves a team in planning what to do in each phase of a project, in doing it, and in studying or checking the results. From here a team makes corrections to plans and looks for improvements in processes that can benefit the next phase of a project (thereby starting the cycle again).

In the ISO (2000) protocol for human-centred design, the PDCA cycle is used to ensure that all stakeholders in a design process publish "quality records" of *how* they went about reviewing plans and actions; knowledge and information; products and processes; and results achieved during a project. The focus of PDCA cycle is on the continuous improvement of work processes, rather than on carrying out a pre-set plan to produce the contents of a solution worked out before the start of a project.

For the design and Learning Methodology, we developed a facilitation tool that includes a set of questions and interventions in design meetings, to guide MDTs in implementing the PDCA cycle in their work process. During a design meeting, the facilitator asks the MDT to present where they are in their PDCA cycle and to discuss findings from activities carried out in the PDCA cycle with colleagues in different departments or stakeholders in the design project.

We also developed standardised formats and digitalised checklists for MDTs to use to manage their PDCA cycle and to carry out design reviews more rapidly. The tools are intended to assist MDTs to produce and share quality records more easily.

Tool 3: Make an Interactive Inventory of Change

Another facilitation tool that we developed for the Design and Learning Methodology involves MDTs in a structured process of interaction and knowledge sharing to improve their design process, which lasts approximately 3 hours. The process takes up an entire room and requires a number of flip-over stands and sheet paper, coloured markers and packets of yellow Post-It notes. At the beginning of the design meeting, the facilitator asks MDT members to split into smaller groups of three to five people per flip-over. Standing around the room next to a flip-over, all groups are asked to simultaneously discuss and describe their individual answers to, and perspectives on, a common set of questions that are related to their current design process. The facilitator asks these questions one at a time, giving groups a set amount of time to deal with each question. Each team member writes his/her answers on a Post-It note and pastes it on the flip-over sheet. After each question is answered, the facilitator asks the groups to move to another flip-over chart, so that they can read what another group has written. For each new question, a new sheet of paper is used, the question is written at the top of the sheet, and a new flurry of notes is added to the sheet.

This facilitation tool creates a rapid-fire inventory of all perspectives on change in the room, enhances interaction between MDT members, and makes discussions of complex and politically charged issues very efficient, while still maintaining maximum room for individual input into complex considerations of how to solve these issues in practice. At the end of the design meeting, the facilitator asks MDT members to collect all flip-over sheets and to paste all answers to one question in clusters on the wall. The facilitator then asks the MDT to scan questions and answers for common patterns in thinking, to filter out overlapping answers, and to glean important directions for team learning from the whole inventory. MDT members then prepare a distilled set of action points, which they take into the next phase of design. The questions and answers are kept as a record of requirements for change, which can be presented to colleagues involved in supporting this change in the organisation, both now and in the future. In this way, the MDT achieves team learning about the state of their multi-disciplinary design processes and about ways to change their processes. The MDT quickly produces a holistic record of requirements for change that is supported by all MDT members, since all team members have contributed to its creation. As a result, the inventory for change can be applied directly in further business activities, immediately following the design session.

Again, these three tools are part of the expansive toolkit that we are developing continuously in practice, and which is being modified to suit emergence of new elements tested for inclusion in the design and learning methodology, based on feedback from client companies.

CONCLUSIONS AND RECOMMENDATIONS FOR PROFESSIONAL PRACTICE

This chapter provided an introduction to a new approach to collaborative Web design, called the Design and Learning Methodology. The approach supports MDTs to learn from design, and thereby to improve their ability to collaborate effectively in design decision making. We introduced a basic model of the Design and Learning Methodology, describing results from the use of the approach in different types of organisations and detailing three facilitation tools developed to help MDTs to engage in both team learning and in multi-disciplinary design processes, simultaneously.

Conclusions from previous research on the Design and Learning Methodology (Evers, 2004), as well as from our ongoing research in organisations, indicates that the approach can support MDTs to:

- Understand what, how, and why they are learning from design, as a team, and to be able to communicate this to other stakeholders in a company or project
- Re-apply learning outcomes using structured and explicit methods in future design activities
- Use their team learning as a critical source for improving design decisions; and
- Consciously track and sustain improvements in the collaborative design process itself, rather than focusing purely on content deliverables and technical issues in Web design

We have found that the Design and Learning Methodology can be implemented at a local level (within one Web design project) and at a meta-level (as a standard approach to all design projects) in organisations. Since most design approaches currently do not tend to offer such a flexible and structured method for facilitating team learning and multi-disciplinary design in one, integrated process, the approach can be seen as an innovative way to improve collaboration in Web projects.

Naturally, there are many factors in Web design projects that are beyond the influence of a facilitator, and there are limitations to the application of the approach across an organisation. For example, the choice to use this approach at all, as opposed to other design approaches, may first require a deep process of intervention on related issues in the organisation in which the model is to be used, in order to change current assumptions, including those regarding the choice of established methods for developing Web sites. This is not a change that can be achieved instantaneously, in all organisational cultures.

REFERENCES

Ball, L. J., Lambell, N., Reed, S., & Reid, F. (2001). The exploration of solution options in design: A natural decision making perspective. In P. Lloyd & H. Christiaans (Eds.), *Designing in Context: Proceedings of Design Thinking and Research Symposium 5,* Delft University of Technology.

Ball, L. J., & Ormerod, T. C. (2000). The influence of co-designers on the generation and evaluation of design alternatives. In S. A. R. Scrivener, L. J. Ball, & A. Woodcock

(Eds.), *Collaborative Design: Proceedings of Co-Designing 2000* (pp. 243-252). London: Springer.

Bekker, M. M., & Long, J. (1998). User involvement in the design of human-computer interactions: Some similarities and differences between design approaches. In S. McDonald, Y. Waern, & G. Cockton (Eds.), *People and Computers XIV—Usability or Else!* (pp. 135-148). UK: Springer-Verlag.

Bourgeon, L. (2002, September). Temporal context of organizational learning in new product development projects. *Creativity and Innovation Management, 11*(3) 175-183.

Buchanan, D. A. (1991). Figure ground reversal in systems development and implementation: From HCI to OSI. In M. I. Nurminen & G. R. S. Weir (Eds.), *Human jobs and computer interfaces.* Amsterdam: Elsevier B.V.

Cooper, A. (1999). *The inmates are running the asylum.* Indianapolis, IN: SAMS Macmillan.

Eisenberg, E. M. (1990). Jamming, transcendence through organizing. *Communication Research, 17*(2), 139-164.

Evers, M. L. (2004) *Learning from design: Facilitating multidisciplinary design teams.* Delft, The Netherlands: Eburon.

Flood, R. L. (1999). *Rethinking the fifth discipline: Learning within the unknowable.* London: Routledge.

Hill, A., Song, S., Don, A., & Agogino, A. (2001, September 9-12). Identifying shared understanding in design using document analysis. In *Proceedings of the 13th International Conference on Design Theory and Methodology, Design Engineering Technical Conferences (DECT 2001).* Pittsburgh, PA.

Homan, T. (2001). *Teamleren: Thoerie en facilitatie.* Schoonhoven, The Netherlands: Academic Service.

International Organization for Standardization (ISO). (2000). *Quality Systems Management series* (9000). Geneva, Switzerland: ISO.

Lei, L. (1994). *User participation and the success of information system development: An integrated model of user-specialist relationships* (No. 73). Rotterdam, The Netherlands, Erasmus Universiteit, Tinbergen Institute Research Series.

Marchman III, J. F. (1998). Multinational, multidisciplinary, vertically integrated team experience in aircraft design. *International Journal for Engineering Education, 14*(5) 328-334.

Olsen, G. R., Cutkosky, M., Tenenbaum, J. M., & Gruber, T. R. (1994). Collaborative engineering based on knowledge sharing agreements. In *Proceedings of the 1994 ASME Database Symposium,* Chicago, IL.

Olson, G. M., Olson, J. S., Storrøsten, M., Carter, M. R., Herbsleb, J., & Rueter, H. (1996). The structure of activity during design meetings. In T. P. Moran & J. M. Carroll (Eds.), *Design rationale: Concepts, techniques, and use* (pp. 217-239). Mahwah, NJ: Erlbaum.

Schwalbe, K. (2000). *Information technology project management.* Course Technology, Cambridge, MA.

Shewart, W. (1980, December). *Economic control of quality of manufactured product* (Reissue ed.). 50th Anniversary Commemorative Issue. Milwaukee, WI: American Society for Quality.

Sole, D., & Edmondson, A. (2002). Bridging knowledge gaps: Learning in geographically dispersed cross-functional development teams. In C. W. Choo & N. Bontins (Eds.), *The strategic management of intellectual capital and organizational knowledge* (pp. 587-605). London: Oxford University Press.

Sonnenwald, D. H. (1993). *Communication in design.* Unpublished PhD thesis, Rutgers, New Brunswick, NJ.

Steiner, M. W., Gabriele, G. A., Swersey, B., Messler, R. W., & Foley, W. (2001, March 6-9). Multidisciplinary project-based learning at Rensselaer: Team advisement, assessment and change. In *Proceedings of NCIIA 5ᵗʰ National Conference..*

Toerpel, B. (2001, September 16-20). Participatory design of collaborative systems — New challenges? *ECSCW 2001 Workshop on Participatory Design.* Bonn, Germany.

Turner, S., & Cross, N. (2000). Small group design activity and requirements on collaborative technologies. *Collaborative Design: Proceedings of Co-Designing 2000* (pp. 253-260). London: Springer.

Valkenburg, A. C. (1996). Shared understanding as a condition for team decision making. *Proceedings of DMD '96,* Istanbul, Turkey.

Van der Veer, G. C., & Puerta Melguizo, M. C. (2003). Mental models. In J. A. Jacko & A. Sears (Eds.), *The human-computer interaction handbook: Fundamentals, evolving techniques and emerging applications* (pp. 52-80). Mahwah, NJ: Lawrence Erlbaum Associates.

Walz, D., Elam, J., & Curtis, B. (1993). Inside a software design team: Knowledge acquisition, sharing and integration. *Communications of the ACM, 36*(10), 62-77.

Zuber-Skeritt, O. (2002). The concept of action learning. *The Learning Organization, 9*(3), 114-124.

Chapter VIII

Information Architecture and Navigation Design for Web Sites

David Benyon, Napier University, Scotland

ABSTRACT

Information architecture concerns how to structure the content of an information space. Information architects design information spaces. Staying with the notion of information space leads us to the realisation that people need to be able to both conceptualise an information space and find their way through that information space to where they want to go. People need to be able to navigate information space. In this chapter we explore two key issues of Web site design; information architecture and the design of navigation support. In order to do this we draw upon theories of information spaces and theories of navigation in urban spaces. From these theories a number of practical features of Web sites are described.

INTRODUCTION

Information architecture has had a relatively short history. Although the term was coined by Richard Saul Wurman in 1975 his interests lie more in the effective presentation of information than in its structure (Wurman, 2001). He has published some excellent books and his Web site is full of great examples. However the term *information design* would probably be a better moniker. In this chapter we have little to say about information design, important though it is (see Jacobson, 2000).

Peter Morville in his introduction to *Information Architecture* (Gilchrist & Mahon, 2004) traces the term back to his efforts, with Louis Rosenfeld that culminated in their 2002 book *Information Architecture for the World Wide Web* (Rosenfeld & Morville, 2002). Information architecture is a growing area of study and, as a result, it changes fast. It is not just the property of Web designers, however. Think of the menu structure on a mobile phone, the layout of the content on a DVD, and even the arrangement of functions on a digital camera — you are thinking about information architecture. Information architecture concerns how to structure the content of an information space. Information architects design information spaces. Indeed many of the ideas presented in this chapter appear in Morville's (2005) recent book *Ambient Findability*.

Staying with the notion of information space leads us to the realisation that people need to be able to both conceptualise an information space and to find their way through that information space to where they want to go. A clean and crisp architecture will aid conceptualisation just as a well-designed city is easier to understand than a rambling place that has evolved over the years (though it may not be so pretty or engaging, something we return to later). The other key feature of a well-designed, geographical space is that there are signposts, maps, and landmarks to help you find your way around. The design of systems to support navigation in geographical spaces such as cities, airports, motorways, and so on can be a useful source of inspiration for Web site designers.

In this chapter we bring together two theoretical positions to provide sound advice on designing for human interaction with Web sites. On the one side is the theory of information spaces (Benyon, 2005) and on the other is the theory of human computer interaction (HCI) as navigation of information spaces (Benyon, 1998; Benyon 2001). Together they enable us to bring much of the knowledge of spatial design gained from the design of cities and other physical spaces to the design of Web sites. First we consider information architecture in general and information architecture in Web site design. We then look briefly at navigation in the geographical world and how some of these ideas can be applied to navigation of information spaces, particularly Web sites. In the conclusion we pull these ideas together to provide clear advice for Web site designers. However, just as architects cannot generally pull standard solutions "out of a hat" for architectural problems, neither can information architects. Information architecture is a design discipline: Information architects need to think hard about their clients and customers' needs, goals, and desires.

INFORMATION ARCHITECTURE

An information space is a combination of things — objects, displays, people, signs, icons, sounds, and so on — that is used by someone to provide information. Information spaces allow people to plan, manage, and control their activities. A Web site is the archetypal information space.

Information architecture is concerned with the design of information spaces. Information architects have to abstract some aspect of a domain and choose how this should be presented to people. The first thing they must do, then, is to decide how to conceptualise the activity they are aiming to support. This is known as defining an ontology (Benyon, Turner, & Turner, 2005). The ontology — the chosen conceptualisation of some activity — is critical and will affect all the other characteristics of the information space. For example, we can consider the Web to be populated by objects such as Web sites, Web pages, links, GIF files, PDF files, MS Word files, and so on. This is our general ontology for Web sites. In a clothes shopping Web site, there may be objects such as women's tops, men's tops, trousers, jackets, and so on. If the designer gets these categories wrong (that is, comes up with a poor ontology) people will find it very difficult to find the things they are looking for. For example, in one well-known clothes shopping site the term Levi's, is not recognised by the search engine, nor does it appear under any other category such as Jeans. The designers of this site have not included Levi's in their ontology, so no one can find them!

In addition to the conceptual objects that constitute the ontology, there are physical and perceptual devices that are used to access the conceptual objects. A key feature of information is that it remains invisible until someone provides an interface to it. Green and Benyon (1996) provide much more detail on this view of information spaces. An information space (or information artefact as it is presented there) must include a conceptual and a physical/perceptual side. Web browsers, mice, scroll bars, radio buttons, drop down menus, clickable links, rollover icons, and all the other widgets that we use constitute the physical/perceptual side of the Web information space. The relationship between physical/perceptual devices and conceptual objects is critical to the design of the space.

If an information space has a coherent design it is easier to convey that structure to the people who visit the site. Other spaces may have grown without any control or moderation. In the former case, often called moderated spaces, it is possible for the careful designer to create maps and signs helping people to orient themselves in the space. In nonmoderated spaces, this is not possible. For example, the Web as a whole is unmoderated so it does seem rather like a wilderness. The only way to find anything is through a keyword search or through following links. Individual Web sites are typically designed with maps and signs.

In some spaces, we are on our own and there are no other people about — or they may be about but we do know about them. In other spaces we can easily communicate with other people (or artificial agents) and in other spaces there may not be any people now, but there are traces of what they have done. The availability of agents in an information space is another key feature affecting its usability and enjoyment. If there is a person behind the ticket counter at the railway station you do not have to consult the timetable. The organisation of a library is something deliberately undertaken to make our search task easier. When we look at the books on a shelf, the well-thumbed volume might attract us. Here we can see traces of previous activity left unintentionally by people over the years. These features arise because people are part of the information space design. Typically they make navigation through it much easier and more pleasurable because it is social navigation.

Ontology

Deciding on an ontology for some domain of activity is deciding on the conceptual entities, or objects, and relationships that will be used to represent the activity. The way that these objects are related is known as a taxonomy. Choosing an appropriate level of abstraction for this is vital as this influences the number of entity types that there are, the number of instances of each type, and the complexity of each object.

A *coarse-grained* ontology will have only a few types of object, each of which will be "weakly typed," that is, will have a fairly vague description. This means that the objects will be quite complex and there will be a lot of instances of each type. Choosing a *fine-grained* ontology results in a structure which has many strongly typed, simple objects with a relatively few instances of each. In a fine-grained ontology the object types differ from each other only in some small way, in a coarse-grained ontology they differ in large ways.

For example, consider the ontology that you (acting as an information architect) choose to help with the activity of organising the files in your office. Some people have a fine-grained structure with lots of types (such as Faculty Research Papers, Faculty Accommodation, Faculty Strategy, etc.) while others have a coarser structure with only a few types (such as Faculty Papers). These different structures facilitate or hinder different activities. The person with the fine-grained ontology will not know where to put a paper on Faculty Research Accommodation, but will have less searching to do to find Minutes of April Research Committee.

A coarse-grained ontology makes storing easy, but retrieval more difficult. In my office I have a large pile of papers. This makes filing a new paper very easy—I just put it on the top. But it makes retrieval of specific papers much more time consuming. My colleague carefully files each paper she receives. So storage takes longer but retrieval is quicker.

Volatility

Volatility is concerned with how often the types and instances of the objects change. In general it is best to choose an ontology that keeps the types of objects stable. Given a small, stable space, it is easy to invent maps or guided tours to present the contents in a clear way. But if the space is very large and keeps changing then very little can be known of how different parts of the space are and will be related to one another. In such cases interfaces will have to look quite different.

Size

The size of an information space is governed by the number of objects which in turn is related to the ontology. Recall that a fine-grained ontology results in lots of object types with fewer instances of each type and a coarse-grained ontology results in a fewer number of types but more instances. A larger space will result from a finer-grained ontology, but the individual objects will be more simple. Hence, the architecture should support locating specific objects through the use of indexes, clustering, categorisation, tables of contents, and so on. With the smaller space of a coarse-grained ontology the emphasis is on finding where in the object a particular piece of information resides.

Topology

The topology of an information space concerns both conceptual and physical objects. The conceptual structure will dictate where conceptual objects are, that is, how things are categorised. The physical topology relates to the movement between and through physical objects and how the interfaces have been designed.

A Web site again provides a good illustration of these issues. How many times have you been to a Web site and tried to find some information only to give up or eventually stumble across it in what seems to you as being a strange place? This is all down to the conceptual information design of the site — the conceptual topology. In many Web sites it is very difficult to get a clear view or understanding of the topology especially as Web sites often try to serve too many different user groups each of which will have a different conception of what should be near to what.

Distance and Direction

Conceptual and physical distance results from the conceptual and physical topologies chosen by the designer. The notion of distance relates to both the ontology and the topology of the space; with the ontology coming from the conceptual objects and the topology coming from how those are mapped onto a physical structure.

Direction can be important in information spaces. For example, when moving between instances of an entity there is always a sense of next and previous. In a large information space such as a corporate Web site it is important to go to the right section to find appropriate information

Other Features

In their discussion of information spaces, Benyon et al. (2005) highlight the range of both conceptual and physical objects that may be present in a space, the various media that are available for presentation of information, whether the space has been designed, and whether there are agents present in a space. Some spaces have a richer representation that may draw upon visual, auditory, and tactile properties, while others are poorer. Issues of colour, the use of sound, and the variety of other media and modalities for the interaction are important components of the information space.

For example, consider the information space of an alarm clock. My clock has the conceptual objects of hours and minutes. Other clocks have an ontology that includes seconds. The perceptual objects could be numbers in a digital display or hands in an analogue display. Both have to support regularly changing (volatile) data. A standard-built clock is typically limited in terms of media (a single sound, the alarm, typically a monochrome display), there are no agents, but the space has been designed for the purpose. A mobile phone has the same conceptual information, but the presentation opportunities are much greater because of the richer media that it has (e.g., you can choose the alarm ring tone). Distance and direction are apparent on my alarm clock when I need to set the alarm time. The display only allows me to cycle through the hours and minutes in ascending order. On my mobile phone I have "little" up and down arrows that makes setting the alarm time much easier.

THE INFORMATION ARCHITECTURE OF WEB SITES

Information architecture for Web sites has to do with how the content of the site is organised and described. Of course, it has to be organised and described for some purpose and so many authors include the design of navigation systems as part of the information architecture. We prefer to deal with this separately in the context of navigation as a whole. Others still might include the design of the information layout as part of the information architecture.

In Jesse James Garrett's (2003) book *The Elements of User Experience*, information architecture sits alongside interaction design in the central *structure* plane of his five level view of Web design (Figure 1). Navigation design along with interface design and information design sits just above on the *skeleton* plane. Above that is the *surface* plane and supporting all this is the *strategy* plane and *scope* plane. Information architecture is about structure. But

Figure 1. Garrett's model of Web site design (Garrett, 2003, p. 33)

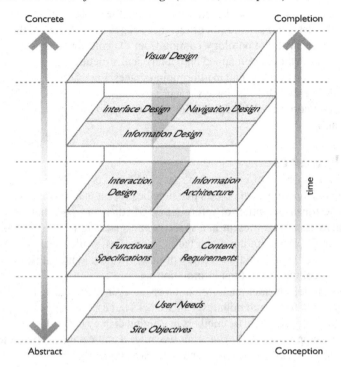

this is not the whole story of Web site design. The strategy, scope, interaction, and visuals also need consideration.

There are many different types, or genres, of Web sites such as news sites, shopping sites, entertainment sites, and information sites. These different types of sites have to serve many different purposes for many different people. Getting an information architecture that is robust enough to serve such multiple interests is difficult, and Web site information architects are in great demand.

The features of Web sites will clearly, vary widely; however, the conceptual objects in Web sites are fairly common: pages; files; different types of files such as PDF, GIF, and JPEG; documents; and links. Physically, sites are distinguished by their use of implementation method. Simple HTML sites have different physical objects for use at the interface than dynamic HTML or Flash sites.

Some sites such as stock exchange sites are of course highly volatile. Any site that aims to provide up-to-date information, for example, airplane arrivals or train departures, has to deal with the volatility of the content. News sites are more volatile than information sites. The key issue for the designers is to get the overall structure of the site — the information architecture — as stable as possible.

Large Web sites are exactly why information architecture for Web sites has become so important. In large sites it is not possible to fit everything onto a single display. There will need to be some complex structure and this requires classification and the development of a taxonomy. Large sites will have a greater distance between objects. Distance in Web sites can be measured by the number of clicks it takes to get from one part of the site to another (Benyon & Wilmes, 2003). We recently worked on a local council Web site with the aim of achieving a *three click rule*. It should be possible to access specific information in three clicks. Of course, this requires getting the ontology of the site at an appropriate level of abstraction.

The topology is another key element of information architecture as it determines how easy or otherwise it is to move through a site. The conceptual topology refers to the way the objects are classified, organised, and related (the taxonomy). The physical topology is concerned with how this structure is presented at the interface — with things such as menu structures and links between the different parts of the site.

Classification Schemes: The Conceptual Topology

As we have seen the choice of an ontology or classification scheme is crucial to how easy it is to retrieve an instance of an object. With a coarse-grained ontology searching for an instance of an object means searching within one of the few types of objects. So to find a particular paper in the pile in my office I have to search through the pile in a serial fashion until I find it. With a fine-grained ontology I search between the types. If I have filed a particular paper in a folder in the filing cabinet, I can search through the folders (i.e., the through the types). There is no simple answer to getting the ontology right; it will be more or less suitable for different purposes.

Whatever the ontology, imposing some structure on how the objects are physically organised will help access to a particular instance. Rosenfeld and Morville (2002) distinguish three exact organisation schemes: (1) alphabetical, (2) chronological, and (3) geographical to which Shedroff (2001) adds continuums (i.e., using some rating scale to rank instances), numbers, and categories. Alphabetical order is exploited in all manner of information artefacts such as phone books, bookstores, and directories of all kinds. Although at first sight an alphabetical organisation is straight forward, it is not always easy, especially where the forenames and surnames are muddled up, or where rogue characters can get into the name. Where is a dot in the alphabet, or a quotation mark? Most mobile phones have an address book with just one object name. Most PDAs distinguish between first and last name. Notice how these two ontologies affect retrieval of instances. Another occasion when alphabetical organisation breaks down is if the formal title of a company or organisation is not the same as the informal name. Recently, while looking in the paper-based phone directory for the phone number for Edinburgh City Council, I finally found it under "C" for "City of Edinburgh"! There was not even an entry under "E" pointing to the entry under "City."

Chronological organisation is suitable for historical archives, diaries, and calendars and event or TV guides. Geographical organisation suits travel subjects; social and political issues; and regional organisations such as wine sites, local foods, and so forth. Organisation by topic or subject is another popular way to structure information, but here it is important to prototype the names of topics with the potential users of a site. Often a topic structure used by people internal to an organisation is different from those outside the organisation.

Task organisation structures the Web site by particular activities that people may want to do; "Buy ticket," "Contact us," and so on aim to structure the site according to task. Audience is another popular structuring method. This can be very effective when there are a few well-defined, different types of users. "Information for staff," "Information for students," and so on helps different visitors find their part of a site.

Hybrid schemes can be used to mix these together and frequently are. Other authors suggest that there are other organisational schemes. For example, Brinck, Gergle, and Wood (2002, p. 152) include "department" as a scheme. They give the following example to illustrate the differences:

Task-based	"Buy a Car"
Audience	"Car Buyers"
Topic-based	"Cars"
Department	"Sales department"

Any information space can be described in terms of three key features: (1) its dimensions, (2) the facets (or attributes) of those dimensions, and (3) the values that these facets can take. This is often called a faceted classification and it can have a great impact on locating instances of the objects. The dimensions come from the ontology — the major concepts in the site. So, a typical travel site has dimensions of cars, flights, hotels, and so on. Each of these has certain common facets (such as price) but also may have their own unique facets: flights go from one city to another; hotels are located in a single city (but maybe part of a chain); and cars generally are rented and returned to the same location, but may exceptionally be returned elsewhere. Ferries have a different pricing structure from planes which have a different structure from trains.

Each if these attributes, or facets, can take certain values. The name of a city, for example, could be just about anything, but the name of an airport could be restricted to a known list of official airports. Classification in terms of the facets of dimensions works particularly

Figure 2. Structure of thesaurus (from Rosenfeld & Morville, 2002, p. 187)

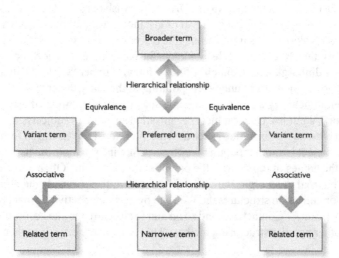

well in small, clearly defined spaces. Music sites classify music in terms of its main facets such as genre, artist, and title. Recipe sites will have facets such as country/region, main ingredient, course/dish, and so on. Wodtke (2003) points out, though, that once such a site includes things such as cooking utensils, the sharing of facets across such different entities as utensils and recipes is no longer possible. Faceted classification has important impact on the user interface that is provided. With clear and known facets and values the interface can be optimised to exploit the structure.

Rosenfeld and Morville (2002) point out the need to consider the granularity of the ontology, as this leads to the breadth versus depth debate in Web site design. Often the same material can be organized as a deep structure — only a few main branches but lots of sub-branches — or as a shallow and broad structure with lots of branches and only a few sub-branches. As a general rule 6-8 links per category is about right. There are many theoretical studies that have been done to try to determine the optimal information structure (e.g., Larson & Czerwinski, 1998; Miller & Remington, 2004). The trouble with these approaches is that there is so much interaction between the ontology, the topology, and the navigational aids that it is difficult to generalise across sites. The nature of the content and how it would naturally be divided up by the people who will be visiting the site must also be considered.

It would be nice if things could be organised and structured into a neat hierarchy, but the problem with a hierarchical structure is that no matter what classification scheme is chosen, some item will not fit nicely into it, and the designer will want to put it under two or more headings. (Note that this happens more often in Web site design with a fine-grained ontology as there are more types of object.) As soon as this happens, the nice clean structure of a hierarchy breaks down and soon the hierarchy becomes a network.

Networks are structures in which the same item may be linked into several different hierarchies. It is a more natural structure but also a more confusing one for people to understand. Often the visitor to a Web site navigates down through a hierarchy and by doing so develops a reasonably clear view of the site structure. However, in a network they may then go back up another branch or may jump from one part of the site to another. In such cases understanding the overall logic of the site is much more difficult. Organising pages into a sequence is ideal for dealing with a straightforward task structure, such as buying a product or filling in a series of questions.

One of the problems with devising a taxonomy is that different people use different concepts to organise things. Another is that people use different words and terms to refer to the same thing. There are synonyms and homonyms. There are slight variations of meaning, and often it is difficult to find a home for an instance of something. A thesaurus is a book of synonyms and semantic relationships between words. Similarly, in information architecture there is often a need to define a thesaurus to help people find what they are looking for. Rosenfeld and Morville (2002) suggest the structure illustrated in Figure 2.

The preferred term is at the centre of the structure. It needs to be chosen carefully so that it will be recognised and remembered by the people using the site. Far too often these terms are chosen by administrative staff and they reflect an administrative view of things. Our university has a heading of "Facilities Services" on its Web site rather than "Catering" and the library is now a "Learning Information Service." Different nationalities will use different words. The preferred term should be linked to any number of variant terms. These are synonyms that people might be expected to use, follow, or type into a search engine. Narrower terms describe subcategories of the term (sometimes called siblings), and these are related to other terms (sometimes called cousins). Moving up the hierarchy takes us to a broader term.

Specifying all these relationships is a lengthy but important activity for the information architect. This structure will be used to explain the conceptual structure to people using the site and to people administrating the site. It will be used in displaying the content on the page as part of the navigation system and to help people searching. This scheme also helps to provide functionality such as "may we also suggest" on a shopping site. The scheme will be used to provide category information for people, navigation bars, and the "breadcrumbs" that show where you are on a site.

Information architecture has become so important that there are now many departments devoted to managing the information or knowledge in an organisation, and there are software systems designed explicitly to help in this process. A key aspect of this is metadata. Metadata is data about the objects in the Web site. It may be data that describes the intrinsic characteristics of the object such as file size, type of file, and so on; it may describe administrative issues such as when the file was created, when it was modified, and who created it; or it may be more descriptive data such as keywords that describe the content in terms of the main facets associated with that type of object. There are standards for describing data such as topic maps (Baxter, 2004) and content management systems that handle specifying and managing metadata and dealing with multiple taxonomies.

NAVIGATION

Information spaces are many and various — from paper documents, to Web sites, to personal organisers, to DVDs, to the complex combination of objects, information artefacts, designs, and people that provide the information in large geographical spaces, such as airports. Information spaces allow people to plan, manage, and control their activities.

Figure 3. Information space and activity space

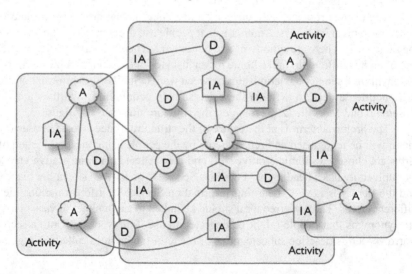

Rarely though, is all the information that someone needs for some activity in one place. We conceptualise the situation as shown in Figure 3. Here the information space, consisting of a variety of information artefacts (IA), agents (A), and devices (D), covers a variety of activities. Accordingly, people have to gather information from a variety of sources; they move through the information space to gather all the information that is required. This is what we call *navigation of information space*.

Navigation is concerned with finding out about and moving through an environment. It includes three different, but related activities.

- Object identification which is concerned with understanding and classifying the objects in an environment.
- Exploration which is concerned with finding out about a local environment and how that environment relates to other environments.
- Wayfinding which is concerned with navigating towards a known destination.

Although object identification is somewhat akin to exploration, the purpose is different. Exploration focuses on understanding what exists in an environment and how the things are related. Object identification is concerned with finding categories and clusters of objects spread across environments, finding interesting configurations of objects, and finding out information about the objects.

Navigation is concerned with both the location of things and with what those things mean for an individual. How many times have you been told something like "turn left at the grocer's shop, you can't miss it," only to drive straight past the supposed obvious landmark. Objects in an environment have different meanings for different people.

Navigation in Geographical Spaces

A lot of work in psychology has been done on how people learn about environments and with the development of "cognitive maps"; the mental representations which people are assumed to have of their environment. These representations are rarely wholly complete or static. Ecological considerations are concerned with the cues that people draw from the immediate environment as they interact with it. People develop knowledge of the space over time and through the experience of interacting with and within a space.

Wayfinding is concerned with how people work out how to reach their destination. For Downs and Stea (1973) and Passini (1994) the process involves four steps; (1) orienting oneself in the environment, (2) choosing the correct route, (3) monitoring this route, and (4) recognising that the destination has been reached. To do this people use a variety of aids such as signposts, maps, and guides. They exploit landmarks in order to have something to aim for.

Learning to find ones way in a new space is another aspect of navigation considered by psychologists (Gärling, Böök, & Ergesen, 1982; Kuipers, 1982). First, we learn a linked list of items. Then we get to know some landmarks and can start relating our position with regards to these landmarks. We learn the relative position of landmarks and start building mental maps of parts of the space in between these landmarks. These maps are not all complete. Some of the "pages" are detailed others are not, and more importantly, the relation between the pages is not perfect. Some may be distorted with respect to one another.

In the 1960s psychologist Kevin Lynch identified five key aspects of the environment; nodes, landmarks, paths, districts, and edges (Lynch, 1961). Districts are identifiable parts of an environment which are defined by their edges. Nodes are smaller points within the environment; those with particular significance may be seen as landmarks. Paths connect nodes. These concepts have endured, though not without criticism. The main issue is to what extent are features of the environment objectively identified. Other writers (e.g., Barthes, 1986) have pointed out that the identification of these features is much more subjective. It is also important to consider the significance and meanings that are attached to spaces by people. Different people see things differently at different times. Shoppers see shopping malls in a different way than skateboarders do. A street corner might feel very different in the middle of the day than it does at night. There are different conceptions of landmarks, districts, and so forth, depending on cultural differences such as race, gender, or social group. The ship's captain can see many different landmarks in the ebb and flow of a river than the novice. Navigation in a wilderness is a wholly different activity from navigation in a museum.

In addition to the five features identified by Lynch (1961), it is generally assumed that there are three different types of knowledge that people have of an environment; landmark, route, and survey knowledge (Downs & Stea, 1973). Landmark knowledge is the simplest sort of spatial knowledge in which people just recognise important features of the environment. Gradually they will fill in the details between landmarks and form route knowledge. As they become more familiar with the environment they will develop survey knowledge; the "cognitive map" of the environment.

Navigation in Information Spaces

In information spaces, the physics are different from geographical spaces and, indeed, some people would consider navigation of information spaces to be quite different from navigation in geographical spaces as there is no body to be moved. However, we treat them as essentially similar activities, with the main difference being that the navigators in information space have to move without the full range of sensory inputs of a physical body. The key thing for us is that design principles transfer from geographic to information spaces.

In information spaces people face similar problems and undertake similar activities as they do in geographical spaces. They may be engaged in wayfinding — searching for a known piece of information. They may be engaged in exploration of the space or in object identification. They will move rapidly between these activities and they will pick up new information from the local environment. Indeed often they will rely on designers putting information in an environment to remind them of different functions and options that are available. This is what Pirolli (2003) refers to as "information scent" (p. 173). Information spaces have different districts, with nodes and paths linking the sections together. Landmarks will help people to recognise where they are in a space and hopefully help them to plan and monitor a route to where they want to go. People will have simple route knowledge of some information spaces and survey knowledge of others.

The essential thing about designing for navigation is to keep in mind the different activities that people undertake in a space — object identification, wayfinding, and exploration — and the different purposes and meanings that people will bring to the space. Of course, designing for navigation has been the concern of architecture, interior design, and urban planning for years, and many useful principles have been developed that can be applied to the design of information spaces.

Responsive Spaces

The practical aim of navigation design is to encourage people to develop a good understanding of the space in terms of landmark, route, and survey knowledge. However, another aim is to create spaces which are enjoyable, engaging, and involving. Design (as ever) is about form and function and how these can be harmoniously united.

One commentator on the aesthetics of space is Norberg-Schulz (1971) another is Bacon (1974). Bacon suggests that any experience we have of space depends on a number of issues. These include:

- The impact shape, colour, location and other properties have on environment
- The features which infuse character
- The relationships between space and time—each experience is based partially on those preceding it
- Involvement

These all have an impact on navigation. Too much similarity between different areas of an environment can cause confusion. The design should encourage people to recognise and recall an environment; to understand the context and use of the environment; and to map the functional to the physical form of the space. Another important design principle from architecture is the idea that to gain a gradual knowledge of the space through use designers should aim for a "responsive environment," ensuring the availability of alternative routes; the legibility of landmarks, paths, and districts; and the ability to undertake a range of activities.

One application of urban design principles to Web sites is described in Benyon and Wilmes (2003). Wilmes used the *serial vision theory* of town planner Gordon Cullen (1971) to design a dynamic site map for a Web site that indicated the distance and direction of the other pages on a site from the current position of the visitor. Cullen's theory was based on the gradual unfolding nature of vistas as one walked through an environment. Wilmes took these ideas and applied them to Web site design, giving each different category on the Web site a distinctive character (a sense of place) through use of colour and texture and allowing the site visitors to see the site unfold as they moved through it. Pages of the site were revealed and got larger as people approached them in much the same way as the vista of a geographical environment changes as a person walks towards it.

Signage

Good, clear signposting of spaces is critical in the design of spaces. There are three primary types of sign that designers can use.

- **Informational signs:** provide information on objects, people, and activities and hence aid object identification and classification.
- **Directional signs:** provide route and survey information. They do this often through sign hierarchies with one type of sign providing general directions being followed by another that provides local directions.
- **Warning and reassurance signs:** provide feedback or information on actual or potential actions within the environment.

Of course, any particular sign may serve more than one purpose, and an effective signage system will not only help people in getting to their desired destination, it will also make them aware of alternative options. Signage needs to integrate with the environment in which it is situated aesthetically so that it will help both good and poor navigators. Consistency of signage is important, but so is being able to distinguish different types of sign. One of the most important in Web site design is the "you are here" sign giving information not just about where you are, but also where you can get to.

Maps and Guides

Maps can be used to provide navigational information and can be supplemented with additional detail about the objects in the environment — they become guides. There are many different sorts of maps from the very detailed and realistic to the highly abstract schematic maps such as Beck's famous map of the London underground.

Maps are social things with their own conventions, symbols, and style. Maps are there to help people explore, understand, and find their way through spaces. They should be designed to fit in with the signage system. Like signs, there will often be a need for maps at different levels of abstraction. A global map which shows the whole extent of the environment will need to be supplemented by local maps showing the details of what is nearby. Maps can be drawn for different perspectives such as a birds-eye view, first-person view, and third-person view. You are here (YAH) maps are also important as they put the visitor into the environment.

Social Navigation

A well-designed environment with good signage and well-designed navigational aids, such as maps, will be conducive to good navigation. However, even in the best designed environment people will often turn to other people for information on navigation rather than use more formalised information artefacts. When navigating in cities, people often ask other people for advice rather than study maps. Information from other people is usually personalised and adapted to suit the individual's needs. People present the information with additional contextual information or with personal anecdotes that help to focus attention on important features of the environment that only a "local" might know.

Even when we are not directly looking for information we use a wide range of cues, both from features of the environment and from the behaviour of other people, to manage our activities. We might be influenced to pick up a book because it appears well thumbed, we walk into a sunny courtyard because it looks attractive, or we might decide to see a film because our friends enjoyed it. We find our way through spaces by talking to or following the trails of others. The whole myriad of uses that people make of other people — whether directly or indirectly — is called *social navigation*.

NAVIGATION DESIGN FOR WEB SITES

The concepts of navigation outlined previously are common to all information spaces. A graphical user interface to a database needs good navigation support, clear signage, and so on. The menu headers are your landmarks or major routes — do you know what lies behind each item on a menu, or are there sketchy areas of the application? As we saw previously,

Figure 4. Wire frame

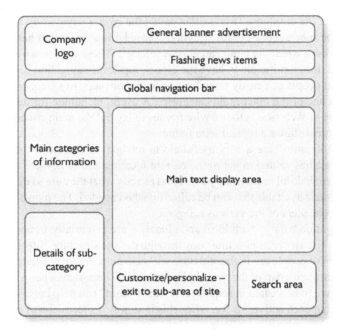

navigational principles apply to electronic and information spaces. But it is perhaps with Web sites that the principles can be more clearly seen. The Web as a space in which people use Internet Explorer or Netscape Navigator to seek out information is a very powerful analogy.

The design of navigation mechanisms is the second main pillar of information architecture (see Figure 1). Of course, there are many different types of visitors to any site that need to be accommodated. Brinck et al. (2002, p. 126) advocate short, efficient paths for the omniscient user or the regular visitor, "distinctive landmarks and orientation cues" for those who tend use rote memorization (i.e., route knowledge), and putting key information in the environment for those using satisfying strategies.

Labels and labelling are key issues in Web site navigation. Recall the discussion of vocabularies mentioned previously and the need to find terms that the site visitors will understand. Miller and Remington (2004) also point to the important interplay between labels and structure of a site. Labels are used for internal and external links; headings and subheadings; titles; and related areas. They are the signage system for the site. Not all labels are text, and iconic labels can be very useful if the context and design is clear. Paying attention to good, consistent, and relevant labels is a critical part of the information architecture. Information architects must develop a clear and unambiguous preferred vocabulary.

There is nothing more confusing for people than if a Web site itself changes the vocabulary, for example, referring to the things it has as "products" one minute and "items" the next. The same labels will be used on search mechanisms as those on the main page and in the names of the pages and the link names.

Navigation support in Web sites is provided through a whole host of methods. It is common to have a navigation bar across the top of a site which points to the main, top-level categories of the ontology. This is often called the *global navigation*. Within each of these there will be subcategories. These might be placed down on the left hand side of the site or may drop down when the main category is selected. These are known as *local navigation*. It is a good design principle to have the global, top-level navigation bar the same on every page so that people can easily jump back to the home page, to a frequently asked questions page, or to one of the other main categories. A useful technique for designing the navigation support of Web sites is to use wire frames to lay out the main structural components of pages. Figure 4 shows a typical wire frame.

"Breadcrumbs" are a very useful aid to navigation that show the trail of categories that someone has visited to get to the current location. Other devices such as indexes and glossaries are helpful in assisting people find exactly what they are searching for. A site map should be made available that can be called up when needed. The map displays the structure and content headers of the various categories.

Navigation bars — both local and global — are essentially signposts and landmarks, leaving the site visitor to pick their way through the site structure. Site maps and good feedback on where people are in the structure will also help. Another alternative is to provide a clear path through a part of the site. This is particularly important when a number of activities or pages have to be visited in sequence. A site "wizard" can help here; it guides people and explains what each activity is for. Often this is simply a succession of pages, such as when buying a ticket or booking a flight.

One of the significant features of the Web as an information space is that many sites support searching. Search engines can be bought, and the better ones are quite expensive but are also effective. Once again the preferred vocabulary should form the basis of searching, and where the synonyms have been defined they too can be used in defining searching terms and in helping people to refine their search.

There are two main problems with searching a Web site. First is knowing exactly what sort of documents the search engine is searching. The second is how to express combinations of search criteria. A frequent failing of Web sites is not to make clear which items are included in the search. Is the content of different documents searched, or is it just the Web pages themselves? Does it include PDF files or MS Word files in which case is it the whole content or just some tagged key words? Sites should indicate what is searched and provide options to search different types of content.

Social Navigation of Information Space

As we mentioned previously, in the real world much navigation is accomplished by interacting with other people. Social navigation of information space encompasses a whole collection of techniques and designs that put people in touch, make people aware of others, and of what others have done (Höök, Benyon, & Munro, 2003). Some designs such as online communities exist solely for the purpose of enabling people to maintain and build links with other people. Other systems are more concerned with making people aware of what others are doing and others with making aggregate knowledge of others available.

Direct social navigation is concerned with putting people in touch with other people; or with artificial agents. When we talk to someone else, the information we get back is often personalised to our needs and the advisor may offer information that changes what we want to do or how we might approach it, making us aware of other possibilities. People can judge to what extent the information given can be trusted depending upon the credibility of the information provider. Even if the information cannot be trusted, it may still be of value as people know where it is from. In information spaces, using person-to-person communication is an important part of the information architecture that is often overlooked.

Direct social navigation comes in many forms. At its most prosaic it consists of a link such as "mail info@website.com" or mail "webmaster." At least these impersonal connections suggest that there is a real person at the end of the line. Having individuals identified by name adds another level of personalisation (but creates difficulties if that person is not answering their mail for a few days). From such beginnings rich webs of direct social navigation support can be developed. There may be an instant messaging facility, video conferencing, and so on.

If other people are not around to provide help and advice then there are a number of systems that try to offer forms of indirect navigation. These might be used to filter out uninteresting information or point people to things that they will find relevant. Just as a newspaper editor filters news into a form that readers of that newspaper like, so filtering systems aim to tailor information to people. (Conversely, the newspaper or TV channel that we choose is selected because we like the way that news is filtered and presented.)

In content-based filtering the information is scanned for specific items that match some criteria. Based on a statistical analysis the system rates the relevance of the information to the person. Usually keyword matching techniques are used to filter the information. The system is supplied with a preference file for each person with keywords that the system should look for in documents.

Recommender systems make suggestions to people for information based on what other people with similar tastes, likes, or dislikes (Konstan & Riedl, 2003). Personal profiles are matched, and the system creates clusters of people with similar tastes. Book recommendations from the Amazon.com site is probably the best example of a mature recommender system. People who subscribe to Amazon can have the system recommend books based on those that they have bought previously and on those that they rank. Amazon also provides recommendations based on what other people have done. "People who bought this book also bought these other ones."

Another method of providing social navigation is to provide a tag so that whenever someone comes upon a new piece of information he/she can see what other people with similar interests, as they have, think of that particular piece of information. Some sort of rating of the information pieces has to be done by the users of the system so the system can create and cluster personal profiles. The more people that rate items, the more accurate the system becomes. Implicit ratings may be things such as the time an individual spends reading an article. Explicit ratings let people score information sources. An excellent example of this sort of social software is eBay, allowing buyers and sellers to see information on previous purchases, sales, and ratings from others. At the end of 2005 there was great excitement as Yahoo acquired two social networking sites, flickr and del.icio.us.

History enriched environments, or *readware* is another technique for social navigation. What other people have done in the past can tell us something about how to navigate the information space. If we get lost in the woods and come upon a trail, a good idea is to follow that trail. In a similar way we may follow a path through the information space. A familiar technique in Web site design is to automatically change the colours on the links in a Web page when a person has visited that page. In some other systems this may be generalised, based on the usage of links. Perhaps the main example of this was the Footprints Project (Wexelblatt, 2003), where ideas of interaction history are associated with an object.

Social translucence is a form of social navigation based on three core principles: (1) visibility, (2) awareness, and (3) accountability (Erickson & Kellogg, 2003). These principles have resulted in a number of *social proxies*: software systems that provide information about other people based on these principles. The best known of these is Babble: a social proxy for meetings, chat, and e-mail. People are represented by *marbles* (coloured blobs), and the space of discussion by a large circle in the centre of the system. The more active people are, the closer to the centre they are, and the marbles gradually move towards the periphery if they do not participate in the chat for some length of time. Other details of the people can be seen in the panes around the edge of the system.

CONCLUSION

Information spaces are made up from three types of things: (1) information artefacts, (2) agents, and (3) devices (Benyon et al. 2005). Information artefacts are objects that aim to provide information about something, but they are static and reactive to interaction. Agents are distinguished by having intentions. They actively try to achieve some higher-level goals. Devices just deal with the syntax of interactions. They are the buttons, wires, and communication channels that are required for the information space to be physically instantiated. Information architects will design some or all of these components of information spaces. In particular they will design the information artefacts and the overall structure of the information space.

Information architecture is concerned with getting the right structure for the site, presenting that structure to people, and helping people find their way through the structure. In order to design a structure an information architect will use all the user-centred design techniques that are useful elsewhere in the design of interactive systems. This will include profiling the users of the site by developing personas; developing scenarios of use; and generating requirements through interviews, questionnaires, and observations. It will involve developing prototype schemes and evaluating them.

Navigation in information spaces is a key activity that people undertake. We can learn much from studying navigation in geographical spaces and indeed apply design principles from urban planning and architecture. The principles of how we find our way in information spaces are the same as those in geographical spaces. The differences are that we have far less sensory cues in information spaces, and the physics are different — we can jump to different parts of the space, fly over data landscapes, and move through virtual walls. In information spaces, design is even more important. Also important is social navigation, and there are a number of applications that seek to provide some form of navigation support.

Navigation of information space is concerned with good design through the use of maps, labelling, and signage. It is also concerned with helping people obtain a survey knowledge of the whole information space. There are three key activities; wayfinding, exploration, and object identification, and it is important that each of these is properly supported. People do not just engage in one of these, they move rapidly between them. Navigation will be more effective and more enjoyable if the information space is a responsive environment; designed to provide a pleasant experience. Providing assistance for social navigation using awareness of other people and what other people have done to help navigate the information space and tailoring and personalising the navigational support is another key aspect of social navigation.

Underpinning the navigational support, however, is the basic architecture. Just as in the geographical world the architecture makes certain journeys possible, so it does in information spaces. The choice of ontology and how the resultant objects are classified, organised, and structured will make some informational tasks easy, some more difficult, and some impossible. Understanding the conceptual information architecture and how that architecture relates to the physical and perceptual devices that are used to provide the interfaces to it is critical to effective Web design.

ACKNOWLEDGMENT
This chapter is based on material from chapters 23-26 of Benyon, Turner, and Turner (2005).

REFERENCES
Bacon, E. N. (1974). *Design of cities*. London: Thomas Hudson

Barthes, R. (1986). Semiology and the urban. In M. Gottdiener & A. Ph. Lagopoulos (Eds.), *The city and the sign*. New York: Columbia University Press.

Baxter, B. (2004). Topic maps. In A. Gilchrist & B. Mahon (Eds.), *Information architecture: Designing information environments for purpose*. London: Facet.

Benyon, D. R. (1998). Cognitive ergonomics as navigation in information space. *Ergonomics, 41*(2), 153-156.

Benyon, D. R. (2001). The new HCI? Navigation of information space. *Knowledge-based Systems, 14*(8), 425-430.

Benyon, D. R. (2005). Information space. In C. Ghaoui (Ed.), *The Encyclopedia of human-computer interaction* (pp. 344-347). Hershey, PA: Idea Group Reference.

Benyon, D. R., & Wilmes, B. (2003). The application of urban design principles to navigation of Web sites. In E. O'Neill, P. Palanque, & P. Johnson (Eds.), *People and computers XVII — Designing for society. Proceedings of Human-Computer Interaction (HCI) 2003*. London: Springer.

Benyon, D. R., Turner, P., & Turner, S. (2005). *Designing interactive systems*. London: Pearson Education.

Brinck, T., Gergle, D., & Wood, S. D. (2002). *Usability for the Web*. San Francisco: Morgan Kaufmann.

Cullen, G. (1971). (reprint 2000). *The concise townscape*. Oxford, UK: Architectural Press.

Downs, R. & Stea, D. (1973). Cognitive representations. In R. Downs & D. Stea (Eds.), *Image and environment* (pp. 79-86). Chicago: Aldine.

Erickson, T., & Kellogg, W. (2003). Social translucence: Using minimalist visualisations of social activity to support collective interaction. In K. Höök, D. R. Benyon, & A. Munro (Eds.), *Designing information spaces: The social navigation approach*. London: Springer.

Gärling, T., Böök, A., & Ergesen, N. (1982). Memory for the spatial layout of the everyday physical environment: Different rates of acquisition of different types of information. *Scandinavian Journal of Psychology, 23,* 23-35.

Garrett, J. J. (2003). *The elements of user experience.* New Riders.

Gilchrist, A., & Mahon, B. (2004). *Information architecture: Designing information environments for purpose.* London: Facet.

Green, T. R. G., & Benyon, D. R. (1996). The skull beneath the skin; Entity-relationship modelling of information artefacts. *International Journal of Human-Computer Studies, 44*(6), 801-828.

Höök, K., Benyon, D. R., & Munro, A. (2003). *Designing information spaces: The social navigation approach.* London: Springer.

Jacobson, R. (2000). *Information design.* Cambridge, MA: MIT Press.

Konstan, J., & Riedl, J. (2003). Collaborative filtering: Supporting social navigation in large, crowded infospaces. In K. Höök, D. R. Benyon, & A. Munro (Eds.), *Designing information spaces: The social navigation approach* (pp. 43-83). London: Springer.

Kuipers, B. (1982). The 'map in the head' metaphor. *Environment and Behaviour, 14,* 202-220.

Larson, K., & Czerwinski, M. (1998). Web page design: Implications of memory, structure and scent for information retrieval. *CHI '98 Human Factors in Computing Systems* (pp.25-32). New York: ACM.

Lynch, K. (1961). *The image of the city.* Cambridge, MA: MIT Press.

Miller, C., & Remington, R. (2004). Modelling information navigation: Implications for information architecture. *Human-Computer Interaction, 19*(3), 225-272.

Morville, P. (2005). *Ambient findability.* Sebastopol, CA: O'Reilly.

Norberg-Schulz, C. (1971). *Existence, space, architecture.* London: Studio Vista.

Passini, R. (1994). *Wayfinding in architecture.* New York: Van Nostrand.

Pirolli, P. (2003). Exploring and finding information. In J. Carroll (Ed.), *HCI models, theories and frameworks* (pp. 157-192). San Francisco: Morgan Kaufmann.

Rosenfeld, L., & Morville, P. (2002). *Information architecture for the World Wide Web* (2nd ed.). Sebastopol, CA: O'Reilly.

Shedroff, N. (2001). *Experience design.* Indianapolis, IN: New Riders.

Wexelblatt, A. (2003). Results from the Footprints project. In K. Höök, K., D. R. Benyon, & A. Munro (Eds.), *Designing information spaces: The social navigation approach.* London: Springer.

Wodtke, C. (2003) *Information architecture: Blueprints for the Web.* Indianapolis, IN: New Riders.

Wurman, R. (2001). Information anxiety 2. Indianapolis, IN: Richard Saul Wurman, Que.

Chapter IX

A Methodology for Web Accessibility Development and Maintenance

Julio Abascal, University of the Basque Country, Spain

Myriam Arrue, University of the Basque Country, Spain

Markel Vigo, University of the Basque Country, Spain

ABSTRACT

Web design and evaluation are currently framed by legal restrictions and social demands for full accessibility. The main reason is that currently most Web sites are not accessible for people with physical, sensory, or cognitive restrictions due to diverse causes, such as disability, use of nonstandard equipment, or special work conditions. Accessibility awareness has advanced considerably in recent years, but designers are still having difficulties in updating or creating new accessible pages. Even though useful tools and sound evaluation methodologies are being designed, they are of no use if they are not integrated into the standard Web design lifecycle, interacting naturally with common design and authoring tools. This chapter introduces the basic concepts related to Web accessibility and proposes a method for including accessibility in standard Web engineering methodologies. The key phases: accessibility, evaluation, and maintenance are described in detail. Finally, a model is proposed for implementing accessibility policy in organizations.

INTRODUCTION

In recent years the Internet has become an essential means of communication. The World Wide Web is particularly used for carrying out many different activities in areas such as business, leisure, learning, and so forth, causing a vertiginous growth in the total number of Web sites in existence. However, most of the currently existing Web sites are inaccessible to varying degrees. For this reason, several categories of users are unable to access a significant part of the information included in the Web. Among the groups of people who find difficulties in accessing the Web are people with disabilities — they are most affected by this situation.

The lifecycle of Web sites is currently very short. In fact, Web designers have to manage the design of new Web sites or new versions of existing Web sites in very short time periods, which has a detrimental effect on the quality and accessibility of the final product. Although significant research is being carried out on Web accessibility, principally on the development of automatic accessibility evaluation tools, accessibility is not being sufficiently considered in the Web site development process. Furthermore, when the issue is considered, the accessibility of a Web application is usually evaluated in the latter phases of the development process, when its implementation is almost complete. As a result, correcting the detected accessibility errors implies a complete redesign of the application which can hardly be afforded. To avoid these situations developers should consider accessibility from the very beginning of the product development process.

There is, in fact, a shortage of development methodologies that incorporate accessibility as an essential property of the product. Such methodologies should be designed and implemented within organizations in order to increase the developers' awareness of accessibility and, as a result, to facilitate the development of accessible Web sites. Not only would these methodologies lead to the production of accessible applications but it would also lead to the development of higher quality products and facilitate their maintenance.

This chapter describes a methodology for the Web accessibility development and maintenance process. The establishment of this methodology in an organization will ensure that accessibility is incorporated as a fundamental characteristic of the product throughout the development process. In addition, it will increase awareness of the importance of Web accessibility within the organization.

WEB ACCESSIBILITY OVERVIEW

Web Accessibility Initiatives

As previously mentioned, most of the currently existing Web sites are to varying degrees inaccessible. Various initiatives have been taken in order to overcome this situation, including the promulgation of laws against electronic exclusion, such as the American with Disablities Act (ADA) and Section 508 of the Rehabilitation Act in the U.S., the Accessibility Act in the UK, and so forth.

The main problem for the inclusion of accessibility criteria in Web site design is that most designers are unaware of the specific needs of people with disabilities. They need inclusive design criteria, often specified as guidelines, in order to be able to design for accessibility. In this sense, the Web Accessibility Initiative (WAI, n.d.) of the World Wide

Web Consortium (W3C, n.d.) has developed many specifications, guidelines, software, and tools for achieving the *design-for-all* paradigm in the Web environment, actively promoting a higher degree of accessibility for people with disabilities.

Web Content Accessibility Guidelines (WCAG Overview, n.d.), created by the WAI, are broadly accepted and used to analyse Web site accessibility. These guidelines determine specific testing techniques or checkpoints. Each checkpoint has a priority (1, 2, or 3) assigned according to its strictness and, therefore, to its impact on accessibility. In addition, three accessibility conformance levels are defined based on these priorities:

- **Conformance level A:** all priority 1 checkpoints are satisfied.
- **Conformance level AA:** all priority 1 and 2 checkpoints are satisfied.
- **Conformance level AAA:** all priority 1, 2, and 3 checkpoints are satisfied.

New versions of these guidelines are currently being produced. The last version of the working draft of WCAG 1.0 was released in November 2005 (Caldwell, Chisholm, Slatin, & Vanderheiden, 2005). This set of guidelines incorporates a new accessibility description, defining the criteria an accessible Web site has to satisfy. According to this description an accessible Web site has to be:

1. **Perceivable:** "Make content perceivable by any user."
2. **Understandable:** "Make content and controls understandable to as many users as possible."
3. **Robust:** "Use Web technologies that maximise the ability of the content to work with current and future accessibility technologies and user agents."
4. **Operable:** "Ensure that interface elements in the content are operable by any user."

These initiatives have heightened awareness of accessibility within the Web developer community and encourage the production of accessible Web applications. Despite this, they have proved to be insufficient, as in most cases an acceptable level of accessibility is not attained.

Accessibility as Quality Measurement

The quality of Web applications should be taken into account, as with any other software product design process. The International Organization for Standardization (ISO) 9126 standard (ISO, 2001) defines six software product quality characteristics: (1) functionality, (2) reliability, (3) efficiency, (4) usability, (5) maintainability, and (6) portability. From this point of view, quality is a composite product property, involving a set of interdependent attributes (Brajnik, 2001). These characteristics can be taken as the attributes that any software product has to fulfil. ISO 9126 also defines a quality model for software product quality that includes both internal quality and quality in use. For evaluation purposes, this standard should be used in conjunction with the ISO/IEC 14598-1 (ISO, 1999) that provides methods for the measurement, assessment, and evaluation of software product quality. Specific models for Web site quality evaluation have also been proposed (see Mich, Franch, & Gaio, 2003). In addition, different approaches for measuring the quality of software products have been proposed, but all of them coincide in the importance of creating adequate metrics in order to efficiently perform the quality evaluation process.

Usability is one of the product attributes that has to be measured, rated, and assessed. This attribute has a bearing on the users' effort in recognizing the logical concept and its applicability, learning its application, operation, and operation control. In addition, usability also refers to the facility with which the user can perform specific tasks in the Web application. Accessibility and usability are closely related, as they both enhance user satisfaction, effectiveness, and efficiency (UsableNet, n.d.). According to Thatcher et al. (2002), accessibility can be understood as a subset of usability. In fact, the concept of accessibility is related to the absence of physical or cognitive barriers to using the functionality implemented in a Web site, such as navigation, information searching, and so forth. Although diverse methods and tools for Web usability evaluation exist (Ivory & Hearst, 2001), accessibility assessment has not been sufficiently developed, even though accessibility measurement, rating, and assessment is essential in determining Web site quality.

As previously mentioned, an accessible Web application has to be perceivable, understandable, robust, and operable (Caldwell et al., 2005). These principles can be understood as the interdependent attributes described in the ISO 9126 (ISO, 2001). However, the conformance level specified in WCAG is not sufficiently accurate. For instance, a Web site fulfilling only all first level success criteria checkpoints would obtain the same accessibility value as another Web site fulfilling all first level success criteria checkpoints and almost all second level success criteria checkpoints. Both of them would have an A level conformance. This illustrates the limitations of current qualitative measurements for performing accessibility comparisons or ratings. These criteria appear to be based on the assumption that if a Web page fails to accomplish one of the guidelines in a level, it is as inaccessible as if it fails to fulfil all of them. That is true for users with specific disabilities, but in general it is essential to have not only a reject/accept validation but a more accurate graduation of accessibility. In other words, in addition to the available qualitative measurements, it is necessary to have quantitative accessibility measurements, such as the ones proposed by Olsina and Rossi (2002). In this way, it will be possible to reveal the accessibility level of a product as a quality attribute of it.

ENGINEERING WEB ACCESSIBILITY

According to Sommerville (1992), a well-engineered software application has to accomplish four key attributes: (1) maintainability, (2) reliability, (3) efficiency, and (4) an appropriate user interface. The last attribute, appropriate user interface, refers to designing the software application, taking into account the capabilities and background of the users. In the current information society any Web application should be designed with the design-for-all paradigm (also called *universal design*) in mind, so that access is guaranteed for all users. Therefore, accessibility must be taken into account in order to develop an application with an appropriate user interface.

Software Engineering Methodologies

Developing Web applications is a complex process which requires adherence to a particular framework or methodology in order to produce good quality products. These methodologies define concrete steps or phases of the development process in order to reduce its complexity.

Software engineering methodologies describe the phases required for software application development, as well as the way in which these phases are integrated into the process model (Pressman, 1992). The most commonly applied software engineering models are the following: *waterfall, prototyping,* and *spiral* models.

The waterfall model is a sequential methodology which establishes a fixed order for the development process. This methodology divides the software methodology into six activities: (1) system engineering, (2) analysis, (3) design, (4) coding, (5) testing, and (6) maintenance.

The prototyping model is based on producing prototypes of the software application in a short period of time. These prototypes are then tested and the results are used to produce subsequent enhanced prototypes until all the requirements are fulfilled.

The spiral model integrates features from the waterfall and the prototyping models and adds an element of risk analysis in the development process. The process model is configured as a spiral where each iteration consists of four major activities: (1) planning, (2) risk analysis, (3) engineering, and (4) customer evaluation.

In all the presented models three main phases are included: (1) definition, (2) development, and (3) maintenance. Requirements research and application analysis are performed in the definition phase, while the design and implementation of the software application take place in the development phase. These phases together constitute the lifecycle of the software application. Selecting one or other methodologies depends on the size and complexity of the software application to be developed, as well as on time constraints.

However, software engineering methods cannot be directly applied to Web application development due to the special features of hypermedia. In order to overcome this situation some new methods have been proposed, that is, hypertext design model (HDM) (Garzotto, Paolini, & Schwbe, 1993) and relationship management methodology (RMM) (Isakowitz, Stohr, & Balasubramanian, 1995), and different methodologies (frequently sharing some features such as some lifecycle stages) have been produced: sequential, iterative, prototype-based, and so forth.

Incorporating Accessibility into the Lifecycle

The objective of this section is to demonstrate the accessibility issues that have to be taken into account and to describe the decisions to be made within each lifecycle phase of a Web application: requirements research, analysis, design, implementation, and maintenance.

A preliminary evaluation of the company must be performed in the product requirements research phase. This preliminary evaluation will determine whether the company is able to proceed to the design of an accessible Web application. It aims to detect any limitations regarding the company's staff, and technical and economical resources in the Web accessibility area. As a result, the company's competence in dealing with upcoming problems is measured, and the most deficient areas are identified. The main obstacles that developers have to face in this stage are the lack of an internal accessibility policy and the shortage of trained staff. These drawbacks are resolved by implementing appropriate policies which may require additional financial resources, and this would have to be weighed up by the company.

It is also essential to analyse the availability of tools to automatically evaluate, develop, correct, and monitor Web accessibility. This analysis is crucial as the selected tools will be used in the rest of the lifecycle phases. Therefore, a detailed analysis would avoid wasting time and effort in the future. Unfortunately, sometimes the lack of financial resources may rule out getting these tools and the human resources to make appropriate use of them. This situation could hinder the achievement of the accessibility goal.

In addition, as it is necessary to recruit disabled users to perform accessibility evaluations with users, it is essential to contact associations of users with disabilities at this stage. Furthermore, the selected user groups should cover the broader range of disabilities in order to perform a comprehensive evaluation. Thus, it is desirable to include groups of users with visual, cognitive, and physical impairments, and also deafness. Furthermore, there is also a wide range of disability within these groups. For example, users with visual impairments can suffer from total or partial loss of vision, colour blindness, tunnel vision, and so forth.

Finally, the availability of experts to conduct manual evaluations has to be taken into account.

Adopting the design-for-all paradigm in the analysis stage is a key point to avoid creating user profiles that would exclude other potential users. Design-for-all philosophy guidelines are aimed at avoiding unnecessary design barriers and promoting the application of user characteristic specifications and their operational environment in a positive way. According to Abascal and Nicolle (2005), the broad diversity of user characteristics makes it extremely difficult to consider all users in this phase. Nevertheless, avoiding unnecessary barriers to accessibility is possible by means of universal design guidelines. In this way, user task analysis produces simple, intuitive, and flexible requirements and specifications.

The results obtained in the analysis phase are formalised in the design stage. Applying techniques related to the previously adopted guidelines, such as Techniques for Web Content Accessibility Guidelines (TWCAG) 1.0 (Chisholm, Vanderheiden, & Jacobs, 2000), is advisable at this stage as it facilitates conformance to accessibility guidelines. These techniques are intended to be independent from the development technology used. It is necessary to identify the most suitable techniques so that the specifications obtained are able to adhere to the principles of accessible Web design. Moreover, the technical restrictions assumed in the previous stage have to be taken into account in the design phase. One of the most frequent and relevant constraints is the shortage of authoring tools which support accessible Web design. This tends to be the main obstacle to overcome.

The next activity to be addressed is the implementation of the product. It is essential to bear in mind the universal design principles in order to make appropriate decisions. Tools that fulfil the Authoring Tools Accessibility Guidelines (ATAG) are helpful as they facilitate the implementation of products based on these principles. When producing content in this stage, especially multimedia content, it is necessary to provide equivalent content if appropriate. This requirement leads to the fulfilment of some of the most relevant checkpoints in the accessibility guidelines, that is, the production of equivalent content that provides the user with the same functionality as the original. For example, attaching a text equivalent to embedded audio content would help to improve deaf users' perception.

The evaluation phase is one of the most relevant phases in the accessible Web application lifecycle. In a design-for-all oriented analysis, results of the design and implementation phases are checked to evaluate the fulfilment of the specifications. In order to reach a reliable conclusion, tools for automatic accessibility validation; repairing and transformation; expert-based evaluation; and evaluation with users must all be applied. After removing all accessibility barriers detected by automatic evaluation tools and by experts, evaluations with users will help to detect the remaining user-specific obstacles. All these evaluation methods are complementary and necessary. However, evaluations with users with disabilities should not be carried out as frequently as automatic ones, due to the difficulty of access and ethical issues that arise when testing incomplete and poor designs with them. In this stage, it is useful to use an error publication framework in order to avoid repeating the same mistakes, thus improving the development process. Producing good quality products should also be an objective of the development process. Therefore, in addition to evaluating compliance with Web accessibility guidelines, it is also necessary to verify the quality of the developed product in the evaluation phase.

Maintenance is a critical phase in any accessible Web site lifecycle. As the Web is essentially dynamic, its contents change frequently. From the Web accessibility point of view, the maintenance phase is understood as the phase where accessibility is monitored in order to measure its evolution. When the content of a Web application is updated, it is difficult to measure if the accessibility level has increased or decreased since up to now only qualitative metrics, such as WCAG conformity levels, have been used. It is advisable to use quantitative metrics, in order to measure more accurately the accessibility level and its evolution through time. Whatever the evolution is (positive or negative), the decisions made and the factors involved must be reported and reviewed. An application which reports these facts and evaluates accessibility quantitatively with a predetermined frequency is a powerful and essential tool within the context of this lifecycle.

The main objective of taking into account accessibility issues during the whole lifecycle is to reach the broader spectrum of end users. Furthermore, it is a methodical and easily maintainable way to manage an accessible Web application.

Process Model for Accessible Web Application Development

Web applications tend to be implemented in short time frames and due to this feature a specific development methodology is necessary, clearly defining the decisions to be made in each phase. Generally speaking, the lifecycle is defined as a group of stages that do not have to follow a determined sequence. On the other hand, a process model defines the sequence followed by the phases of the lifecycle, and it is important to select an appropriate one for accessible Web application development.

According to Nielsen (2001), iterative methodologies fit better when developing accessible Web applications. In this sense, related work can be found at Mayhew (1999) and Granollers, Lores, and Perdrix (2003). The iterative process model, in contrast to the classical waterfall model, enables the development of first prototypes in the earlier phases of the process. This feature facilitates accessibility evaluation during the whole development process. Consequently, accessibility errors are easier to find and fix. As a result, errors are not passed on to subsequent phases and similar errors are avoided in the rest of the process. It is beneficial to use a platform for the reporting of errors detected. In this way, keeping track of errors improves the development process as it avoids the same errors being made again.

In order to determine the appropriate process model it is necessary to take into account that a company may face two possible scenarios: (1) development of a new Web application or (2) accessibility improvement of an existing application. Figure 1 shows how these different scenarios are addressed in different ways.

An initial evaluation has to be performed in order to improve the accessibility of an existing Web application. In this way, accessibility problems will be detected in order to analyse and correct them and avoid passing them on to subsequent phases. Solutions to the errors detected will be implemented in an iterative way, allowing a process of debugging of the application.

It can be seen that both scenarios need to predict and plan accessibility evaluations during the development process. Once the application has been implemented, an evaluation is performed. According to the results, if the objective proposed in the specifications is not met, a re-analysis is carried out. Subsequently, the application will be redesigned. Following this methodology implies the improvement of the prototype with each iteration. When the required accessibility level has been fulfilled (depending on the internal policy or on the client specifications) the development phase will finish and the maintenance phase will start.

In the maintenance phase, periodical accessibility evaluations have to be made in order to know whether the updates made to the application have a detrimental effect on the required accessibility level. If these updates have decreased the overall application accessibility level, the evaluation report must be analysed and the detected errors fixed by designing and implementing new solutions.

WEB ACCESSIBILITY EVALUATION

Web accessibility evaluation is an essential component of the accessible Web development process. Accessibility evaluations should be performed frequently throughout the development process as described in the previous section.

Different methods can be used to carry out these accessibility evaluations, such as manual evaluation by experts, accessibility testing with users, and automatic validation of accessibility guidelines (i.e., TWCAG 1.0, Chisholm et al., 2000). A valid accessibility evaluation methodology should combine all these methods (Abou-Zahra, n.d.). However, the most widespread practice in the Web developer community is to perform only automatic validation of accessibility guidelines, resulting in products with poor accessibility levels.

Manual Evaluation by Experts

As with usability testing, accessibility evaluation also requires performing inspection methods. In this way, heuristic evaluation can be extremely useful as experts are able to evaluate Web applications according to sets of accessibility guidelines. It is well known that some of these guidelines can not be automatically tested as they require human judgement, for instance, checkpoint 14.1 of the TWCAG 1.0 (Chisholm et al., 2000): "Use the

Figure 1. Process model for accessible Web applications

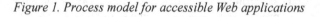
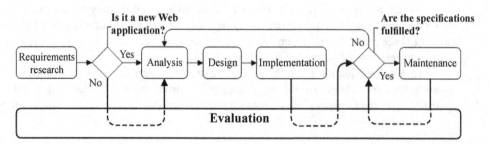

clearest and simplest language appropriate for a site's content." Heuristic evaluations are able to identify many accessibility problems, as well as to evaluate their significance for the overall accessibility goal.

Another convenient technique is performing a walk-through in order to detect any accessibility barrier which obstructs the completion of specific tasks. In this way, experts are able to determine the main executable tasks in a Web site and browse all the particular solution paths by using different browsers and different types of assistive technology such as screen readers, screen magnifiers, mouse emulators, and so forth. This technique will detect the main accessibility barriers for different user groups.

Accessibility Testing with Users

A correct accessibility evaluation methodology requires testing the Web application with different groups of users. This method will detect real accessibility barriers for the end users. This process is even more significant for achieving the overall goal of accessibility when expert evaluation has been performed by people involved in the development of the Web application, as they will be accustomed to the interface features.

This type of test is usually carried out in controlled environments such as testing laboratories where experts can observe and collect data from users. The thinking-aloud technique, consisting of users continuously vocalising their thoughts, feelings, and opinions while interacting with the site, is very useful since it allows the detection of barriers found by users in real time.

In addition, various tasks can be set up in order to encourage users to browse the system, and it may be useful to collect data from this interaction so that usability parameters, such as effectiveness in completing the tasks, can be calculated. If the effectiveness value in performing a specific task is low, its solution paths should be analysed in order to detect any existing accessibility barrier.

Enquiry methods such as questionnaires and interviews are broadly used in usability testing and can also be applied to accessibility testing. The questions within these questionnaires should be designed in such a way that users' answers help evaluators to determine the most significant accessibility barriers in the system.

Automatic Accessibility Guidelines Validation

According to Lang (2003), the advantages of this method are several in terms of cost effectiveness since automatic accessibility evaluation tools, which obtain the evaluation results in a short period of time, are used (e.g., Watchfire WebXACT, n.d.; Web Accessibility Versatile Evaluator [WAVE], n.d.; EvalAccess (Abascal, Arrue, Fajardo, Garay, & Tomás, 2003; etc.).

Development and use of automatic tools of this type are increasing. Currently, there are several Web accessibility evaluation tools with diverse characteristics. Some of them are executed online on a Web server while others need to be downloaded and run locally. Some have to be purchased while others are free. Thus, Web developers have a large selection of tools to choose from. Although this broad choice of tools is of benefit to developers, as they can select the most appropriate tool according to specific conditions, the lack of methods for validating these tools creates a number of problems.

Currently, the results obtained by different tools evaluating the same Web resource frequently differ. Thus, Web developers cannot be sure of detecting all accessibility errors in a Web page by using only one evaluation tool. For this reason, it is advisable to evalu-ate the Web resource with at least two different tools which have dissimilar interfaces and reporting styles. Therefore, Web developers should be familiar with the interfaces of the different tools they use. Moreover, they must get used to interpreting the results produced by different tools. The format of these results can be so unalike that Web developers can become confused when trying to interpret the various issues reported by each of them. Evaluation and Report Language (EARL) (see McCathieNevile & Abou-Zahra, 2005) was developed in order to help in the interpretation of automatic evaluation results.

Accessibility Evaluation Tools

The main objective of this type of tool is to verify the content of a Web page or Web site according to a set of guidelines and to return a report, detailing all errors discovered. In addition, this report can also contain methods, techniques, and/or examples explaining how these errors can be corrected. Some of these tools also offer guidance on error correction. These tools can be classified according to different criteria. The most relevant are the type of service offered and the ability to incorporate new guidelines.

According to the type of service offered a tool can offer:

- Analysis service (returns a report of detected errors), or
- Analysis and repair service (also guides the user in the error correction task)

According to the facility for incorporating new guidelines or new versions of existing accessibility guidelines an automatic accessibility evaluation tool can have:

- Built-in guidelines, so that updating the set of guidelines means modifying the code, and
- Specification of guidelines separated from the validation code, so that guidelines can be easily updated

This second type of tool is also useful for other purposes. For instance, an organisa-tion can define its own style guidelines and validate documents according to them (Takata, Nakamura, & Seki, 2003).

Watchfire WebXACT (n.d.), WAVE (n.d.), and A-Prompt (n.d.) are well-known, free, automatic accessibility evaluation tools which have built-in guidelines. WebXACT can work either online or off-line whereas the current version of A-Prompt works only off-line. Regarding the service they provide, WebXACT offers only an accessibility analysis service, returning a detailed and complete report, while A-Prompt also provides support for error correction. An analysis of these tools can be found in Brajnik (2000) and Blair (2004).

EvalAccess (Abascal et al., 2003) and KWARESMI (Bereikdar, Vanderdonckt, & Noirhomme-Fraiture, 2003) have an architecture where the specification of guidelines is separated from the validation code. Although each one specifies guidelines in a different way, both of them return a detailed report of errors discovered after validating the accessibility of Web content. Another evaluation tool of this type is AccessEnable (Brinck, Hermann, Minnebo, & Hakim, 2002), which is a commercial tool.

Other factors which must be taken into account in order to ensure accuracy when performing automatic accessibility evaluation of Web sites are the correctness and com-pleteness of tools.

Testing Correctness and Completeness of Tools

According to Brajnik (2004), measuring the correctness (whether the tool implements the accessibility tests correctly or not) and the completeness (whether it covers relevant aspects of accessibility) is necessary for determining the efficiency of accessibility evaluation tools.

The correctness of a tool can be seen as the ability to perform the evaluation without producing any false positives (correct items which are marked as errors).

Completeness is related to the number of tests that are performed by the tool. If an automatically detectable error is not tested by a tool a false negative (an error that is not detected) is produced.

Hence, an automatic, validation tool, testing process should report the number of false positives and false negatives detected, as this data will determine the correctness and completeness properties of a tool.

Currently, not all accessibility errors can be automatically detected. As already mentioned, the validation of some accessibility guidelines requires human judgement. Therefore, this type of guideline is usually reported as manual checks or warnings and is not taken into account in testing the completeness and correctness of the tool. Consequently, only the false negatives produced by automatically detectable items are measured for testing the validation tool.

Various methods can be used to test or compare accessibility evaluation tools. For instance, Brajnik (2004) and Diaper and Worman (2003) select several Web sites, evaluate them using different evaluation tools and compare the results obtained. This process allows detecting the differences between the results produced by those tools.

Another method for testing evaluation tools is to define a set of test files which cover all possible accessibility problems and to validate these instead of real Web sites. The problem with this method is the difficulty in defining efficient and comprehensive test files, which increases the development cost in terms of time and effort. For instance, the Access Tool Reviewer (ATR) tool (ATR, n.d.), developed by the Adaptive Technology Resource Centre at the University of Toronto (ATRC, n.d.), employs this method. Some 260 test files have been developed (ATR Test Files, n.d.) in order to test accessibility evaluation tools. Some test files are useful for determining if a tool detects one specific type of error (for instance, one of the test files defines an html document containing only an image without any text equivalent), while others are useful for verifying that valid items are not reported as errors by the tool (for instance, one of the test files defines an html document containing only an image with a valid text equivalent). The ATR tool provides a helpful environment for recording the verified test files and their results (passes or fails). Thus, the developer should manually validate all the test files with the evaluated tool and record each result in the ATR tool, which is quite a tedious task. ATR then records these results in EARL format. According to these results, ATR will automatically calculate the false positives and false negatives produced by the automatic accessibility validation tool.

The advantage of the first method is that the errors detected in the evaluation will also be real-world problems, since the testing is based on real Web sites. Nevertheless, selected Web sites may not have instances of all detectable accessibility errors. Then, results obtained by the first method may not be of use in determining the completeness of the tool. The second method, in contrast, gives a valuable indication of the completeness of the tool. However, of course, it depends on the quality of the test files compiled.

The best approach would be to combine both methods described: performing real Web site based evaluation, as well as test-file-based evaluation.

A Comprehensive Method for Accessibility Evaluation

Accessibility evaluations have to be performed according to a rigorous method in order to ensure their effectiveness. This method should cover the evaluation of all accessibility aspects and should specify all the required steps in the evaluation process.

This section presents a Web accessibility evaluation methodology based on the recommendations issued by the WAI (Abou-Zahra, n.d.). This methodology combines automatic evaluation, manual evaluation, and user evaluation. These three different types of evaluation are required in order to detect all accessibility errors. The evaluator should be conversant with a wide range of techniques and software configurations in order to perform these three types of evaluation. It will require some familiarity with mark-up languages, accessibility guidelines, error correcting techniques, automatic accessibility evaluation tools, browser configuration options, different assistive technologies, and skills in coordinating user groups with different needs. Therefore, the most effective way of performing accessibility evaluations is to establish a group of evaluators, each one having some knowledge of different areas, so the group as a whole has the required background. This would improve the quality of the evaluations. Should it be required, further information on the evaluator groups approach can be found in Brewer (2006). The steps required in order to perform a complete accessibility evaluation will be discussed next.

Identify the Conformance Level the Web Site has to Fulfil

The conformance level the Web site has to achieve is defined in the requirements analysis phase of the lifecycle. It could be determined by the internal accessibility policy of the organization, external requirements (for instance, requirements specified by the client), or external legislation.

Select and Identify the Web Pages to Evaluate

If the Web site consists of a large number of Web pages, a sample of them must be selected. This sample will be manually evaluated, as well as tested with users. The Web pages included in it should be sufficiently representative to ensure that at least one Web page of each type in the site is included. In addition, the Web pages requiring major user interaction and the most visited ones should also be included in the sample.

Perform Automatic Accessibility Evaluation

All the Web pages in the site should be automatically evaluated in order to ensure comprehensive evaluation results, but if the total number of Web pages is too large, a representative sample should be selected. This sample should consist of Web pages from different sections: those that have different design, automatically generated Web pages, those produced according to different sets of guidelines, the most important Web pages for the organization (such as the one containing contact information), and so forth. Another criterion is selecting Web pages according to the most significant tasks in the site (such as Web pages where the user has to fill in a form, view the site map, select a product to buy, and so on).

Different types of automatic evaluation tools (Abou-Zahra, 2006) will be used for this purpose. These tools can be used for evaluating the correctness of the mark-up language or the style sheets (cascading style sheets [CSS]), as well as for evaluating the accessibility of Web pages. As mentioned earlier, it is advisable to automatically evaluate the selected Web pages with at least two different tools (as the results returned may differ). However, all Web pages in the site should be automatically evaluated with at least one tool.

Perform Manual Accessibility Evaluation

Manual evaluation should be carried out for checkpoints which cannot be automatically evaluated and are significant in determining the accessibility level of the Web site. It should be performed at least for those checkpoints whose conformance is necessary in order to achieve the conformance level identified in a previous step.

In addition to performing the manual evaluation, it is also necessary to analyse the layout of the selected Web pages with different browsers and on different platforms. For all configurations the following should be carried out:

- Access the Web pages without loading images in order to analyse if adequate text equivalents are defined for all of them.
- Access the Web pages without loading audio files and ensure that the audio content is also available as text equivalents.
- Change font sizes using the browser options and verify that the text size changes correctly and that the Web pages are still usable.
- Verify that using horizontal scroll is not necessary when changing the resolution of the screen and the size of the browser window. This is useful for determining if there are any references to absolute sizes or positions in the mark-up.
- Verify if the colour contrast is adequate by viewing the Web page or printing it in grey scale.
- Navigate through the Web site using only the tab key without using the mouse, especially in forms, in order to verify that all the elements are accessible. In addition, ensure that the target of all links is clearly defined.
- Access the Web page without loading scripts, style sheets, and applets and verify that all functionalities are available through alternative mechanisms.

It is also necessary to access the Web pages using text browsers such as Lynx (n.d.), screen readers such as Jaws for Windows (n.d.), and talking Web browsers such as IBM Home Page Reader (n.d.). This will verify whether all the information and functions are as easily available when accessing Web sites with special browsers as with graphical browsers. In addition, it is advisable to verify that all information is presented in the correct order, whether accessing with a text browser or with a voice browser. Usability testing techniques such as walk-through are applicable in this step by selecting specific tasks in the Web site and trying to perform them by using different browsers and assistive technology.

Reading through the text, in order to determine if the text is clear and simple, is essential in carrying out a complete manual accessibility evaluation. This aspect of accessibility can also be tested in the next step.

Web Site Accessibility Testing with Users

This step requires coordinating a group of users with different disabilities, diverse levels of technical experience, different levels of familiarity with the Web site, and using diverse assistive technology. These users should evaluate the selected Web pages and navigate through the whole site in order to detect any real error within it. Sometimes these types of evaluations are carried out in controlled environments, such as specific laboratories, but it is also important that users evaluate the Web site in their actual navigation environment. Use of the specific consolidated techniques for Web site usability studies, described in previous sections, such as, thinking aloud, performing specific tasks, and collecting interaction data and enquiry methods is recommended (Nielsen & Mack, 1994; Rubin, 1994).

Documenting the Results of the Evaluation

The results of this process have to be summarised and documented. This results report should contain all the detected errors, clearly identifying the method used for the validation as well as the list of the evaluated Web pages. If an area of the Web site has been omitted from the scope of the evaluation process it should be pointed out in this final report. The more detailed an accessibility evaluation report is, the easier the correction of detected errors will be, so it is desirable to produce as detailed a report as possible. It is advantageous to have a standard organizational template for developing this report as it will facilitate the production of accurate results for the evaluation process. Recommendations for the design of templates for evaluation results reports are available in Brewer 2002c).

Evaluating Accessibility of Dynamically Generated Web Pages

Dynamically generated Web pages have the same presentation, which is defined in a template, but their content may vary as it is obtained from a database. In this case, it is not sufficient to evaluate the accessibility of the template because the dynamically generated content may have accessibility errors and should also be evaluated. In addition to selecting some dynamically generated Web pages for the Web pages sample, it is also necessary to evaluate separately the template and the information contained in the database.

Accessibility of the templates should be evaluated as with the rest of the Web pages. In addition, the information stored in the database should be verified in order to ensure that all the necessary information for generating accessible pages is recorded (for example, equivalent texts for images and audio files).

Finally, it has to be said that, for many reasons, it is difficult to perform frequent accessibility evaluations with impaired users. Thus, the frequency of each type of evaluation (automatic, manual, and with users) need not necessarily be the same, and each one may be performed in different iterations of the lifecycle.

WEB ACCESSIBILITY MAINTENANCE

The maintenance stage can be understood as the accessibility evolution monitoring phase. This process starts once fulfilment of all specifications and requirements have been proved in the evaluation phase. Accessibility maintenance requires performing of automatic accessibility evaluations at a previously defined frequency. Furthermore, Web accessibility has to be evaluated when either a change has been made in the application or new code has been added, as these could cause the nonfulfilment of the accessibility guidelines. The results of these evaluations would monitor accessibility evolution.

In order to know if the changes made in the application have modified the accessibility level, accurate measurements must be carried out. Whatever the accessibility evaluation results are, it is useful to publish the decisions made that have resulted in the present condition of the Web site, in order to fix problems and to avoid them in the future. As developers tend to produce their Web applications in short periods of time and as application updates are also usual, it is useful to automatically monitor accessibility evolution.

An efficient measurement requires design of a metric whose results are accurate and reliable at a given time. Therefore, measurement of Web accessibility in a quantitative way is essential in order to determine the evolution of accessibility of different Web sites in a more rigorous way.

Quantitative Metrics for Web Accessibility

The maintenance phase of the lifecycle requires the definition of quantitative Web metrics. In this section the main factors to be taken into account when defining these quantitative metrics are discussed.

Quantitative accessibility measurements are based on accessibility guidelines, so this section is focused on the WCAG 2.0 guidelines (Caldwell et al., 2005). Thus, the four properties of an accessible Web site are the objects of measurement: Perceivable, Operable, Understandable, and Robust (POUR). The parameters which have to be measured are the following:

- **Depth** of the Web page in the Web site where the error has occurred
- **Number of errors** for each guideline
- Number of times a guideline is **checked**
- The **priority** (or level of success criteria) of the erroneous guidelines should be reflected in the result of the metric, as different priorities impact in different ways.
- The metric should give one value for each accessibility **attribute** (POUR) as well as the overall accessibility value of the Web page.
- **Type** of guideline: related to layout or to content

However, there are also other aspects that have to be taken into account when designing a quantitative metric. In addition to the number of errors (absolute value), the number of times a guideline has been checked must also be measured. This makes it possible to obtain a relative measure which involves real and potential errors. For instance, if a Web page contains only one element which is an image without any text equivalent, this Web page would be completely inaccessible. On the other hand, if one Web page has several elements and one of them is an image which has no text equivalent, it would be more accessible than the former. This is due to the greater number of options the user has while interacting with the Web page.

The navigational context where the error has occurred has to be taken into account in order to measure the accessibility accurately. In some cases this parameter is more illustrative when measuring Web applications. The impact of an error in a deeper Web page within a Web site would be lower than the impact in a Web page which is closer to the home page since the probability of browsing a deeper level page is lower (Lazar, 2003). Therefore, the deeper an error occurs, the less impact it produces.

It is also necessary to distinguish between the types of guidelines. Structural guidelines are those which refer to elements used for the layout of the Web page — such as frames, tables, and embedded objects, such as applets and flash technology. Content guidelines refer to the information provided by elements such as text, images, and audio elements and should have less impact on the accessibility than the former type of guidelines. This is due to the fact that if a structural guideline is not accessible, content elements which may be integrated in these inaccessible structural elements would not be accessible anyway. For instance, a table designed in an inaccessible way, even if it has accessible contents, makes the resulting Web page inaccessible.

As a result, the right combination of all these parameters would ensure an accurate measurement of accessibility.

On the other hand, it would be advisable to use tools that automate the quantitative accessibility measurement. The main problem with integrating the two processes (qualitative and quantitative accessibility evaluation) in a single tool is that automatic validation results are often reported in natural language. A possible error report could be the following: "Guideline 1.1 from WCAG 1.0 has been checked 15 times and has failed 10 times. The guideline has priority 1 and has occurred in the home page."

In order to automatically perform this process, the output report has to be machine-understandable so that integration between tools is easily performed. In this way, the W3C, specifically the Evaluation and Repair Tools Working Group (n.d.) from the WAI is developing EARL. This XML-based language aims at the standardization of the reports produced by accessibility evaluation tools in order to provide interoperability among tools.

IMPLEMENTING THE METHODOLOGY IN ORGANIZATIONS

Establishing an accessibility-driven development methodology in an organization is a complex task that should be performed incrementally in a precisely planned way. Several organization characteristics must be taken into account in this process and significant decisions must be made. First of all, the definition of organizational, internal, accessibility policies is essential in order to implement an appropriate development and maintenance methodology. This means taking into account the available human and material resources in the organization.

Definition of Organizational Accessibility Policies

The commitment of an organization to producing accessible Web content requires the development of internal accessibility policies (Brewer, 2002a). The principal objective of these internal policies should be to establish a development process which incorporates accessibility as an essential property of the product and includes continuous evaluation of this process.

In the case of an organization which does not develop Web applications, but decides to implement and maintain its own accessible Web site, this internal policy can be quite simple. However, if the business of the organization is based on the development of Web applications the implemented accessibility policy will be more complex, as in this case a comprehensive product development methodology, which includes accessibility as the main feature, has to be defined. This policy will become more complex if the development requires external suppliers to develop part of the Web content or Web applications.

Defining an internal accessibility policy that specifies the accessibility guidelines (such as WCAG) to be complied with and at the level of conformance (A, Double-A, Triple-A) will suffice in the first case. An example of this type of policy could be the following:

"[This organization] commits itself to ensuring the accessibility of its Web site. All the Web pages that form the site will conform to the W3C/WAI Web Content Accessibility Guidelines 1.0, with a level of conformance of Double-A by the [date]."

If the main activity of the organization is the development of Web applications, it is necessary to ensure that both the implemented applications and the Web content supplied by external entities or organizations conform to the accessibility guidelines. The end users should be able to access all of its component parts with the same ease (with no differences between the parts implemented by the organization and those from suppliers). The following could be an example of policy for this case:

"[This organization] commits itself to ensuring the accessibility of all the developed Web applications. The new or modified Web content produced by this organization and by the collaborating organizations will conform to level Double-A of the W3C/WAI Web Content Accessibility Guidelines by the [date]. In addition, an accessibility monitoring process will be implemented. Information about the conformance to the W3C/WAI Authoring Tool Accessibility Guidelines will be required from our software providers by the [date]. The Web site of this organization will contain a link to this policy. This policy will be revised in the future in order to consider its modification to reflect new versions of accessibility guidelines."

The involvement of third parties in the development of internal policies requires additional effort, as the Web content developers in those organizations should be trained in the accessibility guidelines specified in the policy. It is sometimes advisable to specify in the internal policy the terms under which these organizations are going to be involved, for instance:

"This internal policy is applied to all the Web content produced or modified by [the organization]. In addition, this organization is performing a number of actions in order to ensure the accessibility of the content provided by external developers or suppliers. These actions are the following:

- Inform about the internal accessibility policy developed by this organization
- Provide links to information on how to implement Web accessibility
- Give incentives for accessible design
- Monitor and provide information on the inaccessible Web content produced

If the Web content developers of the external organizations or collaborators do not produce accessible Web content by the [date] the organization will seek alternative developers."

In some cases, due to the organization's stance on accessibility, it will be necessary to apply an incremental internal accessibility policy, making it possible to establish a date for attaining the A-level of conformance, a later one for Double-A level, and so on. It is also possible to apply the policy to some restricted areas of the Web site and later to extend its applicability to other areas.

Planning Accessibility-Driven Development Methodology Implementation

The accessibility-driven development methodologies implementation plan will vary depending on the type of organization. Some essential steps for successful implementation are described hereafter, although their execution order may change depending on the organization type.

Establish Responsibilities

It is essential that the responsibilities are clearly established within the organization in order to correctly implement an accessibility-driven development process. Then, a manager responsible for aspects of Web accessibility has to be identified, and it is advisable to establish a coordinated group responsible for the implementation plan.

Define and Implement a Clear Accessibility Policy in the Organization

Incorporating a methodology for accessible Web development requires some previous analysis of the accessibility awareness and management in the organization. This preliminary organization evaluation will lead to the definition of an appropriate accessibility policy. A correct accessibility policy should clearly define the accessibility levels that all implemented applications must fulfil.

The implementation of the defined policy can be a complex process since there are many aspects that have to be taken into account, such as resource assignment, selection of appropriate tools, planning of accessibility training courses, and so forth.

It is vital to perform an initial evaluation of the organization before defining a specific internal accessibility policy. The result of this initial evaluation determines the type of policy to be applied. Consequently, if Web accessibility awareness were sufficiently extensive in the organization it would be possible to apply more stringent accessibility policies, requiring a higher level of conformance.

Firstly, it is necessary to find out if the organization has to conform to any external Web accessibility requirement such as legislation on accessibility. If there is any obligation of this kind, the defined internal policy should be at least as stringent as this legislation.

Interviews, accessibility evaluations of the organizational Web site, and evaluations of the methodology applied for Web content development should all be carried out in order to evaluate organization members' knowledge of Web accessibility. Web developers' knowledge about accessible content design has to be especially evaluated, and the type of support for accessibility offered by the currently used development software has to be meticulously analysed.

After defining the accessibility policy, all members of the organization should be informed about it. It is necessary to implement a plan for its initial and continuous development so that awareness about the new organizational policy is disseminated internally as well as externally to clients and Web content suppliers.

Select Suitable Software

It is essential to select suitable development software in order to implement an accessibility-driven development process. The selected software has to comply with the ATAG set of guidelines and has to be installed with the recommended configuration for accessible

Web content development. Some recommendations for selecting appropriate software can be found in Brewer (2002b).

In this respect, the Authoring Tool Accessibility Guidelines Working Group (AUWG) of the WAI periodically performs existing development software validations (Richards, 2002) in order to evaluate their conformance to the ATAG.

There are some applications that evaluate and also assist in correction of the accessibility errors. More information about the existing evaluation and correction tools can be found in Abou-Zahra (2006). These types of tools are useful for evaluating, repairing, and monitoring accessibility of the applications in development. It will be beneficial for the organization to select tools of this kind.

In addition, it would be very useful to obtain an application for publishing the errors or deficiencies found in the selected tools or the common errors made in the development of accessible Web content.

Provide Training

It is essential to plan training options that will satisfy the needs of people with different responsibilities in the organization, in order to successfully implement the development process. Some recommendations on how to prepare training to suit different audiences can be found in Brewer (2000). It is also important to take into account the changes of responsibilities and staff in the organization when planning the training, so that all the training courses should be held as often as required.

Incorporate Accessibility into Each Lifecycle Phase

Accessibility must be taken into account throughout the product lifecycle. This ensures that accessibility errors will be detected and suitably corrected in the early phases of development. Therefore, accessibility should be incorporated into each phase of the lifecycle: analysis, design, implementation, and maintenance.

Currently, some organizations are only concerned with publishing accessible products and not with maintaining their accessibility afterwards, so it is important to highlight the significance of the maintenance phase of the lifecycle. The maintenance phase can be understood as an accessibility monitoring phase, and it must keep track of product accessibility evolution, as modifications and the introduction of new features may affect the accessibility of the product.

Establish an Adequate Process Model which Leads to the Development of Accessible Products

The process model defines the correct sequence of the product lifecycle phases so that selection of an appropriate process model is crucial. Web application development has its own particular characteristics. The lifecycle of these applications is usually quite short and it is important to produce a prototype of the product in a short period of time. These specific characteristics should be taken into account when choosing an appropriate process model. The most suitable process models for developing Web applications have proved to be the iterative ones since they enable rapid production of simple versions or prototypes, which can then be evaluated and improved in subsequent process model stages.

Design a Correct and Accurate Accessibility Evaluation Method

Acessibility evaluation is the most important task and should be performed thoroughly and reiteratively throughout the product lifecycle. Therefore, an appropriate and accurate accessibility evaluation method must be defined in order to obtain useful and comprehensive information on accessibility errors. The completeness and correctness of these evaluations will permit the development of quality products. In addition, an appropriate evaluation method would enable the detection of development methodology failures regarding accessibility. This would lead to a continuous evaluation of the development methodology itself.

Monitoring Accessibility-Driven Development Implementation

Monitoring the development process is as important as implementing it because if regular development process evaluation and monitoring are carried out it enables its deficiencies to be detected. Monitoring the development process can be crucial as it allows it to be enhanced. Therefore, it is essential to specify and plan periodical evaluations which determine the quality of the development process itself, as well as evaluations of all aspects of the internal accessibility policy. These evaluations should also be performed for the Web content developed by suppliers or external developers, and these suppliers should be informed of the results obtained in the evaluations.

If the implemented accessibility policy is incremental, this step is useful in determining whether the organization is ready for the introduction of a more stringent policy in terms of required conformance level or increasing the number of development areas in which the policy is applied.

It is also useful to define a channel for communication with the users in this process, in order to get their opinions, requests, and critiques on the Web content developed by the organization.

CONCLUSION

Useful tools for automatic accessibility evaluation, repair, monitoring, and measurement have been designed, and sound methodologies for accessible design, evaluation, and maintenance have been proposed in recent years. Nevertheless, these tools and methodologies are frequently used in isolation from the standard Web design process. Usually, accessibility is addressed after all the other aspects of the design have been decided, with little scope for in-depth modifications, if they are required, to enable full accessibility. This chapter advocates integration of Web accessibility tools and methodologies in the standard Web design lifecycle. With this approach, accessibility is addressed throughout the process in parallel with other design objectives, and accessibility tools and methodologies are integrated in standard authoring and design tools. This process involves extra effort and requires that companies and institutions make a clear compromise in favour of universal accessibility. Integration of accessibility within the Web software lifecycle is the only way to produce coherent and durable accessible Web sites.

REFERENCES

Abascal, J., Arrue, M., Fajardo, I., Garay, N., & Tomás, J. (2003). Use of guidelines to automatically verify Web accessibility. *Universal Access in the Information Society (UAIS). Guidelines, standards, methods and processes for software accessibility* [Special Issue], *3*(1), 71-79.

Abascal, J., & Nicolle, C. (2005). Moving towards inclusive design guidelines for socially and ethically aware HCI. *Interacting with Computers, 17*(5), 484-505.

Abou-Zahra, S. (Ed.) (n.d.). *Evaluating Web sites for accessibility: Overview*. Retrieved June 9, 2006, from http://www.w3.org/WAI/eval/

Abou-Zahra, S. (Ed.) (2006, March 17). *Web accessibility evaluation tools: Overview*. Retrieved June 9, 2006, from http://www.w3.org/WAI/ER/tools/

Access tool reviewer (ATR). (n.d.). Retrieved December 2005, from http://www.aprompt. ca/ATR/ATR.html

Access tool reviewer (ATR) test files. (n.d.). Retrieved June 9, 2006, from http://www. aprompt.ca/ATR/TestFilesHtml.zip

Adaptive Technology Resource Centre (ATRC). (n.d.). University of Toronto. Retrieved JUne 9, 2006, from http://www.utoronto.ca/atrc/

A-Prompt Project. (n.d.). Retrieved June 9, 2006, from http://aprompt.snow.utoronto.ca/

Bereikdar, A., Vanderdonckt, J., & Noirhomme-Fraiture, M. (2003). KWARESMI — Knowledge-based Web automated evaluation tool with reconfigurable guidelines optimization. In C. Stephanidis (Ed.), *Proceedings of th 10th International Conference in HCI I* (pp. 1504-1508). Mahwah, NJ: Lawrence Erlbaum Associates.

Blair, P. (2004). *A Review of free, online accessibility tools*. Retrieved June 9, 2006, from http://www.webaim.org/techniques/articles/freetools/

Brajnik, G. (2000). *Automatic Web usability evaluation: What needs to be done?* Paper presented at the 6th Human Factors and the Web Conference, Austin, TX.

Brajnik, G. (2001, June 4-6). *A tool for evaluating compliance with accessibility standards*. Paper presented at the 7th Human Factors and the Web Conference, Madison, WI.

Brajnik, G. (2004). Comparing accessibility evaluation tools: A method for tool effectiveness. *Universal Access in the Information Society (UAIS), 3*(3-4), 252-263.

Brewer, J. (Ed.) (2000, November 3). *Overview: Planning Web accessibility training*. Retrieved June 9, 2006, from http://www.w3.org/WAI/training/

Brewer, J. (Ed.) (2002a, October 25). *Developing organizational policies on Web accessibility*. Retrieved June 9, 2006, from http://www.w3.org/WAI/impl/pol.html

Brewer, J. (Ed.) (2002b, October 25). *Selecting and using authoring tools for Web accessibility*. Retrieved June 9, 2006, from http://www.w3.org/WAI/impl/software.html

Brewer, J. (Ed.) (2002c, November 15). *Template for accessibility evaluation reports*. Retrieved June 9, 2006, from http://www.w3.org/WAI/eval/template.html

Brewer, J. (Ed.). (2006, March 23). *Using combined expertise to evaluate Web accessibility*. Retrieved June 9, 2006, from http://www.w3.org/WAI/eval/reviewteams.html

Brinck, T., Hermann, D., Minnebo, B., & Hakim, A. (2002, April 21-22). *AccessEnable: A tool for evaluating compliance with accessibility standards*. Paper presented at the CHI 2002 Workshop: Automatically Evaluating the Usability of Web Sites, Minneapolis, MN.

Caldwell, B., Chisholm, W., Slatin, J., & Vanderheiden, G. (Eds.). (2005, November 23). *Web content accessibility guidelines 2.0 (WCAG 2.0)*. Working draft. Retrieved December 9, 2005, from http://www.w3.org/TR/WCAG20/

Chisholm, W., Vanderheiden, G., & Jacobs, I. (Eds.). (2000, November 6). *Techniques for Web content accessibility guidelines 1.0 (TWCAG 1.0).* Working draft. Retrieved June 9, 2006, from http://www.w3.org/TR/WAI-WEBCONTENT-TECHS/

Diaper, D., & Worman, L. (2003). *Two falls out of three in the automated accessibility assessment of World Wide Web sites: A-Prompt v. Bobby.* In P. Palanque, E. O'Neill, & P. Johnson (Eds.), *Proceedings of the 17th Annual Human-Computer Interaction Conference* (pp. 349-364). London: Springer.

Evaluation and repair tools working group. (n.d.). Retrieved June 9, 2006, from http://www.w3.org/WAI/ER/

Garzotto, F., Paolini, P., & Schwbe, D. (1993). HDM-a model-based approach to hypertext application design. *ACM Transactions on Information Systems, 11*(1), 1-26.

Granollers, T., Lorés, J., & Perdrix, F. (2003). *Usability engineering process model. Integration with software engineering.* In C. Stephanidis (Ed.), *Proceedings of 10th International Conference in HCI* (pp. 965-969). Mahwah, NJ: Lawrence Erlbaum Associates.

Henry, S. L. (Ed.) (2005, November). *Web content accessibility guidelines overview* (WCAG). Retrieved June 9, 2006, from http://www.w3.org/WAI/intro/wcag.php

IBM Home Page Reader (Version 3.04). (n.d.). [Computer software]. IBM Accessibility Center. Retrieved June 9, 2006, from http://www-306.ibm.com/able/solution_offerings/hpr.html

International Organization for Standardization (ISO). (1999). *Information Technology—Software Product Evaluation (ISO 14598-1).* Geneva, Switzerland: ISO.

International Organization for Standardization (ISO). (2001). *Software engineering- Product quality — Part 1: Quality model (ISO 9126-1).* Geneva, Switzerland: ISO.

Isakowitz, T., Stohr, E. A., & Balasubramanian, P. (1995). RMM: A methodology for structured hypermedia design. *Communications of the ACM, 38*(8), 34-44.

Ivory, M., & Hearst, M. (2001). The state of the art in automating usability evaluation of user interfaces. *ACM Computing Surveys, 33*(4), 470-516.

Lazar, J. (2003). The World Wide Web. In J. A. Jacko & A. Sears (Eds.), *The human computer interaction handbook: Fundamentals, evolving technologies, and emerging applications* (pp. 714-730). Mahwah, NJ: Erlbaum.

Jaws for Windows. (n.d.). [Computer software]. Retrieved June 9, 2006, from http://www.freedomscientific.com/fs_products/software_jaws.asp

Lang, T. (2003). *Comparing website accessibility evaluation methods and learnings from usability evaluation methods.* Retrieved from http://www.peakusability.com.au/pdf/website_accessibility.pdf

Lynx (Version 2.8.5). (n.d.). [Computer software]. Retrieved December 2005, from http://lynx.browser.org/

Mayhew, D. J. (1999). *The usability engineering lifecycle: A practitioner's handbook for user interface design.* San Francisco: Morgan Kaufmann.

McCathieNevile, C., & Abou-Zahra, S. (Eds.). (2005, September 9). *Evaluation and report language (EARL) 1.0 schema.* Working draft. Retrieved June 9, 2006, from http://www.w3.org/TR/EARL10/

Mich, L., Franch, M., & Gaio, L. (2003). Evaluating and designing Web site quality. *IEEE Multimedia, 10*(1), 34-43.

Nielsen, J. (2001, May 1). *The usability lifecycle.* Retrieved June 9, 2006, from http://www-128.ibm.com/developerworks/library/it-nielsen3/

Nielsen, J., & Mack, R. L. (1994). *Usability inspection methods*. New York: John Wiley & Sons.

Olsina, L., & Rossi, G. (2002). Measuring Web application quality with WebQEM. *IEEE Multimedia, 9*(4), 20-29.

Pressman, R. S. (1992). *Software engineering: A practitioner's approach*. New York: Mc-Graw-Hill.

Richards, J. (Ed.) (2002, May 28). *Authoring tool conformance evaluations*.Retrieved June 9, 2006, from http://www.w3.org/WAI/AU/2002/tools.html

Rubin, J. (1994). *Handbook of usability testing: How to plan, design and conduct effective tests*. New York: John Wiley & Sons.

Sommerville, I. (1992). *Software engineering*. Reading, MA: Addison-Wesley.

Takata, Y., Nakamura, T., & Seki, H. (2003). *Automatic accessibility guideline validation of XML documents based on a specification language*. In C. Stephanidis (Ed.), Proceedings of the 10th International Conference of HCI (pp. 1040-1044). Mahwah, NJ: Lawerence Erlbaum Associates.

Thatcher, J., Waddell, C. D., Henry, S. L., Swierenga, S., Urban, M. D., Burks, M., et al. (2002). *Constructing accessible Web sites*. Birmingham, UK: glasshaus.

UsableNet—Website Testing Systems (n.d.). Retrieved June 9, 2006, from http://www.usablenet.com/

Watchfire WebXACT. (n.d.). Retrieved June 9, 2006, from http://webxact.watchfire.com/

Web accessibility initiative (WAI). (n.d.). Retrieved Juen 9, 2006, from http://www.w3.org/WAI/

Web Accessibility Versatile Evaluator (WAVE) (Version 3.0). (n.d.). [Computer software]. Retrieved June 9, 2006, from http://wave.webaim.org/index.jsp

World Wide Web Consortium (W3C). (n.d.). Retrieved December 2005 from http://www.w3.org/

Section IV:

Evaluation

Chapter X

Usability
Evaluation

Zhijun Zhang, UsabilityHome.com, USA

ABSTRACT

This chapter introduces the different ways of conducting usability evaluation, which is categorized under four methods: (1) model/metrics based, (2) inquiry, (3) inspection, and (4) testing. Under each method, a list of techniques is described, focusing on when and how each technique should be applied. The chapter also summarizes various studies that compare the effectiveness of different usability evaluation techniques. At the end, guidelines for practitioners and an agenda for researchers are offered. After reading this chapter, the audience should gain an overview of the research and practice of usability evaluation and understand the different criteria for selecting the appropriate technique for a particular project.

INTRODUCTION

Usability evaluation is an important activity in the development of interactive systems. The design of a user interface should go through an iteration of design and evaluation process until usability evaluation shows satisfactory results (Dix, Finlay, Abowd, & Beale, 1998; Nielsen, 1993).

Table 1. The differences between the three usability evaluation methods

Method	User Involved?	Role of Usability Evaluators
Model/Metrics-based	No	Use the model or tool to generate usability measures
Testing	Yes	Observe users using the system; collect and analyze data to identify problems
Inspection	No	Review the user interface and try it out to find problems
Inquiry	Yes	Communicate with users to gain insights into usability problems

Ideally, once a user interface is designed, a tool can be used to take the design as input, and generate usability evaluation results. However, since usability has much to do with human cognitive behavior that is hard to predict, many aspects of usability evaluation still cannot be automated. Therefore, in current practice, usability evaluation typically involves usability experts and representative users.

Usability evaluation can be summative or formative. Summative evaluation aims to collect usability metrics and gain an understanding of the overall usability of the user interface design. Formative usability evaluation is meant to identify usability problems in the design and thus provide input for redesign in order to improve usability.

Typical summative usability measures include task success rate, task completion time, error rate, subjective satisfaction rating, and so forth. It is also possible to summarize all these measures into one number, much like the Six-Sigma approach for quality improvement (Sauro & Kindlund, 2005).

Formative evaluation strives to identify usability problems as much as possible and provide designers the basis for improving the design. Then, based on the priority of the problems and how they may relate to each other, the designers can make decisions on how to modify the design to maximize usability improvement with the available resource.

Operationally, usability evaluation methods can be categorized into the following: model/metrics based, inquiry, inspection, and testing (see Table 1).

MODEL/METRICS-BASED
USABILITY EVALUATION

These techniques are quantitative and are relatively easy to automate. The challenge is to prove that the results generated by the model or the calculated metrics correlate to the actual usability of the system.

Layout Appropriateness

Sears (1993) developed a tool to use a set of metrics for layout appropriateness (LA) to evaluate the usability of the user interface layout based on user tasks. The metrics take into account the sequences of actions users perform and how frequently each sequence is used. The appropriateness of a given layout is computed by weighting the cost of each sequence of actions by how frequently the sequence is performed, which emphasizes frequent methods of accomplishing tasks while incorporating less frequent methods in the design. In addition to calculating the metrics, a tool is developed to generate LA-optimal layout. The designer can compare the LA-optimal and existing layouts or start with the LA-optimal layout and modify it by taking additional factors into consideration.

Web Metrics

Ivory, Sinha, and Hearst (2001) developed 157 metrics for measuring Web pages and Web sites. These metrics assess many aspects of Web interfaces, including the amount of text on a page, color usage, and consistency. They used these metrics to analyze 5,300 Web pages and 330 sites and further developed several statistical models for distinguishing good, average, and poor pages with 93-96% accuracy and for distinguishing sites with 68-88% accuracy. These statistical models can be used by designers to assess the quality of a page or site design and get ideas on how to improve it.

GOMS and Other Models

Card, Moran, and Newell (1983) proposed the goals, operators, methods, and selection (GOMS) rules model. They postulated that users formulate goals that they achieve using methods (procedures for achieving goals). A method is carried out through a set of operators, which are elementary perceptual, motor, or cognitive acts. The selection rules are the control structure for choosing among the several methods available for accomplishing a goal. They also described a model human processor by a set of memories and processors, together with a set of principles of operation.

GOMS model and the model human processor have been used to derive the GOMS technique for user interface evaluation. This technique decomposes user tasks into goals, operators, methods, and selection rules to predict users' task completion time, based on a set of standard processing time for human cognitive, perceptual, and motor processors. It focuses on task completion time for error-free, expert use. This estimated task completion time can be used during the design of a Web or other interface to determine how efficient each design will be for core user tasks. In order to predict a user's learning time, GOMS model has been extended to create natural GOMS language (NGOMSL) (Kieras, 1994).

Similarly, the executive-process/interactive control (EPIC) system (Kieras, Wood, & Meyer, 1997) was developed to simulate the human perceptual and motor performance systems. The EPIC tool can simulate a user's interaction with a user interface system. EPIC has been used to study users engaged in multiple tasks.

The adaptive control of thought-rational (ACT-R) (Anderson, Matessa, & Lebiere, 1997) is a model of the human cognitive process developed and used by cognitive psychologists. It was developed to model problem solving, learning, and memory. Based on ACT-R, adaptive control of thought in information foraging (ACT-IF) (Pirolli & Card, 1998) was developed to model information foraging in Web sites. It is used to simulate user interactions with Web sites in order to predict optimal behavior in large collections of Web documents.

The model can be used to understand the decisions that Web users make in interacting with Web sites to achieve information goals.

NIST WebMetrics

WebMetrics (Scholtz & Laskowski, 1998), developed at the National Institute of Standards and Technology (NIST), consist of a collection of tools for developing and evaluating Web sites and Web applications.

Web Statistic Analyzer Tool (WebSAT), among other similar tools, examines the hyper text markup language (HTML) files of a Web page against usability guidelines and advises the developer about potential usability problems.

Web Category Analysis Tool (WebCAT) lets a usability engineer quickly construct and conduct a simple category analysis across the Web. It is a variation upon traditional card sorting techniques. The usability engineer establishes a set of categories and a number of items. Then, test participants assign items to those categories. The engineer can then compare the actual assignments with the intended usage to make sure that the categories match users' intuitions.

Web Log Based

Web logs are readily available for most Web sites. However, since Web logs are an indirect record of what the user has done, there are limitations in terms of how the logs can be analyzed to accurately represent the usability of a Web site. Nonetheless, because data are available with no extra cost, it is attractive to use the data to uncover some patterns in order to spend more efforts for further investigation.

Commercial products from companies such as WebTrends and Keynote Systems can be used to summarize log data in graphical or report formats in order for the usability evaluator to conduct further analysis.

In the research community, much work has focused on visualizing Web log data for usability evaluators to identify trends and potential usability problems.

Starfield visualization (Hochheiser & Shneiderman, 2001) allows evaluators to interactively explore Web log data in order to gain insights into usability issues. The visualization provides a high-level view of usage patterns such as usage frequency, correlated references, bandwidth usage, hyper text transfer protocol (HTTP) errors, and repeated visits over time. The visualization supports zooming, filtering, and dynamic querying to help the evaluator identify usability problems.

As part of the Web Metrics program, NIST developed tools for analyzing and visualizing Web log data (Cugini & Scholtz, 1999). Framework for logging usability data (FLUD) is a file format and an associated parser for representation of the behavior of Web site users. The VisVIP tool lets the usability evaluator visualize (in 3D graphics) and analyze the navigational paths of Web site users as captured in a FLUD file. VisVIP automatically lays out a 2D graph of the Web site and then overlays the paths of selected subjects to show which pages were visited. A vertical bar indicates how much time users spent at various pages.

USABILITY INQUIRY

In these techniques, usability evaluators obtain information about users' experience with the system by talking to them, observing them using the system in real work (not for the purpose of usability testing), or letting them answer questions (verbally or in written form). These techniques are qualitative and are most suitable in collecting subjective information. The key to these techniques is to have the right users participate and to cover the right issues.

Field Observation

During field observation (Nielsen, 1993), usability evaluators go to representative users' workplace and observe them work, in order to understand how they use the system to accomplish their tasks, and what kind of mental model the users have about the system. This method can be used when users have started to use the system to be evaluated. More than one user in each role should be observed.

With field observation, the usability evaluators should not only look at the use of the system -- like in all usability evaluations, the context of use has to be taken into consideration. The context includes the user's workflow in which the system is part of, the information flow related to the system, and the user's communication pattern (if any) while using the system. Such information should be collected before observing users using the system, by conducting research before the site visit or at the beginning of the site visit.

While observing users use the system, observers should minimize the amount of interruptions to the users. Questions should be held until the user has completed a task, or at least a stage of the task. Observers could ask questions to help understand the user's behavior, and whether the observed behavior is typical for the particular user as well as among all users.

Besides taking notes, after getting the user's permission, observers could also consider using an audio or even a video recorder to record the observation session, or ask users to send screen shots to the observers by e-mail. At the end of the observation session, the evaluators should ask the user for permission for a possible follow-up by phone or e-mail.

After each observation session, the usability evaluators should gather the notes, record observations, identify areas that may need to be clarified with the user observed, and see if anything needs to be adjusted for the next observation session. After all the observation sessions are over, the usability evaluators should put together all the observations, as identified by user ID and role, and identify which ones suggest usability problems. For each potential usability problem, the evaluators should identify which user role has the problem, for what task, and on what screen(s).

Focus Groups

In a focus group (Nielsen, 1993) session, six to nine users are brought together to discuss issues relating to the system. Usability evaluators prepare the list of issues to be discussed beforehand. One of the evaluators plays the role of a moderator during each focus group session. The moderator seeks to gather information from the discussion with regard to the target list of issues. A focus group can capture spontaneous user reactions and ideas that evolve in the dynamic group process.

The moderator plays a critical role in making a focus group session successful. The moderator needs to be skilled in creating an atmosphere in which participants feel at ease and are willing to share their thoughts, keeping the discussion on track without inhibiting the free flow of ideas and comment, and ensuring that all participants get to contribute to the discussion instead of having the discussion dominated by a single participant.

Besides talking, a focus group can include other interactive activities such as real-time surveys, opinion polling, card sorting, and having participants write their comments on sticky notes and put the notes on the printout of some critical screens.

For each study, consider having more than one focus group session, since the outcome of a single session may not be representative and may have focused on a subset of the issues. Besides the moderator, one or more usability evaluators should be present to take notes and possibly ask some questions. With the participants' permission, each focus group session should be video recorded.

Even though technologies have made it possible to conduct real-time online meetings, in most cases, conducting a focus group session using online technologies tends to create a bias in favor of participants with better technology savvy.

Interviews

In this technique, usability evaluators formulate questions about the system based on the kind of issues of interest. Then they interview representative users to ask them these questions to get answers (Nielsen, 1993). This technique is good at obtaining the user's perception of the system, and the user's feedback on system functions that are repeatedly used.

Interviews can be structured or unstructured.

Unstructured interviews are used during earlier stages of usability evaluation. The objective at this stage is to gather as much information as possible concerning the user's experience. The evaluator does not have a well-defined agenda and is not concerned with any specific aspects of the system. The primary objective is to obtain information on procedures adopted by users, their overall satisfaction with the systems, and areas they have the most feedback about.

A structured interview has a predetermined agenda with specific questions to guide and direct the interview. It is more of an interrogation than unstructured interviewing, which is closer to a conversation. A structured interview is designed to uncover the detailed answers to each specific issue:

- When does the problem occur?
- What is the nature of the problem?
- How frequent does the problem occur?
- How severe is the consequence?
- How would the user wish the system to behave differently?

During an interview, the evaluator should ask questions in an open and neutral way—formulate questions in a way that would encourage the user to answer with a full sentence, instead of a simple "yes" or "no" answer. For example, ask, "What do you think of this feature?" and not "Did you like this new feature?" The evaluator should remain neutral and avoid agreeing or disagreeing with the user. Furthermore, the evaluator should not try to explain or even justify the system design to the user.

The evaluator should use probes to obtain further information after the original question is answered. The goal is to encourage the user to continue speaking or to guide the response in a particular direction so a maximum amount of useful information is collected for the topic. Types of probes include:

- **Addition probe:** encourages more information or clarifies certain responses from the user — either verbally or nonverbally, the message is, "Go on, tell me more."
- **Reflecting probe:** encourages the user to give more detailed information. The evaluator can reformulate the question or synthesize the previous response as a proposition.
- **Directive probe:** specifies the direction in which a continuation of the reply should follow without suggesting any particular content. A directive probe may take the form of "Why is this (the case)?"
- **Defining probe:** requires the user to explain the meaning of a particular term or concept.

Ideally, each interview session should be carried out by two evaluators, so that one can take notes while the other is asking the questions. With the permission of the user, the interview session should be recorded. After the interview, it may be necessary for the evaluators to follow up with the user for clarification or important questions that were missed during the interview.

Questionnaires

Questionnaires are a technique for gathering subjective usability ratings from users (Root & Draper, 1983). Each questionnaire consists of a list of questions. For each question, the user is asked to choose one out of a series of choices. The choices typically range from "Strongly disagree" to "Strongly agree," or simply to choose from a numerical scale such as 1 to 9.

When designing a questionnaire, the usability evaluator should pay attention to whether the options provided have a "middle point." Typically a "neutral" answer does not provide much value in understanding the usability of the product. If it is desirable to get a positive or negative answer, then there should not be a middle point in the options (i.e., provide an even number of options).

There are predefined questionnaires that are applicable to most applications. These include the Questionnaire for User Interface Satisfaction (QUIS) by University of Maryland (Chin, Diehl, & Norman, 1988); Computer System Usability Questionnaire (CSUQ) by IBM (Lewis, 1995); and Purdue Usability Testing Questionnaire (PUTQ) by Purdue University (Lin, Choong, & Salvendy, 1997).

Questionnaires can be easily administered over the Web. For the rare case where some users may not have access to the Web, questionnaires can be sent to the users by mail. One challenge with the questionnaire technique is that not all recipients will return the questionnaire. Therefore, there should not be too many questions included in the questionnaire; this would discourage participation.

USABILITY INSPECTION

These techniques involve usability engineers and sometimes software developers, users, and other professionals; they also examine usability-related aspects of a user interface. The inspectors use their knowledge and expertise to uncover potential usability problems in the system. The key is to cover most issues with a limited number of inspectors.

Cognitive Walk-Through

Cognitive walk-through (Polson, Lewis, Rieman, & Wharton, 1992) involves one or a group of evaluators inspecting a user interface by going through a set of tasks and evaluating its understandability and ease of learning. Besides the user interface itself, the input to the walk-through also includes the user profile, especially the users' knowledge of the task domain and of the interface, and the task cases. The evaluators may include human factors engineers, software developers, or people from marketing, documentation, and so forth.

Blackmon, Polson, Kitajima, and Clayton (2002) modified the original cognitive walk-through technique to develop cognitive walk-through for the Web, which uses Latent Semantic Analysis to objectively estimate the degree of semantic similarity (information scent) between representative user goal statements and heading/link texts on each Web page.

Heuristic Evaluation

A heuristic is a guideline or general principle that can guide a design decision or be used to critique a decision that has already been made. Heuristic evaluation (Nielsen & Molich, 1990) is a method for structuring the critique of a system using a set of relatively simple and general heuristics.

The general idea behind heuristic evaluation is that several evaluators independently evaluate a system to come up with potential usability problems. It is important that there be several of these evaluators, and that the evaluations be done independently. Nielsen's experience indicates that having around five evaluators usually results in about 75% of the overall usability problems being discovered.

Heuristic evaluation is best applied at design time, when it is still relatively easy to fix a lot of the usability problems that arise. This technique can be applied very early during the design process. All that is really required to do the evaluation is some sort of artifact that describes the system, and that can range from a set of storyboards giving a quick overview of the system all the way to a fully functioning system that is in use in the field.

Variants of Heuristic Evaluation

Sears (1997) developed heuristic walk-through by providing each inspector a prioritized list of user tasks, a list of usability heuristics, and a list of thought-focusing questions. The inspection is a two-pass process. Pass one is task-based exploration, guided by the list of thought-focusing questions. Pass two is free exploration, guided by usability heuristics. Inspectors detect usability problems in both passes. An empirical study found that heuristic walk-through detected about the same number of usability problems as heuristic evaluation did, but reported much less false positives.

Kurosu, Sugizaki, and Matsuura (1998) developed structured heuristic evaluation, where each usability session was divided into subsessions, with each subsession focusing on one of the following: operability, cognitivity, pleasantness, novice/expert, and disabled users. They reported that their proposed method revealed more than twice the number of problems revealed by heuristic evaluation.

Pluralistic Walk-Through

This technique involves a meeting of usability experts, software developers, and users, where they work on task scenarios and discuss usability issues (Bias, 1994). The idea is to have a diverse group of people to walk through the tasks to identify potential usability problems from different points of view.

While walking through a task, at each step participants are presented with the interface design in the form of a screen panel and are asked to write down separately the action they want to take. Then a discussion begins, in which the users speak first. Only when the users' comments are exhausted do the usability experts and the product developers offer their opinions. After the discussion, the coordinator will tell the participants what actions they are supposed to take according to the user interface design and present the new screen panel after the actions. Thus the walk-through moves to the next step.

Perspective-Based Inspection

This technique asks the inspector to focus on one of several usability perspectives during each inspection session (Zhang, Basili, & Shneiderman, 1999). The combination of these different perspectives should provide a full coverage of all usability issues. An example set of perspectives are novice use, expert use, and error handling. The idea is that by focusing on a subset of issues, each inspection session would be able to uncover a higher percentage of usability problems. During the inspection, evaluators are asked to walk through the representative tasks to make sure that they focus on how users will use the system, instead of just looking at the appearance of the user interface.

Perspective-based inspection can be applied by multiple inspectors, each of which inspects the user interface once using one of the perspectives. It can also be applied by a single inspector, who would inspect the user interface multiple times, each time from one of the perspectives.

USABILITY TESTING

In usability testing, representative users (referred to as test participants) work on typical tasks using the system (or the prototype), and the evaluators use the results to see how the user interface supports the users to do their tasks. During the development lifecycle, it is very important to conduct usability tests before it becomes expensive to change the user interface. When usability testing is toward the end of the lifecycle, few, if any, of the reported usability problems will get fixed because the cost to fix them becomes very high once the system is fully built.

The followed usability testing techniques have been used.

Thinking-Aloud Protocol

Using this technique, during the course of a usability test, the test participants are asked to verbalize their thoughts, feelings, and opinions while interacting with the system (Rubin, 1994). It is very useful in capturing a wide range of cognitive activities.

Thinking aloud allows usability evaluators to understand how the user approaches the interface, and what considerations the user keeps in mind when using the interface. If the user expresses that the sequence of steps dictated by the product to accomplish their task goal is different from what they expected, perhaps the interface is convoluted.

Although the main benefit of the thinking-aloud protocol is a better understanding of the user's mental model during their interaction with the product, there are other benefits as well. For example, the terminology the user uses to express an idea or function should be incorporated into the product design or at least its documentation.

Shadowing Method

This is a variant of the thinking-aloud protocol. With this technique, while the test participate is using the application to complete the tasks, an expert user sits next to the usability evaluator to interpret what the test participant is doing (Zhang, 1996).

This technique can be applied when it is not desirable or not possible for the test participant to think aloud while working on the tasks. It is also useful when the usability evaluator is not familiar with the user interface or the task domain.

Co-Discovery Learning

This is another variant of thinking-aloud protocol. With co-discovery learning, during a usability test, two test users attempt to perform tasks together while being observed (Dumas & Redish, 1999). They are to help each other in the same manner as they would if they were working together to accomplish a common goal using the product. They are encouraged to explain what they are thinking about while working on the tasks. Compared to the thinking-aloud protocol, this technique makes it more natural for the test participants to verbalize their thoughts during the usability test.

To make the technique successful, it is helpful to have two participants who have worked with each other before, and therefore will be able to communicate with each other comfortably and effectively.

Coaching Method

With this technique, during a usability test, the participants are allowed to ask an expert (the coach) any system-related questions. The coach will answer to the best of his or her ability (Nielsen, 1993). Usually the usability evaluator serves as the coach. One variant of the method involves a separate expert user serving as the coach, while the evaluator observes both the interaction between the participant and the computer, and the interaction between the participant and the coach.

The purpose of this technique is to discover the information needs of users in order to provide better training and documentation, as well as possibly redesigning the interface to avoid the need for the questions. When an expert user is used as the coach, the expert user's mental model of the system can also be analyzed by the evaluator.

The evaluator can also control the answers to certain predetermined information. In an extensive series of experiments, one could vary the coach's answers in order to learn what types of answers helped users the most. But this requires skilled and careful coaches since they need to compose answers on the fly to unpredictable user questions.

Question-Asking Protocol

This technique can be used in conjunction with the thinking-aloud protocol. During a usability test, besides letting the test participants verbalize their thoughts as in the thinking-aloud protocol, the evaluators prompt them by asking direct questions about the product, in order to understand their mental model of the system and the tasks, and where they have trouble in understanding and using the system (Zhang, 1996). This is a more natural way than the thinking-aloud technique in letting the test user proactively verbalize their thoughts. It is also useful when the test participants forget or are not used to thinking aloud.

For example, during the usability test, when the test participant says "I'm going to click on the 'View More' button," the usability tester can ask, "What do you expect to see on the next screen once you click on this button?"

Teaching Method

When using this technique during a usability test, the test participants are asked to interact with the system first, so that they get familiar with it and acquire some expertise in accomplishing tasks using the system. Then, a novice user is introduced to each test participant. The novice users are briefed by the usability evaluator to limit their active participation so that they do not become an active problem solver. Then each test participant is asked to explain to the novice user how the system works and demonstrate to him or her a set of predetermined tasks (Vora & Helander, 1995).

This technique is very useful in understanding the user's mental model of the system and verifying if what the user has perceived is the same as what the designer has intended.

Retrospective Testing

If the video of a usability test session has been captured, the usability evaluator can collect more information by reviewing the video recording together with the test participants and asking them questions regarding their behavior during the test (Dumas & Redish, 1999). This technique could be used along with other techniques, especially those where the interaction between the evaluator and the test participants is restricted. It is ideal for the review to happen right after the actual testing session, so that there is a greater chance that the participants accurately remember what they were thinking or trying to do at each step during the test.

Performance Measurement

This technique is used to obtain quantitative data about test participants' performance when they complete tasks during a usability test (Nielsen, 1993). This will generally prohibit an interaction between the participant and the usability evaluator during the test because any interaction will affect the quantitative performance data. It should be conducted in a formal usability laboratory so that the data can be collected accurately and unexpected interference is minimized. Quantitative data is most useful in doing comparative testing, or testing against predefined benchmarks. To obtain dependable results, at least five user participants are needed, while eight or more participants would be more desirable. The technique can be used in combination with retrospective testing, post-test interview, or questionnaires so that both quantitative and qualitative data are obtained.

Remote Testing

Remote usability testing is used when usability evaluators are separated in space and/or time from the test participants (Hartson, Castillo, Kelso, Kamler, & Neale, 1996).

This means that the evaluator(s) cannot observe the testing sessions at the place and time that they are happening. It also means that the participants are usually not in a formal usability laboratory.

There are different types of remote testing. One is *same-time but different-place*, where the usability evaluator can observe the test participant's screen through the computer network, and hear what the test user says during the test, through the network or the speaker telephone. The evaluator can also interact with the participant over the network.

Another type of remote testing is *different-time different-place* testing such as journaled sessions, where the user's test session is guided and logged through a special piece of software as well as additional code added to the system being tested.

Various tools have been developed and used for remote usability testing. An early solution included using CU-SeeMe software for the evaluator to remotely view the participant's computer screen in real time and to interact with the participant through a speaker telephone. More recently, video conferencing technologies such as WebEx are used for doing remote usability testing. Morae Inc. offers a technology that is specifically designed for remote usability testing. The Morae tool not only allows for remote observation and interaction, but also captures the test session, records the user actions, and allows for the evaluator to search for certain actions during post-test analysis.

Using Eye-Tracking Devices

In recent years, the use of eye-tracking devices has been applied to the usability evaluation of Web sites (Duchowski, 2003). Usability practitioners and researchers have been attempting to identify the specific contributions of eye-tracking devices to Web site design and usability evaluation. Many such studies involve the identification of the pattern of the users' visual attention to different parts of the interface, or areas of interest (AOI). Then by trying out different designs and observing their impact on the user's visual attention, the designers can gain insights as to how to lead the user to the important information in order for them to complete the tasks at hand.

Some eye-tracking devices can be obtrusive (e.g., the user needs to wear a helmet), thus may impact the user's performance during the usability test. There are nonobtrusive eye-tracking devices that include a high resolution camera and near infrared light-emitting diodes that are attached to the computer monitor.

EMPIRICAL STUDIES OF USABILITY EVALUATION TECHNIQUES

Much research has been conducted to compare the different usability evaluation techniques. These studies are summarized based on the main variable in the study.

Prescriptiveness

Prescriptiveness means with how much detail a usability evaluation technique provides instruction to the evaluator on how to conduct the evaluation.

Jeffries, Miller, Wharton, and Uyeda (1991) conducted a study in which cognitive walk-through was compared against guideline inspection (i.e., conducting usability evaluation against usability guidelines). The subjects were three software engineers, who used both techniques. The results showed that both techniques detected about 1 of the 6 problems. Among the problems found using guidelines inspection (33 in total number), only about 1 of the 3 were found via the technique itself, with others found as side effect (e.g., while applying a guideline about screen layout, a problem with menu organization might be noted) or through prior experience. Most (30 out of 35) problems detected using cognitive walk-through were via the technique. The reason could be that cognitive walk-through was more prescriptive so that the inspectors were following the technique most of the time. On the other hand, subjects reported that cognitive walk-through was tedious and sometimes required too much detail. As a result, inspectors were only able to finish 7 of the 10 tasks during the evaluation session, which was longer than the session for guidelines inspection.

Nielsen and Phillips (1993) used GOMS and three forms of heuristic evaluation to estimate user performance with two alternative designs for database query tasks. The estimated performance (time to complete tasks) was compared to results from usability testing. The three forms of heuristic evaluation are (1) cold estimates, (2) warm estimates, and (3) hot estimates. For the cold estimates, 12 inspectors were given a written specification of the two designs. For warm estimates, 10 inspectors were given the running prototype of one design and the written description of another design. For hot estimates, 15 inspectors were given running versions of both interfaces. For GOMS, 19 evaluators were given the same specification of the two interfaces as used by the cold estimates. Therefore, GOMS was comparable to the cold estimates situation. The results showed that all methods gave a good estimation of the relative advantage of one design over the other. For absolute user performance (i.e., time to complete tasks), GOMS was always better than the cold estimates, but was not as good as the other two forms of heuristic evaluation. GOMS had much less variance among its 19 evaluators than any form of the heuristic evaluation methods. The variance for GOMS was 19% of the mean, while for the cold, warm, and hot estimates (using heuristic evaluation) the variance was 108%, 75%, and 52% of the mean, respectively.

Desurvire, Kondziela, and Atwood (1992) conducted a study in which a phone-based interface was evaluated by groups of three evaluators of different experience levels by using either heuristic evaluation or cognitive walk-through. The three different experience levels were: (1) experts who had at least 3 years of human factors work experience; (2) software developers; and (3) nonexperts who were not experts in usability or user interface design. The total number of evaluator groups was six, one for each technique and experience level. All groups used task-based evaluation, with six basic tasks representative of the system's usage. User testing data was collected from observing and videotaping 18 potential end users of the system, who performed the same six basic tasks. The identified usability problems were classified into the following three categories:

- Minor annoyance or confusion
- Problem that caused error
- Problem that caused task failure

The results (summarized in Table 2) showed that the groups of nonexperts and software developers had almost the same performance for the two different techniques. But the expert group using heuristic evaluation did better than the expert group using cognitive walk-throughs. Again it was reported that cognitive walk-through was very time consuming. Perhaps this has caused the experts to spend too much time dealing with the inspection procedure, which made their inspection performance poorer.

Table 2. Results from the (Desurvire et al., 1992, p. 95) study: Number of problems detected

Technique	User testing	Heuristic evaluation			Cognitive walk-through		
Evaluators	Users	Experts	Developers	Nonexperts	Experts	Developers	Nonexperts
Problems that did occur	25	11	4	2	7	4	2
Potential problems	29	9	7	1	9	6	2
Minor annoyance or confusion	5	4	2	1	2	2	1
Problems caused error	3	2	0	0	2	0	0
Problems caused task failure	17	5	2	1	3	2	1

In summary, these studies provide evidence that the more prescriptive cognitive walk-through technique seems to be more helpful than guidelines inspection for software developers to detect usability problems (the Jeffries et al., 1991 study); that the more prescriptive GOMS evaluation generates more consistent results among the evaluators than heuristic evaluation (the Nielsen & Phillips, 1993 study); and that neither heuristic evaluation nor cognitive walk-through is effective when used by software developers or nonexperts for usability inspection (the Desurvire et al., 1992 study).

Individual Responsibility

In the studies reviewed in the previous section, inspectors using the same technique all had the same responsibility and were not asked to take different perspectives at different stages of the inspection. In the following studies, inspectors were asked to review the interface with a particular perspective, or focusing on a different set of usability issues during each inspection session. Sometimes, an inspector is asked to review the interface multiple times, changing perspectives from time to time.

In a study by Desurvire (1994), each of the three levels of inspectors — (1) human factors experts, (2) nonexperts, and (3) developers — were asked to study flowcharts of a voice interface (the same interface as in the Desurvire et al., 1992 study described previously) several times, once from each of several quite different perspectives. The perspectives used were of: the inspector's own, a human factors expert, a cognitive psychologist, a behaviorist, a Freudian, an anthropologist, a sociologist, a health advocate, a worried mother, and a spoiled child. All evaluators received the same order of perspectives. For each perspective, after reading a short orientation toward that perspective, the evaluators looked at the flowchart and each of the three tasks and recorded possible user problems.

Table 3. Comparison of problem detection by perspectives (Desurvire, 1994) and other techniques (Desurvire, 1992)

Method	Evaluators	% of problems that occurred	% of potential problems
Perspectives	Experts	37	27
	Developers	29	33
	Nonexperts	34	40
Heuristic evaluation	Experts	44	31
	Developers	16	24
	Nonexperts	8	3
Cognitive walk-through	Experts	28	31
	Developers	16	21
	Nonexperts	8	7

Compared to the study (Desurvire et al., 1992) using the same interface under a similar setup (as described earlier in this section), the author (see Table 3 for comparison) suggested that the perspectives approach may offer substantial promise as a technique to enhance interface evaluations by nonexperts and developers in several dimensions, such as avoiding false positives, finding real problems, and offering suggestions for improvements.

Kurosu et al. (1998) compared heuristic evaluation and structured heuristic evaluation. Each usability session was divided into subsessions, with each subsession focusing on one of the following: operability, cognitivity, pleasantness, novice/expert, and disabled users. Two variations of structured heuristic evaluation were used in the experiment: one with 32 guideline items and the other with 41. There were five subjects for each technique, all nonexpert inspectors. Each subject spent a total of 3 hours inspecting the usability of a walkman. The results were that structured heuristic evaluation with 41 guideline items revealed more than twice the number of problems revealed by heuristic evaluation, and the other condition (with 32 guideline items) revealed about 1.5 times as many problems as revealed by heuristic evaluation.

Zhang (1999) conducted three experiments to compare perspective-based usability inspection against heuristic evaluation. The user interfaces being inspected were a Web-based data collection form (experiment I) and a commercial Web site (experiments II and III). The subjects included both professionals (experiments I and III) and students (experiment II), who worked either individually or in two-person teams. The experimental results showed that on average each inspector using a perspective-based technique detected not only more problems related to the assigned perspective, but also more problems overall. For the combined effectiveness of multiple inspectors, perspective-based inspection showed a significant improvement over heuristic evaluation (30% for three inspectors in experiment I, 90% for four inspectors in experiment II, and 45% for four inspectors in experiment III).

In summary, results from these studies suggest that it is promising to have each inspector focus on a subset of issues or inspect from a specific perspective, especially for nonexpert inspectors in usability inspection.

Inspector Experience

In a study conducted by Nielsen (1992), one voice response user interface was subject to heuristic evaluation by three groups of evaluators: (1) usability novices with knowledge about computers in general but no special usability expertise; (2) single experts who were usability specialists but not specialized in the domain of the interface; and (3) double experts with experience in both usability in general and the kind of interface being evaluated. In the study, the novice inspectors were 31 computer science students who had completed their first programming course but had no formal knowledge of user interface design principles. The single experts were 19 usability specialists. The double experts were 14 specialists in usability for the specific application domain. On average, the novice evaluators each found 22% of the usability problems in the interface; the single experts found 41% of the problems each; and the double experts found 60% each.

Accordingly, it was estimated that to achieve 80% coverage, about two double experts, four single experts, or 16 novices are needed.

In the two Desurvire (1992, 1994) studies mentioned earlier (see Table 2 and Table 3), it is clear that inspector expertise on usability had a substantial impact on the inspection results. Using the same technique, the same number of expert inspectors found 5 times more problems than the nonexpert inspectors.

In two of the studies conducted by Zhang (1999, experiments II and III, as described previously), everything was pretty much the same except that the participants were full-time students in one study, and full-time professionals in another. The results showed that the professionals were able to identify more usability problems than the students, especially when using a nonprescriptive technique such as the heuristic evaluation.

Therefore, evaluator expertise can play an important role in determining the effectiveness of a usability evaluation.

SUMMARY

Different usability evaluation methods and techniques have been developed: practices, and studies. A practitioner needs to be able to decide which technique is the best for a particular situation. Researchers need to continue validating the effectiveness of the different techniques, improving existing ones, and developing new ones. The outcome of such research activities will provide further guidance for usability practitioners.

Practitioner's Guide

Usability professionals should get familiar with the various usability evaluation methods and techniques. Each organization should build a toolbox of such evaluation techniques by building expertise; creating standard procedures and document templates; and establishing the necessary resources such as pools of user participants and the supporting technology that is needed.

For each particular evaluation project, it is important to understand where in the development lifecycle the application is; how many usability evaluators and user participants are available; what kind of usability attributes are the focus for the evaluation; and so forth. Then a tool such as the Usability Advisor (n.d.) can be used to screen the evaluation techniques that can potentially be used for the effort.

Researcher's Agenda

There are many open issues in usability evaluation that need further research. A major challenge is that usability evaluation results vary dramatically when applied by different evaluators. This is highlighted by the series of comparative usability evaluation (CUE) studies, CUE-1 (Molich et al., 1998); CUE-2 (Molich et al., 1999); CUE-3 (Hertzum, Jacobsen, & Molich, 2002); and CUE-4 (Dumas, Molich, & Jeffries, 2004).

CUE-1 and CUE-2 had different teams conduct usability testing of the same user interface (a graphical user interface [GUI] interface in CUE-1 and a Web interface in CUE-2). The results showed little overlap in identifying usability problems among the four and eight independent teams. For example, in CUE-2, 8 of the 9 teams missed 75% of the usability problems, and only one team reported more than 25% of the collective total.

CUE-3 had multiple teams conduct usability inspection and was considered a pilot study with no conclusions. In CUE-4, 17 teams of experienced usability specialists independently conducted either a usability inspection or a usability test of a hotel reservation Web site. This time, there was a strong level of agreement of the usability problems identified. However, there was much less agreement on which usability problems were the highest priority. There was also a significant inconsistency in the granularity of the problems reported. One problem reported by one team is often reported as several more granular problems by another team.

The results from these comparative usability evaluation studies strongly call for further research of the following questions:

- Where do variations of usability evaluation results come from? Is there any systematic way of reducing such variations so that when different people apply the same technique in evaluating a user interface the results would be consistent?
- Why is a significant portion of existing usability problems not uncovered during a usability evaluation? How can we improve these techniques?
- Can we develop a taxonomy of usability problems across the industry with appropriate granularity so that when a usability problem is identified there is a consistent way of reporting it, and it becomes unambiguous for others to understand the problem?
- Can we develop a more objective way of ranking usability problems instead of relying on the evaluator's "gut feeling"?

To study these questions, we need a community of researchers that collaborate with each other and share research agenda and materials. A usability evaluation test bed would also be helpful for researchers to compare research results and build on each other's work.

REFERENCES

Anderson, J., Matessa, M., & Lebiere, C. (1997). ACT-R: A theory of higher level cognition and its relation to visual attention. *Human-Computer Interaction, 12,* 439-462.

Bias, R. (1994). The pluralistic usability walkthrough: Coordinated empathies. In J. Nielsen & R. Mack (Eds.), *Usability inspection methods* (pp. 63-76). New York: John Wiley & Sons.

Blackmon, M. H., Polson, P. G., Kitajima, M., & Clayton, L. (2002). Cognitive walkthrough for the Web. In *Proceedings of the Conference on Human Factors in Computing Systems,* Minneapolis, MN (pp. 463-470). New York: ACM Press.

Card, S. K., Moran, T. P., & Newell, A. (1983). *The psychology of human-computer interaction.* Hillsdale, NJ: Lawrence Erlbaum Associates.

Chin, J. P., Diehl, V. A., & Norman, K. L. (1988). Development of an instrument measuring user satisfaction of the human-computer interface. In *Proceedings of the Conference on Human Factors in Computing Systems* (pp. 213-218). New York: ACM Press.

Cugini, J., & Scholtz, J. (1999). VisVIP: 3D visualization of paths through Websites. In *Proceedings of the International Workshop on Web-based Information Visualization,* Los Alamitos, CA (pp. 259-263). Florence, Italy: IEEE.

Desurvire, H. (1994). Faster, cheaper!! Are usability inspection methods as effective as empirical testing? In J. Nielsen & R. Mack (Eds.), *Usability inspection methods* (pp. 173-202) John Wiley & Sons.

Desurvire, H., Kondziela, J. M., & Atwood, M. E. (1992). What is gained and lost when using evaluation methods other than empirical testing. In A. Monk, D. Diaper, & M. D. Harrison (Eds.), *People and computers VII* (pp. 89-102). Cambridge, UK: Cambridge University Press.

Dix, A., Finlay, J., Abowd, G., & Beale, R. (1998). *Human-computer interaction* (2nd ed.). Upper Saddle River, NJ: Prentice Hall.

Duchowski, A. T. (2003). *Eye tracking methodology: Theory and practice.* London: Springer.

Dumas, J., Molich, R., & Jeffries, R. (2004, July-August). Describing usability problems — Are we sending the right message. *Interactions,* 24-29.

Dumas, J., & Redish, J. (1999). *A practical guide to usability testing* (Rev. ed.). UK: Intellect.

Hartson, H. R., Castillo, J. C., Kelso, J., Kamler, J., & Neale, W. C. (1996). Remote evaluation: The network as an extension of the usability laboratory. In *Proceedings of the Conference on Human Factors in Computing Systems* (pp. 228-235). New York: ACM Press.

Hertzum, M., Jacobsen, N. E., & Molich, R. (2002). Usability inspections by groups of specialists: Perceived agreement in spite of disparate observations. In *Proceedings of the Conference on Human Factors in Computing Systems — Extended Abstracts* (pp. 662-663). New York: ACM Press.

Hochheiser, H., & Shneiderman, B. (2001). Using interactive visualization of WWW log data to characterize access patterns and inform site design. *Journal of American Society for Information Science and Technology, 52*(4), 331-343.

Ivory, M. Y., Sinha, R. R., & Hearst, M. A. (2001). Empirically validated Web page design metrics. In *Proceedings of the Conference on Human Factors in Computing Systems,* Seattle, WA (pp. 53-60). New York: ACM Press.

Jeffries, R., Miller, J. R., Wharton, C., & Uyeda, K. M. (1991). User interface evaluation in the real world: A comparison of four techniques. In *Proceedings of the Conference on Human Factors in Computing Systems* (pp. 119-124). New Orleans, LA. New York: ACM Press.

Kieras, D. E. (1994). GOMS modeling of user interfaces using NGOMSL. In *Proceedings of the Conference on Human Factors in Computing Systems,* Boston (pp. 371-372). New York: ACM Press.

Kieras, D. E., Wood, S. D., & Meyer, D. E. (1997). Predictive engineering models based on the EPIC architecture for a multimodal high-performance human-computer interaction task. *ACM Transactions on Computer-Human Interaction, 4*(3), 230-275.

Kurosu, M., Sugizaki, M., & Matsuura, S. (1998, June 25-26). *Structured heuristic evaluation method (sHEM)*. Paper presented at Usability Professionals Association Annual Meeting, Washington, DC.

Lewis, J. (1995). IBM computer usability satisfaction questionnaires: Psychometric evaluation and instructions for use. *International Journal of Human-Computer Interaction, 7*(1), 57-78.

Lin, H. X., Choong, Y.-Y., & Salvendy, G. (1997). A proposed index of usability: A method for comparing the relative usability of different software systems. *Behaviour & Information Technology, 16*(4 & 5), 267-278.

Molich, R., Bevan, N., Curson, I., Butler, S., Kindlund, E., Miller, D., & Kirakowski, J. (1998, June 25-26). *C omparative evaluation of usability tests*. Paper presented at the Usability Professionals Association Annual Meeting, Washington, DC.

Molich, R., Thomsen, A. D., Karyukina, B., Schmidt, L., Ede, M., van Oel, W., & Arcuri, M. (1999). Comparative evaluation of usability tests. In *Proceedings of the Conference on Human Factor in Computer Systems — Extended Abstracts* (pp. 83-84). New York: ACM Press.

Morae. [Computer software]. Retrieved from http://www.techsmith.com/morae.asp

Nielsen, J., & Molich, R. (1990). Heuristic evaluation of user interfaces. In *Proceedings of the Conference on Human Factors in Computing Systems,* Seattle, WA (pp. 249-256). New York: ACM Press.

Nielsen, J. (1992). Finding usability problems through heuristic evaluation. In *Proceedings of the conference on Human Factors in Computing Systems,* Monterey, CA (pp. 373-380). New York: ACM Press.

Nielsen, J. (1993). *Usability engineering*. Boston: Academic Press.

Nielsen, J., & Phillips, V. (1993). Estimating the relative usability of two interfaces: Heuristic, formal, and empirical methods compared. In *Proceedings of the Conference on Human Factors in Computing Systems* (pp. 214-221). New York: ACM Press.

Pirolli, P., & Card, S. (1998). Information foraging models of browsers for very large document spaces. In *Proceedings of the Working Conference on Advanced Visual Interfaces (AVI) '98,* L'Aquila, Italy (pp. 83-93). New York: ACM Press.

Polson, P. G., Lewis, C., Rieman, J., & Wharton, C. (1992). Cognitive walkthroughs: A method for theory-based evaluation of user interfaces. *International Journal of Man-Machine Studies, 36,* 741-773.

Root, R., & Draper, S. (1983). Questionnaires as a software evaluation tool. In *Proceedings of the Conference on Human Factors in Computing Systems* (pp. 83-87). New York: ACM Press.

Rubin, J. (1994). *Handbook of usability testing*. New York: John Wiley & Sons.

Sauro, J., & Kindlund, E. (2005) A method to standardize usability metrics into a single score. In *Proceedings of the Conference on Human Factors in Computing Systems* (pp. 401-409). New York: ACM Press.

Scholtz, J., & Laskowski, S. (1998, June 5). *Developing usability tools and techniques for designing and testing Web sites*. Paper presented at the 4th Conference on Human Factors and the Web, Basking Ridge, NJ.

Sears, A. (1993). Layout appropriateness: A metric for evaluating user interface widget layout. *IEEE—Transactions on Software Engineering, 19*(7), 707-719.

Sears, A. (1997). Heuristic walkthroughs: Finding the problems without the noise. *International Journal of Human-Computer Interaction, 9*(3), 213-234.

The CU-SeeMe Project. (n.d.). Retrieved June 21, 2006, from http://myhome.hanafos.com/~soonjp/project.html

Usability Advisor. (n.d.). Retrieved June 20, 2006, from http://www.usabilityhome.com/Advisor.html

Vora, P., & Helander, M. (1995). A teaching method as an alternative to the concurrent think-aloud method for usablity testing. In Y. Anzai, K. Ogawa, & H. Mori (Eds.), *Symbiosis of Human and Artifact: Proceedings of the Sixth International Conference on Human-Computer Interaction,* Tokyo, Japan (pp. 375-380). Amsterdam: Elsevier.

WebEx. [Computer software]. Retrieved from http://www.webex.com

Zhang, Z. (1996). *Usability evaluation methods.* Retrieved June 20, 2006, from http://www.usabilityhome.com/

Zhang, Z. (1999). *The design and empirical validation of perspective-based usability inspection.* Unpublished PhD thesis, University of Maryland, College Park.

Zhang, Z., Basili, V., & Shneiderman, B. (1999). Perspective-based usability inspection: An empirical validation of efficacy. *Empirical Software Engineering, 4*(1), 43-69.

Chapter XI

Walkthroughs in Web Usability:
Cognitive, Activity, and Heuristic Walkthrough

Hokyoung Ryu, Massey University, New Zealand

ABSTRACT

The evaluators of a Web site have a need for robust and easy-to-use usability inspection methods to help them to systematically identify the possible usability problems of the Web site being analysed. Three usability inspection methods — heuristic walk-through (HW), cognitive walk-through (CW), and activity walk-through (AW) — are reviewed in this chapter. This chapter discusses the relative advantages and weaknesses of all of the techniques, and suggestions for Web evaluation are offered, with a short Web site example. Based on these analyses, we suggest some changes to Web site evaluation to improve accuracy and reliability of the current walk-through methods; however, this chapter is not a comparison between the walk-through techniques in order to determine which technique is best at detecting usability problems of a Web site.

INTRODUCTION

Studies of human computer interaction (HCI) have established numerous usability inspection methods that can be applied by Web designers without the effort and expense of setting up evaluations with real users. This has ensured that measurement and concern of usability issues can be readily brought into an early Web design process.

The existing usability inspection methods are mostly based on and directed to the evaluation of the user interfaces of software or products that have been the catalyst of the HCI studies thus far. Recently, the relatively new medium — Web-based information systems — has been a driving force to extend the findings and theories from previous studies of HCI, in terms of its different use and use contexts compared with the traditional user interfaces. For instance, the design principles and guidelines of interface design have been rephrased for the Web context (e.g., Nielsen, 2000), likewise some advances of previous psychological theories have also been made for the Web context (e.g., Blackmon, Polson, Kitajima, & Lewis, 2002).

Following these advances, this chapter reviews usability inspection methods based on the walk-through methodology, with the aim of assessing how they collectively provide a reasonable suite of usability inspection tools for Web-based information systems. The first section looks at the theoretical foundations of Web evaluation. In the following sections, we take a brief look at different Web usability inspection techniques and describe the principles and concepts that each method is grounded on. Finally, we discuss the strengths and weaknesses of the methods as they currently exist and suggest improvements for assessing Web sites.

THEORETICAL FOUNDATIONS
OF WEB EVALUATION

Let us first consider the typical situations in which people use a Web site. Quite often, there are two simple ways to access a Web site that the users want to use. Firstly, when they are aware of the Web site that matches their current objectives they will, either type the URL of the Web site, or simply use a previously established bookmark of the Web site. Otherwise they will employ a particular search engine for finding a best-fit Web site for their current objectives. Either way, all of their subsequent actions would be organised by only interacting with the current Web page appearing in a piecemeal and iterative way as follows.

Firstly, it is generally believed that users will analyse the Web page, separating it into several subregions and concentrate on the subregion(s) of the page that is semantically most similar to their current objectives. An action selection process that selects and acts on the relevant widgets from the chosen subregion follows (Kitajima, Blackmon, & Polson, 2000).

In such common Web navigation situations, there seems to be two interaction styles: *recognition-based* and *recall-based interaction*. In general, it is believed that most Web users are completely dependent on the labels, or the information presented on a Web page. Such individuals, especially new or infrequent visitors to a Web page, will have only abstract representations of their tasks and its goal structure with little or no knowledge of the consequences of their actions, so they have a strong tendency to select graphical widgets on the Web page based on how well they semantically match one or more components of their current goal sets. On the contrary, a recall-based interaction style is used by very frequent

Figure 1. Cyclic interaction in the typical Web use situations

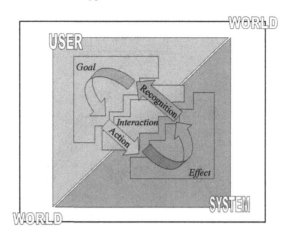

visitors to a Web site, or users of a well-standardised Web site such as an online bookshop site, who would have knowledge of how to decompose a task into a collection of subtasks in order to make effective use of the relevant subregions of the Web site. Therefore, the extensive knowledge of possible actions and the actual consequences of those actions would allow them to easily apply their prior experience to the current Web site use.

The difference between the two interaction styles implies that the evaluation of recognition-based interaction patterns, particularly for novice users, needs to encompass the measurement of congruence between the tasks and the corresponding Web specifications; and the recall-based interaction style used by frequent visitors, or users who have general expectations of a well-standardised Web site, should be evaluated on knowledge transfer as to how their prior knowledge is readily transferable to other situations. This difference also indicates that a set of reasonable speculations about a user's background knowledge and state of mind while carrying out a task should be specified first, which would categorise which interaction style would be the most likely to be used. Hence, the evaluation of Web sites should accommodate the knowledge states of targeted users, which is one of the primary assumptions of the walk-through-based usability inspection methods, for example, CW (Polson, Lewis, Rieman, & Wharton, 1992).

In conjunction with this assumption, the Web use would be mainly as a result of recognising the large number of choices and information content in a single Web page, based on a psychological foundation: *cyclic interaction.*

The concept of cyclic interaction was initially introduced by Card, Moran, and Newell's (1983) *model human processor* as their recognise-act cycle for reifying cognitive constructs of human activities. Further, it has been extensively engineered in Norman's (1986) seven stages model of user activities, stipulating the role of user's goals in the recognise-act cycle. Naturally, the recent HCI theories, for example, *situated action* (Suchman, 1987), *distributed cognition* (Hutchins, 1996), and even *activity theory* (Engestrom & Middleton, 1996; Kutti, 1996; Nardi, 1996), intrinsically follow the accounts of cyclic interaction, but covering a

Figure 2. Categorisation of Web usability problems in terms of cyclic interaction

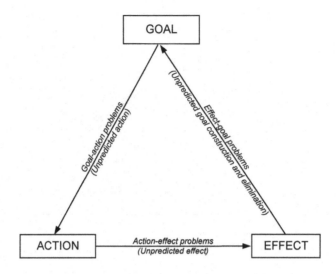

broader context, weighing how actions are informed, how actions are taken, and how users decide on the next step in the various contexts of use.

The key characteristics of cyclic interaction can be expressed simply as shown in Figure 1, which delineates three paths in an interactive cycle: *goal-action path, action-effect path,* and *effect-goal path*. It only illustrates a recognition-based interaction. That is, an action results from the user side having some goal and recognition of the environment. The action leads to system effects on the environment. The new state of the environment (or world) is evaluated, leading to new goals and recognition that in turn leads to new actions, and so on. Indeed, general Web use situations are obviously explained by the three paths in cyclic interaction. For instance, an interactive cycle begins with the reformulation of goals arising from the tasks or relevant visible parts of the current Web page (Ryu & Monk, 2004b). In roughly identifying their immediate subgoals from visible parts of the current Web page, users will seek to take a semantically relevant action or a series of actions on the Web page for accomplishing their current goal set on the goal-action path. It is highly reliant on the repertoire of actions in the specifications of the current Web page, for example, buttons or text links and so on. Accordingly, the chosen action then triggers system effects on the current Web page on the action-effect path. When new system effects are presented, the following effect-goal path deals with changes in what is perceived by the users, and then continues to generate new goals, or eliminate completed goals in their interaction context. This newly organised goal set initiates another cycle, until they accomplish their original goals.

Naturally, the three paths in cyclic interaction suggest three possible usability problems would be concerned in Web evaluation, as sketched out in Figure 2: *action-effect problems, effect-goal problems,* and *goal-action problems* (Ryu & Monk, 2004a).

Firstly, action-effect problems can be thought of as unpredicted effects, compared with user's expectations. To set out these problems in evaluative terms, the concept of *affordance* should be understood first. Gibson (1979) referred to perceptible affordance simply as affordance in line with his theory of direct perception. However, its most basic meaning, in the typical Web use situations, is the effects (or how to operate) a visible object affords. Icons, photos, or widgets on a Web page are often intended to allow users to perceive affordances without learning, or at least to not forget once learned. Another sense of affordance is whether users can perceive how to operate objects (or widgets) and what to accomplish with the objects on the Web page, for example, the link in underlined text affords clicking, a gloved, pointing finger affords clicking, and this clicking leads to a new Web page. Hence, any widget used differently from their own intrinsic affordance would result in action-effect problems.

Second, effect-goal problems refer to whether system effects will generate any new subgoals relevant to the overall goal or eliminate completed subgoals not required in subsequent interactions. To demonstrate this problem in Web evaluation, consider a Web site designed to book accommodation. If the current user goal set has a brief *and-then* goal (Polson et al., 1992) such as *checking availability of a single room* and then *making a reservation with a credit card*, but the first thing the Web page demands is to enter credit card details before checking availability, we see the current Web page (system effects), per se, as providing subgoals inconsistent with the user's current goal set at the time of interaction. For this assessment, we need detailed assumptions of the user's current goal structure of the task being analysed.

Finally, goal-action problems in Web evaluation can be described as mapping between the current goal set assumed by task analysis and the actions available at the time of interaction. As discussed earlier, it is generally believed that Web users would prefer to learn the systems by doing (Polson et al., 1992; Polson & Lewis, 1990), which means they will start with an abstract description of the task they want to accomplish and explore the Web site and select actions they think will accomplish the task. Hence, if the mapping between the current goal set and the actions available is not so obvious, then goal-action problems are inevitable.

Thus far, we have seen the theoretical foundations of Web evaluation and briefly reviewed the assumptions that should be made for evaluating Web sites in terms of the user's cyclic interaction behaviour. We note that walk-through-based usability inspection method, for example, CW operationalises this cyclic interaction behaviour at each action step, to assess if the human information processes are congruent with the expectations of the interface. Therefore, in the following section, three walk-through methods are applied to evaluate a Web site, and the findings are expected to expose the strengths and weaknesses of each walk-through method in Web evaluation.

DETAILED DESCRIPTIONS OF WALK-THROUGHS

There is no formal definition as to which usability inspection methods fall into the walk-through methods. So, as a practical criterion, this chapter first reviews whether a particular usability inspection method complies with the general assumptions of the walk-through approach. Of course, this broad concept means that many usability inspection methods can be described as walk-throughs; however, we note that the essence of the walk-through approach is to take a hypothetical process, that is, simulating step-by-step human informa-

Figure 3. The home page of ITtext

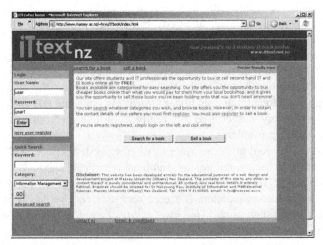

Note: This Web site was developed by a group of students at Massey University.

tion processes and provide an evaluation of the practical situation, how people actually use the system. Therefore, if a usability inspection method conforms to this perspective, it is regarded as a walk-through method.

Three usability inspection methods are considered in this chapter: *heuristic, cognitive,* and *activity walk-through*. It is debatable whether the first method — heuristic walk-through — is a walk-through method, but it is deliberately embraced in this chapter as a contrasting technique against the other two walk-through methods.

An Example: University Students Trading Second-Hand Textbooks

One of the easiest ways to envisage the nature of the walk-through approach is to demonstrate how it can be applied to a real Web evaluation. For this reason, a Web site for University students to trade second-hand textbooks was designed as shown in Figure 3. You can see the Web site and/or try doing the walk-through yourself (www.massey. ac.nz/~hryu/ITbook).

The representative task on this Web site is to trade second-hand textbooks relating to the university's information technology (IT) related courses. We note that this Web site is a walk-up-and-use application, therefore, many users find themselves in the position of needing to use the system without training.

General Procedure of Walk-Through Methodology

While there are many variations of walk-through-based usability inspection, they mostly consist of two phases: a *preparatory phase* and an *analysis phase*. In the preparatory phase, the evaluators are given the basic inputs for the walk-through. The main analytical work follows, during which the evaluators step through each action of every task being analysed. The details of the analysis phase vary with each walk-through technique.

Preparatory Phase

In this phase, four input conditions are considered: (1) *assumptions of targeted users*, (2) *tasks*, (3) *action sequence for each task*, and (4) the *interface* that will be subjected to analysis. The following sets out the inputs of the evaluation of the ITtext Web site.

- **Assumptions of targeted users:** This may be simple such as "people who use the Web site." But the walk-through asks more clarifications of targeted users, including the user's specific background or technical knowledge that can influence the users as they attempt to deal with a Web site. The users' knowledge state of the tasks and of the Web site should both be specified, for example.

  The users of our ITtext Web site would be the university students who have a computer but are not frequent visitors to the ITtext Web site and are seeking to buy the cheapest book for their courses in the university, and generally have an e-mail client system on their computers. It is also assumed that the users have previously seen information about the ITtext Web site so they know the home address and have both the skills and motivation to turn on a computer, operate a mouse, open an Internet browser, and go to the site's home page. The users also possess standard Web navigation skills.

  This assumption seems to be very hypothetical; however, it will justify each decision in the course of the walk-through process.
- **The tasks that the targeted users are to perform on the Web:** The walk-through also needs detailed task analyses of a suite of tasks. They should be the representative tasks that most of the targeted users would like to do. However, it is not cost-effective to analyse all the tasks of a Web site. In general, regardless of the complexity of any Web site, the analyses should be limited to a reasonable but representative collection of primary tasks.

  The selection of representative tasks should be based on the results of needs analysis, task analysis, and/or requirement analysis. For more details of these analytic techniques, please see Kirwan and Ainsworth (1992); Vicente (1999); and Duke and Harrison (1995). As a rule of thumb, some tasks might be sampled from the core functionality of a Web site, that is, the basic functions that the Web site is intended to support. Task descriptions of all selected tasks must include the necessary context, such as the contents of the Web site that the users are most likely to use at each action step.

  For our ITtext Web site, a representative task is examined, which is, logged-in users search and buy an IT book, by logging in the system, searching for a named book, selecting a search result of the named book, and getting a particular seller's details. The search task asks to specify both the title and the categorisation of the named book.

- **A complete, written list of the actions sequences needed to complete the tasks:** There must also be a description of the sequence of actions for each task. These actions might be a machine level operation such as "click the link," or they may be the sequence of several simple actions that a typical user could execute as a block such as "login to the Web site." The decision as to what level of action granularity is appropriate depends on the level of expertise of the targeted users. Our evaluation of the ITtext Web site aims at infrequent visitors to the Web site, so that machine-level operations are considered.

In specifying action sequences, a crucial assumption of the walk-through approach, which has provoked many criticisms against it, even if there may be a major problem with the Web site and digressions from the correct actions may occur, the evaluation merely proceeds to the next steps, as if the correct action had been performed. The critiques of this assumption say that sometimes the wrong actions would indicate true meanings of the usability problems of the current task being analysed, reflecting how to avoid the usability problems in a way that the users are expecting. While this account is highly reasonable, the assumption that the users always choose the correct action would guarantee to widely cover all the possible usability problems in Web evaluation. The action procedures of the representative task in our ITtext example are described next.

- **The specification of the Web site:** The walk-through proposes that the preparatory phase should describe the prompts preceding every action required to accomplish the tasks being analysed, as well as the reactions of the interface to each of these actions. For our example, in carrying out the representative task, the following specifications were given:

Step 0: Initial state
The initial Web page of this Web site is shown in Figure 3.

Step 1
Current system prompt: Figure 3
Action(s): In the Login area in Figure 3, type "user" in User Name textbox and "user1" in Password textbox; then click the Enter button in the login subregion.
System response(s): Logged-in-page appears, as shown in Figure 4.

Step 2
Current system prompt: Figure 4
Action(s): Select Search for a book button
System response(s): Search page appear, as shown in Figure 5.

Step 3
Current system prompt: Figure 5
Action(s): In the Title text box, type "The C++ programming language," select Programming from the Category drop-down list box, then click the Search button.
System response(s): Search Results page appears, as shown in Figure 6.

Step 4
Current system prompt: Figure 6
Action(s): Click the first search result, "The C++ Programming Language (Special 3rd Edition)"
System response(s): Book Details page appears, as shown in Figure 7.

Figure 4. Logged-in page in completion of the action(s) in step 1

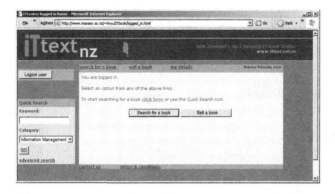

Figure 5. Search page in completion of action(s) in step 2

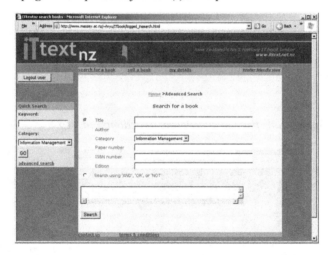

Step 5
Current system prompt: Figure 7
Action(s): Along the Availability row click the Click here link.
System response(s): Sellers detail page appears, as shown in Figure 8.

Step 6
Current system prompt: Figure 8
Action(s): Click the e-mail address cocoman1111 of the first seller
System response(s): E-mail client application is open, as shown in Figure 9.

Figure 6. Search results page in completion of action(s) in step 3

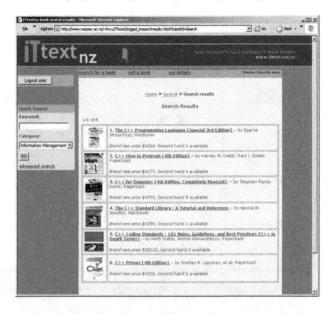

Figure 7. Book details page in completion of action(s) in step 4

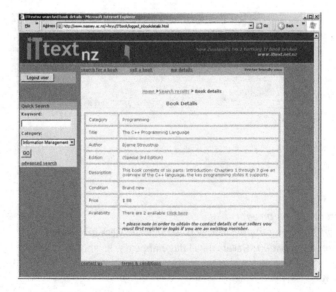

Figure 8. Sellers detail page in completion of action(s) in step 5

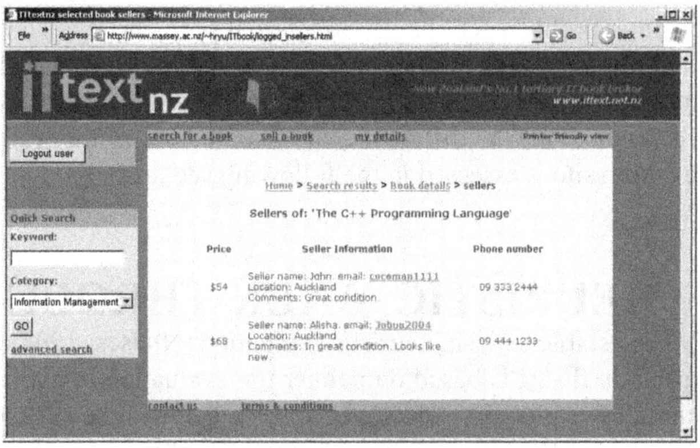

Figure 9. E-mail client application in completion of action(s) in step 6

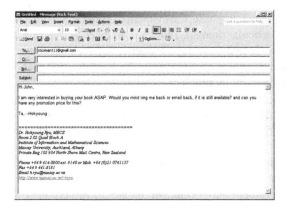

Analysis Phase

In completion of the preparatory phase, the analysis phase of the walk-through examines each action, attempting to evaluate each action against predefined checklists or probing questions. The assessment should be based on the assumptions about the user's background knowledge and goals, which were speculated in the preparatory phase.

The predefined checklists or probing questions limit the analytic outcomes of possible usability problems with a distinct theme of usability problems. For instance, HW judges whether each action conforms to the established 10 usability heuristics (Nielsen, 1994). By contrast, CW (Polson et al., 1992) provides a more detailed evaluation of each action, checking if the simulated user's goals for the following actions can be reasonably assumed to lead to the next correct action. A modified version of the original CW — *cognitive walk-*

through for Web (CWW) (Blackmon et al., 2002) — is specially used in the evaluation of Web sites, and the *low-level interaction walk-through* (LW) (Ryu & Monk, 2004a, 2005) focuses on the other problem set, that is, effect-goal problems, which cannot be explicitly evaluated with the original CW. Finally, the AW (Bertelsen, 2004, p. 253) directs evaluator's attention from the sequence of machine operations to human actions as a meaningful unit of analysis. To demonstrate the different analytic outcomes of the walk-through methods, the same ITtext Web site is assessed in the following sections.

HEURISTIC WALK-THROUGH

It is very contestable to deem heuristic evaluation (Nielsen, 1994) as part of the walk-through approach, in that it is based on neither the evaluation of cyclic interaction, nor a theory of learning by exploration. However, it has a very similar procedure with the other walk-through methods, that is, inputs in the preparatory phase and a step-by-step evaluation in the analysis phase, and assuming the correct action at each action step, which means it is worthwhile to be examined in this chapter, with the additional aim to reveal the strengths and weaknesses of the other walk-through techniques.

HW based on Nielsen's (1994) heuristic evaluation is a simple method for structuring the evaluation of each action step using a set of general Web heuristics.

In the actual analysis phase, the evaluator is provided with a set of heuristics, which is specialised to a particular domain. Table 1 is an extended version of the original heuristics (Nielsen, 1994) to describe common properties of Web usability. While stepping through each action, the evaluator is asked to state which established usability heuristics in Table 1 is violated by each usability problem.

As all of the possible problems are collected, the mean severity ratings of the usability problems are determined in order to assess the relative severity of each of the usability problems. Severity ratings can then be used to allocate the appropriate resources to fix the problems.

The following short report shows the evaluation of our ITtext Web site with HW, conducted by four usability experts. Each identified problem is assessed as to the frequency with which the problem may occur, the impact of the problem if it does occur, and the persistence of the problem. Possible solutions are also discussed by the evaluators to avoid the usability problems.

Heuristic 2: Match Between the System World and the Real World Based on Targeted Users

- **Comments/findings:** In step 3, users might find there was no superfluous information on the Web pages. However, one expert questioned the purpose of the *"Brand new price..."* wording for books on the search results page (see Figure 6). He believed it made users confused as to whether they were buying a second-hand or new book.
- **Problem frequency:** 1 of the 4 evaluators identified this as a usability issue. This problem would occur each time in the system.
- **Problem impact:** Users might be confused as to whether they were buying a new or used book. Users may think that is the actual price.

Table 1. Heuristics of Web usability evaluation, extended from Nielsen (1994)

Web usability heuristics	Description/Examples
Visibility of current Web page status	Users need to know at each Web page as to "Where am I?" and "Where can I go next?" *For example, (1) making sure each page indicates which section it belongs to. (2) internal or external links should be clearly marked; and (3) use the clear URL for distinguish the different Web pages*
Match between the system world and the real world based on targeted users	Word and phrase uses on the Web site must be familiar to the user *For example, (1) a multiple-language support for the Web site of a globalised firm and (2) a Web site for children should use child-friendly phrases.*
Support user control to Web navigation and relevant links	Users often choose system functions by mistake and will need a clearly marked emergency exit to leave the unwanted state. *For example, a "home" button on every page is a simple way to let users feel in control of the Web site.*
Consistent Web design and conformation to standards	Users should not have to wonder whether different words, situations, or actions mean the same thing *For example, consistent wording with links, page titles, and page headers.*
Error prevention with informative contents	Even better than good error messages is a careful design which prevents a problem from occurring in the first place. *For example, (1) use JavaScript to prevent some missing parts before users submit and (2) the essential items to be filled in should be clearly indicated*
Recognition rather than recall	Make objects, actions, and options visible. The user should not have to remember information from one part of the dialogue to another. *For example, (1) if users can recognise where they are by looking at the current page, without having to recall their path from the home page, they are less likely to get lost. (2) The mouseovers for the links should be avoided*
Flexibility and efficiency of use for frequent visitors	Shortcuts may often speed up the interaction for the frequent visitors. *For example,(1) bookmarks and (2) single sign-on process (e.g., Amazon. com)*
Aesthetic and minimal scrolling design	Dialogues should not contain information which is irrelevant or rarely needed. *For example, put the more general information higher up in the contents hierarchy and let users scroll down deeper if they want the details.*
Help users recognise, diagnose, and recover from errors	Error messages should be expressed in plain language. Every error message should offer a solution (or a link to a solution) on the error page. *For example, if a user's search yields no hits, do not just tell him/ her to broaden their search; provide a link that will broaden the search.*
Help and documentation	Even though it is better if the system can be used without documentation, it may be necessary to provide help and documentation. *For example, help pages*

- **Problem persistence:** This would be a persistent problem, confusing new and existing users.
- **Possible solution:** Remove the *"Brand new price..."* wording from the Search Results page to reduce ambiguity.

Heuristic 2: Match Between the System and the Real World Based on Targeted Users

- **Comments/findings:** In step 4, users might feel that on the Book details page (Figure 7) the Click here link could have been worded better. Other links were considered to be well branded.
- **Problem frequency:** 2 of the 4 evaluators identified this area of usability as being an issue. This problem would occur each time in the system.
- **Problem impact:** Although the users could identify what was required of them to obtain details of sellers, they might feel the link could be more "intuitive."
- **Problem persistence:** This problem would only affect new users. Existing users would quickly recognise the link from previous experience.
- **Possible solution:** Changing the Click here link to wording more descriptive such as "view sellers" could solve this problem.

Heuristic 3: Support User Control to Web Navigation and Relevant Links

- **Comments/findings:** In steps 5 and 6, users might identify a key area of functionality that was not provided: an automatically composed e-mail message or message subject line (see Figure 9).
- **Problem frequency:** All four of the evaluators identified this omission in functionality.
- **Problem impact:** This would lead to inconsistent messages being sent to the sellers. It would be likely that wrong information could be sent. The seller could not identify e-mails in regard to the ITtext site, as there was no template subject line.
- **Problem persistence:** This would occur each time the system was used. Problems could be inconsistent and different each time.
- **Possible solution:** An automatically generated message with a subject header referencing the book sale.

Heuristic 10: Help and Documentation

- **Comments/findings:** In step 5, users might not be sure what to do to contact a particular seller (see Figure 8).
- **Problem frequency:** 2 out of 4 identified this omission as a major usability problem.
- **Problem impact:** This would lead to a user's lack of confidence before as to whether they can send an e-mail on their own e-mail client or directly on the Web site. This system uses the e-mail client installed on the user's computer, but if the users do not have any client, they cannot contact a seller with this functionality. If possible, the

Table 2. Different question set for Web evaluation. Extended from Polson et al. (1992), Blackmon et al. (2002), and Ryu et al. (2004a)

Method	Effect-goal problems	Goal-action problems	Action-effect problems
CW	(1) Will the users try to achieve the right effect?	(2) Will the users notice the correct action or control available?	(3) Will the users associate the correct action with the effect trying to be achieved?
CWW	(1) Will the users connect the correct action's description with what they are trying to do?	(2) Will the users connect the correct subregion of the page with the goal, using heading information and their understanding of the sites page layout conventions? (3) Will the users connect the goal with the correct widget in the attended to subregion of the page using link labels and other kinds of descriptive information?	(4) Will the users interpret the system effect to the chosen action correctly?
LW	(1) Will the system effects strongly suggest the subsequent goals? (2) Will the other system effects suggest that the user conceive goals that do not pertain to the overall goal? (3) Will the system effects sufficiently allow the user to recognise (rather than recall) that the goal has been achieved?	(4) Will the users associate the correct action with the affordance of the corresponding object that is relevant to the current goal set? (5) Will the system effects prompt the users to take an incorrect action from the strong affordance of the corresponding object that is not relevant to the current goal set?	(6) Will the correct actions trigger the system effects that are sufficient for the users to justify their action?

Web site has to provide a Web mail system for them to compose an e-mail or simple text message.

- **Problem persistence:** This problem would only affect new users, and the missing Web mail functionality would help the users who do not have their own computer with an e-mail account.
- **Possible solution:** Add a minimal amount of instruction to the Sellers detail page, in order to direct users how to contact a particular seller.

It is generally believed that there are two concerns of HW in Web evaluation. Firstly, according to Hertzum and Jacobsen's study (2001), the HW method significantly suffers from substantial evaluator effects in that multiple evaluators result in the different set of problems depending on their prior experience. Even though this evaluator effect is inevitable in walk-throughs, HW seems to lead to dramatically different outcomes of usability problems in the complex system, compared with the other walk-through methods. Secondly, as Nielsen (1994) claimed, HW tends to pinpoint more salient usability problems such as labels or inconsistent layout between Web pages. How these two issues are dealt with in the other walk-through methods is drawn on possible ways forward.

COGNITIVE WALK-THROUGH FAMILY: CW, CWW, LW

CW was originally proposed by Polson et al. (1992), as an attempt to introduce an informal and subjective walk-through of user interfaces. Since then there have been many variations of the original CW, for example, CWW (Blackmon et al., 2002) and LW (Ryu & Monk, 2004a), in order to deal with some known limitations of the original CW. Yet, the core nature of CW is the same, attempting to provide a detailed step-by-step evaluation of the user's interaction with an interface in the process of carrying out a specific task. Both the narrow focus on a single aspect of usability and the fact that the method provides a more detailed evaluation of ease-of-learning are the nature of the method's strengths and weaknesses against HW.

The evaluation steps through each action sequence, answering the probing questions that address the exploratory learning behaviour, are shown in Table 2. The first question in both the original CW and CWW, "will the users try to achieve the right effect?," refers to whether the users will consider the proposed action as a logical action based on their current goal set at the time of interaction. It can be thought of identifying effect-goal problems, in the sense that the judgement of this question is based on whether the current system status (or system effects) is recognised as their original task, or it clearly tells them what to do. However, the question does not explicitly reflect the nature of effect-goal problems. By contrast, the three probing questions in LW are designed to identify that effect-goal problems, considering how the current system effects would reorganise the current goal set to maintain the subsequent interactions (Ryu, 2003).

The second question of CW is whether the controls are visible or easily perceived. This also indicates whether users experienced success in their choice of proposed actions. The specification of the proposed actions or affordance of the widgets corresponding to the actions on the Web page will determine the outcome of this question. Further, CWW assumes a common Web use situation in which generating an action on a Web page consists of an attention process and an action selection process. An attention process indicates that the users would separate a Web page into subregions and concentrate on the subregions of the page that are semantically most similar to the user's goal. The question (see Table 2) "(2) will the users connect the correct subregion of the page with the goal using heading information and their understanding of the sites page layout conventions?" addresses this level of goal-action problems. In the following action selection process, the corresponding question (see Table 2), "(3) will the users connect the goal with the correct widget in the attended to subregion of the page using link labels and other kinds of descriptive information?" examines whether the proposed actions with the corresponding widgets would be congruent with the user's current goal set. In these two processes, the measurement of congruence between the user's current goal set and the subregions or the widgets is based on latent semantic analysis technique (Laundauer & Dumais, 1997). By contrast, LW simply focuses on the affordances of the widgets on the Web page, considering whether the widgets would provide appropriate affordance resulting in being selected, or not being selected, compared with the user's current goal set.

The final question is to check action-effect problems; whether the controls can be understandable at the time of interaction. That is, if a Web page presents a clear label that connects the proposed action to what users are trying to do and all the other actions seem to be wrong, the users will expect the unique action will trigger the relevant system effects that they want to achieve.

Both the original CW and CWW predominately address goal-action problems which are their intended focus, that is, whether the current user's goal set can clearly be accomplished by the proposed actions. Yet, sometimes answering some of the questions from CW or CWW may be difficult unless there are additional assumptions about how users interpret what they see (Bertelsen, 2004). In other words, both CW and CWW assume that the users are very likely to see the proposed actions on the current Web page and in turn they will choose the actions; however, this assumption is not explicitly supported in the course of the interaction, as what many of the users are able to see depends on what they actually want to do under the real context.

The impact of the problem with CW and CWW can be reduced in two different ways. Firstly, some interaction modelling tools, for example, *state-transition scenarios* (Monk, 1999), and *interaction unit model* (Ryu & Monk, 2005), explicitly specify what the users would like to perceive, and how the perception of system effects would affect the following interactions. Therefore, they can address the concerns identified and point to a possible solution, retaining some of the efficiency of CW or CWW, and at the same time providing more systematic help for the evaluators. Secondly, Bertelsen (2004) claimed that the assumptions that perception and action are separated, and the correct actions are always chosen, are not reasonable. Rather, he emphasised that the basic unit of walk-through analysis should be on the level of human performance that is motivated and directed to human needs in the real context of interaction. Following on from this, he proposed the AW, which is further discussed in the following section.

The basic inputs to the CW family are the same as those of HW. Given this information, the evaluators step through the action sequence and tell an imaginary story about its usability, using the questions specified in Table 2. The answers are based on the evaluators' understanding of both system specifications and the current user's goal set. In the author's experience, as a rule of thumb, an answer scheme, that is, yes, probably yes, probably not, and no, with the credible story of their judgement would be very useful to indicate the severity of possible usability problems. The following analyses present a short CW of our ITtext Web site conducted by the author.

Step 1

Current system prompt: Figure 3

Action(s): In the Login area, type "user" in User Name textbox and "user1" in Password textbox; then Click the Enter button in the login subregion.

System response(s): Logged-in-page appears, as shown in Figure 4.

Criterion of effect-goal problem: Will the user be trying to achieve the right effect?

Yes, the user will be putting their personal identification followed by their password to logon the system as a registered user, which is a general task procedure in other Web use situations and the system effects clearly explain why the logging in is needed.

Criterion of goal-action problem: Will the users notice the correct action or control available?

Probably yes, the user will be seeking the logon process, as the Web page clearly describes why the user has to logon first. In addition, the widgets for logging in are very common, so it is very unlikely to result in some usability problems to our targeted user group who has a general Web navigation skill. However, if the users cannot recall either the correct ID or the password, it is not explicitly described how to sort this problem out on this Web page.

Criterion of action-effect problem: Will the users associate the correct action with the effect trying to be achieved?

Yes, the correct action is clearly worded, and the widget has a strong affordance to be clicked.

Step 2

Current system prompt: Figure 4

Action(s): Select Search for a book button

System response(s): Search page appear, as shown in Figure 5

Criterion of effect-goal problem

Yes, it is very likely that the users will still be attempting to buy a book, so they will be searching for a book first; otherwise they will be seeking to sell a book.

Criterion of goal-action problem

Probably not, actually the button widget 'Search for a book' is very visible, with the support of the description on the Web page, but the subregion on the left side would also be competing in this action step, showing no clear distinction between 'Search for a book' and 'Quick search'. Further, the inconsistent wording 'Click here' above the button 'Search for a book' will make the users confused what the correct action is, even though they will provide the same Web page.

Criterion of action-effect problem

Yes, the correct action is clearly worded, and the widget has a strong affordance to be clicked.

Step 3

Current system prompt: Figure 5

Action(s): In the Title text box, type "The C++ Programming Language," select Programming from the category drop-down list box, then click the Search button.

System response(s): Search Results page appears, as shown in Figure 6.

Criterion of effect-goal problem

Yes, the user will still be attempting to find a relevant book with the answer.

Criterion of goal-action problem

No, there seems to be three issues relevant to failure. Firstly, the Category drop-down list box enlists a lot of competing elements such as programming, information management, and system design. Hence there may be another selection by our users who have little knowledge of the category. Secondly, the paper number is actually used under a particular university system so it will not be clearly understood by many other users. Finally, in some Web sites the first textbox for input is selected as a default, Title textbox in here, so users may not realise they need to select the field first (so they never looked for the control). The first two problems would be relatively major problems, the last one would be minor. In addition, the radio buttons next to both the Title textbox and the bottom textbox may not be clearly understandable as to how these operators would specify the search criterion.

Criterion of action-effect problem

Yes, the standard widgets have a strong affordance to be used.

Step 4

Current system prompt: Figure 6

Action(s): Click the first search result, "The C++ Programming Language (Special 3rd Edition)"

System response(s): Book Details page appears, as shown in Figure 7.

Criterion of effect-goal problem

Yes, the user will still be attempting to find a relevant book with the answer

Criterion of goal-action problem

Yes, the gloved, pointing finger over the icons is a standard within the Web indicating this is a link to a page. In addition, the icons are clearly described by text links next to themselves.

Criterion of action-effect problem

Yes, if the cursor moves over the link, the gloved finger appears.

Step 5

Current system prompt: Figure 7

Action(s): Along the Availability row click the Click here link.

System response(s): Sellers detail page appears, as shown in Figure 8.

Criterion of effect-goal problem

Yes, the user will still be attempting to find a relevant book with the answer

Criterion of goal-action problem

Probably yes, the gloved and pointing finger over the unique link on the content is a standard indicating a link to a page. However, the label 'Click here' does not reveal the exact meaning of the link as to what the link leads them to.

Criterion of action-effect problem

Yes, if the cursor moves over the link, the gloved finger appears.

Step 6

Current system prompt: Figure 8

Action(s): Click the e-mail address of the first seller

System response(s): E-mail client application is open, as shown in Figure 9.

Criterion of effect-goal problem

> Yes, it is part of their original task, and the Web page clearly tells who bids at the cheapest price along with e-mail addresses and telephone numbers. In particular, the e-mail address presents a subsequent task to be followed.

Criterion of goal-action problem

> Yes, the gloved, pointing finger over the unique link is a standard widget indicating it has a link.

Criterion of action-effect problem

> No, the users may have two different expectations. The e-mail client on their own computer will be open by default, or the internal Web mail system on the Web site will be linked to send a message. Whichever, the users will expect that it should specify the e-mail address and the subject heading of the e-mail automatically, such as "Re: The C++ Programming Language (Special 3rd Edition)."

Empirical studies of the original CW, for example, Cuomo and Bowen (1992); Hertzum and Jacobsen (2001); Jacobsen and John (2000); and Blackmon, Kitajima, and Polson (2003), demonstrated that CW has been especially promising. Yet, they also revealed around 15% of usability problems, compared with usability testing, could not be detected by the original CW due to the wrong interpretation or judgement on each question used in the original CW. Of course, the judgements are dependent on the evaluator's personal experience with the method, but it is also affected by the way that the question is expressed. It is thus possible to reduce the effect of the interpretation of the probing questions, employing more specialised probing questions as those of both CWW and LW (Blackmon et al., 2003).

ACTIVITY WALK-THROUGH THROUGH CONTEXTUALISATION

The CW family is a popular theory-based method that is easily applicable for a practical assessment of Web design. They evaluate a Web site based on the knowledge states of the targeted users. Consequently, if the same knowledge states are applied, the evaluation must be the same irrespective of the situations in which the activities take place. However, human activities naturally occur in a context, and that context, to some extent, defines the nature of the activities. The same performance, according to the CW family, that is performed in different contexts may be fundamentally different. Therefore, activities cannot be understood and so should not be analysed outside the context in which it occurs. Most contemporary learning theories, such as *situated cognition* (Suchman, 1987), *constructivism* (Kintsch, 1988) and *activity theory* (Kutti, 1996; Nardi, 1996), emphasised the role of context in learning.

To encompass this context issue in interface evaluation, some studies, for example, Bertelsen (2004) and Quek and Shah (2004), proposed a novel approach based on activity theory (Engestrom & Middleton, 1996; Kutti, 1996; Nardi, 1996). They claimed that the activities in which people are engaged, the nature of the tools (or artefacts) they use in those activities, the intentions of those activities, and the objects or outcomes of those activities should be more focused on an interface evaluation. Following on from this, Bertelsen (2004) proposed the AW method. A note of the walk-through method described in this section is needed. While Bertelsen (2004) provided an exhaustive list of potential questions or issues of his walk-through method, several aspects are not necessary for Web evaluation. Therefore, the author reasonably condensed Bertelsen's AW to guide Web evaluation, considering a number of other studies (e.g., Engestrom & Middleton, 1996; Nardi, 1997; Quek & Shah, 2004).

AW for Web begins with the understanding of relevant contexts in which activities occur. The relevant contexts involve *the environment* in which activities occur, *the targeted users* who perform the activities, *their intentions* that motivate the activities, *the tools and rules* that can be used for the activities. They will help the evaluator to pay attention to how users' actions are informed, how they are taken, and how users decide on the next step in the various contexts of use. The following analyses show the descriptions of the trading activity system.

- **Understand relevant environment in which activities occur:** The community to which targeted users belong is a university. In particular, this activity system is for the students who enrol in one of New Zealand's universities. Generally, undergraduate students must buy a particular textbook for a course, because the basic course structure normally follows the contents structure of the textbook. In contrast, postgraduate students are asked to refer to many recommended books for one course, so a major textbook may not be specified. All the university students who have New Zealand citizenship or permanent residency can have student allowances from the government, which can partially cover the cost of some textbooks. However, it is not sufficient to buy all the new textbooks for their 4 to 5 courses in each semester. Therefore, many students would like to use their second-hand textbooks for buying or selling. This activity of trading second-hand books mostly arises at the beginning of every semester (January and June in New Zealand). Generally, undergraduate students would like to buy more second-hand books rather than graduates, because they tend to take at least four courses in each semester. Currently, the university runs both a Web-based system for small ads and many notice boards in each department building. The current Web page is plain-text based, so the information is very limited. In particular, if the students want to use the Web system, they have to logon first with their university account. Therefore, most of the university students prefer to place their ads on the largest notice board at the library, with the photos of their selling items.
- **Understand the users, their motivations, and intentions of the current activity systems:** Most of the users of this activity system are individual undergraduates. The primary motivation for them is to buy or sell second-hand books. From the seller's perspective, they want to sell the books that they do not need any more at the best bid and very quickly; the buyers seek to find the best quality books at the cheapest price before taking the courses. The notice board at the library is not so big as to contain all their adverts, so if they cannot place their adverts on the notice board, they put their adverts into the Web-based system. Each department has their own small notice board at the foyer of each building, so it is used for adverting more special textbooks

that are dedicated to particular majors. When they find someone who wants to sell or buy, they individually contact them to negotiate the bargain.

- **Understand what tools (artefacts) can be used to accomplish the activities:** There are two different tools in the current activities. The one is the notice boards at the library and each department building. The Web page under the university Web site is also being used for this trading activity. To contact someone, phone calls or e-mails are simply used.

- **Understand relevant rule(s) which can be used to accomplish the activities:** Once potential buyers find an appropriate seller either on the notice board or on the Web page, they tend to contact the seller via e-mail or phone call. In this line of activities, all of them are enthusiastic to buy books at a cheaper price or to sell books at a higher price. In turn, to check whether the book is what they are looking for, they ask the book title and the course name. If it is the one they are looking for, they begin to negotiate the price starting from the seller's bid. After mutually agreeing with a bid, the buyer wants to see the book in person and the buyer and the seller meet in a particular place. As the buyer is satisfied with the book status, he/she will pay the seller in cash. Normally, cheques are not acceptable. In addition, if the buyer and the seller are enrolling in the same major, they mutually check whether the seller has other books to be sold for the major courses, and the buyer would like to purchase other books for the major courses.

Based on the understanding of the relevant contexts of activity systems, the next step — contextualisation — conceptually situates the targeted application, such as the ITtext Web site in this chapter, in the context of use by identifying users' intrinsic activities in which the typical tasks are supposed to be embedded. The procedure for this contextualisation of our ITtext Web site is outlined as follows:

- **Describe the intrinsic human activities in using the Web site:** The students using the ITtext Web site may be oriented to find the books for their own courses in the university. In particular, they seek to find the cheapest and best quality one. From a seller's perspective, they want to sell their books at the highest offer and quickly. If the buyers find the book they are looking for from this Web site, they contact the sellers in order to buy it quickly, negotiating the price. When they are satisfied with the price and the status of the book, they are willing to buy it as quickly as they can.

- **Describe the actions for the intrinsic human activities and the objects or outcomes that these actions are directed to:** The potential buyers are oriented to getting the best and cheapest book when using the Web site. For this reason, they will search the books, contact the sellers as quickly as they can, and negotiate with them. The outcomes of this line of actions will be the cheapest book obtained. Reversely, the sellers want to sell their books as quickly as possible, so they will put the details (e.g., photos) of their books and carefully decide what prices will attract possible buyers. After being contacted, both parties are enthusiastic to negotiate the price in a reasonable price range.

- **Consider other artefacts of realising the activity independent of the application:** Most of the students at the university use the notice boards to trade their second-hands at the end of the semester or at the beginning of semester. Sometimes, local newspapers are being used, only if the bulk of items need to be sold, because the cost of the advert in the newspapers should be justified. Considering the wide use of Instant Messenger by the students, the contacts with this artefact are applicable.

- **Consider the user's horizon of expectation:** The students have quite a lot of experience trading or buying something on the Web. In this textbooks trade, the buyers are very likely to search for the book using the title of a course rather than the title of a particular book, because different books may have the same title. In addition, both the buyers and the sellers want to check whether the other party has other books to trade.

- **Consider the application as being a mediator between various activities by situating it in a web of activities where it is used, and analysing contradictions or tensions between these activities:** The ITtext Web site mediates the seller and the buyer on the Web-based system, thus the application should not only be usable but it should also support effective contacts between the seller and the buyer. Especially, the negotiation between the seller and the buyer should be considered first. That is, the sellers want to sell their books at the best offer, and the buyers would like to buy them at the cheapest price.

- **Consider the historical development of the web of activities and the historical predecessors of the application:** Currently, the preferred medium of these activities is the notice boards at the library and at each building. The use of these physical notice boards has proven to be less effective for trading books.

This contextualisation step would be used for the evaluators to verify whether each task is corresponding to the user activities in which the application is going to be embedded. That is, if a particular task is not likely to take place, compared with the current user's activity, the redesign of the task itself would be firstly considered rather than simply following walkthrough analysis. In our ITtext Web site, the task in step 3 is accomplished by filling in the title and categorisation of a particular textbook on the search page. It is very straightforward if our users are aware of the title of the textbook; otherwise, there is no meaning in terms of the current user's horizon of expectation. In addition, the task in step 6 considered the e-mail contact as the primary user's activity; however, the negotiation process via e-mails would not be so effective in the user's activity. Considering the wide use of Instant Messengers by the university students, the negotiation process can be supported by this mediating artefact in order to support intrinsic human activities in using this Web site. Consequently, the tasks in step 3 and step 6 must be redesigned before taking the walk-through analysis.

In completion of this verification of each task in terms of contextualisation, the evaluators can step through each action, using the probing questions as shown in Table 3. For a short AW, step 6 of our ITtext Web site was taken; however since the machine operation is not necessarily making sense as purposeful actions for the users, the more neutral formulation is used in this example — "contacting the seller to negotiate."

Step 6
Current system prompt: Figure 8
Action(s): contacting the seller to negotiate
System response(s): Figure 9
Criterion of effect-goal problem: *Will the system effects match users' horizon of expectation so that they will be confident that progress has been made?*

Probably not, simply, the application supports the contact with one of the sellers via e-mail. However, the users will expect the negotiation process between the sellers and themselves to buy the book as soon as possible.

Criterion of goal-action problem:

(i) Will the required machine operation make sense in the context of users action towards the goal?

No, it only looks like an e-mail link rather than an indication of the negotiation process.

(ii) Will the users associate the correct machine operation with the affordance of the corresponding object?

Yes, but this is only for e-mail link.

(iii) Will the user be able to develop matching actions in the situation?

Probably yes, if the users can refer to the two e-mail addresses on the Web page, they can send the same e-mail to both sellers for a simple negotiation.

(iv) Will the user need instruction to be able to use the application?

No, because there is no machine operation to be matched with the current user's expectation.

Criterion of action-effect problem: *Will the machine operation match user's horizon of expectation?*

No, the negotiation process should be considered first.

Table 3. Web evaluation question set in activity walk-through, extended from Bertelsen (2004)

Method	Effect-goal problems	Goal-action problems	Action-effect problems
		(2) Will the required machine operation make sense in the context of users action towards the goal?	
AW	(1) Will the system effects match users' horizon of expectation so that they will be confident that progress has been made?	(3) Will the users associate the correct machine operation with the affordance of the corresponding object? (4) Will the user be able to develop matching actions in the situation? (5) Will the user need instruction to be able to use the application?	(6) Will the machine operation match user's horizon of expectation?

As a final stage, Bertelsen proposed that, together with the outcomes of the walk-through, the evaluators should review how well the sequence of machine operations matches the user's operations or actions, and the consistent flow of operations throughout the task. In our ITtext example, there are three possible conflicts between the system specification and the user's expectations: (1) logging in first before finding the textbook they are looking for, (2) specifying a textbook search without any references to course names or majors, and (3) no negotiation process support between the seller and the buyer.

Loosely speaking, the other walk-throughs leave considerations of context and environment as afterthoughts, often considered only when a given interventions fails. Instead, AW can provide a systematic way of identifying and understanding important contextual factors in a particular situation, using historical factors to guide evaluators of the current Web site and situating performance within the real context within which it actually takes place. Yet, it has not been widely tested, so it is very difficult to tell what extent AW can be employed in the usability inspection domain. Nonetheless, it is very obvious that the benefits of contextualisation processed in AW are the most important advance over the CW family. In particular, it can easily spot various alternatives of design solutions, which is not expected in the CW family.

DISCUSSION AND CONCLUSION

Thus far, we reviewed the three walk-through methods that can be used in the Web evaluation context. Table 4 summarises the walk-through methods.

Table 4. Appropriate use of the walk-through methods in Web evaluation

Method	Description	Proposed to use	Main advantages	Main disadvantages
HW	Three or four evaluators separately review an interface and categorise and justify problems based on a short set of heuristics	In the course of the design process check for immediate possible usability problems	A fast and ease-of-use evaluation method	Lack of details and the very subjective explanation of the problems
CW family	A method that employs task scenarios to assess the user's cognitive process	A relatively formal usability session	A deep account of how users would like to use the system, given the users' goals	Lack of consideration of the context where the actions occur
AW	A method that includes the use contexts into the evaluation to assess the intrinsic user's activities	In a very early design process to get extensive insights of the contextual reasons for possible usability problems	A detailed explanation of the contextual issues in Web use situation	May be tedious and unable to cover the entire use contexts

As discussed earlier, it is not intended that this chapter provides a comparison between the usability inspection methods, in order to determine which technique is best at detecting usability problems of the Web site. Rather, we want to examine the strengths and weaknesses of each walk-through method, so that they can collectively serve to provide a reasonable suite of usability inspection tools for Web sites.

In summary, firstly, we noted that the review-based inspection methods, such as the design principles or guidelines, have successfully generated a set of characteristics with which to define successful Web interfaces; however, this sort of inspection does not provide the detail that task-based usability inspection can. In contrast, the task-based usability inspection methods, such as HW, CW, and AW allow a greater number of usability problems to be identified, because the methods follow a narrow path of analysis for each task, one after the other. Although HW is not a true walk-through method, it can provide insights into how well each task follows the general Web heuristics. However, it does not provide a true evaluation of task performance, nevertheless, its ease-of-use can compensate for the lack of detail in Web evaluation. Therefore, it might be very useful in the course of the design process for designers to have an immediate check of possible usability problems.

Although there are a small numbers of studies to draw on, an extensive success of the CW family in Web evaluation seems to be obvious. It would appear to yield roughly the same number of problems as the other inspection methods, and in some cases slightly more; further, it allows the evaluators to gain knowledge of how the users actually use the Web site, rather than simply focusing on the individual tasks being analysed (e.g., Blackmon et al., 2003; Blackmon et al., 2002; Cuomo & Bowen, 1992; Hertzum & Jacobsen, 2001; Jacobsen & John, 2000). Yet, we noted that they emphasise task performance irrespective of the context where the actions (or activities) occur, so that the Web evaluation is enhanced by adding the context to walk-throughs, such as happens with AW. Therefore, AW can be performed in a very early design process to get extensive insights into the contextual reasons for possible usability problems that may occur. The CW family, by comparison, would be useful to identify usability problems with a detailed design specification.

In conclusion, Web evaluation tends to be a very subjective activity. To lessen this issue, this chapter reviewed the walk-through methods because they provide a strict procedure to examine each task and include more explicit questioning with which to detect usability problems for Web sites. Yet, different walk-through methods have their own strengths and weaknesses, so that several methods will be needed by the evaluators to ensure good Web evaluation coverage in different design stages.

ACKNOWLEDGMENTS

The author owes much of these works to the students who developed the Web site used in this chapter. Also, the author thanks Sue Pritchard, Chris Messom, and Ramesh Lal for their thorough comments and helpful suggestions on the first draft of this chapter.

REFERENCES

Bertelsen, O. W. (2004, October 23-27). *The activity walkthrough: An expert review method based on activity theory.* Paper presented at the 3rd Nordic Conference on Human-Computer Interaction, Tampere, Finland.

Blackmon, M. H., Kitajima, M., & Polson, P. (2003, April 20-25). *Repairing usability problems identified by the cognitive walkthrough for the Web.* Paper presented at the Special Interest Group Computer-Human Interaction Conference on Human Factors in Computing Systems, Ft. Lauderdale, FL.

Blackmon, M. H., Polson, P. G., Kitajima, M., & Lewis, C. (2002, April 20-25). *Cognitive walkthrough for the Web.* Paper presented at the Special Interest Group Computer-Human Interaction Conference on Human Factors in Computing Systems, Minneapolis, MN.

Card, S. K., Moran, T. P., & Newell, A. (1983). *The psychology of human-computer interaction.* Hillsdale, NJ: Lawrence Erlbaum Associates.

Cuomo, D. L., & Bowen, C. D. (1992, October 12-16). *Stages of user activity model as a basis for user-system interface evaluation.* Paper presented at the The Human Factors Society 36th Annual Meeting, Atlanta, GA.

Duke, D., & Harrison, M. (Eds.). (1995). *Interaction and task requirements.* New York: Springer-Verlag.

Engestrom, Y., & Middleton, D. (1996). *Cognition and communication at work.* Boston: Cambridge University Press.

Gibson, J. J. (1979). *The ecological approach to visual perception.* Boston: Houghton Mifflin.

Hertzum, M., & Jacobsen, N. E. (2001). The evaluator effect: A chilling fact about usability evaluation methods. *International Journal of Human-Computer Interaction, 13*(4), 421-443.

Hutchins, E. (1996). *Cognition in the wild* (2nd ed.). Cambridge, MA: MIT Press.

Jacobsen, N. E., & John, B. E. (2000). *Two case studies in using cognitive walkthrough for interface evaluation* (CMU-CS-00-132). Working paper, Computer Science department, Carnagie Mellon University, Pittsburgh, PA.

Kintsch, W. (1988). The role of knowledge in discourse comprehension — A construction integration model. *Psychological Review, 95*(2), 163-182.

Kirwan, B., & Ainsworth, L. K. (Eds.). (1992). *A guide to task analysis.* London: Taylor & Francis.

Kitajima, M., Blackmon, M. H., & Polson, P. (2000, September 5-8). *Comprehension-based model of Web navigation and its application to Web usability analysis.* Paper presented at the Annual Conference of British Computer Society Human Computer Interaction Specialist Group.

Kutti, K. (1996). Activity theory as a potential framework for human-computer interaction research. In B. A. Nardi (Ed.), *Context and consciousness: Activity theory and human-computer interaction* (pp. 17-44). Cambridge, MA: MIT Press.

Laundauer, T. K., & Dumais, S. T. (1997). A solution to Plato's problem: The latent semantic analysis theory of acquisition, induction, and representation of knowledge. *Psychological Review, 104,* 210-240.

Monk, A. (1999). Modelling cyclic interaction. *Behaviour & Information Technology, 18*(2), 127-139.

Nardi, B. A. (1996). Studying context: A comparison of activity theory, situated action models, and distributed cognition. In B. A. Nardi (Ed.), *Context and consciousness: Activity theory and human-computer interaction.* Cambridge, MA: MIT Press.

Nardi, B. A. (Ed.). (1997). *Context and consciousness: Activity theory and human-computer interaction.* Cambridge, MA: MIT Press.

Nielsen, J. (1994). Heuristic evaluation. In J. Nielsen & R. L. Mack (Eds.), *Usability inspection methods* (pp. 25-62). New York: John Wiley & Sons.

Nielsen, J. (2000). *Designing Web usability*. Indianapolis, IN: New Riders.

Norman, D. A. (1986). Cognitive engineering. In D. A. Norman & S. W. Draper (Eds.), *User centered system design* (pp. 29-61). Hillsdale, NJ: Lawrence Erlbaum Associates.

Polson, P. G., Lewis, C., Rieman, J., & Wharton, C. (1992). Cognitive walkthroughs — A method for theory-based evaluation of user interfaces. *International Journal of Man-Machine Studies, 36*(5), 741-773.

Polson, P. G., & Lewis, C. H. (1990). Theory-based design for easily learned interfaces. *Human-Computer Interaction, 5*(2-3), 191-220.

Quek, A., & Shah, H. (2004, September 2-3). *The activity theoretical iterative evaluation method.* Paper presented at the 3rd Nordic Conference on Cultural and Activity Research, Copenhagen, Denmark.

Ryu, H. (2003, April 5-10). *Modelling cyclic interaction: An account of goal-elimination process.* Paper presented at the Special Interest Group Computer-Human Interaction Conference on Human Factors in Computing Systems, Ft. Lauderdale, FL.

Ryu, H., & Monk, A. (2004a). Analysing interaction problems with cyclic interaction theory: Low-level interaction walkthrough. *PsychNology, 2*(3), 304-330.

Ryu, H., & Monk, A. (2004b, November 22-24). *A brief account of interaction problems.* Paper presented at the OZCHI, Wollongong, Australia.

Ryu, H., & Monk, A. (2005). Will it be a capital letter: Signalling case mode in mobile devices. *Interacting with Computers, 17,* 395-418.

Suchman, L. A. (1987). *Plans and situated actions: The problem of human-machine communication.* New York: Cambridge University Press.

Vicente, K. J. (1999). *Cognitive work analysis: Towards safe, productive and healthy computer-based work.* Mahwah, NJ: Erlbaum.

Chapter XII

User-Centered Evaluation of Personalized Web Sites:
What's Unique?

Sherman R. Alpert, IBM T. J. Watson Research Center, USA

John G. Vergo, IBM T. J. Watson Research Center, USA

ABSTRACT

In addition to traditional usability issues, evaluation studies for personalized Web sites and applications must consider concerns specific to these systems. In the general case, usability studies for computer-based applications attempt to determine whether the software, in actual use, meets users' needs; whether users can accomplish their goals in using the software; whether users can understand and use the application (whether they comprehend what they can do and how); the rate, frequency, and severity of user errors; the rate of and time duration for task completion; and so on. But in the case of user-centered evaluations of personalized Web sites, there are additional questions and issues that must be addressed. In this paper, we present some of these, based on our experience in usability studies of a personalized e-commerce site.

INTRODUCTION

Personalized Web sites attempt to adapt and tailor the user experience to a particular user's preferences, needs, goals, interests, knowledge, or interaction history. A personalized site adapts its content, content structure, the presentation of information, the inclusion of hyperlinks, or the availability of functionality to each individual user's characteristics and/or usage behavior. Such a site may place specific information, which it "thinks" you will be interested in, at a distinguished or obvious location on a Web page. Another personalized site may choose to add or elide specific content or hyperlinks to additional information based on what it "knows" about the current user's knowledge or interests. An e-commerce site that knows what model laptop you own may only show accessories compatible with that model. A site that displays information about movies and theater schedules may use knowledge of the user's postal code to display only theaters within n miles of the user's location. A personalized news site may elect to show (or not) today's baseball scores, depending on whether the user has viewed this sort of information in previous site visits. A book seller may use knowledge of the books you have ordered in the past to recommend new works by the same author or other authors of the same genre, or may suggest additional books purchased by other users that have bought the same book as you are now ordering. Data about the user, used to drive the site's personalizations, may be obtained by information explicitly provided by the user and by inferences made by the system based on previous user interactions.

The personalization approach begs many questions, Do personalized Web sites actually improve the user's experience when using such sites? Do specific personalization features improve and others detract from user experience? Does personalization actually add value to users? Is the site not only usable but acceptable, attractive, and desirable to users?

Personalized Web sites are a specific example of the more general field of adaptive systems. The literature of the evaluation of adaptive systems is replete with evaluative studies of how well the "system" works. These evaluations have focused on algorithms and user model representations for programmatically "implementing" the systems' adaptive behavior, including determining how well the detection and gathering of implicit information about users' functions, how appropriately are inferences drawn about users, and how robust are the systems' techniques for using such information to provide some type of adaptive functionality. For example, evaluations of adaptive systems might consider whether the system's inferences about the user indeed coincide with the user's prior behavior (Weibelzahl & Weber, 2003). As another example, "evaluators need to check if [the system's] inferences or the conclusions drawn by the system concerning the user-computer interaction are correct since it is not necessary that there will be a direct one to one mapping between raw data and their semantically meaningful counterparts" (Gupta & Grover, 2004). Thus many adaptive system evaluations focus on how well the system functions in an (objective) application-centered sense. Many such studies focus on an individual personalization technique, such as recommender systems or collaborative filtering (e.g., Mobasher, Dai, Luo, & Nakagawa, 2001; Zhu & Greiner, 2005). Still others have focused on success of a personalized site as measured by the number of site visits and return visits, number of purchases on an e-commerce site, click-throughs to suggested content, and so forth.

Of course, many of these measures are useful and must be considered in the evaluation of a personalized site. However, evaluations of personalized Web sites must also consider the more subjective user-centered perspective, and the literature is considerably sparser in this regard. User satisfaction is only partially determined by the accuracy of the algorithmic implementation and, further, user satisfaction may not be achieved even in systems that do provide accurate information (Swearingen & Sinha, 2001). In a user-centered design approach, design decisions are based on the experimentally validated value to users of a system's features and facilities (Vredenburg, Isensee, & Righi, 2001). Thus user-centered evaluations must involve the testing of the system by (and for) users. Some of the existing evaluation literature has suggested using an evaluator who attempts to take the role of a "typical" user of the system; but we have learned from experience (Alpert, Karat, Karat, Brodie, & Vergo, 2003; Karat, Brodie, Karat, Vergo, & Alpert, 2003) that testing must involve actual intended users of the system because doing so may elicit results that are unexpected based solely on the system developers' analysis, and reveals more accurately the real user's perspective.

In the general case, usability studies for computer-based applications attempt to determine whether the software, in actual use, meets users' requirements; whether the software performs as it should in supporting users as they attempt to accomplish specific tasks; whether typical users are successful in achieving their goals; whether users can understand and use the application (whether they comprehend what they can do and how); the rate, frequency, and severity of user errors; the rate of and time duration for task completion; and so on. The goal is to test "how well the functionality fits user needs, how well the flow through the application fits user tasks, and how well the response of the application fits user expectations" (Usability First, n.d.). Usability testing may involve such abstract issues as the appropriateness of an overall system metaphor and such low level details as the placement of widgets on the screen, the use of color, and the wording of textual content. Usability testing informs the design of interactive software by obtaining the user's perspective regarding the design, rather than simply relying on the intuitions of the designers and implementers of the software.

Even when researchers have spoken directly to the idea of evaluating the usability of adaptive or personalized systems, they have not addressed the entire problem: Such discussions often revolve around traditional usability issues or around Boolean comparisons of a whole system with and without its entire adaptive functionality (Weibelzahl, Lippitsch, & Weber, 2002). Of course, standard usability issues must be addressed when evaluating adaptive systems: We do care whether users can accomplish their goals using the system, and further, whether they can accomplish their goals faster or more accurately using a system that adapts to their needs than when using a system that does not. And usability evaluations and system evaluations will have interdependencies: If the system's personalization mechanisms simply do not function well, the user will lose confidence in the system and all of its personalized recommendations (McLaughlin & Herlocke, 2004). But there are other factors that must be considered, issues that go to the heart of the user experience.

As in the design of any software, developers of personalized solutions begin with what they consider to be "good ideas" regarding the sorts of adaptations that would serve users, using intuitions about users and the software's functionality. And as in case of other interactive software, these intuitions must again be verified by contact with actual users at some time before application deployment. In the case of personalized applications, however, additional questions that go beyond traditional usability must be addressed by user-centered evaluative studies. The functionality offered by personalized applications must not only match users' needs and, perhaps even more importantly than before, their expectations, but also their desires and level of trust in computational systems. User studies in this domain must not only assess ostensibly quantitative measures such as time-to-task completion, but qualitative issues such as users' confidence and belief in the system's recommendations, personalizations, and other adaptive behaviors. We must determine not only whether the system is usable for performing tasks, but also whether it is acceptable to users and enhances, rather than degrades, the user experience. In this paper, we discuss some of these issues that go beyond the purview of traditional usability evaluations.

The issues discussed in this paper are derived from user studies of personalized Web sites in a particular e-commerce context, specifically the Web site of a large computer hardware, software, and services provider (Alpert et al., 2003; Karat et al., 2003). As such, the issues themselves are derived from empirical evaluations. They may be considered a step moving toward the full realization of the issues and factors that must be addressed in personalized Web site evaluations.

USER-CENTERED PERSONALIZATION MEASURES

As mentioned previously, there are many proposals in the adaptive systems literature aimed at evaluating whether the application or Web site in question performs its adaptations correctly or accurately. And usability studies of (nonpersonalized) Web sites have shown that ease of use can increase the number of revisits and purchases (e.g., Nielsen, 2003). We touch only gently on general usability issues here. Instead, this discussion focuses on the user's views and opinions of personalized adaptations, not only whether they work as intended, but even if they do so, whether users want the Web site to be making and using inferences and data about the user to influence or direct an adaptive presentation to the user. Evaluations of adaptive and personalized applications must ultimately address the question, do the adaptive features actually improve the user's experience when using the site? (see also Chin, 2001). Designers, researchers, and developers may have many ideas for personalized functionality for a Web site that they think would provide users with some benefit. But actual users when confronted with such features may find them useless or, worse, objectionable. The intuitions of the builders of (personalized and all) interactive software must be confirmed by actual potential users of that software.

Here we introduce some of the questions and issues that must be addressed when performing user-centered evaluations of personalized Web sites. These must be addressed in addition to traditional usability concerns, which we will not discuss but that, of course, must be incorporated into the user-centered evaluation. For example, fundamental to any evaluation is whether the site (and its adaptive behaviors) supports users in accomplishing their goals. Or, even more specifically related to personalization, does the inclusion of personalized features make the user more "efficient" and decrease time-to-goal completion. These are important, and ignoring such issues would be foolish. In this paper, we only touch on these more traditional concerns but go further in discussing issues that are of a more subjective nature and relate to the overall user experience, not simply quantitative efficiency measures such as time-to-task completion.

Do Users Want the Personalized Behavior?

Beyond whether site adaptations support the user in accomplishing tasks and goals, the next question we must ask in a user-centered analysis of a personalized site is whether users actually desire the personalizations the site intends or purports to provide. For example,

Alpert et al. (2003) found many users were not pleased with a site's attempts to infer their needs, goals, or interests to thereby provide user-specific adaptive content. A number of study participants declared they would prefer that the site not attempt to infer their intentions, declaring their opinion that "computers are not smart enough" to do a good job of inferring users' goals and plans, and therefore personalized interactions may be based on specious inferences. "Users say things like 'don't stereotype me -- just give me the options because I prefer choosing for myself rather than having the computer tell me what's good for me'" (Nielsen, 1998).

One type of adaptive system behavior is to intervene while a user is working. The intervention might be to offer advice relating to the user's plan for achieving particular goals; to offer just-in-time instruction related to information currently in view; to offer additional, related information or an alternative or associated product; and so on. In a user-centered view of the system, the question is, is an intervention wanted or timed correctly? For example, "Clippy" is the assistive agent in Microsoft Office applications (who by default appears in the form of an interactive paper clip), who offers advice on how to accomplish goals while using the application. The question is, should Clippy intervene while users are working, and when? Overwhelmingly, at least anecdotally, users dislike the assistive agent and its interventions, and many users disable the advice-giving assistance. Problems here include not wishing to be interrupted while focusing on actual work. This can be considered the annoyance factor and may be based on the cognitive load of having to interrupt a plan to focus on advice for an alternative plan. Perhaps more important is the fact that the assistant often does a poor job of inferring the user's goals and plans. Thus, not only is the interruption unwanted, but the advice is not useful anyway! Due to the extensive use of these application products, many users are wary of computer applications' attempts to infer their needs and simply do not trust them to be smart enough to do a good job at it.

Questions Regarding the Use of Prior User Behavior for Adaptive Site Behavior

In personalized Web sites, a user may attempt to find or explicitly ask for information on a particular topic, and the site uses information explicitly provided by the user and implicitly inferred about the user to find and (perhaps adaptively) display or recommend pointers to the appropriate information. The first question this raises is, what implicit information does the site use in making personalization decisions? Where (sites, pages, topics, products, etc.) has the user browsed before? Which search hitlist items has the user clicked on before? Does the site use information about the user's apparent current information needs, for example, current task and inferred goals; recent needs; needs some time in the past; general long-term interests; where the user navigated and the topical or product information the user viewed; or information gathered about other users? How does a personalized site adapt to individual users — that is, on what information are the system's adaptations based?

First, personalized sites typically use information explicitly provided by users about themselves, in either questionnaires or in the course of performing actual tasks (e.g., the user's mail zip code is obtained when the user makes a purchase; this can later be used to provide information personalized by location, such as nearby movie theater listings). In the case of multi-user systems such as Web sites, personalized systems may also use information about other users, including their behavior on the site (e.g., for collaborative filtering, what did other users purchase?). In addition, intelligent personalized sites use implicit information gathered about the user, based on the user's previous behavior on the site. This includes information obtained by observing the user's previous navigations (e.g., what topics, products, genres did the user look at before?) and clickstream data (e.g., what links did the user click?).

An application-centered evaluation of such a site might ask questions about how well the system's algorithms perform, for example, does the collaborative filtering engine accurately display the most popular related items? (McLaughlin & Herlocke, 2004). A user-centered evaluation of such an application must ask at least two questions. First, does it make sense — in the context of this site — to use prior user behavior to decide what to present to that user? And, do users want such personalized site features and have it based on their own previous performance and/or the previous behavior and decisions of other users?

Personalized content, based on implicit information, such as previous navigation paths, also met with mixed reactions in our previous studies. The notion of basing content on previous navigation was rated positively by participants overall, but some participants were so adamant in their disapproval of this feature, and their opinions were so clear and passionately articulated, that they must be considered by developers of personalized sites. One participant stated the explicit-implicit problem succinctly: "I like to have more control and less assumptions made." Other participants expressed skepticism that this feature could be implemented in a way that would make it generally valuable to them. Specifically, participants expressed some level of concern about a site's ability to do this well enough to be useful. The overarching message was, "adapting content based on past navigation would be a nice thing, but we don't believe you can do it well, so don't do it at all."

Clearly, using a particular user's previous behavior is not always useful: "I viewed pages about x before, but I have very different goals and needs now; don't bias what I can view based on what I did before." Participants mentioned "shifting goals" as a problem that they believe would not be handled well by systems that use inferred goals to guide current and future presentations. They asserted that their needs, even on a single site, change over time, and they do not want adaptive behavior of the site to be based on their obsolete goals. As Nielsen (1998) puts it, "Having the computer personalize the website to the user assumes that the computer can guess the user's needs. This is difficult to do and even more difficult when you consider that the same person may have different desires at different times."

Refining this result further, adapting content based on immediate context was met with favor by our participants. For example, personalized recommendations can be based on the content of the Web page that is currently visible. It appears that using the immediate or current context to influence concurrent or immediately ensuing content is seen to be useful, whereas attempting to infer current goals based on navigation or other information from the past was not universally welcome. Overall, participants agreed that there ought to be a logical "limit" regarding how far back into one's past history the site should look for implicit information about goals and interests, and further that this limit should be the current "session." That is, the consensus view was that a user's past history should have a limited life span: It is acceptable for the site to adapt content based on the user's current task and navigation context and even the user's context and history since he/she logged on today, but it should not look at past behavior beyond this point to a disjoint time or session in the past.

A further complicating issue relating to the implicit gathering of information about a user's past interaction history is: Is all navigation behavior and clickstream data even relevant or meaningful, shifting goals notwithstanding? Therefore exactly when should such information not be collected by the site? Participants in our studies did not want data collected implicitly about them — and "remembered" in their profile — during exploratory sessions on a site unless they specifically authorize it. As one participant explained, "Hey, I might just be knocking around the site for a while...it doesn't mean anything, and you'll fill up my profile with a lot of junk if you implicitly collect that information. Wait until I know that I'm really after something before you start collecting data about what I'm doing, and let me tell you when that is."

Consideration of Context

Some personalization features are based on the behavior, attitudes, likes and dislikes, navigation, or purchases of other users. For example, many existing e-commerce sites recommend additional "related" products to the user when a purchase transaction is about to be completed: "People who bought this product also bought products X, Y, and Z." This is a simple form of collaborative filtering or recommender technologies (e.g., Burke, 1999; Resnick & Varian, 1997; Schafer, Konstan, & Riedl, 2001). When applied in the context of e-commerce, these technologies use the buying behavior of prior customers to attempt to "predict" which products a new customer may be interested in purchasing. But in our user studies, some participants expressed objections such as, "I am not like other people, I have different needs." Additionally, this feature might be perceived simply as an intrusive marketing ploy: One of our participants found it to be an "obnoxious" attempt at marketing more products.

Looking a bit deeper, it appears that user attitudes about collaborative filtering may in fact be influenced by a variety of factors including the type of e-commerce site involved, the particular product being purchased, the type of user, and the reason an item is being purchased. Our previous evaluation studies involved a specific class of user, a particular type of e-commerce site, for a particular category of products and services: Users were business managers buying computer equipment for their enterprises, driven by specific business requirements in their actual jobs. What other customers purchased is not interesting or important to these users. The upshot is that our users had equivocal reactions to a feature that is nonetheless in extensive use: Collaborative filtering is clearly viewed by users as a benefit in other e-commerce settings, such as book and music sellers like Amazon.com. The clear conclusion is that individual personalization strategies, such as recommender systems, are not necessarily effective or beneficial across the spectrum of users and activities. Instead, user opinions and desires regarding such technologies may depend on multiple dimensions of the e-commerce scenario in question, such as the type of product being purchased, whether the purchase is for one's self or for one's company, and whether subjective parameters such as taste or genre are relevant to the item being purchased.

Confidence in and Understanding of the Site's Personalizations

As we can already see, usability measures for personalized systems are significantly interconnected; For example, if a user does not trust that the site is capable of making reasonable inferences regarding his/her current goals, the he/she will not want the site's (perhaps specious) adaptations. From the user's perspective, then, an important question is, do users believe computer systems can do the proposed adaptations well (enough to be useful)? Are users confident that a site can perform the personalized adaptation without annoying them or wasting their time? As we have noted, in our previous studies we found that the confidence issue is so important that some participants disclosed that they do not want any information that has been collected implicitly by the site to become a part of their persistent personal profile. Instead, they wanted only information explicitly provided by them to be remembered by the site: "I want the stored information to be based on what I told you, not what you think I've said."

Especially if the site is making decisions regarding the customizing of information shown to individual users, are users confident the site is giving them "good" or the "best" information available? "When the user knows that a screen has been adapted to them, it is natural for them to wonder just what has been adapted to them. What might a different user see? Are they missing out on something?" (Kay, 2001). These thoughts may intensify a user's lack of confidence in an individually customized site. In a survey of Web users, 94% said that being able to trust the information on a site is *very* important or somewhat important to them as they decide to (re)visit a Web site (80% said very important; 80% also said that it is very important that the site be easy to navigate) (Consumer Reports WebWatch, 2002).

Confidence in the site also relies heavily on being able to make sense of the site and its behaviors. In a user-centered analysis of a personalized site, one ought to ask, does the user understand what is being adapted due to personalization, and why? The issue is one of determinism and comprehension. "To navigate through web-sites (e.g., presentations, online-shops, or learning courses) the user requires a mental model of the site's structure" (Weibelzahl & Weber, 2001, p. 74). It may be difficult to form a coherent model of the structure, content, and behavior of a site when these change over time and circumstance (although Weibelzahl & Weber argue that an adaptive site may require building a less complex mental model than a nonadaptive site). A site may be more difficult to understand and learn to use when multiple instances of the same user-system interaction result in different behavior by the system. Does the user understand what is changing and why it is changing? These are questions that must be addressed in a user-centered evaluation of a personalized site. Does the user understand why the site is "adapting" its behavior and output? Is the system predictable: "Will the user know, with a reasonable degree of certainty, what will happen when (s)he takes an action?" (D'Hertefelt, 2000). Can the user understand how the site behaves and is he/she disconcerted by the fact that the content shown in a specific context is not always the same? Is the user experience degraded because the ability of the user to understand and predict what the site will do is diminished? Paramythis, Totter, and Stephanidis (2001) refer to this issue as transparency. Users want to readily be able to make sense of site behavior, to understand a site's rationale for displaying particular content. When past behavior or other nonobvious implicit information is used to generate content, the users' confused reaction — "Where did this come from?" — conveys to users the notion that they are not in control. On the other hand, content whose origin is obvious or readily inferable is met with favor, while content that is based on something the user, or other users, did at some temporally distant time is often met with disapproval.

Users seem to have similar expectations of a dialog with a software application or Web site as with other people. That is, it appears that users desire responses from a Web site to follow logical conversational conventions (Grice, 1975; Searle, 1969); for example, they expect responses to be relevant to the ongoing dialog and to be as informative as required but not more so. This result coincides with the experimental work of Reeves and Nass (1999). After conducting numerous studies, Reeves and Nass concluded that users' expectations regarding their interactions with computers and other media are based in large part on social interactions in real life, that is, users expect computers to obey rules that come from the world of interpersonal interaction. When a site provides more information — or, in some manner, other information — than what is expected, the user may not immediately know what to make of the "extra" information. In discussing many features, we heard from our users that they want to understand, without difficulty, why and how the computer side of the ongoing bilateral conversation, represented by the content the Web site displays, chose to "say" what it has displayed.

Further, does a user's need to understand what is happening vary with the type of personalized site? If personalized adaptation is based on, say, previous navigation, the resultant application behavior may not always be clear to the user. For example, the simple collaborative filtering mechanism implemented on the Amazon site is explained as "Customers who bought [this book] also bought…" Thus the attempt is made to have users understand this simple personalization. On the other hand, when personalized results for a particular search query result in differing output at different times, does the user understand why the results differ? During usability evaluation, we must also be sure that when a site does explain its behavior, the explanation is satisfactorily informative from the user's perspective.

Andersen, Andersen, and Hansen (2001) assert that users of adaptive e-commerce sites wish to be *surprised* by the site, but in a very different manner than what is being discussed here. They mean pleasantly surprised in terms of value-added services as a reward for using the site. First, they state that users wish to see recommended products related to what they are already purchasing. We saw in our user study that this is dependent on the e-commerce context: Users of book seller sites (as in Andersen et al.) may wish to have this feature, whereas in many other product-purchasing contexts this is not a welcome feature. Andersen et al. also state that users wish to be *surprised* by special offers associated with use of the site (e.g., lower prices than in brick-and-mortar stores and flexible delivery options). On the other hand, users do not wish to be *surprised* in the conventional sense; if they ask, "What color is the sky?" they do not expect a response about shoe sizes in North America.

Confidence and trust in a site of course also touch on the broader issue of privacy. The importance of this issue is brought into relief by a survey in which Web users were asked to rate their confidence in various types of organizations and enterprises (businesses, newspapers, banks, charities, government, etc.). Web sites rated among the lowest, and the overwhelming reason was lack of trust regarding the handling of private information (Consumer Reports WebWatch, 2002). For a given site then, usability evaluations must also determine whether users are willing to divulge information about themselves to the site. Do users of the site under evaluation believe that the value added by the site's personalization features is worth the user-perceived risk in disclosing private information? Are they confident that the site will use the personal information in ethical ways? Is an official privacy statement — in which the site spells out a legally binding description of how it will use and disseminate (or not) personal information — necessary?

Who is in Control?

In our previous studies regarding personalized Web sites, the most important issue to users was their fervent desire to be — or at least feel like they are — "in control." "The feeling of security experienced by a user of an interactive system is determined by the user's feeling of control of the interactive system" (D'Hertefelt, 2000). The issue is one of trust, and again has interdependencies with other issues, such as confidence and comprehensibility. "An interactive system that allows the user to feel in control should in the first place be comprehensible" (D'Hertefelt, 2000). But also, does the user trust that the inferences the personalized site has made about him are correct? "People usually do not know the reasons behind some of the personal recommendations, which often results in their distrust of the personalization mechanism" (Wang & Lin, 2003). Is there a way for the user to understand the kinds of inferences the site is making? Should there be? Can the user correct the inferences and other profile information? How granular is the control — that is, is it simply on/off for all adaptation, for subsets of the adaptation features? What is the accuracy rate required for the adaptation to become a net benefit to the user? If content or features are elided as a result of inferences made about the user, can the user easily "see" what they are missing: While users may feel that at times personalization may be useful, they also believe the application must provide ways to view the "full," nonpersonalized or nonadapted content or information (Nielsen, 1998). Can the user view, and even modify, his/her personalization profile? These are the sorts of questions that must be addressed in a user-centered evaluation of a personalized Web site.

In our studies, this control issue emerged most strikingly in terms of being in control of one's profile, the persistently stored personal information collected by the site about the user. As noted previously with regard to confidence and trust in a site, users ask, "What are you going to do with this data; can I trust you to maintain 'intimate' information about me?" While this result is certainly no surprise, it is prevalent among all users and is a strongly emotional issue. As such, it can be considered a "deal breaker" — users will not provide personal information and will not perform transactions on a Web site that in their opinion cannot be fully trusted to use profile information in an ethical and private manner. Andersen et al. (2001) also discuss this issue. Users want to be able to review, modify, delete, or add personal information to their profile at any time. This should be another focus of usability evaluations of personalized Web sites, to determine how the users of the specific site feel regarding these issues and what might be done to ameliorate their concerns (for example, Kay and her colleagues have attempted to address these sorts of "feeling in control" issues in personalized systems with scrutable user models and adaptations; see, e.g., Kay, 2001; Czarkowski & Kay, 2005).

Of course, there is a delicate balance that must be maintained between adaptability of the system and the user's sense of control: "Increasing the flexibility can also increase complexity and diminish comprehensibility" (D'Hertefelt, 2000). Thus the need for actually testing personalized sites with users is further intensified — personalized systems attempt to balance adaptability versus users' sense of control, and usability testing must be performed to determine whether the site has succeeded in this balancing act.

How Much Work is Involved on the Part of the User?

Web site users are loath to spend extra time and effort to enter personal information, even to enable a site to "know" more about them for personalization purposes. Nielsen (1998) invokes the notion of the paradox of the active user to explain this user behavior and preference. When encountering a new application, users wish to immediately engage in actual tasks, tasks that further their own goals. This is especially true when visiting Web sites; users have a specific goal in mind (e.g., purchasing a CD) when they visit an e-commerce site, and have little desire to first enter into an extended session of entering information about themselves before being able to accomplish that goal. "Web users are extremely impatient and want to get something useful out of a site immediately" (Nielsen, 1998).

An alternative to lengthy data-entering sessions is a technique known as "permission marketing" (Godin, 1999), in which a user's profile or user model is incrementally constructed over time as the user interacts with a service or product provider, such as an e-commerce site. In this scenario, customers are asked only for information sufficient to complete a specific transaction or obtain a particular service, but over time a more complete user profile is obtained. An important aspect of permission marketing is that users receive an observable and immediate benefit in return for the small amount of information explicitly provided to the site and are therefore motivated to comply.

Notably, in our e-commerce studies in which permission marketing was evaluated, users rated the feature very highly. Users also expect that information explicitly entered once will persist — that is, users do not want to be asked by the site to enter the same information at a later time for a subsequent transaction or interaction.

The clear implications for usability evaluations are to determine whether users consider the explicit entering of personal information onerous or annoying, and whether there is consensus among users regarding the implied cost-benefit relationship. Do users ultimately find benefit in the site's personalization features in spite of the amount or level of work involved in enabling the site to personalize or adapt its interactions?

WHAT IS THE SAME?

The aforementioned discussion focuses on what is different about evaluations of personalized Web sites and systems, that is, what distinguishes evaluations of such sites from other Web sites. It enumerates questions and issues that must be addressed in the assessment of personalized sites from a user-centered perspective, including asking not only is the site usable, but does it provide functionality and affordances users actually desire, that provide obvious value to users, and that users will choose to use. The evaluation process must address these many questions posed previously. The pragmatics of evaluating these issues is where things are the same as other thorough and comprehensive user-centered assessments. The techniques and approach are the same, the focus and issues addressed are expanded.

As for other types of Web sites, user-centered evaluations of personalized sites certainly ought to involve a system prototype that users can view and perhaps minimally interact with. Upon deciding what personalized features you wish to potentially incorporate into the site, a prototype that reifies those features should be constructed. Evaluation studies should be performed early in the design process using site prototypes; this can be a money- and effort-saving technique if designers' initial intuitions regarding adaptive features and functionality do not match users' opinions of them. This savings may be greater in the case of adaptive functionality than traditional software because the former may involve techniques that are difficult and time consuming to implement. As Paramythis et al. (2001) suggest, "Eliciting user feedback regarding the modeling process requires that at least a prototype of the system exists." Taking this a step further, initial user testing should begin when only a prototype exists, that is, before the site is fully implemented, so that many design and implementation decisions are made prior to the expense and time of building the full site.

A reasonable method of putting the site and its personalization behaviors in front of users without the expense of actually building the system (including its adaptive functionality, which is often complex to implement) is to use paper prototypes, a technique often used in formative usability evaluations. Here, drawings of potential screens are shown to potential users, providing a sense of what the fully implemented system would look like. The images may be skeletal wire frames of the proposed screens or fully rendered realistic images of actual Web pages. Here, drawings of potential screens are shown to potential users who may express their opinions of particular screens, including their content and affordances. Usability study experimenters may be "in control," demonstrating the proposed site design to focus groups or individual users by walking the study participants through scenarios of interaction, an approach much like the Design Walk-through technique for usability evaluation (Vredenburg et al., 2001). Or participants may discuss what they would choose to do at the interface, what actions they would take to accomplish some scenario-based goal. Experimenters can then show the appropriate image of the site's response to the user action — for example, a new Web page or the same page with updated information — and the evaluation process iterates over several scenarios.

Evaluations of design ideas might be also performed with prototype Web pages built using presentation software, such as Microsoft® PowerPoint®, thus using digital images on a screen rather than paper. Realistic screen shots can be created using a graphical drawing and editing tool. Taking this notion a step further, in addition to being able to show users static screen images, PowerPoint possesses the ability to easily add programmatic behaviors to provide true interactivity, without the cost of a full, "real" implementation of the actual system. Users cannot only see what screens might look like in the implemented site, but can push buttons, enter text, and in general "use" the interactive prototype, whose behaviors mimic the ultimate implementation, in hands-on, scenario-based interactions. This technique offers a prototype for user testing of greater fidelity than merely showing static screen images and gives users a truer sense of the look-and-feel of the site.

Of course, this implies that driving the evaluation should be realistic scenarios of use of the Web site. Each scenario should involve a "story" in which the user must accomplish a particular goal by using the Web site. The full corpus of scenarios must include ones that exercise the personalization features the site offers. For example, a scenario of use for a computer-purchasing site might involve the goal of purchasing a memory card that is compatible with a particular computer (Alpert et al., 2003; Karat et al., 2003).

One approach might be to contrast performing a particular scenario using two different prototype sites, with and without specific personalization features that might or might not support the user in accomplishing specific goals. Experimenters can walk users through interaction with mock-site prototypes, or users can use, hands on, a minimally interactive prototype, to accomplish this same scenario goal with the two prototypes. Or the walk-through or interaction may occur with only a single prototype, one that incorporates and demonstrates a particular personalization feature. Then, experimenter-led discussions with focus groups and with individual study participants, written and oral questionnaires, time-to-task completion, number of clicks, and keyboard interactions — those materials and procedures typically incorporated into user evaluations of interactive systems — would also be employed (as in the personalization evaluation studies reported in Alpert et al. (2003) and Karat et al. (2003).

For example, questionnaires might list features such as "The site will conduct constrained searches for accessories and upgrades, searching only among those that are compatible with the products you already own," and study participants would be asked to rate each feature in terms of its value to the participant using a Likert scale ranging from "Highly valuable" to "Not at all valuable." Evaluations must interrogate whether the personalization features actually helped the user accomplish his/her goals. Questionnaires might include assertions, including such general statements as, "I believe the system helped me in accomplishing my goals" and "The site did not understand very well what I wanted to do and did not offer information helpful to accomplishing my goals," and more specific statements such as, "When I wanted to purchase memory compatible with my laptop, I found the site helped me in accomplishing my goal" and "When I wanted to purchase memory compatible with my laptop, it was helpful that the site showed only those accessories that are compatible with my particular computer model." Assertions might also probe the affective issues that have been discussed; for instance, "I liked when the site tried to understand what I was trying to accomplish," "I'm comfortable with the Web site trying to figure out what my goals are," and "The site should not try to infer what I'm trying to accomplish and should let me be completely in control." These too would require Likert ratings from "I strongly agree" to "I strongly disagree." Group and individual discussions should be sure to focus as well on issues such as the desirability or acceptability of the site's attempts to infer users' needs and goals, and how well the system's intervention indeed facilitated the success of goal achievement.

CONCLUSION

Design of personalization or user-adaptive systems (or any software technology) cannot occur in a vacuum, specifically, it cannot usefully proceed without assessing the value and usefulness to users of the concepts proposed and implemented by researchers and developers. Is the overall user experience enhanced due to the inclusion of personalized features and functionality?

We can see that many of the presented user-centered measures interact and overlap: User trust and confidence in a Web site will plainly be affected by the quality of the system's inferences regarding what the user wants to see; if a user cannot understand why particular information is being displayed, he/she will have less confidence in the site; if the user is confused by the site's actions, they will feel less in control of the user-system interaction, and so on. The measures may be evaluated with and by users as individual items or joined to form more complex evaluation issues. In either case, the evaluation of personalized Web sites must consider several features, issues, and questions, including:

- Do users desire the particular personalization adaptations provided by the site?
- Do adaptations that apparently succeed in one application context (e.g., collaborative filtering on Amazon.com) necessarily enhance the user experience in the context of the site being evaluated?
- Is the site using appropriate information for its adaptations (e.g., previous navigation, explicitly entered information, previous click-throughs, etc.)?
- Do users find the site's adaptations predictable and acceptable, or unintelligible and even unnerving?
- Are users confused by seeing information they did not explicitly request?

- Do users have confidence and trust in the site based on experiencing its personalized adaptations?
- Are users satisfied with the amount of work they must perform to allow the site to personalize user interactions?
- Do users have an adequate sense of being in control (even though the site may behave differently at different times and circumstances)?
- Are users willing to relinquish control to the extent required to allow the site to personalize interactions?

Many of the questions, issues, and measures we have raised and studied are qualitative (and at times, emotional) in nature. Assessments of personalization features will of course vary across Web site domains, user types, and individual users. Researchers, usability professionals, and developers need to have a broad sensitivity to the issues we have listed, and will be well-served by investing in appropriate user-centered studies before implementing personalization features on their Web sites.

REFERENCES

Alpert, S. R., Karat, J., Karat, C.-M., Brodie, C., & Vergo, J. G. (2003). User attitudes regarding a user-adaptive ecommerce Web site. *User Modeling and User-Adapted Interaction, 13*(4), 373-396.

Andersen, H. H. K., Andersen, V., & Hansen, C. B. (2001). Establishing criteria for evaluating intelligent agents in e-commerce. In S. Weibelzahl, D. Chin, & G. Weber (Eds.), *Empirical evaluation of adaptive systems*.

Burke, R. (1999). Integrating knowledge-based and collaborative-filtering. In *Proceedings of the AAAI 1999 Workshop on AI and Electronic Commerce* (pp. 14-20).

Carroll, J. M., & Rosson, M. B. (1987). The paradox of the active user. In J. M. Carroll (Ed.), *Interfacing thought: Cognitive aspects of human-computer interaction*. Cambridge, MA: MIT Press.

Chin, D. N. (2001). Empirical evaluation of user models and user-adapted systems. *User Modeling and User-Adapted Interaction, 11*, 181-194.

Consumer Reports WebWatch. (2002, April 16). *A matter of trust: What users want from Web sites*. Retrieved from http://www.consumerwebwatch.org/dynamic/web-credibility-report-a-matter-of-trust.cfm

Czarkowski, M., & Kay, J. (2005). Scrutability as a core interface element. In C.-K. Looi et al. (Eds.), *Artificial Intelligence in Education, Proceedings of AIED-2005* (pp. 783-785). Amsterdam: IOS Press.

D'Hertefelt, S. (2000, January 3). *Trust and the perception of security*. Retrieved from http://www.interactionarchitect.com/research/report20000103shd.htm

Godin, S. (1999). *Permission marketing: Turning strangers into friends, and friends into customers*. New York: Simon & Schuster.

Grice, H. P. (1975). Logic and conversation. In P. Cole & J. Morgan (Eds.), *Syntax and semantics 3: Speech Acts* (pp. 41-58). New York: Academic.

Gupta, A., & Grover, P. S. (2003). Proposed evaluation framework for adaptive hypermedia systems. In *Proceedings of the Third Workshop on Empirical Evaluation of Adaptive*

Systems. Retrieved from http://www.easy-hub.org/hub/workshops/ah2004/proceedings.html

Karat, C. M., Brodie, C., Karat, J., Vergo, J. G., & Alpert, S. R. (2003). Personalizing the user experience on IBM.com. *IBM Systems Journal, 42*(4), 686-701.

Kay, J. (2001, July). Scrutability for personalised interfaces. *ERCIM News* (No. 46). Retrieved from http://www.ercim.org/publication/Ercim_News/enw46/kay.html

McLaughlin, M. R., & Herlocke, J. L. (2004). A collaborative filtering algorithm and evaluation metric that accurately model the user experience. In *Proceedings of the 27th Annual International Conference on Research and Development in Information Retrieval* (pp. 329-336). New York: ACM Press.

Mobasher, B., Dai, H., Luo, T., & Nakagawa, M. (2001). Improving the effectiveness of collaborative filtering on anonymous Web usage data. In *Proceedings of the IJCAI 2001 Workshop on Intelligent Techniques for Web Personalization (ITWP01)*.

Nielsen, J. (1998, October 4). Personalization is over-rated. *Jakob Nielsen's Alertbox*. Retrieved from http://www.useit.com/alertbox/981004.html

Paramythis, A., Totter, A., & Stephanidis, C. (2001). A modular approach to the evaluation of adaptive user interfaces. In S. Weibelzahl, D. Chin, & G. Weber (Eds.), *Empirical Evaluation of Adaptive Systems, Proceedings of Workshop Held at the Eighth International Conference on User Modeling*. Retrieved from http://art.ph-freiburg.de/um2001/documents/paramythis.pdf

Reeves, B., & Nass, C. (1999). *The media equation: How people treat computers, television, and new media like real people and places*. Stanford, CA: CSLI Publications/Cambridge University Press.

Resnick, P., & Varian, H. R. (1997). Recommender systems. *Communications of the ACM, 40*(3), 56-58.

Schafer, J. B., Konstan, J., & Riedl, J. (2001). E-commerce recommendation applications. *Journal of Data Mining and Knowledge Discovery, 5*(1/2), 115-152.

Searle, J. R. (1969). *Speech acts: An essay in the philosophy of language*. London: Cambridge University Press.

Swearingen, K., & Sinha, R. (2001). *Beyond algorithms: An HCI perspective on recommender systems*. Paper presented at the ACM SIGIR 2001 Workshop on Recommender Systems.

Usability First. (2004). *Introduction to usability*. Retrieved from http://www.softwareevaluation.de

Venkatesh, V., & Agarwal, R. (2005). *Turning visitors into customers: A usability-centric perspective on purchase behavior in electronic channels*. Retrieved from http://disc-nt.cba.uh.edu/chin/speakerseries/Venkatesh-Agarwal.pdf

Vredenburg, K., Isensee, S., & Righi, C. (2001). *User centered design: An integrated approach*. Upper Saddle River, NJ: Prentice Hall.

Wang, J.-C., & Lin, J.-P. (2000). Are personalization systems really personal — Effects of conformity in reducing information overload. In *Proceedings of the 36th Hawaii International Conference on System Sciences*. Retrieved from http://computing.breinestorm.net/conformity+information+personalization+study+edu/.

Weibelzahl, S., Lippitsch, S., & Weber, G. (2002). Advantages, opportunities, and limits of empirical evaluations: Evaluating adaptive systems. *Künstliche Intelligenz, 3*(02), 17-20.

Weibelzahl, S., & Weber, G. (2001). Mental models for navigation in adaptive Web-sites and behavioral complexity. In T. Arnold & C. S. Herrmann (Eds.), *Cognitive Systems & Mechanisms. Abstracts of the Fifth Annual Meeting of the German Cognitive Science Society in Leipzig, KogWis 2001* (p. 74). Leipzig: Leipziger Universitätsverlag.

Weibelzahl, S., & Weber, G. (2003). Evaluating the inference mechanism of adaptive learning systems. In P. Brusilovsky, A. Corbett, & F. de Rosis (Eds.), *User Modeling: Proceedings of the Ninth International Conference* (LNAI 2702, pp. 154-168). Berlin: Springer.

Zhu, T., & Greiner, R. (2005). Evaluating an adaptive music-clip recommender system. In S. Weibelzahl, A. Paramythis, & J. Masthoff (Eds.), *Proceedings of the Fourth Workshop*

Chapter XIII

Remote Usability Evaluation of Web Interfaces

Naouel Moha, University of Montreal, Canada

Ashraf Gaffar, Concordia University, Canada

Gabriel Michel, University of Metz, France

ABSTRACT

Usability testing is a process that employs a sample of future users to evaluate software according to specific usability criteria. With the unprecedented growth and reach of the Internet, it is hard to reach representative users of Web sites across the world. The new branch of remote usability testing has emerged as an alternative. While it is prohibitively expensive to conduct usability testing on a global range of users, it is technically possible and is more feasible to remotely collect the necessary information about usability problems and to analyze them the same way we do local tests. In this chapter, we present systematic methods and tools to support remote usability testing and evaluation of Web interfaces.

INTRODUCTION

Before launching a Web site on the Internet, one should test and validate it in order to ensure that the software fulfills the criteria defined in the requirements stage. The costs and the benefits of usability tests are largely demonstrated by the human-computer interaction (HCI) community (Karat, 1990; Pressman, 1992). Therefore, different types of usability labs have been proposed and implemented in order to offer organizational, physical, and software infrastructure to support and conduct these tests. These laboratories are used to observe, gather, and analyze different data generated during test sessions.

However, research shows that only large companies and big research centers can afford fixed usability labs because of their relatively high costs. Small companies have neither enough financial resources to equip themselves with usability labs nor the expertise to conduct usability tests (Moha, Li, Seffah, & Michel, 2004). Furthermore, for small companies, investing in the equipment of such a system is not an economically viable solution. A usability lab requires large investment in terms of well-equipped rooms and qualified personnel in order to successfully undertake usability tests.

Moreover, fixed usability labs cover only local population. But Web interfaces are often dedicated to a large public and accessible by users across the world. Users have different languages, different cultures, and are geographically separated. Taking these factors into account is essential for effective use of Web sites. Besides translating a Web site or a Web-based application into different languages, cultural views and concepts for different populations should be integrated in the design in order to be well perceived. After these aspects have been considered and modifications added, the resultant Web interfaces need to be tested to ensure the new versions are equally usable by different populations (Nielsen, 1996). It is technically impossible to test those interfaces by physically displacing testers and test materials to different countries. It is equally costly to invite representative users to a local test lab because it necessitates acquiring the staff and the material and financial resources to support the tests, making it prohibitively expensive.

Mobile usability labs essentially emerged to compensate for the economical and logistical disadvantages of fixed test platforms. However, these laboratories provide only a subset of the facilities offered in fixed labs. And above all, they do not remedy the major disadvantage of fixed labs: the recruitment of a sufficiently large number of test subjects that accurately represent the population of actual users.

An emerging trend to efficiently solve this problem is to test the usability of Web interfaces remotely. Several companies are building software to support the infrastructure needed for remote testing. The idea is based on enabling small and big companies alike, employing usability professionals or not, to integrate remote usability tests in their software development process; remote usability tests appear to be a less expensive and effective solution.

Remote Usability Testing

Remote usability tests can be defined as the usability tests where the testers performing observation and analysis are separated in space and/or time from the participants (Hartson, Castillo, Kelso, Kamler, & Neale, 1996). One of the undeniable advantages of remote usability testing is the fact that it is a cost-effective solution; it enables testing a large panel of participants in their own environment by remotely located testers and observers. In addition to identifying major usability problems similar to those found in traditional lab testing, remote tests uncover more problems because of the larger number of test participants (Tullis, Flieschman, McNulty, Cianchette, & Bergel, 2002).

The emphasis of this chapter is on systematic methods and tools to support remote usability testing and evaluation of Web interfaces. It also presents the advantages and limitations associated with the different infrastructures for conducting usability testing (Moha et al., 2004). First, we will go over the roles and limitations of both fixed and mobile labs. Then, we will present the advantages and challenges of remote usability tests. The results of a study conducted on remote usability testing methods and tools will also be presented. Finally, the concept of internationalization will be illustrated through a case study.

USABILITY TESTING

Usability testing is not directly concerned with testing for bugs in the application source code, or testing for matching colors and working hyperlinks in the interface. Rubin (1994) defines usability testing as a process that employs participants who are representative of the target population to evaluate the degree to which a software system meets specific usability criteria. The International Organization for Standardization (ISO) 9241-11 defines usability testing as a structured approach to evaluate the quality in use of an interactive system and measure the degree of effectiveness and efficiency of the system in accomplishing its goals as well as the degree of users' satisfaction.

Due to the wide range and diversity of Web users, usability testing of Web applications requires a sufficient number of users for Web sites. The agreement on how many test participants are considered "sufficient" greatly varies among experts. The number depends on the type of Web site, the target audience, and the budget available to perform tests. Originally, Nielsen and Landauer (1993) provided a mathematical model to argue for the sufficiency of five users in usability testing. They claim that 85% of the usability problems in any software are found by the first five users. This became an "industry standard" for some time. Contrarily, others recommend a large number of users (Faulkner, 2003; Perfetti & Landesman, 2002; Spool & Schroeder, 2001). Consequently, Spool and Schroeder (2001) performed a large experiment to measure the relationship between the number of users and the number of usability errors found in tests. They concluded that many more users are needed to find the satisfactory level of 85% of errors. Indeed, serious usability problems were found first in tests 13 and 15. They showed that five users only found approximately 35% of the problems in the interface, which is unacceptable as an industry standard. In 2003, several experts organized an ACM panel to debate the issue from different sides (Bevan et al., 2003). In this debate, Cockton (Bevan et al., 2003) indicated that the break even on cost-benefit of usability testing varies depending on specific cases, and that in some cases one user is enough, while in other cases even 100 users will be too few. After great controversy and many discussions, Nielsen (2004) recently called for caution and pointed at the danger of quantitative studies. He warned against using unnecessary numbers, calling it "number Fetishism" in qualitative research. Therefore, we believe that determining the number of users in a usability test should be left to individual cases. Our own experience with testing Web sites aligns with the majority of usability experts regarding Web-based applications. In this particular field, the number of users needs to be sufficiently large and versatile to suite the global reach of the Web.

DEFINITIONS, ROLES, AND LIMITATIONS OF FIXED AND MOBILE LABS

While recommendations and procedures proposed by usability experts provide general rules and guidelines for testing, the type of software under test as well as users and context may affect the selection of the test environment. In some occasions, it is equally possible to run tests in a fixed or mobile environment. In other occasions, careful considerations may show great advantages of one environment over the other. In this section, we go through the forces and challenges behind setting up and conducting tests in both fixed and mobile labs.

Fixed Usability Labs

Typical usability labs are equipped with audio visual materials necessary to capture observation data. They contain the entire software infrastructure for controlling test sessions and realizing the analysis of collected data.

Traditional usability labs include two rooms separated by a one-way mirror (Figure 1). A front room, intended for use by the participants to perform the test, simulates the user environment. The term participant designates the user who has been selected — and possibly recruited — for testing the software. In the other room, the back room, are observers who can watch the participants in action. Generally, there is also a reception hall for the participants' convenience. These traditional laboratories allow the observers to watch and study the participants' behavior while performing the test. Walls between the front and back room are usually sound proof, allowing observers to talk and exchange ideas between themselves during the tests without disturbing the participants. Recently, some usability labs started offering the possibility to observe the observers and provide feedback to help improve the testing techniques.

Figure 1. Fixed usability laboratory

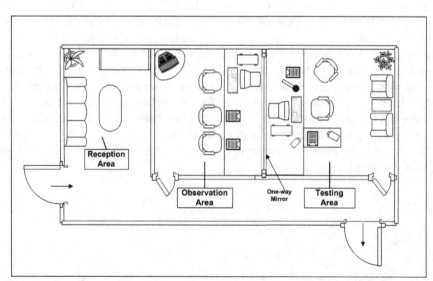

Limitations of Fixed Usability Labs

In spite of their considerable contribution to software engineering and to the comprehension of HCI, common laboratories do have some limitations. The first constraint is that fixed labs are costly in equipment and software for analysis and observation.

As a matter of fact, the cost of a typical infrastructure for fixed labs is estimated between $100,000 and $150,000 including the cost of management and test analysis software. Therefore, only big companies or research centers can afford usability laboratories. Furthermore, there has to be dedicated rooms, making it even less suitable for small companies.

The second constraint is that fixed labs force the participants as well as the testers and the observers to move and gather all in the same place and at the same time. It becomes difficult to recruit a representative sample of the target population since participants' moving is costly and sometimes practically impossible. Moreover, the number of participants is often limited due to financial reasons and restricted availability. Tests that involve more than few users are often plagued by the delay or absence of some participants. This would often void parts of the test session even when all preparations and testers are ready. It is also common for some persons to arrive late, making tests run behind schedule and causing a chain of delays to other participants. Contingency plans and standby participants are not always feasible as they impose more loads on test resources and time.

For all of these reasons, a test session does not typically count more than 10 participants. Thus, the tests results are deducted from a small sample and consequently their reliability is limited.

A third constraint that cannot be ignored is that the tests are realized out of the participants' natural work environment. Even when the front room is made to simulate a work environment, in reality it hardly resembles one, and it cannot be made "perfect." Additionally, the typical work environment varies significantly between individual users. For this reason, test results can be biased. The test environment and workstations are not familiar to the participants. Feeling surrounded and watched by the observers and by the testers, even when they are concealed in the back room, the participants are generally anxious about not being able to achieve assigned tasks. We have observed this behavior repeatedly during tests that we conducted within our lab. The environment and the formal character of tests have a negative influence on the participant's behavior and on their own actions and consequently, on the pertinence and the reliability of test results.

Mobile Usability Labs

A mobile usability lab generally comes in the form of a suitcase, which contains all necessary equipment for conducting usability tests. In general, the suitcase contains a camera, a laptop and eventually a camcorder and a video recorder. The equipments used in mobile labs are not excessively expensive. Rubin (1994, p. 57) estimates the approximate cost of the basic equipments between $10,000 and $15,000. When taking the costs of necessary software into account, the total cost amounts from $15,000 to $20,000, which constitutes an undeniable advantage in comparison with fixed labs. Moreover, these equipments are portable; so, it is easy to install it in the participant's place of work and conduct the tests in their work environment. Nevertheless, the observers and the testers are still forced to move, and for similar reasons as mentioned in the Fixed Usability Labs Section, the number of participants is often limited. In addition, even though the users are in their own work environment, they are still influenced by the presence of the observers and the testers.

REMOTE USABILITY TESTS

Remote usability tests can be defined as the usability tests where the testers, performing observation and analysis, are separated in space and/or time from the participants (Hartson et al., 1996).

Advantages of Remote Usability Tests

Remote usability testing has several advantages over traditional labs testing. It allows testing with many more participants with diverse backgrounds. The tests are performed with reduced budget, and they take less time. In addition, the participants are hardly influenced by the test environment. During an empirical study carried out by Tullis et al. (2002), usability tests of Web sites have been performed within a traditional usability lab on 8 participants and on 29 remote participants via the Internet with the aim of comparing and determining the efficiency of these two techniques. The study has shown that both techniques enable the testers to collect the most significant problems. However, remote tests enable researchers to get the most reliable subjective affirmations of Web sites because of the significant number of participants involved, but also considering the fact that users are not influenced by the test environment. As a result, they can provide feedback closer to their perception.

Another advantage is that neither the participants nor the testers need to make costly or timely travel. Indeed, the testers test and interact with the participants remotely. The testers themselves can also be geographically remote to each other and collaborate all together during the same test session. Consequently, it is possible to take advantage of the expertise of professionals and specialists, who are located in many places across the world. In addition, participants' sample can be broad, diverse, and international, which is a determining advantage, especially if it is for developing specific applications that target a foreign population (Dray & Siegel, 2004).

Moreover, since there is almost no environmental influence while conducting remote usability tests, participants feel at ease, and as a result, their comments are more reliable. Participants can remain anonymous, which makes their comments even richer. In this case, testers focus only on recording a user's screen and possibly their interactions with the keyboard. In addition, tests made in the participant's real work environment in his/her office or at his/her home reveal relevant problems related to specific work environments that could not be detected otherwise (Tullis et al., 2002).

Finally, remote testing often involves the transfer of large multimedia files in audio and video format as well as data logs. Real time remote interaction like Internet video conferencing is also gaining popularity. The recent advances in software and hardware technologies are allowing it to be feasible. Just a decade ago, it was practically impossible to run advanced remote usability tests as we have now. The much greater bandwidth available to Internet users today make it possible to remotely run the tests and send back the collected information in large amounts. However, some tests do not require a real time connection between testers and the participant. There is no constraint of time as the test can be done at anytime. Data is collected automatically by a software agent. When the test is finished, these agents send back the collected test results to the testers via Internet (Hilbert & Redmiles, 1998).

Challenges

In spite of all their advantages, remote usability tests have some challenges to be addressed.

It is difficult to remotely control the participant's environment. Indeed, participants can be distracted by their family or their colleagues during the tests or suddenly stop the test session (Bartek & Cheatham, 2003). In some cases, this disruptive environment can be considered as part of the final user's environment, and hence recorded and included in test information and analysis. Thus, this loss of control can be seen as an advantage because the collected data truly reflect the participant's work environment.

In addition, the limited scope of visual feedback leads to information loss because of nonverbal communication and participants' attitude. Although the participants have a camera, practical considerations often allow only their face to be captured; the rest of the body gestures, in particular the hands and the room where the participant is located, are hard to visualize even when they may be important to consider in a usability test.

Another disadvantage of remote usability tests is that they involve a more significant workload for the preparation and the setup of tests like putting the questionnaires online, or ensuring the feasibility of remote tests.

Despite these challenges, remote usability tests propose a viable alternative for certain types of tests. For example, they are particularly adapted to tests of Web applications, desktop applications, and Web sites (Tullis et al., 2002) and for test sessions not longer than 3 hours (Bartek & Cheatham, 2003). More research and technology advances are gradually widening the range of remote testing applicability.

REMOTE USABILITY TESTING METHODS AND TOOLS

Methods and tools to support remote usability testing and evaluation of Web interfaces have been surveyed in order to provide practical materials for performing such tests.

Remote Evaluation Methods

Hartson et al. (1996) identified three main categories of remote methods: (1) video conferencing via the Internet; (2) instrumented remote evaluation; and (3) semi-structured remote evaluation.

Video Conferencing via the Internet

This mechanism allows testers to remotely observe and interact with users and locally record video data in real time. Lotus Sametime (n.d.) and NetMeeting (n.d.) are among the tools for performing video conferencing.

Instrumented Remote Evaluation

An application and its interface can be instrumented with embedded code to collect and return a journal or log of data representing user actions. This category includes surveys, questionnaires, and automated usage tracking. WebQuilt, a proxy-based approach, is a Web logging and visualization system. It helps Web design teams run both local and remote usability tests and analyze the collected data (Hong, Jeffrey, Waterson, & Landay, 2001).

Semi-Instrumented Remote Evaluation

The user and the system gather the data, and evaluators look only at data that relate to usability problems. This method is known as the user-reported, critical incident method (Castillo, 1997). The user-reported, critical incident method is defined as a usability evaluation method that involves real users located in their own working environment, doing everyday tasks and reporting critical incidents without direct interaction with evaluators (Castillo, 1997). However, not all users have the ability to recognize and report critical incidents effectively. Mainly, "homemade" programs and tools enable usability testers to perform this semi-instrumented evaluation.

Synchronous vs. Asynchronous

In general, synchronous remote testing is the current preferred method when applicable (Brush, Ames, & Davis, 2004). Synchronous testing allows the tester to be present at the same time the remote user is performing the test, hence capturing essential information and observations not recorded by the testing software. Synchronous testing can be done using software tools that allow the evaluator to view the remote user's screen. Audio connections may be established and voice recorded synchronously by the software or separately by using phone lines in real time. Asynchronous tests can be done by electronically distributing the software and the test procedures and providing a way for the results to be captured and returned to the evaluator. Asynchronous tests with simple tools may cause important user feedback and real-time debriefing to be lost. Even when user movements and comments are recorded along with their interaction activities and screenshots of their interface, it is hard to fully resynchronize them again for later analysis. Therefore, synchronous remote testing is currently more accurate than asynchronous testing in most circumstances. Morae (n.d.) is one of the commonly used tools in the market for synchronous remote testing. A large scale survey was conducted to evaluate actual use of usability tools by industrial settings and usability experts (Moha, Li, Gaffar, & Seffah, 2005). Among the wide range of general and specialized usability tools available today, the study showed that Morae was predominantly used by most. Other tools included in-house developed tools to suit specific needs. This remote testing software allows observing users and their interaction with Web applications. It records users' behavior and synchronizes it with the collected test data for more accurate usability analysis. In the next section, we provide a review of most of the tools commonly used in remote testing and their applicability in different test phases.

Remote Usability Tools, Procedure, and Roles

The platforms for conducting remote usability tests can be equipped with various software and material mechanisms ranging from a simple camera and a microphone to powerful and efficient software for control and remote observation. The aim of all these mechanisms is to make the execution of real usability tests as efficient as those performed in traditional labs.

Usability and empirical studies generate a huge quantity of both qualitative and quantitative raw data that needs to be analyzed in order to draw conclusions and to make objective and valid recommendations. That is why tool support is essential to help in capturing and classifying data as well as in data analysis (statistics, data mining, neural networks).

Moha et al. (2005) showed that many companies have developed a little assortment of homemade tools for their own usability studies. But, these tools are not adapted for tests other

Figure 2. Classification of remote usability testing tools

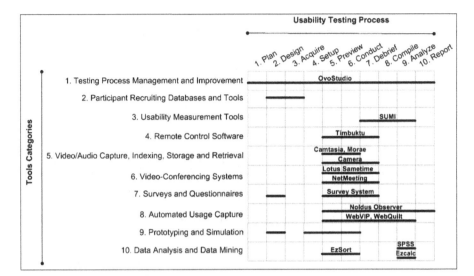

than those for which they were intended. It is in this perspective that we have conducted a study of a wide range of other tools. This study focused on finding, comparing, and analyzing several tools with the aim of developing a platform for remote usability tests. The platform provides an infrastructure for designing and controlling test sessions as well as analyzing test results with the help of various tools. A classification of the tools found on the market has also been established with respect to the usability testing process that we had defined.

The quality of the way tests are conducted has a great impact on the pertinence of results (Manning, Dalton, & Amato, 2003). The procedures, in which tests are conducted, have much more impact on test results than the equipment that is used.

Based on the analysis of previous work on local usability testing process (Mayhew, 1999; Nielsen, 1993; Rubin, 1994) as well as some emerging standards such as ISO 13407 and the usability maturity model, we adopted and combined the common features in some of them. We added some modifications to be more suitable for remote testing. Some major milestones were redefined for the new paradigm. These milestones need to be done differently since they proved to have major impact on the accuracy of the tests results. They include activities associated with hiring the remote participants, setting the remote environment, conducting the remote tests and pre-tests as well as retrieving and compiling the data results collected from different sources.

The procedure of remote usability testing comprises 10 phases to cover all activities needed for a comprehensive remote test.

1.   **Plan:** This activity consists of producing a testing plan which answers the following questions: what, why, how, when, and where to test.
2.   **Design:** It consists of defining the profile of the participants; selecting and adapting the research methods; and preparing the required equipment for conducting the tests.

Figure 3. The remote testing process model

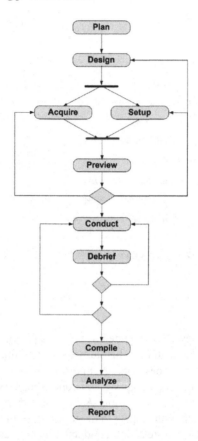

3.   **Acquire:** Generally needed for large tests, this step consists of remotely selecting, hiring and interviewing participants.
4.   **Setup:** During this step, the hardware equipment and the software tools needed for tests are deployed, installed, configured, and tested.
5.   **Preview:** Most often neglected even after being highly recommended by experts, this step focuses on conducting a series of pilot tests to ensure that the test environment, materials, and resources are appropriate and functional. It is also an opportunity for any last minute refinement of the test design and the acquisition of additional equipments and materials.
6.   **Conduct:** The real test is performed in this step. Several quantitative and qualitative data are remotely gathered including participant feedback, video observations, and screen snapshots.
7.   **Debrief:** This step refers to remotely interviewing the participants and reviewing with them their reactions during the test and getting their feedback.
8.   **Compile:** The data are aggregated, consolidated, annotated, and properly archived to facilitate their later retrieval and analysis.

9. **Analyze:** Using appropriate data analysis and data mining techniques, this step aims to transform the qualitative and quantitative test results into findings and patterns.
10. **Report:** This step consists of transforming findings and patterns into recommendations. This step generally delivers a report that states all the findings and recommendations.

In each of the phases, several tools can be applied. Figure 2 depicts the applicability of common tools in each of the test phases. These commercial tools allow testers to reduce the workload related to the preparation and the execution of remote usability tests. Some tools such as OvoStudios and Noldus Observer cover a big part of the testing process while others cover only one step. Each of the tools presented in this classification have been studied and tested for applicability.

Figure 3 presents the workflow of the different steps. Some steps can be done in parallel such as the Acquire and Setup steps while others are performed sequentially. The decision-making boxes allow us to check if the previous steps have been performed correctly, otherwise it is required to go back to the previous steps to fix the issues.

People's Roles and Responsibilities

Here, we identify and describe the different actors involved in the usability testing process as well as roles and responsibilities. Each person involved can have several roles. Each role refers to some responsibilities and functions carried out by this person.

*   **Monitors:** They are responsible for managing and ensuring the smooth functioning of test sessions. A monitor is, in a way, the conductor or a test moderator.
*   **Coordinators:** Their tasks are to select, recruit, and schedule participants for the tests.
*   **Evaluators:** They are the primary persons responsible for testing the product; analyzing and documenting the results; and providing the report to the development team.
*   **Data loggers:** They attend preview, conduct, and debrief steps. The data loggers also help the evaluators to compile usability data into electronic format. In formal test sessions, data loggers use predefined data collection sheets or computers to record all usability data needed to be collected.
*   **Observers:** They observe the users during tests sessions. Normally, they do not intervene during the tests, but provide their feedbacks at the end of each session. Any person who has an interest in the test and in the product being tested can participate as an observer. Observers may include different stakeholders of the product, the designers, and the project development team.
*   **Users/participants:** They are a representative sample of people who use the system and are selected to test it. They may be end users who use the system to complete their tasks, or indirect users who use it for other purposes such as system administrators, installers, or demonstrators. They perform the tasks handed to them by the evaluator and provide their comments.

Figure 4 presents a use case diagram that illustrates the associations between the actors and the different steps of the remote testing process.

Figure 4. User roles in the user-oriented testing process

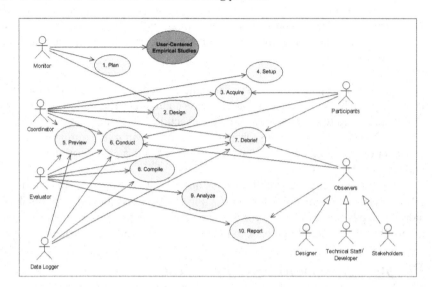

USABILITY AND INTERNATIONALIZATION: A CASE STUDY

To sell software in another country besides the country of origin, the interface may need to be modified. Translation of text included in the interface is not always enough to make it equally acceptable and usable by the new population. Simple translation often causes problems when it fails to integrate the cultural aspects of the target country. Cultural aspects are essential in order for the product to be accepted. Significant research has been done to study the effect of international and cultural aspects on user interfaces (Bastien & Leulier, 2001; Del Galdo & Nielsen, 1996; Hofstede, 1997; Maner, 1997). They focus on challenges associated with the creation of Web sites intended for use by different cultures and propose solutions to guide Web designers. Culture is the beliefs, norms, myths, and structural elements of a given organization, tribe, or society (Nakakoji, 1996). This case study illustrates some impediments associated with the global reach of Web sites and testing them for usability, which illustrates the necessity of remote usability testing over traditional methods.

Internationalization of a Web Site

The internationalization of a Web site corresponds to the first stage in the process of adjusting a Web site for an international audience. One first isolates the elements which are specific to local cultures in the country of origin (texts, format of the numbers, of the dates, etc.). These elements are then modified into a format which the end user is accustomed to.

The latter process corresponds to localization which is the adaptation of the software to a new country. The same interface can be localized several times to suit different local populations, or a single version can be made general enough to cover multiple populations.

Cultural Form Aspects

The meaning of certain cultural form aspects such as icons and metaphors can vary by the country. It is preferable to avoid using symbols that have cultural connotation which may be unclear to a foreign user. The use of the American mailbox with a small flag to indicate the arrival of new mail is one example. This metaphor is commonly used in many Web sites but users outside North America will not necessarily recognize the symbol as representing a mailbox, full or empty. For an international Web site, a more efficient and universally recognized symbol would be the envelope.

In general, the following symbol groups can be confusing and misunderstood in a Web site intended for a general audience:

- Hand gestures
- Images whose interpretation is multiple
- Symbols with religious connotations such as crosses or stars
- Forms and shapes related to particular cultures (traffic signs such as the "Stop" sign and sport signs)

A better solution in integrating a different culture in software is to work directly with users belonging to that culture from the very start of the internationalization process and to create tests adapted to these cultures and performed on representative users. The same approach can be more effective for testing software intended for users with special needs such as the handicapped, the elderly, and children. Hence, distant user tests on the various versions of the site are essential to ensure the acceptability and success of the Web site by the actual users of the new cultures.

Case Study

A usability test was performed to evaluate the effectiveness of a Web site in terms of language used by multicultural users. (De Wet, Blignaut, & Burger, 2002) The results indicate that — as one example — South African developers should take into account the fact that African-speaking people find it easier to search information in Afrikaans (in contrast to English). South Africa has a multicultural population (different origins, cultural backgrounds, and languages). The dominant cultures are African, Anglo-Saxon, Indian, and Afrikaans. South Africa is a country with 11 official languages, and this clearly indicates that many South African users use the interfaces in a second or even in a third language and not necessarily in their original language. Thus, in order to create a Web site for this country, it is necessary to know the cultural or subcultural groups for which it is intended. And for a designer of a Web site who is not a sociologist or a native of this country, it is a very difficult task, and distant test users prove to be absolutely essential.

To address this new challenge, we provide a solution in form of a remote usability test. Figure 5 illustrates the environment setup for conducting this remote test. Multi-disciplinary teams located in several countries observe, collaborate, and communicate during a test. Remote usability tests open borders for Web applications to cross local markets toward an

Figure 5. Remote usability tests performed in South Africa from Canada

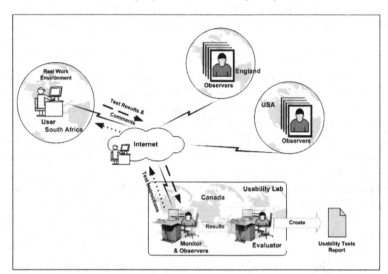

international audience by enabling the integration of cultural and linguistic parameters. Only testing gives accurate feedback about the level of acceptance of these parameters.

Several companies have international reach and have several testing and research labs in different countries. They are relying more on remote accessibility and virtual meetings for planning, development, and testing. Remote usability and the distributed nature of involved parties are suitable to this already-distributed nature. While the main goal of remote testing is to access test participants remotely, testers and experts can also be distributed in several places. In the case of a Web site designed by a Canadian company for a South African public, remote tests are valuable in testing the usability of the Web site. We visualize the schema of setting up the remote usability test as in Figure 5. The testers are located in Canada and interact remotely in synchronous or asynchronous mode with a sample of the target population located in South Africa. The test participants are equipped with a microphone and a camera in order to visualize their behaviors during the test sessions. Other people located in Canada, in England, or in United States also participate in the tests as observers or actors. The actors are usability professionals (ergonomists, interface developers, designers, etc.) who collaborate with the testers in Canada and share their expertise. This type of remote test enables us to obtain the reaction of the target population with the prototype before its launching on the Web, and this without physically displacing the target population or the testers. Thus, remote usability tests open borders to Web sites and Web applications designed for a local public toward an international public.

After a product has been sold, appreciated, and accepted in a given country, its success cannot be guaranteed in another country even if they speak the same language. The interface and the interaction bring cultural values that only remote tests will enable to reveal (Bastien & Leulier, 2001). Remote tests can thus be used for verifying the acceptability of products (although usability is an essential aspect).

CONCLUSION

In this chapter, we analyzed the advantages and disadvantages of fixed and mobile laboratories and we compared them with remote usability tests. We also proposed a set of tools and methods to support remote tests. In general, remote usability tests enable us to have the same results as the tests made in a lab. As we have seen, in some cases, these results turn out to be richer and more reliable. However, the two techniques of tests, on site and remote, that support the three types of laboratories, are complementary. They bear different advantages and disadvantages depending on the type of performed tests. One of the undeniable advantages of remote usability testing is the fact that it is a cost-effective solution; it allows testing a large panel of participants in their own environment by remote testers and observers with various cultures and professional competences. An increasing number of software, Web applications, and Web sites are designed for both national and international markets. Remote usability tests meet the need to test those products on a sample of the target population. Moreover, remote tests create an environment to allow multi-disciplinary teams located across the world to collaborate and exchange ideas during tests sessions. Remote usability tests open borders for Web applications to cross local markets toward an international audience by testing the success and acceptability of software after integrating new cultural and linguistic parameters. Only testing in remote locations will give accurate feedback about the level of acceptance of these parameters. Moreover, the development of the remote user tests will transform the profession of ergonomists: They can interact with other professionals with different cultures, and thus develop intercultural skills, since a professional may familiarize themselves with other working manners, other strategies of problem resolution, and other working methods and techniques. This intercultural and professional enrichment is an opening to the world for the usability and HCI professionals.

REFERENCES

Bartek, V., & Cheatham, D. (2003). *Experience remote usability testing, Part 1: Examine study results on the benefits and downside of remote usability testing.* Retrieved July 31, 2005, from http://www-106.ibm.com/developerworks/library/wa-rmusts1/

Bastien, C., & Leulier, C. (2001). *Les aspects ergonomiques de l'internationalisation des sites Web. L'ergonome (Ergonomic aspects of internationalization of Websites).* Retrieved July 31, 2005, from http://www.lergonome.org/pages/internationalisation.pdf

Bevan, N., Barnum, C., Cockton, G., Nielsen, J., Spool, J., & Wixon, D. (2003, April 5-10). The "magic number 5": Is it enough for Web testing? [Extended abstracts]. In G. Cockton & P. Korhonen (Eds.), *Proceedings of the CHI '03, International Conference on Human Factors in Computing Systems*, Ft. Lauderdale, FL (pp. 698-699). New York: ACM Press.

Brush, A. J., Ames, M., & Davis, J. (2004) A comparison of synchronous remote and local usability studies for an expert interface [Extended abstracts]. In *Proceedings of the CHI '04 Human Factors in Computing Systems*, Vienna, Austria (pp. 1179-1182). New York: ACM Press.

Butler, S., & Gunther, R. (2005). Ovo Studios [computer software]. Retrieved June 8, 2006, from http://www.ovostudios.com/

Castillo, J. C. (1997). *The user-reported critical incident method for remote usability evaluation*. Unpublished masters thesis, Virginia Polytechnic Institute and State University, Blacksburg.

De Wet, L., Blignaut, P., & Burger, A. (2002). Comprehension and usability variances among multicultural Web users in South Africa. In *Proceedings of the CHI 2002, International Conference on Human Factors in Computing Systems, extended abstracts*, (pp. 526-527). New York: ACM Press.

Del Galdo, E. M., & Nielsen, J. (1996). *International user interfaces*. New York: Wiley.

Dray, S., & Siegel, D. (2004). Remote possibilities? International usability testing at a distance. *ACM interactions, 11*(2), 10-17.

Faulkner, L. (2003). Beyond the five-user assumption: Benefits of increased sample sizes in usability testing. *Behavior Research Methods, Instruments, & Computers, 35*(3), 379-383.

Hartson, H. R., Castillo, J. C., Kelso, J., Kamler, J., & Neale, W. C. (1996). Remote evaluation: The network as an extension of the usability laboratory. In *Proceedings of the ACM Conference on Human Factors in Computing Systems (CHI '96)*, Vancouver, British Columbia, Canada (pp. 228-235). New York: ACM Press.

Hilbert, D. M., & Redmiles, D. F. (1998). Agents for collecting application usage data over the Internet. In *Proceedings of the 2nd International Conference on Autonomous Agents*, (pp. 149-156). New York: ACM Press.

Hofstede, G. (1997). *Cultures and organizations: Software of the mind. Intercultural cooperation and its importance for survival*. New York: McGraw-Hill.

Hong, J. I., Jeffrey, H., Waterson, S., & Landay, J. A. (2001). WebQuilt: A proxy-based approach to remote Web usability testing. *ACM Transactions on Information Systems (TOIS), 19*(3), 263-285.

Hong, J. I., Jeffrey, H., Waterson, S., & Landay, J. A. (2001). WebQuilt [computer software]. Retrieved June 8, 2006, from http://guir.berkeley.edu/projects/webquilt/

International Organization for Standardization (ISO). (1998). *Ergonomic requirements for office work with visual display terminals (VDTs) — Part 11: Guidance on usability information technology — Software production evaluation (ISO 9241-11)*. Geneva, Switzerland: ISO.

International Organization for Standardization (ISO). (1999). *Human-centred design processes for interactive systems (ISO 13407)*. Geneva, Switzerland: ISO.

Karat, M. C. (1990). Cost-benefit analysis of usability engineering techniques. In *Proceedings of the Human Factors Society 34th Annual Meeting*, Orlando, FL (pp. 839-843).

Lotus Sametime. (n.d.). *IBM Lotus instant messaging and Web conferencing (Sametime, Version 6.5.1)* [Computer software]. Retrieved July 31, 2005, from http://www.lotus.com/products/product3.nsf/wdocs/homepage

Maner, W. (1997). *Internationalization of user interfaces*. Retrieved July 31, 2005, from http://web.cs.bgsu.edu/maner/uiguides/internat.htm

Manning, H., Dalton, J. P., & Amato, M. (2003, July 28). *The myth of the infallible usability lab test*. Forrester Research. Retrieved July 31, 2005, from http://www.forrester.com/ER/Research/Brief/Excerpt/0,1317,17239,00.html

Mayhew, D. J. (1999). *The usability engineering lifecycle: A practitioner's handbook for user interface design*. San Francisco: Morgan Kaufmann.

Moha, N., Li, Q., Gaffar, A., & Seffah, A. (2005, September 27-30). Enquête sur les pratiques de tests d'utilisabilité. In *Proceedings of the IHM'05, 17ème Conférence Francophone sur l'Interaction Homme-Machine*, (pp. 115-122). New York: ACM Press.

Moha, N., Li, Q., Seffah, A., & Michel, G. (2004, November 22-24). *Towards a Platform for Usability Remote Tests via Internet*. Paper presented at the OZCHI2004, University of Wollongong, Australia.

Morae. (n.d.). *TechSmith Morae Usability and Web Site Testing*. Retrieved July 31, 2005, from http://www.techsmith.com/products/morae/default.asp

Nakakoji, K. (1996). Beyond language translation: Crossing the cultural divide. *IEEE Software, 13*(6), 42-46.

NetMeeting Windows. (n.d.). [Computer softare]. Retrieved July 31, 2005, from http://www.microsoft.com/windows/netmeeting/

Nielsen, J. (1996). *International usability testing*. Retrieved July 31, 2005, from http://www.useit.com/papers/international_usetest.html

Nielsen, J. (2004, March 1). *Risk of quantitative studies. Alertbox*. Retrieved July 31, 2005, from http://www.useit.com/alertbox/20040301.html

Nielsen, J., & Landauer, T. K. (1993, April 24-29). A mathematical model of the finding of usability problems. In S. Ashlund, K. Mullet, A. Henderson, E. Hollnagel, & T. White (Eds.), *Proceedings of ACM INTERCHI'93 Conference on Human Factors in Computing Systems*, (pp. 206-213). New York: ACM Press.

Noldus Information Technology (2005). Noldus Observer [computer software]. Retrieved June 8, 2006, from http://www.noldus.com/site/doc200401012

Perfetti, C., & Landesman, L. (2002). *Eight is not enough*. Retrieved July 31, 2005, from http://webdesign.templatemonster.com/web/web-design-basics/website-usability/eight-is-not-enough-for-usability-testing.2643.html

Pressman, R. S. (1992). *Software engineering: A practitioner's approach*. New York: McGraw-Hill.

Rubin, J. (1994). *Handbook of usability testing: How to plan, design, and conduct effective tests*. New York: John Wiley & Sons.

Spool, J., & Schroeder, W. (2001). Testing Web sites: Five users is nowhere near enough. [Extended abstracts]. In *Proceedings of the CHI 2001, International Conference on Human Factors in Computing Systems, extended abstracts*, (pp. 285-286). New York: AMC Press.

Tullis, T., Flieschman, S., McNulty, M., Cianchette, C., & Bergel, M. (2002, July). *An empirical comparison of lab and remote usability testing of Web sites*. Paper presented at the 2002 Annual Meeting of the Usability Professionals' Association Conference, Orlando, FL.

Chapter XIV

Modelling Interactive Behaviour with a Rational Cognitive Architecture

David Peebles, University of Huddersfield, UK

Anna L. Cox, University College London, UK

ABSTRACT

In this chapter we discuss a number of recent studies that demonstrate the use of rational analysis (Anderson, 1990) and cognitive modelling methods to understand complex interactive behaviour involved in three tasks: (1) icon search, (2) graph reading, and (3) information retrieval on the World Wide Web (WWW). We describe the underlying theoretical assumptions of rational analysis and the adaptive control of thought-rational (ACT-R) cognitive architecture (Anderson & Lebiere, 1998), a theory of cognition that incorporates rational analysis in its mechanisms for learning and decision making. In presenting these studies we aim to show how such methods can be combined with eye movement data to provide detailed, highly constrained accounts of user performance that are grounded in psychological theory. We argue that the theoretical and technological developments that underpin these methods are now at a stage that the approach can be more broadly applied to other areas of Web use.

INTRODUCTION

With the rapid increase in Internet use over the past decade there is a growing need for those engaged in the design of Web technology to understand the human factors involved in Web-based interaction. Incorporating insights from cognitive science about the mechanisms, strengths, and limits of human perception and cognition can provide a number of benefits for Web practitioners. Knowledge about the various constraints on cognition, (e.g., limitations on working memory), patterns of strategy selection, or the effect of design decisions (e.g., icon style) on visual search, can inform the design and evaluation process and allow practitioners to develop technologies that are better suited to human abilities.

The application of cognitive psychology to human-computer interaction (HCI) issues has a long history going back to Card, Moran, and Newell's (1983) introduction of the goals, operators, methods, and selection rules (GOMS) task analysis technique and model human processor (MHP) account of human information processing in the early 1980s. Since then, their cognitive engineering approach has developed into a family of methods (John & Kieras, 1994; Olson & Olson, 1990) which are widely used to produce quantitative models of user performance in interactive tasks.

Another, more recent approach to modelling human performance in interactive tasks has emerged in the last decade from theoretical and technological advances in research into cognitive architectures. Cognitive architectures are theories of the fundamental structures and processes that underlie all human cognition, of which there are several currently in existence including EPIC (executive process / interactive control; Kieras & Meyer, 1997), Soar (Laird, Newell, & Rosenbloom, 1987; Newell, 1990), and ACT-R (Anderson & Lebiere, 1998; Anderson et al., 2004). An important feature of these architectures is that they are all implemented as computer programming systems so that cognitive models may be specified, executed, and their outputs (e.g., error rates and response latencies) compared to human performance data.

Originally ACT-R and Soar were theories of central cognition only and did not explicitly specify mechanisms for perception or motor control. EPIC however, was unique in that from its inception it incorporated processors for cognition, perception, and motor control. Recent adaptations to ACT-R (Byrne & Anderson, 1998) and Soar (Chong & Laird, 1997) have now ensured that both architectures incorporate perceptual motor components that allow models to include visual attention processes and manual interactions with a keyboard and mouse. This is an important development for the study of HCI as cognitive models can now be *embodied* (Kieras & Meyer, 1997) in the sense that the architectures are now able to simulate perceptual-motor contact with computer interfaces and devices and so capture the complex interactions between the task environment, cognition, and perceptual-motor behaviour.

Modelling interactive behaviour with an embodied cognitive architecture has a number of advantages over the traditional cognitive engineering approach exemplified by GOMS and its relatives. Perhaps the most important of these is that computational models can actually execute the task, allowing a direct test of the sufficiency of the hypothesised processes. Second, although most cognitive architectures contain built-in timing parameters taken from the psychological literature, unlike cognitive engineering models, they do not require prior estimated times for all subcomponents of a task. In addition, some architectures — such as ACT-R and Soar — contain learning mechanisms which allow them to model various effects of practice on performance. This allows cognitive architectures to be used to model novel tasks, novice users, or tasks involving components without prior time estimates.

One of the promises of embodied cognitive architectures is that, once they are equipped with sufficient knowledge, they will begin to provide a priori predictions of user performance and eventually evolve into artificial users that can be employed to evaluate novel tasks and environments (Ritter, Baxter, Jones, & Young, 2000; Young, Green, & Simon, 1989). In this chapter we will describe one of these architectures, ACT-R, and show how it has been used to provide detailed and sophisticated process models of human performance in interactive tasks with complex interfaces. ACT-R is an appropriate choice for this discussion because, in contrast to other cognitive architectures, ACT-R also embodies the rational theory of cognition (Anderson, 1990) which analyses cognitive phenomena in terms of how they are adapted to the statistical structure of the environment. Rational analysis and ACT-R's mechanisms have been used recently to provide novel insights into Web-based interactions. The chapter proceeds as follows: First we describe the basic assumptions and mechanisms of rational analysis and the ACT-R cognitive architecture. We then show how these have been used to develop a model of information foraging on the Web and discuss the model in relation to a rational analysis model of the task and the data from eye-tracking studies of interactive search. In the final sections of this chapter we briefly outline ACT-R models of two interactive tasks; graph reading (Peebles & Cheng, 2003) and icon search (Fleetwood & Byrne, in press). Although neither of these studies involves a specifically Web-based task, they both describe user interaction with items commonly found on Web pages. They are also illustrative of a methodology that combines task analysis, eye tracking, and formal modelling to provide a detailed account of the cognitive, perceptual, and motor processes involved in the performance of the task. These studies are also useful because in both cases the model is validated by comparing the simulated eye movements with those recorded from human subjects. Both studies, therefore, are clear demonstrations of a novel approach to understanding interactive behaviour that can be applied to Web-based tasks.

RATIONAL ANALYSIS

Rational analysis (Anderson, 1990) is a method for understanding the task an agent attempts to complete. It assumes that humans have evolved cognitive mechanisms that are useful for completing tasks that we encounter in our environment, and that these mechanisms work in an efficient way to complete these tasks. Therefore, rather than concerning ourselves with firstly trying to define the cognitive mechanisms required by the agent to solve the task, rational analysis suggests that we should consider the structure of the task itself, the environment in which it is encountered, together with some minimal assumptions about the computational limitations of the system. From these initial statements the analysis proceeds by the specification of an optimal solution to the problem and the comparison of human behavioural data to see how close an approximation it is to the optimal solution.

By identifying the best way to complete the task (the optimal strategy) we can often infer what the cognitive mechanisms of a rational agent must be as although humans do not always complete tasks in the most optimal way their behaviour is usually similar to the optimal strategy. That is, humans usually behave in such a way that they appear to be try-ing to complete their tasks in the most efficient manner, that is, they try to maximise their returns while minimising the cost of achieving their goals.

Figure 1. The modular structure of ACT-R 6.0

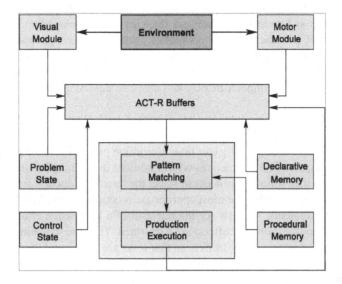

Rational analysis has been applied to several aspects of human cognition (see e.g., Oaksford & Chater, 1998), from the original analyses of memory, categorisation, causal inference, and decision making conducted by Anderson (1990), to more recent analyses of exploratory choice (Cox & Young 2004; Young, 1998) and the updating of memory during tasks in dynamic environments (Neth, Sims, Veksler, & Gray, 2004).

THE ACT-R COGNITIVE ARCHITECTURE

ACT-R is a theory of human cognition developed over a period of 30 years by John Anderson and his colleagues (Anderson & Lebiere, 1998; Anderson et al., 2004) that incorporates the theory of rational analysis. It is a principal effort in the attempt to develop a unified theory of cognition (Newell, 1990). As a cognitive architecture, ACT-R attempts to specify the basic cognitive structures and processes that underlie all human cognition.

Figure 1 illustrates the components of the architecture relevant to our discussion. ACT-R consists of a set of independent modules that acquire information from the environment, process information, and execute motor actions in the furtherance of particular goals. There are four modules that comprise the central cognitive components of ACT-R. Two of these are memory stores for two types of knowledge: a declarative memory module that stores factual knowledge about the domain, and a procedural memory module that stores the system's knowledge about how tasks are performed. The former consists of a network of knowledge chunks whereas the latter is a set of *productions*, rules of the form "IF <condition> THEN <action>": the condition specifying the state of the system that must exist for the rule to apply and the action specifying the actions to be taken should this occur. The other two cognitive modules represent information related to the execution of tasks. The first is a control state module that keeps track of the intentions of the system during problem solving, and the second is a problem state module that maintains the current state of the task.

In addition to these cognitive modules there are four perceptual-motor modules for speech, audition, visual, and motor processing (only the latter two are shown in Figure 1). The speech and audition modules are the least well-developed and, at present, simply provide ACT-R with the capacity to simulate basic audio perception and vocal output for the purpose of modelling typical psychology experiments. The visual and motor modules are more well-developed and provide ACT-R with the ability to simulate visual attention shifts to objects on a computer display and manual interactions with a computer keyboard and mouse.

Each of ACT-R's modules has an associated *buffer* that can hold only one chunk of information from its module at a time, and the contents of all of the buffers constitute the state of an ACT-R model at any one time. Cognition proceeds via a pattern matching process that attempts to find productions with conditions that match the current contents of the buffers. There then follows a process to select the "best" production from those that match the conditions, after which the most appropriate production "fires" and the actions (visual or manual movements, requests for the retrieval of a knowledge chunk from declarative memory, or modifications to buffers) are performed. Then the matching process continues on the updated contents of the buffers so that tasks are performed through a succession of production rule firings. As an example, two production rules (written in English rather than in ACT-R code) that instantiate part of a search task may look something like this:

IF	the goal is to find the meaning of "eudaimonia" (control state)
AND	there is nothing in declarative memory about "eudaimonia" (declarative)
THEN	set the goal to search the WWW for "eudaimonia" (control state)
IF	the goal is to search the WWW for "eudaimonia" (control state)
AND	the Web browser is open (problem state)
THEN	look for the menu labelled "Bookmarks" (visual)
AND	update the problem state to "looking for Google" (problem state)

The processing in ACT-R's modules is serial but the modules run in parallel with each other so that the system can move visual attention while also moving the mouse and attempting to retrieve knowledge from declarative memory. ACT-R processes also have associated latency parameters taken from the psychology literature. For example, it typically takes 50 ms for a production to fire and the time taken to move the mouse cursor to an object on the computer screen is calculated using Fitts' Law (Fitts, 1954).

ACT-R implements rational analysis in two ways. The first is its mechanism for retrieving knowledge chunks from declarative memory which is based on the notion of activation. Each chunk in declarative memory has a level of activation which determines its probability and latency of retrieval, and the level of activation for a chunk reflects the recency and frequency of its use. This enables us to understand how rehearsal of items in a short-term memory task can boost the activation levels of these chunks and consequently increase the chances of recall/retrieval from declarative memory. The level of activation of a chunk falls gradually over time, and without retrieval or activation spreading from chunks in the current goal, it may fall below a threshold level which then results in retrieval failure. This enables ACT-R models to forget knowledge without having to explicitly delete chunks from the declarative memory store.

The second way that ACT-R implements rational analysis is in its mechanism for choosing between alternative production rules. According to rational analysis, people choose between a number of options to maximise their expected utility. Each option (i.e., production rule) has an expected probability of achieving the goal and an expected cost. It is assumed that when carrying out computer-based tasks people interact with the task environment and choose actions that will optimise their efficiency (i.e., maximise the probability of achieving the goal while minimising the cost, usually measured in units of time). At each decision step in the cycle, therefore, all possible production rules that match against the current goal are proposed in a choice set, and the one with the highest level of efficiency is chosen and executed.

ACT-R has been used to model a wide range of cognitive phenomena (Anderson & Lebiere, 1998), and in recent years, with the inclusion of the perceptual-motor modules, it has been applied to a number of complex interactive tasks in the area of HCI and human factors research, for example, menu selection (Byrne, 2001), cell phone menu interaction (St. Amant, Horton, & Ritter, 2004), and driving (Salvucci & Macuga, 2002). Although individually these models do not yet offer us a virtual "user" which can be sat in front of a Web browser and asked to complete any goal, together they provide us with insights into how and why users behave in particular ways, for example, when searching for information on the Web. In this chapter we will concentrate on three particular areas of work that are relevant to understanding Web behaviour: icon search, graph reading, and information foraging on the WWW.

MODELLING INTERACTIVE BEHAVIOUR

In the following section, we will summarise a number of recent studies which employ rational analysis, cognitive modelling, eye tracking, or a combination of all three, to understand human performance in Web-based or HCI tasks. We first discuss recent efforts to model information foraging and interactive search on the WWW. These studies show how ACT-R and rational analysis can be successfully applied to explain different aspects of people's behaviour when conducting interactive search tasks. This can include both high-level behaviours such as backtracking through Web-pages and low-level behaviours such as patterns of visual attention obtained from eye-tracking studies. We then describe two studies which combine experimental data collection, eye movement recording, and cognitive modelling methods using ACT-R to provide detailed accounts of the cognitive, perceptual, and motor processes involved in the tasks. These studies were chosen because both develop a detailed process model which not only captures the human response time data from the experiment, but also provides a close match to the patterns of visual attention revealed by the eye movement study. This level of detail in modelling is still relatively uncommon and the strong constraints added by seeking to match model and human eye movement scan paths during the course of the task provide a further validation of the models.

Information Foraging on the World Wide Web

Information foraging theory (IFT; Pirolli & Card, 1999; Pirolli, 2005) describes an account of information gathering behaviour based on the ecological behaviours of animals when foraging for food. The account can be applied to situations in which people are searching for information in a number of different situations such as in a library or on the WWW.

The theory rests on rational analysis in that it proposes that human behaviour is directed by the objective to maximise gain and minimise effort, and that this process is sensitive to changes in the environment. In contrast to animal studies, where the assumption is that animals seek to reduce the ratio of calorie intake to energy expenditure, the assumption in IFT is that people attempt to reduce the ratio of information gained to time spent.

The way in which the environment is structured determines the costs of search for information. For example, the structure of a Web site will determine how many pages the user has to navigate through in order to satisfy his/her goal. When searching for information on the WWW, many people make use of search engines. After entering some key words the user is presented with a list of search results which are usually ordered in terms of their relevance to the key words. Each of the results returned can be considered to be a "patch" of information. The user has to choose to either investigate one of the patches or to redefine their search criteria. Conducting another search using different key words will result in a change in the environment. This process is known as *enriching* the environment as it is hoped that the result is that the cost of obtaining the required information will be reduced compared to the perceived cost of obtaining it in the previous environment. Decisions about whether or not to pursue a particular information patch or to continue enriching the environment are based on a number of factors such as the perceived value of the information returned, the perceived costs of acquiring that information, interface constraints, and previous knowledge.

The decision to forage within a particular patch of information is based on an ongoing assessment of information *scent*. Information scent is the perception of the value of the distal information based on the proximal information available, that is, it is an estimate of the relevance of the information contained on a yet unseen page based on the cues from the icon or wording of the link on the page currently viewed. The theory predicts that as more time is allocated to within-patch foraging, the rate of information return increases but only up to an optimal point, after which the rate starts to decrease. Therefore, after a particular amount of within-patch foraging (searching within a Web site) it becomes more profitable to move to the next patch (select another Web site from the list of search results) even though there are still pages within the previous patch that have not yet been visited.

SNIF-ACT

Scent-based Navigation and Information Foraging in the ACT architecture (SNIF-ACT) (Pirolli & Fu, 2003) is a model of human behaviour in an interactive search task. The model makes use of ACT-R's spreading activation mechanism so that the information scent of the currently viewed Web page activates chunks in declarative memory as does the spreading activation from the goal. Where these two sources of activation coincide there are higher levels of activation and this indicates a high degree of relevance between the goal and the page being attended to. This activation is what ultimately drives the behaviour of the model. The model includes the use of search engines to provide a set of search results and the processing of the page that is returned. The links on the page are attended to and eventually one of the links is selected.

The behaviour of the model is compared to user behaviour and successfully demonstrates that people tend to select the highest scent item in a list. SNIF-ACT does this by assessing the information scent of all the links on a page and then choosing the highest one.

The model is also able to explain the point at which a user abandons a particular Web site and returns to the search results in order to select another item from the list or selects a link that takes them to another Web site. If the mean information scent of the currently viewed page is lower than the mean information scent of a page on another site the model selects that action that takes them to the other site.

Eye-Tracking Experiments in Interactive Search

When presented with a list of search results or items on a menu within a Web site (i.e., a patch of information), the user has to choose between selecting an item which will move him/her to another patch and doing some assessment on either the currently attended item or some other item in the list (i.e., consume the information presented within the current patch). As has been mentioned previously, IFT proposes that the user will make use of the information scent of the items to guide their behaviour. If the information scent of a particular item in the list is higher than the rest (i.e., that item appears to be relevant to the task and the user believes that clicking it will lead them to better information) then the item will be selected.

Eye-tracking experiments have been used to investigate what people attend to when conducting interactive search tasks (Brumby & Howes, 2004; Silva & Cox, 2005). Participants were given an information goal and a list of items and asked to select the label that they thought would lead to the information they required. Brumby and Howes demonstrated

Figure 2. A simplified scan path of a participant performing an interactive search task

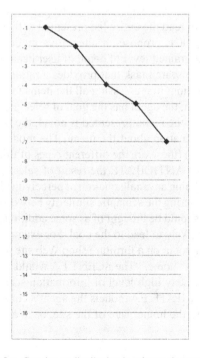

that people often examine only a subset of the list before selecting the target item, and that this behaviour is affected by the relevance of the other items in the list. When the other items in the list are more relevant to the goal (i.e., they have high levels of information scent), people tend to look at more items in the list and also tend to look at individual items on more occasions than when the items are irrelevant. When there are a number of items with high scent (i.e., two or more items look like they would lead to relevant information) people need to consider more items than when only one item looks sensible.

However, one limitation of this work is that the analysis of eye-tracking data is rarely sensitive enough to determine whether a lack of fixation of the eyes on an item really means that people have not assessed the relevance of the item. In order to address this, Silva and Cox (2005) additionally employed a recognition task in their study in order to assess the level of processing of each item in the list.

Figure 2 represents a simplified scan path of a participant completing one of these tasks. The items are represented on the y axis with time along the x axis. The highlighted item is the target item and was selected by the participant. The figure demonstrates how the user starts at the top of the list and scans down the list fixating items in the list. Some of the items (3 & 6) are skipped over. The results from Silva and Cox's (2005) recognition task suggest that in such cases the lack of fixations of particular items in the menu can be explained by parafoveal processing. However, parafoveal processing can only explain lack of fixations on up to two items below the last fixation (i.e., items 8 & 9) and cannot explain why the user does not attend to other items in the list (i.e., items 10 to 16).

SNIF-ACT would be able to produce a trace that would match the behaviour of users in these studies in terms of which items from the menus the user selected. However, the model does not account for the fact that some of the items in the menus were not assessed by the users as it assumes that users have knowledge about information scent of all the items in the list and then selects the item with the highest level of scent. Consequently, SNIF-ACT is unable to provide us with any explanation for why users should choose to select an item when they have not even read the entire list presented to them.

Cox and Young (2004) propose an alternative model to that of SNIF-ACT that is able to capture this fine-grained level of detail of user behaviour. Their model is a rational analysis of an interactive search task that provides a rational explanation of why the user would select an item without first assessing all the items in the list.

In interactive search, the agent has the goal of selecting the item that will lead to goal completion. However, as the menu presented is novel, the first thing that the model has to do is to gain some information about the menu. The model therefore includes two types of exploratory acts (EAs) (these are the different types of things the model can do): assess information SCENT and ANTICIPATE the result of selecting this item. The SCENT EA should be thought of as being an amalgamation of perceiving the label, reading the label (at a lexical level), and considering the semantic similarity between the label and the current task. The ANTICIPATE EA should be thought of as some additional cognitive effort that considers whether the label is likely to lead to the goal. For example, given the goal of finding an armchair for your living room on a furniture shop Web site, imagine the model considering the first item in the menu "home." The SCENT EA would return a moderately high rating as the label has a moderately high level of information scent given the goal ("home" and "armchair"). The ANTICIPATE EA models the agent's consideration of whether the label *home* is likely to lead to the home page of the site, or to a list of home furnishings. Each of these EA types has a cost associated with it with the ANTICIPATE EA type being more expensive in mental effort than the first type. There is also a fixed cost of moving attention from one item in the menu to the next.

Before assessing any items, the model "knows" the number of items in the menu and considers each of these items to be equally (ir)relevant to completing the task. The scent ratings of the items in the menu are used as the basis for determining the new relevance (R) value of an item following an assessment. On each page, the set of relevancies R_i are mapped into a set of probabilities P_i by the transformation $P_i = \text{odds}(R_i)/\sum\text{odds}(R_j)$, where odds(R) is defined in the standard way as odds(R) = R/(1–R). Note that $\sum P_i = 1$, reflecting the fact that exactly one option on the page leads to the goal.

When the model is run on a set of menus it demonstrates how different patterns of information scent result in different behaviours. As Brumby and Howes (2004) demonstrated, the levels of information scent of both the goal item and the distractors affect behaviour. However, it is also interesting to note that the model predicts that just the change in position of the goal item relevant to the distractors results in different patterns of behaviour: Sometimes the model predicts that users will scan to the bottom of the menu before selecting the target item, and other times they will select the item immediately after assessing the item leaving other items in the menu unassessed. To explain how this occurs we will compare the behaviour of the model when the high scent item is in position two (as an example of occurring early in the menu) and in position 12 (as an example of occurring late in the menu) in more detail. In both examples, initially, all 16 menu items are rated equally and all have an R value of 0.06. The relevance values are translated into efficiencies (E) which are then used to determine which of the EAs is most likely to lead to the goal and therefore which EA is executed in each cycle. In the first cycle, the EA that proposes assessing the scent of the first item in the menu is rated as having the highest E value due to it having the lowest cost. Consequently, the model assesses the first item which gets rated as very low scent. As a result, the new R value of this item is set at 0. On the next cycle, the EA that proposes SCENT assessment on the second item in the list is the most efficient (due to the lower cost) so this item gets assessed. This behaviour continues until the model assesses the high scent item.

In menus where the high scent item occurs early on in the menu, the second item in the menu gets an R value of 0.5097 which raises the probability that this item will lead to the goal to 0.6220. On the following cycle the R value of the high scent item leads to an E value of 0.008 while the second best item (an item yet to be assessed) has an R value of 0.06 which results in an E value of 0.006. Although the E values of the two EAs are very similar, one is larger than the other, and this is what determines which EA is chosen.

In our example of a menu where the high scent item occurs later on in the menu, the relevance of each of the low scent items that have already been assessed falls to 0. When the model assesses the twelfth item its R value is 0.5097, which raises the probability that this item will lead to the goal to 0.6220. On the following cycle the R value of the high scent item only has an E value of 0.005 while the item with the best efficiency (an item yet to be assessed) has an R value of 0.05 which results in an E value of 0.006. The result is that the model continues to assess each item in the menu until it reaches the bottom because the efficiency of conducting a SCENT assessment of a new item is greater than the efficiency of conducting the ANTICIPATE assessment on the high scent item in position 12. This has the effect of slowly increasing the probability of the item in position 12 leading to the goal.

The detail of the model explains that the reason the behaviour is different for the two types of menus is because the detail of the mathematics of the rational analysis. Comparisons of the traces of the model with the empirical data suggest that the model provides a good explanation of the cognitive processes involved in this task. This suggests that participants make an assessment of the relevance of a label to the current goal and then, together with the estimated relevance of previous items, choose to either (1) select that item as the one that will lead to the goal, (2) conduct some further assessment of the current item, or (3) move on to another item and assess that. Which of these EAs is chosen is driven by the pattern of information scent that has been experienced so far.

The model provides us with an explanation of how and why the position of the goal and the quality of the distractor items affect the behaviour of the participants on the task. Regardless of the pattern of scent of the menu, the model predicts that the agent will tend to stop exploring the menu as soon as it comes across a menu item that has high information scent (self-terminates) if this is encountered early in the menu. On menus where there is one high scent item among a set of low scent items and the high scent item occurs later in the menu, the agent continues to assess the other items in the menu before conducting further assessment of the high scent item and finally selecting it. The model enables us to explain why we see these different patterns of behaviour on menus which have such similar patterns of information scent. This is due to the effect of the interdependence of the probability that each of the items will lead to the goal. The actual point on the menu at which the model swaps from one behaviour to the other is sensitive to a number of factors such as the length of the menu and the costs of the EAs. It would appear therefore that it is in the nature of interactive search that there are close calls which suggest that people can rationally do either behaviour and that a number of factors have an effect on the behaviour of participants exploring real menus.

Together the two models described previously provide us with a good understanding of how people perform search tasks on the WWW. SNIF-ACT and the rational model explain different aspects of the interaction: SNIF-ACT demonstrates the higher level, page by page, link following behaviour seen in such tasks, whereas the rational model explains the lower level interactions with just one page. Given information about the information scent of the items on a new Web site both models are able to make predictions about user behaviour on the site.

Modelling Graph Reading

Peebles and Cheng (2003) conducted an experiment, eye movement study and cognitive modelling analysis to investigate the cognitive, perceptual, and motor processes involved in a common graph-reading task using two different types of Cartesian graph. The purpose of the study was to determine how graph users' ability to retrieve information can be affected by presenting the same information in slightly different types of the same class of diagram. The two types of graph, shown in Figure 3, represent amounts of UK oil and gas production over two decades. The only difference between the two graph types is in which variables are represented on the axes and which are plotted. In the *Function* graphs, the *argument* variable (AV: time in years) is represented on the x-axis and the *quantity* variables (QV: oil and gas) on the y-axis whereas in the *Parametric* graphs, the quantity variables are represented on the x and y axes and time is plotted on the curve.

Figure 3. Function and parametric graphs used in Peebles and Cheng (2003) depicting values of oil and gas production for each year

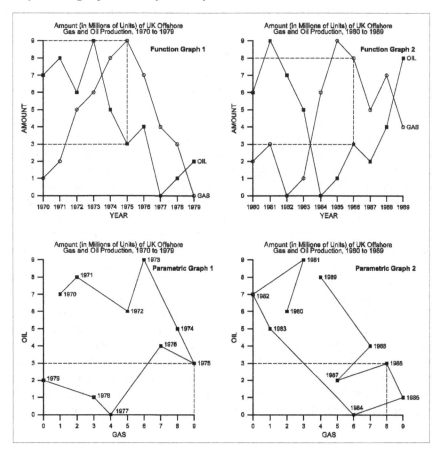

Notes: The graphs on the left (labelled 1) show years 1970 to 1979 while those on the right (labelled 2) show years 1980 to 1989. Dashed lines indicate the optimal scan path required to answer the question, "when the value of oil is 3, what is the value of gas?"

In the experiment, participants were presented with the value of a "given" variable and required to use the graph to find the corresponding value of a "target" variable, for example, "when the value of oil is 2, what is the value of gas?" This type of task has typically been analysed in terms of the minimum sequence of saccades and fixations required to reach the location of the given variable's value and then from there to the location of the corresponding value of the target variable (Lohse, 1993; Peebles & Cheng, 2001, 2002; Peebles, Cheng, & Shadbolt, 1999). Experiment participants (some of whom had their eye movements recorded) completed 120 trials, each participant using only one graph type. The 120 questions were coded into three classes (QV–QV, QV–AV, and AV–QV) according to which variable's value was given and which was required (QV denotes a *quantity* variable, oil or gas, and AV denotes the *argument* variable, time). On each trial, a question (e.g., "GAS = 6, OIL = ?") was presented above the graph and participants were required to read the question, find the answer using the graph on the screen and then enter their answer by clicking on a button labelled *Answer* in the top right corner of the window which revealed a circle of buttons containing the digits 0 to 9. RTs were recorded from the onset of a question to the mouse click on the Answer button.

The RT data from the experiment, displayed in Figure 4, showed that the graph used and the type of question asked both had a significant effect on the time it took for participants to retrieve the answer. This was all the more surprising because, for two of the three question types, participants were faster using the less familiar parametric graphs by nearly a second.

The results of the eye movement study were also surprising. It was found that in 63% of trials (irrespective of the graph used or question type being attempted), after having read the question at the start of a trial, participants redirected their visual attention to elements of the question at least once during the process of problem solving with the graph. This was not predicted by the simple minimal fixation sequence account outlined previously but two possible explanations may be provided: (1) participants initially encode the three question elements but are unable to retain all of them in working memory and retrieve them by the time they are required to do so, or (2) to reduce the probability of retrieval failure, participants break the problem into two sections, the first allowing them to reach the given location and the second to then proceed to the target location corresponding to the solution.

Peebles and Cheng (2003) constructed two ACT-R models of the experiment (one for each graph type) that were able to interact with an exact replica of the experiment software. The models consisted of a set of productions to carry out the six basic subgoals in the task; (1) read the question; (2) identify the *start location* determined by the given variable; (3) identify the *given location* on the graph representing the given value of given variable; (4) from the given location, identify the *target location* representing the required variable; (5) identify the *target value* at the target location; and (6) enter the answer. Many of the productions were shared by the two models, the main difference between them being the control structure that sequences the execution of the productions. Figure 4 shows that the mean RTs

Figure 4. Mean response times for experimental participants and ACT-R models for each question type (Peebles & Cheng, 2003)

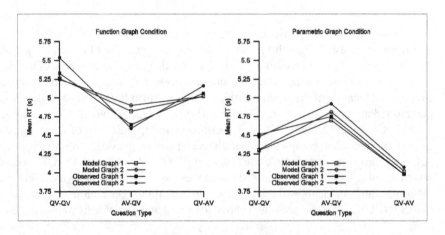

from the parametric and function graph models are a good fit to the observed data (R^2 = .868, RMSE = 0.123, and R^2 = .664, RMSE = 0.199 respectively). Perhaps more importantly however, were the insights into the observed eye movement data that came from the modelling process itself. When ACT-R focuses attention on an object on the screen, representations of the object and its location are created in the system's visual buffers which can be accessed by productions. Eventually these representations go into declarative memory with initial activation values and, as long as these values are above a certain threshold, they can be retrieved by the cognitive system and replaced in a buffer. However, ACT-R includes a mechanism by which the activation of representations in declarative memory decreases over time which allows it to simulate processes involved in forgetting. These mechanisms played a crucial role in the ACT-R models' ability to capture the eye movement data observed in the experiment. At the start of each trial, the models read the three question elements and during the problem solving these elements are placed in declarative memory. As a consequence, at least one question element must be retrieved from memory at each stage of the problem in order to continue. However, as soon as a question element is placed in declarative memory its activation starts to decay and, as a consequence, the probability that it cannot be retrieved increases. Typically, if a retrieval failure occurs, an ACT-R model will halt as it does not have the appropriate information to solve the problem. During the process of model development it was found that on a significant proportion of trials the model was not able to retrieve question elements at the later stages of the trial because their activation had fallen below the retrieval threshold. As a consequence new productions had to be added to allow the model to redirect attention to the question in order to re-encode the element and then return to solving the problem. This was precisely the behaviour observed in the eye movement study. This is illustrated in Figure 5 which compares screen shots of the model scan path and eye movements recorded from one participant for the same question using

Figure 5. Screen shots showing an experimental participant's eye movement data (left) and the ACT-R model's visual attention scan path (right) for the QV–QV question "oil = 6, gas = ?" using the 1980's parametric graph

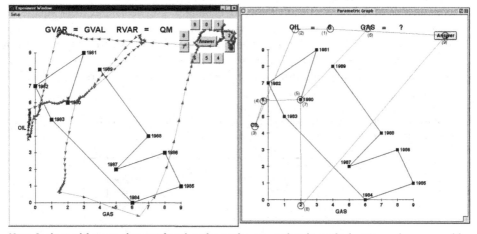

Note: In the model screen shot, numbered circles on the scan path indicate the location and sequence of fixations.

the 1980's parametric graph. The numbered circles on the model screen shot indicate the sequence of fixations produced by the model. The pattern of fixations in both screenshots is remarkably similar.

Modelling Icon Search

Fleetwood and Byrne's study of icon search (2002, in press) is a another demonstration of how an ACT-R cognitive model can provide a detailed account of the cognitive and perceptual processes involved in a common HCI task that closely matches people's response times (RTs) and patterns of eye movements. Fleetwood and Byrne's model differs from that of Peebles and Cheng (2003) in that it incorporates eye movements and movement of attention (EMMA) (Salvucci, 2001), a computational model of the relationship between eye movements and visual attention. EMMA can be easily integrated into the ACT-R architecture, allowing models to make more detailed predictions of actual eye movements, rather than simple shifts of visual attention.

One of the main aims of Fleetwood and Byrne's research is to investigate the notion of icon "quality" (defined in terms of an icon's distinctiveness and visual complexity) and to examine the effect that differences in quality may have on identification performance. They created three classes of icon (examples of which are shown in Figure 6). "Good" quality icons were designed to be easily distinguishable from others based on the primitive features of colour and shape. All icons in this set were a combination of one colour (from six) and one shape (from two).

In contrast, "poor" quality icons were designed to be distinguishable only by a relatively careful inspection but to be relatively indistinguishable in a large distractor set. These poor quality icons were all of the same basic shape and colour (a combination of black, white, and shades of grey). An intermediate class of "fair" quality icons was also designed with shapes more distinctive than the poor quality icons but more complex than the good quality icons, and with the same range of greyscale colours as the poor quality icons. The main effect of the manipulation was to produce a different similarity structure for each class of icons. Good quality icons could be identified as a single combination of features, for example, "yellow triangle." In contrast, fair quality icons were defined by more than one combination of features (typically three, for example: "grey rectangle; black square; black diagonal-right"), some of which were shared with other icons. In the poor quality group, icons were defined by an average of four feature combinations and many more of these were shared by several other icons in the group. From the visual search literature, it can be predicted that search time will increase as icon distinctiveness decreases. An additional

Figure 6. Examples of icons of good, fair, and poor quality used in the experiment of Fleetwood and Byrne (in press)

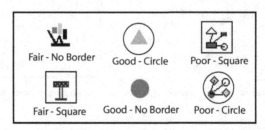

factor in Fleetwood and Byrne's (2006) study also known to affect search time (at least for certain stimuli) is the number of distractors in the display, with search time increasing with the number of distractors in the search set. In their experiment, Fleetwood and Byrne had search sets of 6, 12, 18 and 24 icons.

In the experiment, participants were required to find, as rapidly as possible, different quality target icons in search sets of differing sizes. On each trial, a target icon and file name were presented followed 1500 ms later by a button labelled *Ready* for the participant to click when he/she felt ready to continue. When this button was clicked, the target icon was replaced by the search set and the participant had simply to look for the target icon and click on it as quickly as possible; when an icon was clicked upon, the next trial started. Participants completed a total of 144 trials, involving all levels of the search set and icon quality variables, and on each trial the participant's RT (the duration between clicks on the Ready button and an icon in the search set) was recorded. The results of the experiment (shown in Figure 7) revealed that, as predicted, both icon quality and search set size had a significant effect on search time.

To provide an explanation of their data, Fleetwood and Byrne (2006) produced an ACT-R model of the task that was able to interact with the same experiment software as the participants. As described previously, each experiment trial is comprised of two stages, the first where the target icon and its file name are encoded and the second in which it is sought. The model has a set of seven productions to carry out the first stage: (1) locate the target icon and (2) encode an attribute pair (e.g., "grey rectangle"), (3) look below the icon and (4) encode the associated file name, and finally (5) locate and (6) click on the "Ready" button. In the second stage, the model locates and attends to an icon with the previously encoded target feature and then shifts visual attention to the file name below it. If the file name matches the target file name, visual attention is returned to the icon and the mouse clicks on it. If the file name is not the target, however, the model continues the search by locating another icon at random with the same target features. This sequence of events requires four productions and takes 285 ms to complete.

Figure 7. Response time by set size and icon quality for Fleetwood and Byrne's (in press) revised model and the experiment data.

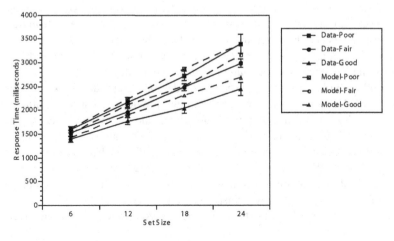

Figure 8. Mean number of shifts of visual attention per trial made by Fleetwood and Byrne's (in press) revised model relative to the mean number of gazes per trial made by participants

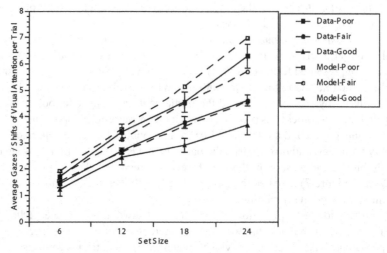

Figure 7 reveals a close correspondence between the mean RTs produced by the model and those of the experiment participants ($R^2 = .98$, RMSE = 126ms) and shows that an ACT-R model based on the similarity structure of the search set and the strategy of identifying a single combination of features and random search can provide a reasonable account of the data. However, Byrne, Anderson, Douglass, and Matessa (1999) had shown in an earlier study of visual search in a menu selection task that alternative strategies can produce similar aggregate RTs, necessitating the incorporation of eye movement data to add further constraints on the proposed theory. As a result, Fleetwood and Byrne (2006) carried out an eye movement study to test their model further and found two major discrepancies between the observed eye movements and the patterns of visual attention produced by their model. First, they found that, although the model successfully reproduced the patterns of visual attention across the icon quality and set size conditions, for all conditions the number of saccades per trial produced by the model was significantly greater than those recorded in the experiment. Second, when analysing the eye movement data, Fleetwood and Byrne found that patterns of icon search were not random as their model predicted, but were systematic, in the sense that participants sought to minimise the distance between successive fixations, typically looking at target icons closest to their current fixation point. This produced a search pattern that revealed a systematic scanning of areas of the display.

Both of the discrepancies between the model and human data are explained by Salvucci's (2001) EMMA model. It is been demonstrated previously that the relationship between eye movements and visual attention is not direct, and that people often do not move their eyes to their focus of attention (e.g., Henderson, 1992; Rayner, 1995). EMMA attempts to capture this relationship by providing an account of if and when eye movements occur, and if they do occur, the location of their landing relative to their targets. Integrating EMMA into ACT-R allows models to simulate actual eye movements rather than just visual attention shifts and provides a more realistic output to be compared with human eye movement data. In addition, EMMA predicts that efficient search strategies minimise average saccade distance, resulting in search patterns in which objects nearest to the current fixation point are examined soonest.

Fleetwood and Byrne (2006) modified their model's search strategy according to the EMMA account and incorporated EMMA's eye movement computations into their model, resulting in a greatly improved fit (shown in Figure 8) to the human eye movement data ($R^2 = .99$, RMSE = 0.58).

CONCLUSION

In this chapter we have presented a number of recent examples of research that we believe clearly demonstrate the value of rational analysis and cognitive modelling in the study of complex interactive behaviour. Such tasks typically involve the complex interaction of three elements: (1) the perceptual and cognitive abilities of the user; (2) the visual and statistical properties of the task environment; and (3) the specific requirements of the task being carried out. The use of rational analysis and an embodied cognitive architecture such as ACT-R allows all three of these elements to be brought together in an integrated theoretical account of user behaviour. Rational analysis provides a set of assumptions and methods that allow researchers to understand user behaviour in terms of the statistical structure of the task environment and the user's goal of optimising (i.e., reducing the cost/benefit ratio of) the interaction. Developing cognitive models of interactive behaviour in a cognitive architecture such as ACT-R allows researchers to specify precisely the cognitive factors (e.g., domain knowledge, problem-solving strategies, and working memory capacity) involved. In addition, the recent incorporation of perceptual-motor modules to cognitive architectures allows them to make predictions about users' eye movements during the entire performance of the task, which can be compared to observed eye movement data — a highly stringent test of the sufficiency and efficacy of a model. The use of these methods has increased rapidly over the last 5 years, as has the range of task interfaces being studied. Although we are still a long way from achieving the goal of an artificial user that can be applied "off the shelf" to novel tasks and environments, the models of interactive behaviour described here demonstrate a level of sophistication and rigour still relatively rare in HCI research. As these examples illustrate, developing more detailed accounts of interactive behaviour can provide genuine insights into the complex interplay of factors that affect the use of computer and Web technologies, which may inform the design of systems more adapted to their users.

NOTE

All correspondence to: David Peebles, Department of Behavioural Sciences, University of Huddersfield, Queensgate, Huddersfield, HD1 3DH, UK; D.Peebles@hud.ac.uk.

REFERENCES

Anderson, J. R. (1990). *The adaptive character of thought*. Hillsdale, NJ: Lawrence Erlbaum Associates.

Anderson, J. R., Bothell, D., Byrne, M. D., Douglass, S., Lebiere, C., & Qin, Y. (2004). An integrated theory of the mind. *Psychological Review, 111*(4), 1036-1060.

Anderson, J. R., & Lebiere, C. (1998). *The atomic components of thought*. Mahwah, NJ: Lawrence Erlbaum Associates.

Brumby, D. P., & Howes, A. (2004, July 30-August 1). Good enough but I'll just check: Web-page search as attentional refocusing. In *Proceedings of the 6ᵗʰ International Conference on Cognitive Modelling*, Pittsburgh, PA.

Byrne, M. D. (2001). ACT-R/PM and menu selection: Applying a cognitive architecture to HCI. *International Journal of Human-Computer Studies, 55*, 41-84.

Byrne, M. D., & Anderson, J. R. (1998). Perception and action. In J. R. Anderson & C. Lebiere (Eds.), *The atomic components of thought*, (pp. 167-200). Mahwah, NJ: Lawrence Erlbaum Associates.

Byrne, M. D., Anderson, J. R., Douglass, S., & Matessa, M. (1999). Eye tracking the visual search of click-down menus. In *Proceedings of the ACM CHI'99 Conference on Human Factors in Computing Systems* (pp. 402-409). New York: ACM.

Card, S. K., Moran, T. P., & Newell, A. (1983). *The psychology of human-computer interaction*. Hillsdale, NJ: Erlbaum.

Chong, R. S., & Laird, J. E. (1997). Identifying dual-task executive process knowledge using EPIC-Soar. In *Proceedings of the 19ᵗʰ Annual Conference of the Cognitive Science Society* (pp. 107-112). Mahwah, NJ: Lawrence Erlbaum Associates.

Cox, A. L., & Young, R. M. (2004). A rational model of the effect of information scent on the exploration of menus. In *Proceedings of 6ᵗʰ International Conference on Cognitive Modeling: Integrating Models*, (pp. 82-86). Mahwah, NJ: Lawrence Erlbaum Associates.

Fitts, P. M. (1954). The information capacity of the human motor systems in controlling the amplitude of movement. *Journal of Experimental Psychology, 47*, 381-391.

Fleetwood, M. D., & Byrne, M. D. (2002). Modeling icon search in ACT-R/PM. *Cognitive Systems Research, 3*, 25-33.

Fleetwood, M. D., & Byrne, M. D. (2006). Modeling the visual search of displays: A revised ACT-R/PM model of icon search based on eye tracking data. *Human Computer Interaction, 21*, 153-197.

Henderson, J. M. (1992). Visual attention and eye movement control during reading and picture viewing. In K. Rayner (Ed.), *Eye movements and visual cognition: Scene perception and reading*, (pp. 261-283). New York: Springer-Verlag.

John, B. E., & Kieras, D. E. (1994). *The GOMS family of analysis techniques: Tools for design and evaluation* (Tech. Rep. No. CMUHCII94106). Pittsburgh, PA: Carnegie Mellon University, Human-Computer Interaction Institute.

Kieras, D. E., & Meyer, D. E. (1997). An overview of the EPIC architecture for cognition and performance with application to human-computer interaction. *Human-Computer Interaction, 12*, 391-438.

Laird, J. E., Newell, A., & Rosenbloom, P. S. (1987). SOAR: An architecture for general intelligence. *Artificial Intelligence, 33*, 1-64.

Lohse, G. L. (1993). A cognitive model for understanding graphical perception. *Human-Computer Interaction, 8*, 353-388.

Neth, H., Sims, C. R., Veksler, V. D., & Gray, W. D. (2004). You can't play straight TRACS and win: Memory updates in a dynamic task environment. In K. D. Forbus, D. Gentner, & T. Regier (Eds.), *Proceedings of the 26ᵗʰ Annual Meeting of the Cognitive Science Society* (pp. 1017-1022). Hillsdale, NJ: Lawrence Erlbaum Associates.

Newell, A. (1990) *Unified theories of cognition.* Cambridge, MA: Harvard University Press.

Oaksford, M., & Chater, N. (Eds.). (1998). *Rational models of cognition.* UK: Oxford University Press.

Olson, J. S., & Olson, G. M. (1990). The growth of cognitive modeling in human-computer interaction since GOMS. *Human Computer Interaction, 5,* 221-265.

Peebles, D., & Cheng, P. C.-H. (2001). Graph-based reasoning: From task analysis to cognitive explanation. In *Proceedings of the 23rd Annual Conference of the Cognitive Science Society* (pp. 762-767). Mahwah, NJ: Lawrence Erlbaum Associates.

Peebles, D., & Cheng, P. C.-H. (2002). Extending task analytic models of graph-based reasoning: A cognitive model of problem solving with Cartesian graphs in ACT-R/PM. *Cognitive Systems Research, 3,* 77-86.

Peebles, D., & Cheng, P. C.-H. (2003). Modeling the effect of task and graphical representation on response latency in a graph reading task. *Human Factors, 45,* 28-46.

Peebles, D., Cheng, P. C.-H., & Shadbolt, N. (1999). Multiple processes in graph-based reasoning. In *Proceedings of the 21st Annual Conference of the Cognitive Science Society* (pp. 531-536). Mahwah, NJ: Lawrence Erlbaum Associates.

Pirolli, P. (2005) Rational analyses of information foraging on the Web. *Cognitive Science, 29,* 343-374.

Pirolli, P. L., & Card, S. K. (1999). Information foraging. *Psychological Review, 106*(4), 643-675.

Pirolli, P., & Fu, W.-T. (2003, June 22-26). *SNIF-ACT: A model of information foraging on the World Wide Web.* Paper presented at the Ninth International Conference on User Modeling, Johnstown, PA.

Rayner, K. (1995). Eye movements and cognitive processes in reading, visual search, and scene perception. In J. M. Findlay, R. Walker, & R. W. Kentridge (Eds.), *Eye movement research: Mechanisms, processes, and applications,* (pp. 3-22). New York: Elsevier.

Ritter, F. E., Baxter, G. D., Jones, G., & Young, R. M. (2000). Supporting cognitive models as users. *ACM Transactions on Computer-Human Interaction, 7,* 141-173.

Salvucci, D. D. (2001). An integrated model of eye movements and visual encoding. *Cognitive Systems Research, 1*(4), 201-220.

Salvucci, D. D., & Macuga, K. L. (2002). Predicting the effects of cellular-phone dialling on driver performance. *Cognitive Systems Research, 3,* 95-102.

Silva, M., & Cox, A. L. (2005, August 31-September 2) *Eye-movement behaviour in interactive menu search: Evidence for rational analysis.* Paper presented at the BPS Cognitive Section Conference 2005, University of Leeds.

St. Amant, R., Horton, T. E., & Ritter F. E. (2004). Model-based evaluation of cell phone menu interaction. In *Proceedings of the CHI'04 Conference on Human Factors in Computer Systems* (pp. 343-350). New York: ACM.

Young, R. M. (1998). Rational analysis of exploratory choice. In M. Oaksford & N. Chater (Eds.), *Rational models of cognition* (pp. 469-500). UK: Oxford University Press.

Young, R. M., Green, T. R. G., & Simon, T. (1989). Programmable user models for predictive evaluation of interface designs. In *Proceedings of CHI '89: Human Factors in Computing Systems* (pp. 15-19). AMC Press.

About the Editors

Panayiotis Zaphiris is a senior lecturer at the Centre for Human-Computer Interaction Design, School of Informatics of City University, London. Before joining City University, he was a researcher at the Institute of Gerontology at Wayne State University from where he also got his PhD in human-computer interaction (HCI). His research interests lie in HCI with an emphasis on inclusive design and social aspects of computing. He is especially interested in HCI issues related to the elderly and people with disabilities. He is also interested in Internet related research (Web usability, mathematical modelling of browsing behavior in hierarchical online information systems, online communities, e-learning, Web-based digital libraries, and finally, social network analysis of online human-to-human interactions).

Sri Kurniawan is a lecturer at the School of Informatics of the University of Manchester and a visiting lecturer at the Centre for Human-Computer Interaction Design, School of Informatics of City University, London. She joined the University of Manchester upon completion of her PhD in HCI and her postgraduate research assistantship at the Institute of Gerontology, Wayne State University. Her research focuses on facilitating access to information for people who are technologically-frail, including older persons and persons with disabilities. She has published numerous articles and has been invited to provide seminars and keynote speeches in the areas of assistive technology, HCI for technologically-frail user group, and design and evaluation of user interfaces for this user group.

About the Authors

Julio Abascal (BSD, physics, Universidad de Navarra, 1978; PhD, informatics, Universidad del País Vasco-Euskal Herriko Unibertsitatea, 1987) is a professor of the Computer Architecture and Technology Department of the University of the Basque Country, Spain, where he has worked since 1981. In 1985 he co-founded the Laboratory of Human-Computer Interaction for Special Needs that has participated in several R&D projects at national and international levels. His research activity is focused on the application of HCI methods and techniques to assistive technology, including the design of ubiquitous, adaptive, and accessible user interfaces. Currently he coordinates a research group aiming to develop methods and tools to enhance physical and cognitive accessibility to the Web. He has been the Spanish representative in the IFIP Technical Committee 13 on HCI since 1991, and the former and founder chairman (in 1993) of IFIP WG 13.3 Human-Computer Interaction and Disability. Currently he serves as a member of the Management Committee of COST 219 ter Accessibility for All to Services and Terminals for Next Generation Networks.

Sherman R. Alpert has been at the IBM T. J. Watson Research Center (USA) since 1987. He received a BS in computer science from the State University of New York at Stony Brook and an MA in computing in education from Columbia University's Teachers College where he has pursued additional graduate studies. He has been involved in research and software development in a variety of domains including educational technology, HCI, multimedia, funds transfer systems, and object-oriented programming and design. He has published widely in these fields, including a book on object-oriented software design, *The Design Patterns Smalltalk Companion* (1998). He serves on the advisory board and editorial boards of several journals as well as conference and program committees.

Myriam Arrue is an engineer in informatics (Universidad del País Vasco-Euskal Herriko Unibersitatea, 1999). After her graduation she joined the industry to work on Web application development. In 2001 she moved to the Laboratory of Human-Computer Interaction for Special Needs (UPV-EHU) to work on the IRIS European Project on tools for automatic Web accessibility evaluation. Currently she is a lecturer in the Department of Computer Architecture and Technology (UPV-EHU), and she is finishing her PhD on Web accessibility design methods. She is a member of the WAI Evaluation and Repair Tools Working Group.

David Benyon is a professor of human-computer systems at Napier University, Edinburgh, Scotland. His research focus is on navigation of information space, a new view of HCI that focuses on how people find their way around the information spaces created by new media. He has also published on semiotics and new media and on applying experientialism to new media. The book, *Designing with Blends* is due to be published by MIT Press in 2006. In 2005 he published *Designing Interactive Systems* with Phil and Susan Turner, the latest and most up-to-date textbook on HCI and interaction.

Anna L. Cox is a lecturer in HCI at UCLIC, University College London. She received her PhD in cognitive science from the University of Hertfordshire in 2002.

Madelon Evers helps companies design innovative, interactive products and services. With a PhD in design, she focuses on creative and qualitative processes in cross media and multimedia projects. Evers started out as multimedia publisher for Jumbo (games) and Meulenhoff (edutainment). In 1995 she founded Human Shareware (The Netherlands), an international design consultancy firm. Clients include broadcasters, publishers, marketing agencies, nonprofits, insurance, and information and communication technology (ICT) companies. Evers is often invited as speaker and guest lecturer on design at European universities and professional training institutes. Her mission is to embed human-centred design in organizations, so that products and services can better serve human needs.

Rod Farmer is a recent PhD graduate from the Department of Computer Science and Software Engineering at The University of Melbourne, Australia. He currently lectures in applied linguistics at the Horwood Language Centre within the University of Melbourne. He possesses a BA (*magna cum laude*) in arts and computer science. Possessing over a decade of experience in the Australian ICT industry, he has provided HCI and software engineering consulting services to several of Australia's largest defense, corporate, and charitable organizations. His research interests include HCI, software engineering, computer-assisted language learning, philosophy of mind, natural language processing, multimodal interaction, and machine learning.

Catherine Forsman is currently an independent consultant, providing training and assistance in usability and usability testing, analyzing users and users' tasks, and reviewing products and documentation. From 1996 to the present, Catherine has worked on numerous projects for major American and European companies such as Siemens, *NY Times*, Goldman Sachs,

MapInfo, and Delta Airlines. Her most current endeavor is documenting user behavior in the United States after hurricane Katrina in New Orleans.

Ashraf Gaffar is a part time faculty member at Concordia University (Montreal, Canada). His research combines software engineering, interface design, and usability testing. He participated in the design and building of Concordia's first usability lab. He also participated in several usability tests jointly with industrial and research partners like Daimler Chrysler and the Natural Sciences and Engineering Research Council of Canada (NSERC).

Rebecca A. Grier is a human-systems engineer with Aptima (USA) in the interaction engineering team. Primarily, her work entails domain analysis and knowledge elicitation to inform the system requirements and user interface design for software and Web-based systems. Prior to joining Aptima, Grier worked in the Human Factors Group at SBC. In this position, she conducted usability tests and participated in the design of a variety of telecommunication systems. She earned her PhD in human factors/experimental psychology from the University of Cincinnati.

Paul Gruba is a senior lecturer at the Horwood Language Centre within the School of Languages at The University of Melbourne, Australia. His work is widely recognized in L2 listening assessment and serves as the basis of the listening section of the Web-based Language Assessment Project at UCLA. Gruba is also known as an expert in computer-assisted language learning. He has served as a research consultant to Australia's largest online, task-based teaching resource, the Virtual Independent Learning Centre (VILC). At the University of Melbourne, Gruba acts as deputy director for the Horwood Language Centre.

Marie Jefsioutine is faculty research fellow in digital media at University of Central England, Birmingham Institute of Art and Design and is involved in design and usability research. Jefsioutine has worked in digital media for over 10 years, previously at the BBC Open University and Goldsmith's College. She studied experimental psychology at Sussex University, and has an MSc in computing, cognition, and psychology from Warwick University. Memberships include the Design Research Society, the BCS HCI Group, the Museums Computer Group, and The British Association of Counseling & Psychotherapy. She contributes to conferences and publications in the field of design, e-learning, and museums.

John Knight is director of User-Lab at Birmingham Institute of Art and Design. His work includes academic and commercial research in usability and accessibility. He studied at University College Wales and completed an MSc in user-interface design at London Guildhall University. He has worked for a variety of major international clients including McCann Erikson, The British Council, and Honda. He is a longstanding member of The BCS HCI Group, Design Research Society, The Usability Professionals' Association, and an associate editor of *The Design Journal*. As a regular contributor to *Usability News*, he reviews HCI and design issues for Leonardo and Interactions.

Philip Kortum is currently a professor in the Department of Psychology at Rice University in Houston, Texas (USA), having recently joined the university after working for almost a decade at SBC Laboratories. Kortum has performed extensive work in the research and development of user-centric systems in both visual (Web and equipment design, image compression) and auditory domains (telephony operations and interactive voice response systems). He received his PhD in biomedical engineering from the University of Texas at Austin.

Gabriel Michel is an associate professor in the University of Metz (France). He has been an ergonomist and usability labs specialist for about 10 years. His main research interests include usability testing, Web accessibility (for disabled people, seniors, and children), and intercultural problems (in learning and in the interfaces).

James T. Miller is currently a principal member of the technical staff at SBC Laboratories, Inc. (USA). For the past several years, he has been responsible for the development, testing, and evaluation of products for consumer and business customers on the Web. In addition to this work, he has been responsible for developing and evaluating a number of telephony products, interactive voice response systems, and telephones. He received his PhD in psychology from the University of Colorado at Boulder.

Naouel Moha is a PhD candidate in computer science at the University of Montreal (Canada). She worked during the last 2 years as a research assistant with a specialized research group in HCI at Concordia University. Naouel Moha has been involved in collaborative projects with industrial and research groups including the Interaction and Cognition Lab Team at the University of Metz (France) and the Usability Professional Association in Montréal (Canada). Her main research interests include remote usability testing; methods and process for conducting tests; and human-centred, software engineering.

Elizabeth D. (Betty) **Murphy** was selected to lead the Census Bureau's Human Factors and Usability Group, after 7 years as a research psychologist with the U.S. Census Bureau. She holds a PhD in psychology from the University of Maryland and an MA in psychology from George Mason University. Betty has over 20 years of experience in conducting human-factors evaluations for government agencies. Her areas of specialization include the usability and accessibility of human-computer interfaces, focusing on the design and evaluation of Web-based, national censuses and surveys. Betty has authored or co-authored over 40 papers in journals and conference proceedings.

Theresa A. O'Connell is a well-published, usability engineering researcher and practitioner. After senior positions with major information technology firms, she formed Humans and Computers, Inc. (USA). She played a major role in machine translation evaluation in the DARPA Machine Translation Initiative. Her research includes human interaction with personal autonomous intelligent agents. Access to technology for users with physical disabilities is an area of expertise. Her consulting track record includes integrating usability engineering practices into over 100 software development projects in North America and Europe, in fields ranging from telecommunications to finance, and for industry and government clients.

David Peebles is a senior lecturer in cognitive psychology in the Department of Behavioural Sciences, University of Huddersfield, UK. He received his PhD in cognitive science from the University of Birmingham in 1998.

Hokyoung Ryu is a lecturer of information systems at Massey University in New Zealand. He is also a member of the British Computer Society. Ryu obtained his doctorate at the University of York (UK) in psychology. Ryu is active on how new information and communication technologies (ICTs) such as interactive TV and mobile systems, will change human social behavior in the community or person-to-person relationship.

Napawan Sawasdichai holds a BA in industrial design from the King Mongkut's Institute of Technology Ladkrabang (KMITL) and an MA in graphic design from the Rochester Institute of Technology (RIT). She received her PhD from the Institute of Design at Illinois Institute of Technology (IIT) in 2004 for research in the area of user-centered communication design, for which she developed a framework to formulate alternative design strategies for structuring and presenting information to better serve user purposes and enhance user experience in processing information through Web-based media. She is currently a full-time faculty at the Department of Industrial Design, Faculty of Architecture, King Mongkut's Institute of Technology Ladkrabang in Thailand. Her current research interest concerns information design in new media.

John G. Vergo is researcher and program manager for Component Business Modeling (CBM) in the Business Informatics Group at the IBM T. J. Watson Research Center in Hawthorne, New York. His research interests include CBM, enterprise analysis methods, research strategy, HCI, user-centered design methods, multimodal user interfaces, e-commerce user experiences, speech recognition, natural language understanding, scientific visualization, 3D graphics and software development methods. He has a BS in mathematics and psychology from the University at Albany, and an MS in computer science from Polytechnic University.

Markel Vigo is an engineer in informatics (Universidad del País Vasco-Euskal Herriko Unibersitatea, 2004). After his graduation he joined the Laboratory of Human-Computer Interaction for Special Needs (UPV-EHU) to collaborate on research projects on Web accessibility. Currently he is working on his Ph.D on Methods and Tools for Web Accessibility Measuring, Monitoring, and Maintenance.

Zhijun Zhang received his BA degree in computer science from Peking University, Beijing, China, in 1990. He developed interactive computer software for 3 years before starting his graduate study at the University of Maryland, where he became interested in software usability and conducted research in usability evaluation. He received his PhD degree in computer science from the University of Maryland in 1999. He has worked for various organizations in the field of human factors and usability, as an intern, full-time employee, or consultant. Most recently, he has been a technology researcher (focusing on emerging technologies for user interaction) and enterprise architect at a large financial service company. Zhang maintains the UsabilityHome.com Web site, which hosts information about various usability evaluation methods and techniques.

Index

M

maintainability 187
map 178, 258
mental model 5, 154, 264
micro-planning 83
mobile phone 18, 133, 139, 166, 169
mobile usability lab 277
multi-disciplinary design 148
multi-disciplinary design team 148

N

natural language 96
navigation 174
navigation design 165
normative modelling 88

O

observation 139

P

Paris-ile-de-France.com 52
participants 114
participatory prototyping 142
perceptual mechanisms 22
performance measurement 219
permission marketing 267
persona 111
personal interests 48
personality 124
personalization 259
personalized Web site 257
photographs 24
physical distance 169
pluralistic walk-through 217
pre-motor theory 23
prescriptiveness 220
probe 215
process analysis 13
product use 135
prototyping model 189

Q

qualitative study 42
quality 187

question-asking 218
questionnaires 215

R

recall-based interaction 230
recognition 26
recognition-based interaction 230
recommendation 113
recruiting 114
reflecting probe 215
Rehabilitation Act 186
relationship management methodology
    189
remote testing 219, 280
remote usability evaluation 273
remote usability test 219, 278
requirements definition 2
responsive space 177
retrospective testing 219

S

salient visual element (SVE) 23
scenario-based design 94
search behavior 49
shadowing 218
shopping 113
signage 177-182
situated action 91, 231
situated task analysis 95
social navigation 178
software development life cycle 2, 79
software engineering 8, 131, 188
South Africa 285
stakeholder 7, 142
store visit 121
structured interview 214
survey 114
synchronous remote testing 280
systematic search 35

T

task 82, 235
task-as-activity 82
task analysis 78
task flow 120
teaching 219